APPNA QISSA II

A History of the Association of Physicians
of Pakistani descent of North America
2004–2016

MAHMOOD ALAM

ASSOCIATION OF PHYSICIANS OF PAKISTANI
DESCENT OF NORTH AMERICA
WESTMONT, ILLINOIS
USA

APPNA QISSA II: A History of the Association of Physicians of Pakistani descent of North America 2004–2016

ISBN 978-0-9981773-0-4

© Copyright 2016 Mahmood Alam, Association of Physicians of Pakistani descent of North America
Published by the Association of Physicians of Pakistani descent of North America
www.APPNA.org

Printed and bound in the United States of America

Price US $30.00

About the Title
APPNA, the acronym for the Association of Physicians of Pakistani descent of North America, also means *Ours* in Urdu language (official language of Pakistan). *Qissa* is story, tale or a fable in Urdu (and in Persian)). *APPNA QISSA II* means Our Story, volume 2.

About the Cover
Calligraphy artwork contributed by Dr. Shamsuddin Akhtar. *Ilm* or علم in Urdu means knowledge, a concept that is crucial to the salvation of humankind.

CONTENTS

ACKNOWLEDGEMENTS

I am humbled by the support I received from all the friends who cared to spend their valuable time and expertise in helping me to complete this book. I am grateful to past presidents, Aslam Malik, Muhammad Suleman, and Omar Atiq, for their invaluable role as advisors, contributors, and reviewers. A very special thanks to past president Mubasher Rana for his determination and tenacity to help initiating and completing this overwhelming job of compiling the history of APPNA from 2004–2016. I am also grateful to M. Nasar Qureshi, who let me carry the project throughout his presidency in 2016 with complete liberty and the independence required to complete the job.

I am grateful to the editors, Nasir Gondal, Aslam Malik, Wasique Mirza, and Mubasher Rana for their assistance in contributing and editing not only the original text but also painstakingly taking the time to edit the contributions from past presidents, alumni associations, and chapters. My hats off to all of them for endorsing the project and putting up with my urgent requests, inquiries, and untimely phone calls.

Special thanks to Arif Agha, Naheed Usmani, Aisha Zafar, Saima Zafar, Shahid Yousuf, Asif Rehman, Sajjad Savul, A.R. Piracha, Rubina Inayat, Shahzad Iqbal, Sabir Ali Khan, Rizwan Naeem, Adeel Butt, Faisal Cheema, Tipu Ahmad, Tariq Cheema, Atiya Khan, Rizwan Karatela, Babar Rao, Riffat Chughtai, Ayesha Najib, Samrina Haseeb, Shahid Sheikh, and M. Khalid Riaz. All of them, amongst many others, were instrumental in moving this project forward.

And my heartfelt appreciation also goes out to Jennifer Wozniak-Watson, Karolina Strack, and Nicholas Suh from APPNA office for their untiring support for the project.

A special thanks to Manzoor Tariq and Mohammed Haseeb for procuring two separate unrestricted grants from BIOTRONIK along with Imran Jaffer and Mehran's donations, which were invaluable earmarked contributions for the project. In addition, JSMUANNA and the Alabama Chapter also donated $500 each. Nadeem Kazi, Mubasher Rana, Arif Muslim, A.R. Piracha, and Omar Atiq matched my personal contribution of $1,000 each. They all helped actualize this initiative.

A very special thanks to my daughter Zainab for serving as an editor and for holding my hand from the very first day on this project, helping to set the tone of this book as I desired. I dearly value the last minute effort of my son, Omar, for reviewing a number of chapters to pick up some of the inadvertent spelling mistakes. And finally to my life partner Lubna for her unwavering and continuously level-headed support that was much needed during the most frustrating moments of this venture, a very loving thank you.

FOREWORD

Near the end of 2014, as I sought advice from various APPNA leaders to plan for my upcoming presidency in 2015, Dr. Mahmood Alam shared his feelings about lack of institutional memory and long range planning in APPNA. He proposed putting together a sequel of *APPNA Qissa* covering the time period of 2004–2015. I liked the idea very much and requested him to consider taking the lead on this important task. At its 2015 spring meeting, APPNA Council unanimously approved the project and appointed Dr. Alam as the project director of APPNA history. I am convinced we could not have found a better person than Dr. Alam to undertake the compilation and documentation of APPNA history over the last 12 years. His commitment to APPNA is above reproach. Dr. Alam has virtually lived APPNA during the period covered in this history book and missed only three council meetings since 2003. Besides spending many hours every day for more than a year, he needed to take several weeks off from his medical practice and his other engagements including precious family and holiday time to work on this book. We cannot thank him enough for his commitment and hundreds of hours of hard work he donated to complete this herculean task.

I would also like to sincerely thank all the APPNA members and associates who generously donated their skills and time towards writing the book. The book could not have been a reality without their commitment and contributions. I have been personally involved in reviewing and editing most chapters of the book. I must say Dr. Alam has painstakingly compiled the details and made sure the facts are accurately depicted. He has also provided varying perspectives on each topic. Each chapter provides a gripping account of the events during the period. APPNA is a big organization with lots of facets and components. Doing justice to all is a great challenge. However, I have no doubt the readers will find Dr. Alam has been able to cover all venues objectively and without bias.

Another important task was to raise funds for the book. We are very thankful to individuals and industry who donated generously for the book. Their names are acknowledged elsewhere in the book.

Reviewing the manuscript, I learnt a lot about APPNA and its tremendous achievements and challenges over the years. This book will indeed serve as a great resource of knowledge about our beloved organization. It will provide us opportunity to celebrate our successes and learn from our challenges; the occasions where we failed initially, but then succeeded. As President Theodore Roosevelt said, *"The more you know about the past, the better prepared you are for the future."* Let us leave this book for our future generations as an account of how a group of committed and caring people came together and made a difference in the world.

Long Live APPNA
Mubasher Rana
President APPNA 2015

PREFACE

Established in 1978, the Association of Physicians of Pakistani Descent of North America (APPNA) is an ethnic professional association of medical doctors. These Pakistani-physicians came to North America in pursuit of higher training and education. Majority of them then settled in the United States and Canada during the last fifty years. APPNA, a not-for-profit organization, has a rich history of its work in the fields of education, philanthropy, and advocacy—the work that is carried out by its selfless volunteers across North America and in Pakistan on daily basis.

APPNA QISSA II covers organizational history from 2004 to 2015, with inclusion of the key events until the end of September 2016. This new book is an addition, not a new edition, to the first book on APPNA's history that covered the first twenty-five years (1978–2003). *APPNA Qissa II* is a continuation of tale of APPNA adventure and a successor to the first venture. The account of all the materials presented in this book is well-referenced. Moreover, at least two independent reviewers looked at the contents of potentially contentious discussions before it was decided to make those narratives part of the book.

The active membership of APPNA has steadily increased from 1,000 to about 3,500 during the last fifteen years. The tremendous growth of the organization during this period is a testament to the work done by several committees under the leadership of their chairs. I have duly attempted to acknowledge and recognize Social Welfare and Disaster Relief, Advocacy, Young Physicians, Research Education and Scientific Affairs, MERIT, and Telemedicine committees, including APPNA Sehat and HDF, by highlighting their work in separate chapters. A section on the work of APPNA Chapters is also added to encompass their activities. These narratives are in part extracted from the minutes of the general body and council meetings and from the published reports in APPNA Newsletters and Journals. Efforts were made to fill any ostensible gaps with verifiable oral accounts by various leaders. Moreover, numerous past and present committee chairs were given the opportunity to review the written material for veracity of the facts and to add any missing information. I fear that even with utmost care to include everyone whose work has made, and continues to make APPNA a great organization, there will be inadvertent omissions for which I apologize in advance.

The period of APPNA's history covered in this book happened right in front of my eyes. I was not a silent observer. In fact, I sought to play my part during the most productive years of my life to promote APPNA's mission. Therefore, putting together the factual details was not arduous. I needed help to present those historical details with unbiased objectivity that is true to the core of this organization. I was fortunate enough to have support of skilled reviewers and editors whose contributions were instrumental in shaping this book. I had asked my daughter, Zainab B. Alam, and APPNA journal co-editor Dr. Wasique Mirza to help me with the project, and they served as editors from the very beginning. I also had the honor of having Dr. Mubasher Rana, APPNA President 2015, as the prime mover for the history project. Dr. Rana, over the period of eighteen months, proved to be the best advisor and most involved editor of *APPNA Qissa II*. Dr. Nasir Gondal was also always available for his input and editing of some of the most challenging chapters, besides making a major contribution in the chapter on Advocacy, Civil Liberties, and Social Justice. Last but not the least, I needed a senior advisor who would not only have an insight of APPNA since its founding but also be helpful in reviewing the manuscript to ensure fairness in the narratives of APPNA history. I was lucky enough to have Dr. Aslam Malik to do that job.

I desired to put meaningful art work on the cover that would reflect, at least in part, on the contents of *APPNA Qissa II*. It was a tough decision. However, in the archives of APPNA, I found some intriguing work by Dr. Shamsuddin Akhtar, published in the Winter 2010 issue of the APPNA Journal. Dr. Akhtar's artwork on the three lettered Urdu word, *ilm* "علم" or knowledge is an end product of education that is one of the core values of APPNA's work. The pursuit of knowledge indeed promotes tolerance, understanding and peace.

In the archives of APPNA, I came across great action pictures for the period we intended to cover in *Qissa II*. However, I was not sure how could it be possible to put all the pictures together with the narratives of

QISSA II. I also realized that pictures speak louder than words especially when compiling history of a vibrant organization like APPNA. Therefore, conceptualization of a separate pictorial book led to the omission of an album section from *Qissa II*. A Visual History of APPNA since 1978 onwards remains an extension of the history project that can hopefully be accomplished in the near future.

From the very beginning, despite it being a daunting task, I was determined to write a comprehensive account of APPNA's history—in a way that does not shy away from the issues we confronted, challenges we faced, differences we had, and the lessoned we learned—in order to develop a roadmap for the future. The success of this effort will be determined by its readers. I have put together this work with utmost earnestness in order to appraise the tremendous work done during this period. I hope the reader will enjoy this historical account and would appreciate our sincere effort.

Mahmood Alam
Edison, New Jersey
October 2016

This book is dedicated to all the

Volunteers of APPNA

APPNA would not exist if it were not for the
selfless dedication of its volunteers who help
further its mission to promote and serve healthcare,
educational, social, advocacy, disaster relief and
charitable activities both at home and abroad.

And
to the loving memories of our pioneering
founders, leaders, and educators.
Though they may not be with us, they
are forever in our hearts and in the
flame that illuminates APPNA.

Mushtaq A. Khan

13th President, 1991–92

DOW MEDICAL COLLEGE 1965

Recipient of APPNA Gold Medal in 2003

August 11, 1943–January 05, 2005

Dr. Mushtaq Khan was the founder of the Pakistan Physicians Society of Illinois. After joining APPNA in 1980, he moved through the ranks to serve as its President (1991–92). He had also been President of Dow Alumni (DOGANA) and its executive director. Over the years, he chaired numerous APPNA meetings and worked with utmost dedication. The last summer meeting he chaired was in 2001 at Chicago. He also helped to purchase and organize the present central APPNA office in Westmont, Illinois during his presidency. During his tenure as APPNA president, the first APPNA membership directory was produced and the APPNA Gold Medal was initiated.

M. Ayub Khan Ommaya

3rd President, 1981–82

KING EDWARD MEDICAL COLLEGE 1953

1930–July 11, 2008

Dr. M. Ayub Khan Ommaya was a distinguished graduate of KEMC. Dr. Ommaya enjoyed worldwide recognition as a master Neurosurgeon, superb researcher, and inventor. He studied physiology of the brain and emotions at Oxford (UK) as a Rhode Scholar, completing it with honors in 1956. Dr. Ommaya was awarded fellowship of Royal College of Surgeons of England in 1960 and a year later he obtained his D Phil in Clinical Biology from Oxford. In 1964 he was named Hunterian Professor at the Royal College of Surgeons and in 1968 he received certification of the American Board of Neurological Surgery. He served as the section chief of Applied Neuroscience Research and Surgical Neurology at the NIH for over a decade. He also served as chief of neurosurgery at NIH from 1975–1980. Dr. Ommaya is the inventor of Ommaya Reservoir that is used to treat aggressive brain cancers. In 1982 the Government of Pakistan honored him with *Sitara-e-Imtiaz*.

Raana Saboohi Akbar

24th President, 2003

KING EDWARD MEDICAL COLLEGE 1975

Recipient of APPNA Gold Medal Award in 2011

May 31, 1951–December 03, 2009

Dr. Raana S. Akbar relentlessly served the North American Pakistani and Muslim community since 1976. She always took special pride in serving KEMCAANA and APPNA. Her dedication to her alma mater and APPNA only ended with her passing in 2009. Dr. Akbar was a visionary who always led the community with the highest ethical and moral standards. She was the pioneer of advocacy for young physicians, social justice, and civil liberties. The Michigan State Medical Society recognized her work twice; with its Community Service Award and then with its National Leadership Award. The Governor Granholm of Michigan appointed her to the Saginaw Valley State University's Board of Control. Dr. Akbar was also a guiding force in the local Muslim community in Saginaw, MI. She led the efforts to build a new Islamic Center in Saginaw, where she also taught high school level classes at the Sunday School for twenty years.

Raza Ali Dilawari

Past Chair Research Education and Scientific Affairs Committee (RESA)
KING EDWARD MEDICAL COLLEGE 1968
Recipient of APPNA Lifetime Achievement Award in 2011

September 28, 1946–September 18, 2011

Dr. Raza Dilawari was a distinguished member of APPNA. He also had a lifetime commitment to promoting educational and academic endeavors in the medical sciences. He served as the Chair of the RESA committee for several years. Dr. Dilawari took charge of RESA when APPNA was struggling to maintain its accreditation with Accreditation Council on Continuing Medical Education (ACCME). He led the RESA committee to organize CME sessions of the highest academic standards. He was the guiding light for the initiation of the APPNA Mentorship Program for young physicians. At the time of his passing, Professor Dilawari was Assistant Dean for Clinical Affairs at the University of Tennessee at Memphis, and the Vice Chairman of the Department of Surgery at Methodist University Hospital.

Parvez Rasul

Chair APPNA Board of Trustees 2011
Co-Chair APPNA Summer Meeting 2006
Past President Pakistani Physicians Society (PPS), IL (1990–91)
NISHTAR MEDICAL COLLEGE 1965

October 1, 1943–October 12, 2012

Dr. Parvez Rasul completed his residency at Michael Rees Hospital in Ophthalmology in 1974. He was on the faculty of the Univ. of Illinois in Chicago. He was a board certified ophthalmologist who served the Chicago community for over 36 years. Dr. Rasul will perhaps be best remembered for his perpetual efforts to elevate the standards of care in Ophthalmology through his commitment to Al-Shifa Trust Eye Hospitals and his humanitarian work for the people of Pakistan after the earthquake of 2005 and at other times. He retired as the chair of the Board of Trustees of APPNA on December 31, 2011. Dr. Rasul regularly volunteered his professional services at APPNA free clinic and generously treated the needy at his private office.

Hassan Imam Bukhari

8th APPNA President, 1986–87

Past Chair APPNA *Sehat* Committee

KING EDWARD MEDICAL COLLEGE 1963

Recipient of APPNA Gold Medal Award in 1996

1938–2015

Dr. Hassan Bukhari was trained as general and peripheral vascular surgeon at Baylor University in Dallas, Texas, where he entered into private practice in 1972. Dr. Bukhari served APPNA in many capacities and chaired various committees before he assumed presidency in 1986. He was also entrusted with the management of the APPNA Lifetime Dues Investment Fund, which he managed with the help of Finance Committee until 2000. Later he became interested in the APPNA *Sehat* project for Pakistan and served as its Chair for several years. Dr. Bukhari remained active in PAK-PAC as one of its directors until his death. He also organized the yearly CME in Pakistan for decades under the auspices of the College of Family Physicians of Pakistan.

1

APPNA

From Ethnic Professional Organization to Grassroots Movement

In the first *APPNA Qissa* published in 2004, the authors have suggested that the survival and continued progress of APPNA beyond its 25th anniversary is a testament to its continued success.[1] The humble beginning of the Association of Pakistani Physicians (APP) as an educational and charitable organization of medical professionals that started in 1977 had successfully evolved into a dynamic association by 2002.[2] By that time, APPNA was recognized as the leading democratic organization of the Pakistani diaspora in the US. APPNA had a track record of successfully working for the causes of foreign medical graduates in collaboration with other medical organizations of immigrants in the US. APPNA had also worked and proposed recommendations to improve the curriculum of medical education in Pakistan. Moreover, APPNA *Sehat* had provided a successful model for basic healthcare in rural Pakistan.

In the first two decades (1977–1996) since APPNA's inception, a handful of alumni associations of the premier medical colleges from Pakistan came together under one banner and provided strength and legitimacy to APPNA's being the sole national representative of Pakistani physicians. However, the growth of local chapters in the last two decades (1997–2016) and their recognition as the component societies of APPNA is the major factor that has transformed APPNA into a grassroots organization. These regional chapters have branded APPNA as a North American organization that is playing a pivotal role in organizing Pakistani-descent community at major metropolises and smaller cities, alike. Besides organizing health-care days and free health clinics, chapters are getting increasingly involved in advocacy efforts, catering to young physicians' needs, holding health awareness campaigns like those on obesity, heart disease, and participating in cancer walks to name a few. (see page 123 in, "Chapter Activism in APPNA Comes of Age")

Organizational behavior is a very well-studied subject and remains an area of continued research. Organizational behavior is influenced by both internal integration and external adaptation.[3] The growth of any organization depends on how the organization reacts to these pressures, and APPNA is no exception. Internal integration reflects on how an organization promotes unity of purpose while respecting cultural diversity. In APPNA, ethnic divides do exist and at times some members have exploited these differences for political gains. Fortunately, these smoldering issues never gained enough momentum to hurt the organization. The most plausible explanation to APPNA's strength despite these differences is its unity as Pakistani-Americans. Everyone is united for the cause of Pakistan. Moreover, the continued growth of APPNA chapters has played a positive role in promoting unity and dissipating divisions. Most volunteers work on the common goal of promoting and strengthening the Pakistani community, regardless of their ethnicity or alumni affiliation. Therefore, one can argue that internal integration has further enhanced APPNA's growth. Nevertheless, there were indeed numerous internal organizational challenges that APPNA faced and dealt with as it moved forward in promoting its core values. (see detailed discussion page 163 in in the chapter, "Inside APPNA—Organization Building, Challenges and Opportunities")

External adaptation has been a significant challenge for APPNA in the post 9/11 era. The creation of Homeland Security in the US apparently impacted Pakistanis more than any other Muslim immigrant group. The visa denials first surfaced in 2003; a majority of young physicians from Pakistan were delayed from joining their residency training hospitals under stricter scrutiny for visa clearance. APPNA took the challenge head-on and left no stone unturned in safeguarding the right of Pakistani physicians to enter the US for educational and training purposes. Moreover, the issues of racial profiling and discrimination stemming from media promoted

Islamophobia continues to threaten Pakistani-American community. Stereotyping of Muslims due to the radical acts of a few is a growing challenge that we face today. Many Muslims including Pakistani-Americans and even non-Muslims (e.g., Sikhs) have been targeted or killed in acts of violence due to Islamophobia. APPNA has partnered with different civil liberty organizations to educate lawmakers in our efforts to stand against the rising tide of anti-Muslim bigotry. Furthermore, APPNA has taken a stand on issues of social justice in Pakistan over the years. APPNA membership has always been vocal in support of the rights of various minorities and women. In recent years, APPNA has also denounced the alarming wave of physician killings in the most vociferous way. Confronting these issues has made APPNA stronger, and deepened its legitimacy as the leading Pakistani organization of ex-patriates in the western hemisphere. (See page 87 for details in Chapter, "APPNA Advocacy for Young Physicians, Civil Liberties, and Social Justice").[4]

It would be a fair statement to say that APPNA is the most democratic organization of ex-patriate Pakistanis in the world. The officers of the organization have been elected every year by the general body since its inception in 1978. Moreover, only the elected presidents or officers of the component societies are represented in the APPNA Council; a key decision making body of the association. This practice is a hallmark of democratic societies that are built from the bottom up. Issues pertaining to APPNA elections are discussed in the chapter on "Democratic APPNA," page 149.

Another yardstick of organizational success is maintenance of its core values with a proven track record of its achievements. APPNA's core values are briefly stated in the preamble and are also enlisted in six point aims and objectives of the constitution.[5] The preamble reads, *"We the physicians of Pakistani descent, out of our conviction for our profession and motherland, do hereby proclaim the establishment of the Association of Physicians of Pakistani descent, so that collectively we all can: uphold ethical and moral values, engage in social and professional activities, support educational and intellectual pursuits, upgrade medical care and thus glorify our Association."*

These core values were redefined under the Vision and Mission statements of APPNA at a dedicated strategic planning meeting held on February 5–6, 2011 at Saint Louis, MO:[6]

Vision: To become the premier organization of physicians of Pakistani-descent in North America that best promotes and serves healthcare, educational, social, and charitable activities.

Mission: APPNA is a professional, nonpolitical, equal opportunity organization, which promotes excellence in healthcare, research, education, and humanitarian activities. It facilitates the transfer of healthcare expertise and resources to deserving communities. It also provides advocacy, caters to cultural and social needs, is a vehicle for charitable projects and seeks to nurture young physicians.

These statements encourage us to examine how APPNA has fared in working towards the promotion of its core values. On October 8, 2005, when a deadly earthquake struck areas in northern Pakistan, APPNA stepped up and took the lead in relief efforts needed in the aftermath of this disaster and continued to work for the relief projects that were undertaken for the next two years. Similarly, in the devastation and human displacement following the floods in Pakistan over the years (2010–2014) and the Karachi heatwave related casualties of 2015, APPNA immediately responded to the help of the needy and destitute and provided humanitarian aid along with its partners in Pakistan. Furthermore, in the US from hurricane Katrina to Sandy and beyond, our members at the local chapters have actively volunteered in medical and disaster relief. APPNA owes a great deal to its volunteer unsung heroes whose dedicated service and passion for charitable work has established it as a leading medical relief organization of expatriates Pakistanis. APPNA's charitable work is summarized in the longest chapter of this book page 9 "Giving back to the community."

The pursuit of education and scientific development and assisting newly arriving physicians from Pakistan are the core values for which this organization has aspired for since its inception. These efforts have been intensified in the recent years. The formation of the standing Committee on Young Physicians (CYP) in 2004 has spearheaded the efforts in coaching, mentoring, and educating our young physicians. APPNA remains the single source of guidance to young Pakistani physicians seeking higher education in the US. The role of CYP in this regards cannot be over emphasized and is recounted on page 69 in chapter, "APPNA Caters to Young Physicians from Pakistan."

The 2007 creation of the Medical Education & Research International Training & Transfer-of-technology (MERIT) committee in addition to the continued efforts of Research Education & Scientific Affairs Committee (RESA) in fulfilling the educational needs of our North American physicians have contributed significantly to achieving educational goals that are inherent to APPNA's core values. The role of these two committees in achieving our educational goals in Pakistan as well as in the United States is elaborated on page III in chapter, "APPNA on Medical Education—The roles of RESA, MERIT, and Telemedicine."[7]

The formation of the Human Development Foundation (HDF) at the time of the 50th anniversary of Pakistan in 1997 was a gift from APPNA to the Pakistani people. It was a paradigm shift with regards to how we viewed the suffering of a common people as inhumane and then took charge to propose a comprehensive plan to deal with it in a holistic model of poverty alleviation through education, healthcare, and economic development. This move was a step forward from the APPNA *Sehat* model that ran successfully for basic healthcare delivery in areas of rural Pakistan. APPNA membership continues to support HDF work with letter and spirit. As HDF grew, APPNA *Sehat* was phased out. This transition has been eloquently discussed on page 59 in chapter, "From APPNA *Sehat* to Human Development Foundation."[8,9]

The Pakistani American Political Action Committee, commonly known as PAK-PAC is another brainchild of APPNA, which was established in 1989. PAK-PAC continues to play a role in lobbying with US legislators for the interests of Pakistan and the Pakistani-American community. A critical appraisal of PAK-PAC in historical perspective is discussed in the chapter on advocacy.[10]

The Association of Pakistani-descent Cardiologists of North America (APCNA) also owes its creation to APPNA. APCNA's founders have been active members of APPNA. The need for a specialty group of cardiologists and cardiac surgeons of Pakistani-descent was felt for quite some time. APCNA was founded in 2004 during the American College of Cardiology annual scientific sessions held in New Orleans, LA. APCNA has been playing a significant role in "Healthy Heart" awareness campaign and research with special focus on heightened coronary disease related morbidity and mortality especially in Pakistanis. The theme of the year 2009 as well as 2013 in APPNA was focused on "Healthy Heart." Moreover, provision of free pacemaker banks and performance of coronary interventions on indigent Pakistanis has become a common practice offered by APCNA members visiting Pakistan.[11]

Similarly, other specialty groups of Pakistani-Americans physicians are stemming from APPNA. Dental APPNA was organized and became an active affiliate organization in 2008. Most of the other specialty groups were formed in the recent past (2013–2015). Some of them are APPNA—Pediatrics, APPNA—Hematology Oncology, APPNA—Chest Physicians, APPNA—Gastroenterology, APPNA—Nephrology, APPNA—Anesthesia and Pain Medicine, and APPNA—Radiology. Every year, the APPNA summer convention provides a platform for all the affiliates to have meetings, network, and promote ideas in achieving common goals.

APPNA has emerged as the sole representative of Pakistani physicians in North America over the past 40 years. APPNA's success lies in maintaining its centrist position while accommodating all the ideologies in a fairly secular organization with a common goal of serving Pakistani people in North America as well as in Pakistan. Everyone who is poised to carry the mission of APPNA forward finds his or her place in the organization. This book expounds on the great work of the organization primarily focusing on the last last thirteen years (2004–2016)—the work of APPNA that is not very well known to its own members and Pakistani-American physicians.

Are we a grassroots organization? According to one political mobilizer: "People at the grassroots are anxious to do something. They are especially anxious to do something MEANINGFUL—at least to them. They are politically-minded people who—when they find a cause worthy of their time, energy, and means—are willing to let go of inhibitions, fears, and preconceptions and jump into the cause with unusual passion."[12] It is indeed the characteristic of APPNA. The rest is history!

End Notes:

1   *APPNA Qissa*, 1978–2003, Literary Circle of Toledo, OH—2004, page 57
2   A short historical perspective of APPNA, Zaheer G. Ahmad, MI, APPNA Journal, 4:1, 11–12
3   Don Hellriegel, John W. Slocum, and Richard W. Woodman, Organizational Behavior. St. Paul, MN: West Publishing Company, 1989, 304–305.

4   Dr. Nasir Gondal made a significant contribution to the Chapter on Advocacy and Social Justice

5   APPNA constitution and Bylaws, 2014 edition, Preamble, Aims and Objectives; 4–5

6   APPNA Newsletter, 21:1, Spring 2011: Report on APPNA Strategic Planning Meeting, 6–7

7   A special article written by Dr. Naheed Usmani on the creation, work, and progress of MERIT deserved its inclusion in the Appendices of this book.

8   Dr. Omar Atiq, APPNA Sehat, Crown Jewel of APPNA.

9   Dr. Atiya Khan provided the article on HDF for *APPNA Qissa* that is placed in the appendices

10 Mrs. Riffat Chughtai, Dr. Mohammad Suleman, and Irfan Malik contributed to the information on Pak-Pac.

11 A detailed report on a decade of services by APCNA submitted by its past president and executive director, Dr. Rizwan Keratela, is also included in the Appendices of this book.

12 See: http://www.renewamerica.com/grassroots.htm—How the grassroots works

2

Giving Back to the Community[1]

The Social Welfare and Disaster Relief

The Social Welfare and Disaster Relief Committee (SWDRC) of APPNA was conceived by the founders as two distinct standing committees: The Social Welfare Committee, and the Disaster Relief Committee.[2] However, their roles were merged to fulfill the mission in a single committee with common goals, both short term in the face of an urgent need, and long term planning to sustain such projects. Although, work under this committee was steadily carried out throughout the 1990's, it is commonly believed that APPNA was reborn as a social welfare and disaster relief organization in the wake of 2005 earthquake in northern Pakistan and Azad Kashmir. Since then, SWDRC has undertaken numerous ventures, adopted projects, and completed most of the programs it has initiated. The following mission and scope of the work done under SWDRC were conceived as we marched forward with our work from 2002–2016.

Mission

A team of dedicated individuals to support health, education and humanitarian causes.

Goals

Disaster Relief and Humanitarian Activities

- Provide resources to assess the needs of disaster-affected areas.
- Provide immediate and long-term medical services through volunteer healthcare professionals.
- Assist in rebuilding the infrastructures in affected areas.
- Collect and deliver relief goods and monetary assistance to the affected people.

Healthcare and Education

- Provide monetary support for immediate health care needs of deserving individuals.
- Provide treatment oversight by establishing a second opinion center in USA.
- Train Pakistani professionals, to improve healthcare delivery through primary prevention.
- Help organizing free health education and screening in Pakistan.
- Conduct joint ventures with medical colleges and hospitals to provide free state-of-the-art surgeries to indigent patients.
- Expand and improve schools for the indigent in Pakistan through cooperation with established educational organizations.
- Provide leading edge equipment to medical colleges and public hospitals in Pakistan.
- Assist medical students and medical graduates from Pakistan to support their training goals.

Values

SWDRC values compassion, trust, dedication, law abidance in accordance with 501c3 guidelines of US Internal Revenue Service.

Social Welfare and Disaster Relief in Pakistan

"With faith, discipline and selfless devotion to duty, there
is nothing worthwhile that you cannot achieve."
MOHAMMAD ALI JINNAH.[3]

The true mantle of an organization is not known until it is faced with adversity. It is easier to reach the limits of one's endeavors with the goals defined and tasks at hand clearly in sight. However, we have to play with the cards we are dealt with and it changes everything. History has shown us time and again that crises arrive without any warning. These challenges test us and our ability to deal with the stresses. These situations test the strongest, whether they can stand up to the challenge or run away. There are always those who take the challenge and move forward, and in doing so show the world what transcendent leadership is all about.

Thirty-Seven Seconds of Jolt and Devastation

On October 8, 2005, in the early hours of a dark and cold morning, an unthinkable tragedy struck northern areas of Pakistan and Kashmir on both sides of line of control. It was unprecedented in magnitude and the devastation, which followed. The earth shook and rumbled with a magnitude of 7.6 on the Richter scale, shaking the ground to its core. Though a mere 37 seconds, it created havoc and devastation across the region making helpless souls scramble for safety in areas of no refuge. The majestic foothills of the Himalayas witnessed their tranquility shattered and picturesque valleys crumbed under the wrath of nature's fury. The boundaries of Eurasian and the Indian tectonic plates run through Pakistan like a line of fracture from the Arabian Sea in the South in a North Easterly direction towards Kashmir.

This was a moment that screamed for saviors. Leadership was thrust upon the worthy and this was the moment, in which APPNA and its Social Welfare and Disaster Relief Committee (SWDRC) stepped up, embracing the challenge with open arms.

Pakistan Earthquake Relief Work (2005–2007)

- Over $2 million were collected and disbursed for earthquake relief work. *
- Medical and surgical supplies valued at several million US dollars were collected and distributed.
- Over 559 tents worth $84,000 were distributed within weeks of the disaster.
- APPNA donated 2645 galvanized tin roofs worth $26,000 used in shelters before winter 2005.
- Over 200 APPNA doctors traveled on their own expense and worked pro-bono rendering medical and surgical services in numerous makeshift hospitals and walk-in clinics and at numerous established hospitals in the catchment area.

The Treasurer of APPNA 2006, Dr. Shahid F. Usmani (FL) reported in his spring meeting report that APPNA (central office) raised $1,520,342 for the Pakistan earthquake relief efforts.[4] However, this figure does not include funds that were collected later in 2006. Moreover, there were also significant amount of funds that were raised by the component societies and were spent by them collaborating with different charitable organizations of their choice in the aftermath of earthquake. The figure of over $2 million raised is an educated guess.

First Responders to Earthquake Relief

(Left to right) Dr. Nighat Agha, Dr. Saeed Akhtar, Dr. Rehana Kauser, Dr. A.R. Piracha, Dr. Afzal Arain, Dr. Murtaza Arain, General Usmani, Dr. Saeed Bajwa, Dr. Shaheer Yousaf, and Dr. Parvez Malik.[5]

The history of APPNA relief efforts for earthquake 2005 would be incomplete without mentioning the first responders to the crises.

Dr. Saeed Akhtar (PK), a lifetime member of APPNA and a renowned US-trained urologist and transplant surgeon, was one of the first person to respond to the crisis. He opened the doors of his house in Islamabad Pakistan to accommodate as many US doctors as possible. He closed his medical practice down for 2 months. Dr. Sobia Hafeez from Islamabad also joined him in the pursuit of minimizing death, destruction, and disease in the aftermath of earthquake. Dr. Akhtar took the leadership role in the coordinating efforts for relief work. His home and Shifa International Hospital where he worked became the base camp for most APPNA first responders.[6] At one time there were 16 guests in his home for the relief operations.

Dr. A. R. Piracha (WV), Dr. Murtaza Arain (IL), Dr. M. Afzal Arain (CA), Dr. Azam Khan (AZ), Dr. Tehmina Khan (CA), Dr. Rabia Khan, Dr. Waheed Akbar (MI), Dr. Parvez Malik (NJ), Dr. Rehana Kauser, Dr. Saeed Bajwa (NY), Dr. Shaheer Yousaf (MD), Dr. Tahseen Cheema, and many others went to join hands with the relief efforts and arrived in Islamabad on October 17, 2005. These doctors were received by Senator Nighat Agha, Senator Tahira Latif, President of PIMA Dr. Tariq, Dr. M. H. Qazi, Medical Director Shifa, Dr. Habib ur Rahman, Dr. Masooma Saeed, and Dr. Sobia Hafeez (PK), Communications and Control Coordinator.

Dr. Mohammad Suleman (LA) led the 2nd group of volunteers a few days later.[7] Dr. Amjad Gulzar Shaikh, an orthopedic surgeon from London, UK, was also among the first responders. Dr. Parween Khan, a pediatrician, was part of the second group and she also represented Pakistani Civic Association of Staten Island, NY. Dr. Arshad Saeed (Canada) joined the Canadian Forces DART in Pakistan. Dr. Mushtaq Sheikh (NY) joined his son Major Dr. Fareed Sheikh at MASH unit on October 23, 2005. Dr. M. Raza Khan, Dr. Naheed Usmani (MA), Dr. Syed Iftikhar Hussain (MA), Dr. Taimur Zaman (NJ), and Dr. Ayaz Samdani (WI) were also among the first responders. Dr. Hussain Malik (PA), Dr. Javed Akhtar (PA), Dr. Zahid Chohan (NY), and Mr. Amir Sheikh, an orthopedic prosthesis specialist from Chicago, IL also left for Pakistan on November 6, 2005. Dr. S. Tariq Shahab (VA) also joined a relief team to Pakistan that established a camp at "Garhi Dupatta" in Kashmir. Scores of other volunteers also joined the relief work later in the December of 2005. Among them were: Dr. Mahmood Alam (NJ), Dr. Nadeem Kazi (AZ), Dr. Ahsan Rasheed (CA), Dr. Zia Mansoor, Dr. Saba Mansoor, Dr. Rubina Inayat (FL), Dr. Omar Naseeb (IL), Dr. Saud Anwar (CT), and Dr. Rizwan Naeem (TX).

Shifa International Hospital Islamabad

Shifa Hospital opened its doors specially to expatriate Pakistani consultants to help perform the surgeries on the seriously traumatized patients. The hospital President and CEO, Dr. Zaheer Ahmad (PK), designated 100 beds for the disaster relief with free services to the injured. Dr. Tahseen Cheema and Shaheer Yousaf both orthopedic surgeons, Dr. Afzal Arian, general surgeon, Dr. Rehana Kauser, an anesthesiologist, Dr. Parvez Malik, a plastic/reconstructive surgeon, and Dr. Saeed Bajwa, a renowned neurosurgeon from upstate New York were among those who performed surgeries in the acute phase of the tragedy. Shifa hospital also acted as a base camp for those who served at various field hospitals established by Pakistan Islamic Medical Association (PIMA) in Muzaffarabad, Bagh, Balakot, Rawalakot, Batgram, Mansehra, and Abbottabad. Patients requiring major surgeries and amputations were airlifted to facilities like Shifa hospital and Pakistan Institute of Medical Sciences (PIMS). In addition, APPNA volunteers also served at Holy Family Hospital Rawalpindi and Rawalpindi General Hospital, Pakistan.

Devastation and Interventions at Ground Zero

According to Dr. Pervaiz Malik, lifetime APPNA member and past president of IMANA, in comparison to the 2004 tsunami in Indonesia, where death-to-injury ratio was high, the 2005 earthquake in Pakistan was in a sense more devastating due to the extremely large number of injuries.[8]

Thus the makeshift hospitals in the earthquake areas and underequipped hospitals of Islamabad, Abbottabad, and Rawalpindi were overcrowded with injured patients with fractures, spinal cord injuries and gangrenous extremity wounds requiring amputations. There were an estimated 70,000 patients of all ages whose treatment was rendered by hundreds of local and foreign doctors with the help of innumerable volunteers and healthcare workers. In the initial phase of the tragedy, operating rooms were working around the clock and invariably two to three surgeries were performed at the same time in one operating room.

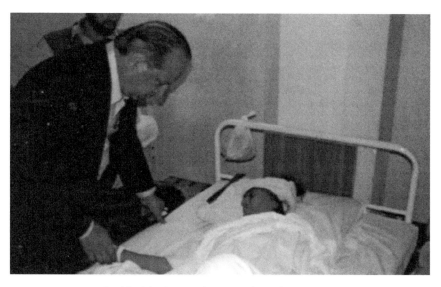

Dr. Afzal Arain examines a patient after surgery

Dr. Afzal Arain wrote an account of two weeks long work of first responders in APPNA Journal[9]: *"We had our first meeting at Shifa Hospital the same day we arrived with various volunteer organizations… There was a continuous flow of injured patients on "charpaees" (a bed made of wood and ropes). One wondered where all of these were going. Patients were fast tracked and got very timely care…We met the director of PIMS hospital Dr. Fazle Hadi. He stated that they were performing an average of 170 surgeries a day. He mentioned that they had ten operating rooms but only seven were furnished. He said if we could furnish three more surgery rooms it will increase their efficacy by 33%… We had a meeting and decided to refurbish the rooms at PIMS. The estimated cost was $50,000 and APPNA and IMANA each donated $25,000 and next day the equipment was ordered."*

Human Development Foundation

Dr. Ijaz Qayyum, a surgeon from Chicago, IL also left in early November to serve with HDF Pakistan team. In addition, Dr. Yasmin Khan from Dallas, TX also joined the work that was facilitated by Col. (R) Azhar Saleem, the Executive Director of HDF Pakistan. Many other board members of HDFNA including Dr. M. Khalid Riaz and Dr. Naheed Qayyum from Chicago area also joined the relief efforts. Later, a team of "courageous five," as Dr. M. Sohail Khan puts it in the APPNA Newsletter of Winter 2005, joined HDF efforts in Muzaffarabad. These team members were Dr. Raheela Hafeez, pediatrician from Dallas, TX; Dr. Jabeen Fatima, family physician from Leesville, LA; Dr. Shazia Malik, psychiatrist from St. Louis, MO; Dr. Naila Khateeb, pediatrician from Leesville, LA; and Dr. Anita Afzal, child psychiatrist from St. Charles, LA.[10]

APPNA Sehat

APPNA Sehat in Islamabad had its own relief project, which provided food and shelter in the initial days after the earthquake under the direction of Late Dr. Hassan Bukhari (1938–2015) and its executive director Dr. Shafique ur Rehman. Sehat staff distributed 12 metric tons of non-perishable food and built 175 makeshift homes. Ajmaira village was adopted under this project for a period of six months to supply all amenities to the victims.

AAPI

A delegation of American Physicians of Indian Origin (AAPI) led by AAPI president Dr. Vijay Koli also visited the earthquake-affected areas.[11]

Officers and SWDR Volunteers in 2005

President Hussain Malik (PA), President elect AR Piracha (WV), Immediate past President Omar Atiq (AR), Secretary, Nadeem Kazi (AZ), Treasurer, Mahmood Alam (NY), Chair SWDR Committee Javed Akhtar (PA), Co-Chair Afzal Arain (CA), Members, Nadeem Zafar (TN), Waheed Akbar (MI), Mushtaq Sheikh (NY), Naveed Iqbal (NY), Asim Malik (NY), Muhammad Ali (FL), Saud Anwar (CT), Saima Zafar (IA), M. Shahid Yousuf (MI), Faisal Cheema (NY), Rubina Inayat (FL), Rizwan Khalid (NY), Rizwan Naeem (TX), Imtiaz Arain (IL), Sajid Chaudhary (FL), Mansoor Alam (IL) and numerous other volunteers including but not limited to Iqbal Ahmed (MA), Tariq Malik (MA), Zahra Ayub (MA), Saad Ayub, (MA), Nadeem Afridi (MA), Syed Imran Ali, Rifat Zaidi, Abdul Majeed (NY), Faheem Butt (NY), Sarwar Ghuman (NY), Qazi K. Haider (NY), Iqbal Jangda (NY), Mohammad Aslam (NY), Shahid Sheikh (OH), Abdullah Jafri (TX), Kashif Ansari (TX), Avais Masud (NJ), Amer Akmal (NJ), Mohammad Zubair (NJ), and Salim Chowdhery (NJ) worked with local communities and hospitals to collect funds and medical supplies.

APPNA Chapters

There were unprecedented initiatives taking place at most of the 20 chapters of APPNA in 2005. Both funds and in kind donations were collected for the relief efforts. The local print and TV media at numerous metropolises highlighted the Pakistani-Americans on the life after earthquake. Significant contributions came from the Connecticut, Illinois, Mid-Southern, New England, New Jersey, New York, Ohio, and Texas Chapters.[12]

APPNA's work with MASH[13]

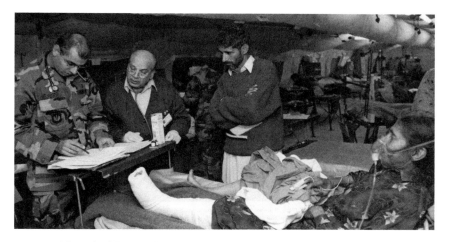

Major (Dr.) Fareed Sheikh with his father Dr. Mushtaq Sheikh from Elmira, NY --Working at the M.A.S.H. facility in Muzaffarabad, AJK

The disaster in Pakistan killed more than 80,000 people and rendered over 3.5 million people homeless. The U.S. Government mobilized its 212th M*A*S*H (Mobile Army Surgical Hospital) from Germany and sent it to Muzaffarabad on October 23 to help with the relief efforts. It provided 84 beds and a staff of 200 persons including our own APPNA Member and Pakistani American, Major (Dr.) Fareed Sheikh from the US Air Force. Dr. Fareed was joined by numerous physicians from the US, including his father, Dr. Mushtaq Sheikh, an internist from Elmira, New York. Dr. M. Raza Khan (IL) also joined MASH and he describes how he got to MASH unit: *"Being an internist with ER (emergency room) experience I volunteered my services with APPNA Earthquake team as soon as the magnitude of the human and property devastation became apparent and the need for urgent*

*medical relief became obvious. M.A.S.H. of American Military (was) set up
in Muzaffarabad where an Internist was needed to relieve the only internist,
Dr. Mushtaq Sheikh, who had been working nonstop for almost a month."*

The help from APPNA came in the form of physicians, medical students, and specialists from every field of medicine. MASH was one of
the best-organized health care facilities and was functioning according to
American standards. More than 20,000 patients were treated at MASH
in Muzaffarabad. This unit, worth $4.5 million, was handed over to the
Pakistani Military as a gift on February 16, 2006 so that it would continue
to serve earthquake stricken people of Pakistan as a temporary Combined
Military Hospital (CMH).

Canadian DART in Pakistan Earthquake

The prime minister of Canada announced that their Disaster Assistance
Response Team (DART) would be deployed to the earthquake-affected
region in Pakistan.[14] DART was fully operational on October 23, 2005.
DART consisted of a total of 215 military personnel, out of which 51
formed the medical platoon. APPNA lifetime member, Lt. Col. Dr. Arshad
Saeed (Dow) was one of the medical team members of DART.

Lt. Col. Dr. Arshad Saeed from Canada treating a
child at DART facility, Muzaffarabad, AJK

DART established static medical clinic and one of the Reverse Osmosis Water Purification Units (ROWPU) in the town of Garhi Dupatta, located 15 Km southeast of Muzaffarabad. Personnel were also located at Hatian Bala and in Muzaffarabad to support ROWPU operations and a small detachment of liaison and support staff was stationed in Islamabad. Canada also leased a (Kamov-32A) medium lift helicopter to distribute relief goods, deploy medical teams, and to evacuate patients from the mountainous terrain.

DART provided medical treatment to 11,782 patients, 7,000 of whom were treated by mobile medical teams, 2,637 in the static medical clinic, and 2,145 of whom received immunizations. Prior to DART's redeployment back to Canada, DART's winterized medical unit was donated to Pakistan Red Crescent Society operating in Garhi Dupatta in order to carry on the medical care. DART personnel returned to Canada on December 9, 2005.

APPNA and Relief operation at Abbottabad[15]

Dr. Naheed Usmani, President of New England Chapter of APPNA (APPNE) 2006 and Dr. Iftikhar Hussain were also passionately involved in earthquake relief with their chapter. Dr. Usmani describes her involvement as follows: *"Since a number of APPNE members were from Abbottabad and Mansehra area, APPNE decided to partner with first responders Abbottonian Medical Association (AMA, a doctor-run NGO in Abbottabad) and their Disaster Management Cell at Ayub Teaching hospital (ATH) in order to provide the relief goods, and for the purchase of ambulance. APPNE also worked on Mobile Rehabilitation Service with AMA for physiotherapy/OT services for amputees and injured."*[16]

Dr. Amjad Gulzar Shaikh, a London (UK) based orthopedic surgeon and a graduate of Sindh Medical College, Karachi, class of 1981, was among the first responders who provided most needed care of orthopedic surgery for the earthquake victims at Ayub Teaching Hospital in Abbottabad. In 2005 he co-founded Rehabilitation Response, a registered UK charity that provides humanitarian aid to the developing world. Besides providing valuable equipment for the surgeries, APPNA volunteers also worked alongside with Dr. Shaikh in the acute phase of the tragedy.

APPNA rebuilds *Kathai*, A village of HOPE![17,18]

A paramedic from New York was dropped to the devastated region of Kathai by a chopper. He communicated to Dr. Saeed Akhtar about the bleak situation in Kathai after the October 8 earthquake; no food, no shelter, and no access to roads due to landslides. APPNA adopted *Kathai* village, population 1150, situated 55 kilometer north of Muzaffarabad near the Line of Control with India. It is a valley close to the town of Chinari where significant death, disability, and destruction happened: 122 died, 87 were injured and 10–15 individuals were permanently disabled. About 235 houses were demolished including a girls' school in Kathai. Immediate response included all weather tents, blankets, sleeping bags and food. APPNA was able to nearly rebuild this adopted village with the help of Pakistani Army unit there. Dr. Waheed Akbar (MI) (past president APPNA) summarizes the role of Army: "*The Pakistani army (was) working full force, very courteous, and omnipresent. As we watched their interaction with the villagers, we were impressed by the general respect that they evoked by their dedicated commitment and hard work. The villagers were obviously grateful to "the Jawaans" (general infantry) of the Pakistani army. The Major in-charge of the APPNA's adopted Kathai village told us that he was covering 16 villages, with a population of about 26,000.*"[19]

Tents, blankets, food, and a large marquee tent for the completely demolished girls school was provided and supplies were airlifted to this valley that was otherwise cut off from the main road for several weeks after the earthquake. A medical clinic was also established where a fair number of Pakistani-American physicians had the honor to serve. Dr. Javed Akhtar, APPNA past president and Chair of the SWDR committee summarizes his team's efforts: "*We (APPNA) adopted Kathai as "APPNA Village." APPNA in Urdu language means "Ours." Things have changed a bit between November 10 when I first visited Kathai and December 24, the day of my last visit. Everyone had food and tents. Temporary shelters from the sheets and materials we provided are built with the help of Pak army and locals. They have enough food through March (the roughest time of the year because of harsh winter there). A girls and boys school is running in the tents we provided. We are especially proud of the marquee tent shipped from here (US) and it took a US Chinook helicopter to airlift it from Islamabad to Kathai. It is housing 72 girls (in) school. We found children playing cricket outdoors, a popular sport in Pakistan.*"[20]

The supplies were airlifted from Islamabad to Kathai village.
Dr. Nadeem Kazi is carrying the box and Dr. Saba Mansoor
is stepping out of the chopper among others.

Dr. Saeed Akhtar and Dr. Sobia Hafeez from Shifa International Hospital Islamabad
escorted a group of APPNA physicians to Kathai Village from Islamabad

The Girls middle school at Kathai was completely rebuilt with a total donation of $175,000 and $90,000 towards that funding came from the Arizona Chapter. This building was three times larger than the demolished building. The new building was inaugurated by Dr. Nadeem Kazi on December 23, 2007. This school was also visited by Dr. Mahmood Alam in December of 2008 since the work was still in progress.[21, 22]

Dr. Hussain Malik poses with Kids at Kathai village
during his visit in November 2005.

There was no running water in Kathai due to landslides. The villagers had to go down about 1,000 feet to fetch the water. APPNA offered $50,000 and requested the Army Engineering Corp if they could rebuild the blocked channel. APPNA also helped to run two schools for boys and girls in partnership with the "Read Foundation" in the area adjacent to Kathai.

APPNA Rehabilitation Projects in Earthquake Areas[23, 24]

There were huge numbers of amputees and paraplegics left in the wake of the earthquake and long-term rehabilitation was needed for the affected people. There were 719 amputations and 659 paraplegic patients officially recorded from different hospitals in Frontier (NWFP) and Punjab provinces. Within the short period of 6–12 months, APPNA helped establish two rehab centers in the cities of Rawalpindi and Mansehra, fully equipped to offer physical therapy and artificial limbs.

PIPOS-APPNA Rehabilitation Center of Mansehra[25]

The Pakistan Institute of Prosthetic and Orthotic Sciences (PIPOS) is Pakistan's primary prosthetic treatment center and the only school for prosthetic and orthotic sciences in South Asia when it was built. PIPOS was established by the German non-profit GTZ in 1979 and is affiliated with Peshawar University. The PIPOS-APPNA Rehab Centre, situated in the District Headquarter Hospital (DHQ) of Mansehra, has been fully operational since February 2006. The center was well equipped with the machinery necessary for the manufacturing of prostheses (artificial limbs) and orthoses (body supports). APPNA's New York Chapter had pledged US $200,000 as three-year funding for this project. In the year 2006–2007, the center had provided physiotherapy, prosthetic and orthotic services to 593 patients. The center manufactured and fitted 271 assistive devices with 103 prostheses and 168 orthoses. All services were provided free of cost to the patients.

APPNA Rehabilitation Center at Rawalpindi General Hospital (RGH)[26, 27]

This project was undertaken by APPNA due to the personal interest of APPNA President 2006, Dr. A.R. Piracha with commitment of Professor of Orthopedics, Dr. Salim Chaudhary at RGH, whose dedication was instrumental in completing this project in record time. A budget of $286,000 was allocated for this project by APPNA. An existing building was remodeled and expanded to construct three operating rooms as well as a connecting bridge between the units and the operating theater.

The center was located on the campus of Rawalpindi General Hospital and comprised of the following:
- Physiotherapy unit.

- Orthopedic workshop and Artificial Limb Center.
- Orthopedic Rehab Ward
- Orthopedic and Spinal Operating rooms.
- Orthotic experts visited the center in late 2005 and early 2006
  to install prosthetic limbs on earthquake amputees. This rehab
  center fitted 666 patients with prosthetic limbs. These patients also
  underwent the necessary physiotherapy in order to learn the use of
  artificial limbs and are seen at the center for follow-up visits.

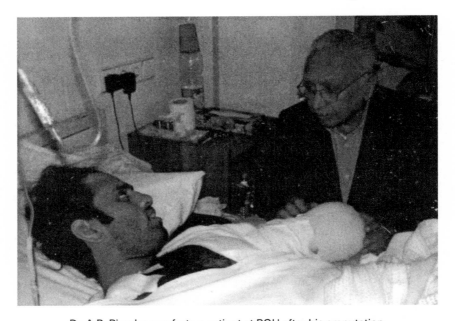

Dr. A.R. Piracha comforts a patient at RGH after his amputation.

US Medical Students volunteer in
Earthquake hit areas during Summer 2006

Six medical students of Pakistani descent from around the United States
went on an APPNA sponsored trip to work in Pakistan Islamic Medical
Association (PIMA) medical clinic at Muzaffarabad for a 2-week rotation
in July 2006. They experienced first-hand patient care and visited numerous buildings and homes that were destroyed by the earthquake. They witnessed the survivors' resolve to rebuild and return to a normal life.

"My experience with the APPNA rehabilitation centers in Mansehra and Rawalpindi General Hospital was extremely positive. I watched from beginning to end how the patient received a prosthetic limb. I was very impressed with the way that, there was so much attention to detail in the making of prosthesis as well as how well trained and knowledgeable the staff was. It was clear to see how much of a difference a prosthetic made in an amputee's life. And then to see that they were given physical therapy reassured me that the staff was doing as much as possible to improve the quality of the patients' lives. The only thing they needed was some level of occupational therapy so that the patients will would again be able to return to their normal routines." —Henna Qureshi (APPNA 2006 Medical Students Relief Mission member)

APPNA Earthquake Rehabilitation and Reconstruction Projects: An Overview [28]

APPNA Orthopedic and Rehab Center, Rawalpindi	Completed, 2006
APPNA Rehab Center, Mansehra	Completed, 2006
APPNA Dispensary, Topa Soon, Dist. Rawlakot	Completed, 2007
APPNA Police Hospital, Abbottabad	Completed, 2007
APPNA Girls School, Khatai, Dist. Muzaffarabad	Completed, 2007–2008
Village of Hope—Children Campus, Dist. Mansehra	Completed, 2006
TCF School—APPNA Campus, Mohri Farman Shah, Dist. Poonch	Completed, 2007–2008
Saba Trust Orphanage—APPNA Block, Rawalpindi	Completed, 2007

APPNA Disaster Relief Conference, December 22–23, 2005 [29]

In the midst of earthquake relief efforts, Dr. Hussain Malik cancelled APPNA 2005 winter meeting in Lahore. Instead, APPNA in collaboration with the National Commission on Human Development (NCHD), and Aga Khan University Karachi (AKU) arranged a timely and thought provoking conference titled "POST DISASTER HEALTH CARE SYSTEMS IN PAKISTAN: A NATIONAL AND INTERNATIONAL CHALLENGE." Dr. M. Saud Anwar, the Chair of the scientific committee of the conference, expressed *this conference is envisioned as the first organized step towards enhancing the current healthcare system to be better equipped for the later phases of the current challenge and future disasters.*

The conference attracted a wide range of experts with experience and knowledge of disaster preparedness and building of a healthcare system equipped with disaster relief management. The participants from Pakistan were represented by the Government of Pakistan, Dr. Mussadiq, Principal Rawalpindi Medical College (RMC), Dr. Nasim Ashraf (past president APPNA) of National Commission (PK) on Human Development, Dr. Junaid Razzak, Aga Khan University, Higher Education Commission (HEC), Pakistan Medical and Dental Council (PMDC), Pakistan Medical Association (PMA), PIMA, Ayub Medical College (AMC) Abbotabad, Punjab emergency and ambulance services, Rescue 1122, and Pakistan Army. Among the international groups the participants represented, Johns Hopkins University, Harvard Medical School (Dr. Stephanie Rosborough), USAID, Save the Children, Rush University Medical Center, IL, University of Connecticut, Hartford, Arizona Department of Health Services, American College of Surgeons, WHO collaborating center, Center for Public Health Preparedness and Disaster Response, American Medical Association (AMA) (Dr. James James), and Ephesus Emergency Medicine Training and Research Center, Izmir, Turkey (Dr. James Fowler), to name a few.

The recommendations and the disaster conference declaration were summarized by APPNA's President elect, Dr. Piracha. The meeting was concluded by Dr. Raza Bokhari, president Rawalpindi Medical College Alumni Association of North America (RMCAANA) 2005 and conference chair, who thanked all the participants especially Dr. Umar, Professor of Medicine at RMC and Dr. Saud Anwar for their role in the success of this conference.

Disaster Conference Summary[30]

The important guiding Principles of Disaster Planning and Management were identified in this International Conference and are summarized below.

1. The current situation and management plans though helped in dealing with the aftermath of disaster are not enough at this time from long-term management perspective.
2. It is critical for sustenance of disaster plans to have alliances and partnerships amongst different stakeholders.
3. The disaster plan and management of a country remains a responsibility of the government and its administration should seek support from other stakeholders.
4. The use of coordination, collaboration, communication, and capacity building is of paramount importance.
5. Investment in education of masses and disaster managers remains a cornerstone of effective future plan.
6. Work should be services based, along with data-driven research.
7. Development of accountability, transparency, and trust between stakeholders would help ensure sustainability and collaboration.
8. All stakeholders must continue to learn from the current experience.
9. A paradigm shift is needed in the mindset of the government from reactive processes to preventive and preparedness and safety culture.
10. The success of disaster management process is dependent on the political will and understanding of the administration.
11. Effective preparedness may require a multi-prong approach including top down and bottom up approaches working simultaneously to meet in the middle and improve the situation.

APPNA Responds to Baluchistan Earthquake 2008[31]

Hours and minutes often make the difference between life and death for the victims of disasters. The Baluchistan earthquake struck on October 29, 2008. Immediately, telephonic contacts were established with APPNA's Pakistan based network through Zeeshan Piracha and damage assessment was undertaken. Immediate action was taken by the SWDRC under the leadership of Dr. Shahabul Arfeen (IA) (Chair) and Dr. Mansoor Alam (IL)(Co-Chair). Numerous chapters of APPNA responded to the appeal by the committee. Initial help comprised of food and basic provisions for 100 families for a month. Past President, Dr. A.R Piracha also helped to facilitate APPNA's relief work through his contacts in Quetta. A total of

$100,000 was raised through the efforts of APPNA chapters during the fall of 2008. Immediate release of $50,000 to the affected area was instrumental in building 60 homes for the internally displaced people in the village of Kharboz. Dr. Tariq Cheema and Dr. Mahmood Alam made a visit to meet with inhabitants of houses built with APPNA donations in December 2008. Some communities, such as the one in New Orleans, decided to give part of their own funds ($20,000) for the earthquake in addition to the contributions given to Edhi Foundation (PK) and Red Crescent Society of Pakistan.

APPNA Relief Work in Pakistan Floods

APPNA has always stepped forward when any calamity strikes Pakistan and APPNA's response to the floods (2007–2015), which wreaked havoc in Gilgit-Baltistan, southern Punjab, and Sindh were no exception. The membership of the organization at large, its leadership and the SWDRC rose to occasions by joining hands with the international and local disaster relief agencies. Dedicated members provided all the support they could; from healthcare and equipment to combat these disasters in acute phase and then in the months to come when late effects of displacement and disease made life miserable. In 2007, APPNA raised $15,000 for the Pakistan floods relief. The funds were distributed through Edhi Trust, Pakistan Medical Association, and Red Crescent.[32]

Flood Relief 2010[33]

APPNA's efforts towards the 2010 floods were supported generously by the membership and communities all across the continent and raised a total of $1,343,630.00. Dr. Zeelaf Munir (DE), APPNA president 2010 made an urgent visit to the flood ravaged areas right away. The efforts of helping the flood victims were divided in three phases.

Phase 1 *Immediate relief:* by helping with rescue efforts and providing food, shelter, water, clothing, and supplies of daily living. Alumni and medical college based social organizations working on ground partnered with APPNA.

Phase 2 *Intermediate relief:* in this phase, the above-mentioned efforts were continued. In addition, a huge multi-center vaccination campaign was started to prevent water borne diseases. This project was in collaboration with American Academy of Pediatrics [AAP] and Pakistan Pediatric Association [PPA]. The areas served by APPNA included Mardan,

Nowshera, Samar Bagh, Multan, Muzaffargarh, Sunawan, Taunsa, Kot Addu, Makli, Thatta and Shahdad Kot. APPNA also collaborated with the USAID and other agencies to obtain grants for its relief projects.

Phase 3 *Rehabilitation*: SWDRC recommended adopting a village in the flood affected area in collaboration with the Human Development foundation [HDF].

Dr. Zeelaf Munir at groundbreaking of Samarbagh village; a co-sponsorship of APPNA-HDF to rebuild the village completely destroyed by the flood in 2010

President Munir appointed a task force, which comprised of three members from HDF and four members from APPNA. APPNA was represented by Dr. Manzoor Tariq (MO) (President-elect 2011), Dr. Nasar Qureshi (Secretary 2010), M. Javed Akhtar (Former SWDRC Chair 2006) and Dr. Jamil Farooqui (Chair SWDRC 2010). APPNA and HDF adopted Samar Bagh, a village in Mardan. The village was reconstructed by building houses, school, and a community health unit. The project also included the development of sewerage systems, roads, and the provision of clean drinking water by installing a water purification plant. The cost of the project was $777,357.00. This included the initial reconstruction and running cost for three years. This cost was equally shared by HDF and APPNA.

Dr. Farooqui visited Samar Bagh in November 2010 and inaugurated the "Concept Launching Event" for the Model village. Later in December 2010, Dr. Zeelaf Munir, Dr. Manzoor Tariq, Dr. Atiya Khan, and Dr. Javed Akhtar were among others who participated in the "Groundbreaking Ceremony" for this project.

Flood Relief in Southern Punjab 2010[34]

Physicians based in Nishtar Medical College organized relief work. A not-for-profit organization PWS MINAR run by Mr. Seyal and Dr. Durre Sabih, in collaboration with Professor Inayatullah, Dr Salma Tanweer and others delivered a great deal in flood relief efforts of 2010. It was mostly in Khangarh area where west bank of Chanab had crested. APPNA got involved in this work right from the outset.

The work included construction of houses. Out of them 120 were built anew and additional 400 got significant repairs. One hundred and ten water hand pumps were installed. One water filtration plant was installed in village Gurmani from donations of APPNA members Abdul Jabbar and Babar Cheema of Louisville, KY. Numerous medical camps were conducted and thousands of patients treated in a wide area right up to Rojhan at the Sindh border with the help of army helicopters, boats and army trucks. Hundreds of local doctors participated voluntarily. Medicines worth lacs of rupees dispensed. Follow up camps were also done in most areas.

APPNA's SWDRC donated $13,000, Nishtar Alumni of North America (NANA) donated $30,000, and APPNE chapter donated $20,000 (A total of 63,000 dollars by APPNA and its affiliates) to this relief work. In addition to that, bulk of donations were raised locally. Dr. Jamil Farooqi, Chair SWDRC 2010, Dr. Haroon Durrani President NANA 2010 and Dr. Manzoor Tariq President 2011, personally visited the area and the work. The involvement of Dr. Fauzia Wali Khan of APPNE and Dr. Rashid Piracha, Past President APPNA was crucial in bringing in the donations. Dr. Nasir Gondal's personal efforts brought together the Multan based team and APPNA along with its affiliates.

American Academy of Pediatrics
DEDICATED TO THE HEALTH OF ALL CHILDREN™

141 Northwest Point Blvd
Elk Grove Village, IL 60007-1019
Phone: 847/434-4000
Fax: 847/434-8000
E-mail: kidsdocs@aap.org
www.aap.org

November 24, 2010

Dr. Zeelaf Munir, President
Association of Physicians of Pakistani Descent of North America
6414 South Cass Avenue
Westmont, IL 60559

Executive Committee

President
O. Marion Burton, MD, FAAP

President-Elect
Robert W. Block, MD, FAAP

Immediate Past President
Judith S. Palfrey, MD, FAAP

Executive Director/CEO
Errol R. Alden, MD, FAAP

Board of Directors

District I
Carole E. Allen, MD, FAAP
Arlington, MA

District II
Henry A. Schaeffer, MD, FAAP
Brooklyn, NY

District III
Sandra Gibson Hassink, MD, FAAP
Wilmington, DE

District IV
Francis E. Rushton, Jr, MD, FAAP
Beaufort, SC

District V
Marilyn J. Bull, MD, FAAP
Indianapolis, IN

District VI
Michael V. Severson, MD, FAAP
Brainerd, MN

District VII
Kenneth E. Matthews, MD, FAAP
College Station, TX

District VIII
Mary P. Brown, MD, FAAP
Bend, OH

District IX
Myles B. Abbott, MD, FAAP
Berkeley, CA

District X
John S. Curran, MD, FAAP
Tampa, FL

Dear Dr. Munir:

I would like to extend my personal thanks for the matching contribution of $35,500 to the American Academy of Pediatrics. Your gift spurred our membership into increasing their donations for disaster relief funds for Pakistan.

Your contribution was made to the Friends of Children Fund and designated for Disaster Relief, where it will be used to provide assistance to children in Pakistan. To date, the Academy has been working with the Pakistan Pediatric Association to provide funding for medicine and vaccines for children in flood affected areas.

I am pleased to recognize Association of Physicians of Pakistani Descent of North America as a member of the *Della Robbia Club*. Your organization's name will be listed in the Honor Roll of Giving published in the *AAP News* in September of 2011.

If you have any questions or would like additional information, please do not hesitate to contact our Development office at (888) 700-5378.

Sincerely,

Brad Hutchins
Director of Development

Thank you for Munir and the APPDNA for supporting the AAP and our friends of Children Fund

P.S. Please retain this letter as your official tax receipt. No gifts or services were provided in exchange for this contribution. The American Academy of Pediatrics is chartered as a 501(c)(3) educational and philanthropic organization and your gift is tax deductible as allowed by law.

BH/gkg

The program was Very Successful.

Brad

Medical Relief in Floods of 2010

Dr. Mubasher Rana (CA) (APPNA president 2015) shared his experience, *"When floods hit Pakistan, we knew we had to go back and help. I took two weeks off from my practice and went to Pakistan as a representative of APPNA. The arrangements for my visit were made through Relief International (USA). Qasba Gujarat is about 1.5-hour drive from Multan and is close to Kot Addu in District Muzaffargarh in Southern Punjab. As I drove to my destination, the effects of the flood became increasingly apparent. Whole villages were destroyed. Roads were badly damaged and bridges washed away. People were living in tents or partially built shacks. These poor people had very little to begin with and had lost all they possessed. Besides, volunteering in Dr. Qadeer's clinic, I organized Medical Camps in various villages. The devastation of the flood and its consequences were apparent. We saw 40–50 patients per day. I realized there were infectious diseases which were rampant; diarrhea, malaria, skin abscesses, and upper respiratory infections. Moreover, you could immediately identify the widespread malnutrition, especially in children.*"[35]

Dr. Mubasher Rana in an open air medical clinic for the flood victims

Munirabad and Farooqabad Villages: [36]

One of the tasks assigned by KEMCAANA (King Edward Medical College Alumni Association of North America) Executive committee to Dr. Mubasher Rana during his volunteer visit to Kot Addu was to identify a village which KEMCAANA could adopt and rebuild. Dr. Rana identified the village of Farooqabad and assembled a team of local volunteers under the leadership of Mr. Babar Mughal to do the rebuilding. KEMCAANA built 100 houses at $1000 each.[37]

Dr. Manzoor Tariq and others at the opening ceremony
of Munirabad Village in December 2011

After the success of Farooqabad village, APPNA adopted flood-affected
Munirabad village after assisting in the acute phase of disaster with provision of clean water, shelter, and medical supplies in 2011. Dr. Aisha Zafar
(Chair SWDRC 2011) and Dr. Ayesha Najib (MD) were actively involved
in fundraising. SWDRC raised $60,000 on 27th night of Ramadan that
included a generous donation of $25,000 from Dr. Manzoor Tariq (MO).
That evening was memorable for SWDRC. Dr. Aisha Zafar personally
made several dozen calls throughout the late night and early morning
and membership responded generously. Never before in APPNA's history
was a project an overnight reality such as Munirabad. Response exceeded
expectations and APPNA was able to build 28 more homes than originally
promised. A total of 128 homes were built by the same team as Farooqabad
at a cost of $1,000 per residence. The cement brick homes had an addi-
tional feature that being of an attached bathroom with its own septic
system. Previously mud and thatch huts were the norm. The official inauguration took place on December 24, 2011. APPNA also provided clothing
and 1,600 pair of shoes to the children of Munirabad in 2012. These would

be the first pairs of shoes they had worn in their lives. In the same year, the St. Louis chapter provided the initial money for a dispensary that was also established in the Munirabad village that treated about 400 patients a month. The cost of running the dispensary was $600 per month. A water purification plant was also donated at the cost of $4,500. Dr. Mubasher Rana, (Chair SWDRC 2012) and his team's efforts were instrumental in completing the job. In the words of Dr. Manzoor Tariq, *"Revisiting the village after one year (2012), it was amazing to see the world of difference APPNA made for the villagers. Everyone was residing comfortably in their homes, clothed warmly, and filled with nothing but prayers and love of APPNA."*

Munirabad School

APPNA built a primary school in Munirabad that opened its doors in 2011. In four short years, it has become a model school. It was declared the best among thirty local schools by National Commission of Human Development (PK). Currently, there are 125 students enrolled, who otherwise would not have attended school. Four dedicated teachers provide quality education to sixty-five girls and sixty boys every day up to fifth grade. APPNA donated $26,000 for the maintenance of this school in 2015. Presently, this school is being supervised by *Tameer-e-Millat* Foundation (PK).

APPNA activist and President KEMCAANA 2014, Dr. Ayesha Najib (AZ) introduces a student of the Munirabad School: *"Meet Zubair. It was the devastating floods of 2010 that opened school doors for 12-year-old Zubair. His family lost their house and all their possessions. Then APPNA came, which built his one room house and established a primary school in his village that transformed his life.*

Zubair's father is a "Tandoorchi." He expected his son to follow the same path, but his son had dreams. He wanted to attend school and make his own path. When APPNA School opened in Munirabad, this dream became a reality for Zubair. Our volunteers saw his drive and convinced his father to send him to school. He excelled in school and covered five grades in three years. He recently stood first in his district for fifth grade exams." [38]

More recently, it was decided that APPNA Munirabad Primary School will be expanded to high school level. More land has been acquired and a new school will be built in collaboration with the Citizens Foundation (TCF). The Washington DC /Virginia/Maryland chapter will sponsor the project. APPNA raised $50,000 and the remaining $150,000 has been donated by the DC chapter.

Floods in 2011 and Sajawal Home Project

In September of 2011, areas of Sindh province were badly hit with floods. Again APPNA membership responded with commitment to rebuild homes for the internally displaced and by providing vehicles for economic assistance. SWDRC helped building 100 homes at cost of $1200 per home in village Rahib Amaro in Sajawal Sindh in partnership with "Shine Humanity." The money for this project was donated by APPNA Southern California Chapter.

Floods in 2012 and 2014

Torrential monsoon rains and flash floods hit Pakistan in August and September 2012. There were over 200 reported dead and nearly 1000 were injured. Almost 2 million acres of land was affected resulting in billions of Rupees loss in agricultural produce. SWDRC collected over $15,000 for the flood victims and distributed money through Akhuwat Foundation, Patient Welfare Societies, and Edhi Trust in Pakistan.

In 2014, $25,240 was donated to Akhuwat Foundation to help flood victims. Also in 2014, $10,841 was donated to Mukhtaran Mai Girls' School in Meerwala, District Muzaffargarh. Another $10,000 was donated to St. Albert School in Faisalabad run by Sisters of Loretto to support the deserving students.

Motorcycle Rickshaw Project

To help with earnings for the families in the flood affected areas of Sanghar, Badin, and Mirpurkhas, APPNA raised $35,000 and distributed 34 Rickshaws in 2012. Dr. Abdul Majeed (LMC) led this project.

Karachi Heat-wave—2015

The 2015 Karachi heat-wave death toll had been estimated at well over 1,000. Temperatures in much of Southern Pakistan reached 49°C (120°F) in the shade. With urban cement structures and lack of air conditioning human life became unbearable. Experts surmised that it was a symptom of global warming. Coinciding with the month of fasting in which no food or water is to be taken dusk to dawn, rapid fluid loss resulted in severe dehydration especially of the vulnerable. Morgues were filling beyond capacity as corpses were heaped one upon the other. Hospitals were unable to cater to the deluge of infirm, hyperthermic, and dehydrated patients. Failure of the electric grid left fans, air conditioners and water pumps nonfunctional. The media reported the daily death toll and hardship in Karachi.

APPNA is actively followed on social media of which Facebook and APPNA's own website are popular visiting sites. The rapid response of SWDRC to this human catastrophe gained the support of Pakistani expatriate community. The donors rushed to APPNA website to donate. It was a grassroots response. Donations in all sums were received from the community and ranged from $5–$5,000 and other denominations. These included one of $5 from a little girl who apologized that it was all she could afford. It was this trickle that grew into a torrent and APPNA was receiving well over $1000 per hour in its first 24 hours of the appeal.

A Pakistan Link (CA) newspaper article July 3, 2015 reported the following:

Dr. Mubasher Rana (CA), APPNA President, stated, *"APPNA has a strong and longstanding tradition of helping in charitable causes. The situation in Karachi and Southern Sindh is very grim and resources in Pakistan are limited. People are in dire state in this holy month of Ramadan. It is imperative we do whatever we can to relieve their suffering and illness. APPNA will continue to play its part in providing medical and social relief."* Dr. Aisha Zafar (IN), Chair Social Welfare and Disaster Relief Committee stated, *"After providing funds for acute care like medicines and food, we are now focusing on providing water coolers for clean water in hospitals in Karachi."*

The outpouring of support from APPNA members and expatriate Pakistanis alike was very heartening. The Karachi heat-wave funds raised were $121,000 and most of this money was given to several hospitals in Karachi including Civil, Jinnah, Qatar, Children's cancer hospital, Patient Welfare Association, SIUT (Sind Institute of Urology and Transplantation) and Cytogenetics Lab at Jinnah Hospital, which has been an APPNA project. These funds were used for medical supplies, medicines and treatment of indigent patients as well as provision of food and water in some areas.

Pakistan Earthquake 2015

Pakistan was shaken with yet another earthquake in 2015. Fortunately, the damage and destruction was not as much as previous earthquakes. APPNA raised $15,000 for tents and blankets, distributed with the assistance of Dr. Saeed Akhtar (PK).

Healthcare Projects

Cytogenetics Lab Project in Karachi Pakistan [39, 40, 41]

Genetic diagnosis is an essential element for treating childhood leukemia. Most patients at National Institute of Child Health (NICH), Karachi, Pakistan, are investigated and treated free of cost. As 99% of the patients cannot afford to pay for their investigations and treatment, the Child Aid Association (CAA)(PK) made a provision that all patients receive free treatment according to international protocols.

Children at the opening of APPNA sponsored Cytogenetic Lab in Karachi at the hospital where their cancer was cured with free world class treatment

APPNA was approached for assistance and decided to support the Cytogenetic laboratory as a center of excellence; a prelude to the first Bone Marrow Transplantation in public sector in Pakistan. This was a joint effort of APPNA, Department of Cytogenetics at Texas Children's Hospital, Houston, TX, CAA, and the NICH. The role of Dr. Rizwan C. Naeem, a geneticist who was on the faculty at Texas Children's Hospital at that time, was instrumental in this collaboration. It was made possible due to investment of precious time and expertise of Pakistani Physicians and monetary donations by the members in order to establish a genetic diagnostic laboratory at NICH. Dr. Nadeem Zafar, a pathologist from Tennessee, also played a significant role in this venture. The APPNA fundraising efforts for the support of Cytogenetics laboratory resulted in collection of $41,000 in Ramadan of 2004. As a result, we were able to start funding the project. The Cytogenetic laboratory at NICH in Karachi was formally inaugurated on December 27, 2007 by the children who benefitted from the Institute. Another grant of $7,200 was given for the equipment to be used for administering chemotherapy at the children's hospital in 2009.

APPNA supports Medicine & Endocrine Foundation (MEF) Jinnah Postgraduate Medical Centre Karachi (JPMC), 2007–2008 [42]

This project was started by concerned citizens as a partnership between the government and private philanthropists, in response to the paucity of effective Endocrine services available to Karachi's indigent patient population. Jinnah Postgraduate Medical Center in Karachi was selected as the venue for this project. APPNA donated $15,000 in support of this joint venture in which Dr. Shahabul Arfeen (IN) played a major role.

In addition to providing high quality medical services, the MEF-supported Medical Unit II is now the premier teaching unit at JPMC, and has already produced numerous highly trained and motivated physicians that have gone on to continue the good work all over Pakistan. In recognition of the stellar work being done by the MEF, the Ministry of Health in Islamabad expressed an interest in adopting the MEF model of public-private partnership as a blueprint for improving all government-run hospitals in Pakistan.

Pediatric Intensive Care Project at Faisalabad Medical College [43, 44]

Around October 2009, we were notified that several children had died in Faisalabad Children's hospital due to lack of ventilators. Dr. Shahid Sheikh (OH), a graduate of Punjab Medical College (PMC) spearheaded a campaign along with SWDRC co-chair, Dr. Nadeem Zafar and raised $70,000. A generous grant of $50,000 was also received from Islamic Relief (USA) for this project.

Later in 2011, the APPNA-Ohio chapter, in collaboration with Punjab Medical College Alumni Association (PMCAANA) and APPNA-SWDRC, expanded the project to upgrade Pediatrics and Neonatal Intensive Care Units (PICU/NICU) and raised over $200,000 to establish PICU/NICU at PMC. PMCAANA also coordinated education of young physicians, nurses, and respiratory therapists on Pediatric ICU care including ventilator management. Now it is a thriving and fully functional tertiary care PICU/NICU which is self-sustaining. It is able to provide care free of charge to the children in need and have saved lives of estimated 1,000 children every year.

Rawalian Burn Center [45]

In 2006, a small group of physicians recognized the need for a burn treatment center that would be available to the public in the Rawalpindi/ Islamabad area of Pakistan. Until that time, there was no burn center in public sector in the Rawalpindi/ Islamabad area. The mortality rate in the Rawalpindi area for major burns was extremely high at 73.8% as compared to other neighboring countries. Therefore, a small burn center was established by the Rawalpindi Medical College Overseas Foundation (RMCOF) in collaboration with APPNA and the Rawalpindi Medical College Alumni Association for North America (RMCAANA). The space for this facility was provided by Holy Family Hospital in Rawalpindi. The initial staff consisted of one plastic surgeon, two medical officers, six nurses, and fifteen other staff members. The initial facilities included a burn ICU, a hydrotherapy unit, inpatient dressing rooms, outpatient clinic, library, and a seminar room.

A review conducted after two years of operation showed a total of 1,546 outpatients, 1,956 consultations, 1,610 surgeries, and 97 patients admitted in the hospital of which 55 recovered and were discharged. These results revealed that mortality had been reduced from 73.8% to 46%. At this point, an effort was made to convince the Punjab government to assume responsibility for this facility that had been funded from private donations and the limited resources were now exhausted. After a very long and arduous process, the Punjab Government assumed responsibility for the Burn Center in 2010. The following audit, which was conducted at the 5-year mark, 2.5 years after the facility had been administered by the government, the total number of patients admitted had climbed to 596, of which 365 were discharged, showing a mortality rate of 40%.

APPNA Institute of Public Health, Karachi, Pakistan[46]

Dr. Javed Suleman (NY) (President APPNA 2013) presented the idea of APPNA Institute of Public Health (AIPH) at the 2013 APPNA fall council meeting held in Houston, TX. It was proposed, if APPNA could provide the seed money for the establishment of AIPH this would bring APPNA's name as the institution builder. During the banquet, Dr. Suleman raised $80,000 in donations and pledges that were later sent to Jinnah Sindh Medical University (JSMU).

AIPH opened its door in 2014 with the help of Dr. Lubna Baig as its first Dean, a graduate of Dow Universities of Medical Sciences. She received her PhD from University of Calgary, Canada. She has extensive teaching and management experience in public health.

AIPH offers Master of Public Health (MPH) and Master of Science in Public Health (MSPH). In addition, AIPH offers multiple short courses on various topics like curriculum planning, child abuse, sexual harassment at work & anti-harassment laws, qualitative research, health research, and urban emergency management.

The goal of AIPH is to develop public and private partnership models of primary health care, support government in policy formulation through empirical studies and provide support for their implementation, monitoring and evaluation. AIPH plans to produce competent public health professionals, by teaching accredited competency based curriculum.

APPNA's support for the Visually Impaired— LRBT and Rotary Club of Pakistan[47]

APPNA has been collaborating with *Layton* Rahmatulla Benevolent Trust (LRBT) since 2005. Dr. Aisha Zafar worked hard on this work from 2012–2015. LRBT website claims that they treat 1 out of 3 eye patients in Pakistan. In 2015 alone, more than 12 eye camps were held with APPNA sponsorship. For the three eye camps held in Karachi, APPNA also held free medical camps and around 1,000 patients were seen in each camp. It costs $73 to treat pediatric cataract, $28 for adult cataract and $40 for squint surgery. APPNA worked with Rotary Pakistan and eye surgeries are funded through them at local district hospitals. This is being supported by Pakistan Association of Memphis TN as an annual project. APPNA donated about $20,000 dollars in 2015. In another program, $2,000 was donated to Amigos Welfare Trust (PK) for blind persons to provide white canes and audio recordings.

Health Education Campaigns

APPNA Hepatitis C Awareness Campaign in Pakistan[48]

The APPNA Hepatitis C Initiative begun in 2011 under the leadership of Dr. Maqbool Arshad (WI). The Hepatitis C Initiative committee was established after an exploratory meeting held at Lahore Gymkhana Club in 2011. APPNA delegates visiting from the U.S. also held a town hall meeting at Lahore, along with politicians and medical professionals. It was felt that Hepatitis C had almost reached an epidemic level in Pakistan, which would lead to the deaths of millions of innocent citizens.

The committee after deliberations felt that a comprehensive educational campaign should be launched to raise awareness about Hepatitis C. The re-use of needles, transfusion of contaminated blood, and use of unsterilized hospital surgical and diagnostic equipment remain the major sources of Hepatitis C infection in countries like Pakistan. The barbers, beauty parlor workers, and unscrupulous dentists and physicians are also responsible for the spread of hepatitis C along with infections like HIV and other blood borne illnesses.

The committee then initiated the work of creating educational materials for public and medical professionals alike. Funds for this work were raised from members of APPNA. Islamic Relief also contributed funds in this effort.

Individuals who participated in this campaign included Dr. Manzoor Tariq, Dr. Jameel Tareen, Dr. Muhammad Nadeem, Dr. Aisha Zafar, Dr. Sajid Chaudhry, Dr. Ahmed Malik, Professor Fasiha Kanwal, and Dr. Maqbool Arshad, as chairman of this committee. A network of interested and influential Gastroenterologists and Hepatologists were included from Pakistan. Key roles were played by a number of individuals including Professor Saeed Hameed of Agha Khan University and Professor Hasan Abbas Zaheer of Pakistan Institute of Medical Sciences (PK) and the Director of Safe Transfusion Program. General Suhaib Ahmad and Professor Arif Siddiqi of Allama Iqbal Medical College (PK). Hematologists and hospital safety committee members of JPMC and Indus Hospital, Karachi also participated.

Guidelines for dialysis centers to prevent blood borne infections were developed with the efforts of Dr. Ahmad Malik. Hospital sterilization protocols and blood safety program guidelines were developed and printed after a meeting of experts that was held at Pearl Continental Hotel, Lahore, in December 2012. Experts from Jinnah Postgraduate Medical Institute, Aga Khan University Hospital, Indus Hospital, Karachi, and Allama Iqbal Medical College, Lahore assisted in developing guidelines for blood safety, surgical instrument disinfection protocols, and methods of preventing the spread of Hepatitis C. These guidelines and protocols were published and distributed in hospitals and medical colleges throughout Pakistan.

Another meeting was held in December 2013 at the Avari Hotel, Lahore, where experts in the field from Pakistan, the representatives of the World Health Organization-Pakistan region, and other stakeholders participated. The public health guidelines were developed and published to help stop the spread of the disease.

During this effort, educational booklets, posters and animated videos were developed. It was carried out with active participation of the staff of King Edward Medical College Alumni Association in Lahore, as well as expert consultation was provided on voluntary basis by Mrs. Sara Ikram, who oversaw the development of posters and videos as well as booklet for the campaign. Students from King Edward Medical University also participated in the development of this program.

APPNA sponsored Pakistan Hepatitis Day has been actively observed with lectures, seminars, and rallies throughout Pakistan since 2012. More than 40 medical institutions, including all major medical universities, hospitals and clinics participate in these activities annually. There has been participation from rural areas and small cities in this campaign as well. Over the last five years, the campaign has reached all corners of Pakistan. APPNA have made presentations to the Federal Minister of Health and Coordination, Chief Minister of Punjab, and the government and-health professionals in Khyber Pakhtunkhwa Province.

There are estimated 12–15 million people in Pakistan suffering with Hepatitis B and C. This number is mounting every day. A large number of these people would die early with liver failure either due to cirrhosis or cancer of liver. It is felt that without a comprehensive plan of action to curb the disease by the Government of Pakistan, which enforces the elimination of unscrupulous practices of unsterilized use of all the vehicles of this blood borne disease, the epidemic of Hepatitis C cannot be addressed by the educational campaign of NGO's alone.

APPNA receives Dr. Zakir Husain Award for Polio Eradication help in India:[49]

The Polio epidemic was worst in Uttar Pradesh (UP) before it was completely eradicated in India. In 2002 UP had 1241 cases, which were 65% of total global cases. APPNA donated $11,000 to Federation of Aligarh Alumni Association (FAAA) for holding camps in polio affected areas of UP in 2005. FAAA, through Aligarh Muslim University (AMU) initiative funded the camps at various locations in UP. At the annual convention of FAAA held in August 2008, APPNA was given Dr. Zakir Hussain award for community service in India for helping in polio eradication. Dr. Farzana Bharmal (GA) received this award on behalf of APPNA who appreciated the generosity of Dr. Hussain Malik, president 2005 and the efforts put forth by Mr. Hasan Kamal, Dr. Shahid Rafique, Mr. Mohammed Inamullah, Dr. Rizwan Naeem, and Dr. Nadeem Zafar.

Polio Eradication Campaign in Pakistan

The United Nations Children's Fund (UNICEF) and APPNA members donated over $125,000 from 2011–2015 to support UNICEF's work in Pakistan. With over 90% of all donations to UNICEF going directly to its programs for children, such support has helped save and protect countless young lives.

The Race to End Polio in Pakistan[50]

In 2015, Dr. Ariba Khan explained and made her case for Polio eradication in Pakistan, *"Today, we stand at the threshold of a polio-free world with only TWO countries remaining endemic to this disease: Pakistan and Afghanistan. A large number of cases may be asymptomatic but continue to transmit the disease. The most devastating consequence of polio infection is the acute flaccid paralysis. It is known that for one case of flaccid paralysis there maybe 200 to 300 asymptomatic cases. Unfortunately, there is no cure for polio."[51]*

We are very close to eradicating polio and the total number of cases at the end of 2015 were reported to be 54. There were only 16 in FATA, 17 in Khyber Pakhtunkhwa, 12 in Sindh, 7 in Baluchistan, and 2 in Punjab makes it 54 to eradicate.

Strategies such as social mobilization, political advocacy and using a public health approach; our members have an opportunity to participate in the eradication of polio, Dr. Khan pleaded. APPNA has been assisting Rotary Pakistan, which has large networks that have the direct access to grassroots rural people in Pakistan.

Social Welfare Initiatives

Smile Again Foundation

The tragedy of permanent facial disfigurement in Pakistan due to acid attacks on the victims needs no elaboration. Sadly, little exists for treatment and restoration of facial features by surgery. The "Smile Again Foundation" sought to raise funds during 2006 Annual Summer Meeting of APPNA in Chicago, IL. APPNA members donated $9,000.

Social Sector Support Service or Karachi Street Children Project

In Karachi, Pakistan, the Social Sector Support Service (SSSS) provides support in the form of education and vocational training to youth who cannot afford the 'luxury' of conventional schooling. The Karachi Street Children Project provides vocational training for the children wandering in the slums of Karachi. The venues for these services are 2 educational/vocational training schools in Lyari suburb. SSSS launched this project in 2001 with the institute for male children and later followed up with the girls' program in 2005. There were approximately 120 girls and 60 boys studying in these schools. APPNA donated $31,000 to these schools in 2007 and made more donations in 2008. This support continued through 2009 and a total of $8,500 were raised in 2009.

Kachra Kundi School

Kachra Kundi is a small settlement outside Karachi in Ghulam Hussain Goth. Ms. Uzma Bawany (Thaakat Foundation USA) wrote to APPNA, *"In any given day 100 tons of waste is dumped here from morning to night. Hundreds of villagers in this area make their living by picking through burning garbage in search of aluminum, coppers, metals and plastics. The surprising thing is, this trash isn't for free. The villagers must pay for ownership to sift through what each truck leaves here. Villagers are covered in flies and 15–20 people live in each shack made with recyclables and garbage. This community is not guarded from danger, rain, heat or pollution. They struggle every day."*

In 2012 APPNA donated for 2 classrooms at a school near Kachra Kundi largely funded by Thaakat Foundation (USA). In the latter half of 2015 APPNA donated $5,452, which allowed Thaakat Foundation to finish the project that had stalled in September 2015 owing to funding issues. Dr. Aisha Zafar had met the Thaakat Foundation delegation at the August 2015 summer meeting at Kissimmee, FL. APPNA had also partially funded the East Africa Famine Relief Campaign of Thaakat Foundation. The campaign in 2011 was based on provision of a nutritious mix Plumpy'nut® in Somalia which was famine ravaged.

Memorial School Project with TCF:

In October of 2014, three physicians of Pakistani descent lost their lives in a tragic plane crash in Palos Hills, IL USA. An APPNA/Citizens Foundation School is now being built to honor Late Dr. Tauseef Ahmad (Neurosurgeon), Late Dr. Maria Javed (Interventional Cardiologist), and her husband Late Dr. Ali Kanchwala (pulmonologist). This School will be built in Karachi and will have 180 students. The cost is $215,000. The friends and family of the three doctors along with TCF have already raised $100,000.

Clean Water Project in Thar, Sindh[52]

Liaquat Alumni of APPNA initiated Thar Clean Sweet Water Project under SWDRC in 2015 and raised $120,000. Dr. Abdul Majeed, President Liaquat Alumni Association (2015) made a special trip to the region in late August to understand the need and assess ways of providing water to the people of Thar; one of the most drought stricken area of the world. This included an exhaustive tour of the desert where he met numerous persons with knowledge of various technical aspects of this project.

Dr. Majeed reported, *"We were able to complete an 8 km underground water pipeline and built 3 underground water tanks with capacity of 10,000 gallons each, all in one of the most remote areas of Tharparkar. This will serve about population of 3,500 in 3 large villages and a similar or even higher number from the surrounding areas will also benefit."* On December 22, 2015, the pipeline was inaugurated by Dr. Mubasher Rana, President APPNA, Dr. Amjad Aziz, physician practicing in Hyderabad, Pakistan and Dr. Abdul Majeed (NY).

Dr. Majeed further reported that the second part of this project is to install more than 50 water pumps, which is expected to be completed in the first quarter of 2016. This project would have not been completed without generous donations and resolve of many APPNA members to provide wholesome water for the people of Thar. A few of them include Dr. Kimat Khatak (MA), Dr. Nusrat Haque (NY), Dr. Muhammad Aslam (OH), and Dr. Malik Nadeem Abid (NY).

"We must also extend our special thanks to Drs. Khalid Memon (Member SWDRC), Aisha Zafar (Chair SWDRC), Mubasher Rana (President APPNA), and Ms. Jennifer Wozniak (Administrator APPNA Office). This project would not have been possible without their dedication and hard work. It would be unfair if we did not thank our friends in Pakistan, Dr. M. Amjad Aziz and Chaudhry Ahsan Ul Haque, for their relentless support on the ground," Dr. Majeed added.

Peshawar School Attack and APPNA Support Initiative

Dr. Asif Rehman (NY) and Dr. Mubashar Rana (President and President-elect 2014) had pledged to support Lady Reading Hospital with ambulance golf carts during their visit to Peshawar in December 2014. In 2015, SWRDC pledged to continue and finish this noble initiative. Army Public School (APS) Peshawar tragedy funds generated $28,000, which were sent for stretchers and medical carts. APPNA also raised $10,000 in support of a scholarship fund to honor Madame Qazi, principal of APS Peshawar, who sacrificed her life in defense of her students during the terrorist attack along with 134 other innocent victims.

Internally Displaced Persons (IDP) Relief Initiative [53, 54]

In 2009, Pakistan saw one of the largest displacements of individuals in the country's 62-year history. In the wake of a peace agreement with the government of Pakistan, the Taliban took over large parts of *Malakand* division. Subsequent military action led to the exodus of almost three million internally displaced persons (IDP) to various areas of Khyber Pakhtunkhwa (KPK) province.

APPNA's response to this humanitarian crisis was with vigor. APPNA members and its various component societies made unprecedented efforts. APPNA's SWDRC partnered with Khyber Medical College Alumni Association of North America (KMCAANA). With APPNA's funding, most of the ground work was undertaken by KMC's Social Welfare Society (SWS). SWS is a non-denominational, non-political, volunteer run organization and an affiliate of Pakistan Red Crescent Society with a 30-year history of delivering healthcare in times of disaster and peace. Within five days of the May 2, 2009 IDP crisis, SWS established a large medical camp where 15 volunteer doctors saw over 700 patients on the first day. Several similar medical camps were established over the following weeks and months. IDPs were also provided daily necessities and three BLS (basic life support) equipped ambulances were provided to two major trauma center hospitals in Peshawar and Swat. APPNA's Executive Director at the time, Dr. Tariq Cheema, personally went to Pakistan to oversee the delivery of this $120,000 ambulance project. The Vice Chancellor of Khyber Medical University, Dr. M. Hafizullah and Chief Justice of Peshawar High Court, Justice Tariq Pervez oversaw the project and financial accounts in Pakistan. APPNA-SWDRC worked very closely with a subcommittee created by Khyber Alumnus including Drs. Naeem Khan (IL), Mohammed Taqi (FL), Arshad Rehan (OH) and Fauzia Wali Khan (MA). APPNA raised over $200,000 for various IDP projects under the leadership of SWDR Chair, Dr. Aisha Zafar in 2009. In addition to Khyber SWS, funds were also utilized through Edhi Trust and Red Crescent Society.

APPKI (Kentucky/Indiana chapter) was the first component society to raise $14,000 for the IDPs in the first 24 hours. The Cincinnati chapter donated $30,000 for an ambulance for the IDPs in the Swat area. APPNE, (New England chapter) raised $60,000 to help the IDPs and the orphanage of Khapal Kor in Swat. The Virginia chapter also donated $30,000 for the IDPs.

In 2014, $22,280 was donated to the Hasan Foundation (USA) to support IDPs. In the same year, $13,325 was donated to the Alasar Academy in Ustarzai Payan village in Tehsil and District Kohat to support the orphan and other deserving students who are IDPs. In 2014, $21,443 was donated to Social Welfare Society of Khyber Medical College who forwarded it to Frontier Constabulary (FC) Peshawar to support families of FC soldiers who were beheaded by Taliban (See www.fc.gov.pk).

Stranded Pakistanis in Bangladesh

Dr. Arif Qureshi, a philanthropist from upstate New York and a lifetime member of APPNA, has donated $100,000 every year since 2006 to OBAT, the organization that helps stranded Pakistanis in Bangladesh (OBAThelpers.org).[55]

Giving Back to the Local Community

Disaster Relief in the US

As APPNA evolved over the decades, its mission to give back to the community strengthened. The leadership broadened their focus beyond the boundaries of a social and educational forum to providing help to needy and the victims of natural calamities. One of the central challenges for APPNA in the post-9/11 world was to balance their love for their country of birth with the love of their adopted homeland, and how APPNA maintains its ties with Pakistan, while remaining a North American organization.[56] Since then, APPNA, has stepped up to aid in relief effort, not only in Pakistan but also in the US and around the globe.

Hurricane Katrina relief work [57]

Early in the morning on August 29, 2005, Hurricane Katrina struck the Gulf Coast of the United States. When the storm made landfall, it had a Category 3 rating on the Saffir-Simpson Hurricane Scale. It brought sustained winds of 100–140 miles per hour, and stretched some 400 miles across. The storm itself did a great deal of damage, but its aftermath was catastrophic. APPNA raised $91,278 for hurricane Katrina.[58] Dr. Mohammed Suleman, past President of APPNA and also former President of Jefferson County Medical Society, along with other Pakistani physicians stayed behind in their hospitals rendering help. He was also interviewed by British Broadcasting Corporation (BBC)

- APPNA provided immediate financial, material and logistic help to the Katrina victims.
- APPNA physicians organized free mobile clinics in collaboration with the city of Houston to provide immediate health care services to the relocated Katrina victims.
- APPNA co-sponsored a summer camp in 2006 for Katrina affected children relocated in Germantown, TN.
- In collaboration with the city of Houston and IMET, APPNA organized a two-day training program for the teachers and healthcare responders on how to deal with childhood psychosocial trauma due to such disasters.

- APPNA financially helped over 40 families affected by hurricane Katrina through Jefferson Muslim Association of New Orleans.

As a result of the support provided to the local population, when the earthquake struck Baluchistan, Pakistan in 2008, the New Orleans community lent a helping hand to the victims of disaster in Pakistan.

APPNA sponsored Hurricane-Affected Children camp invention, 2006

This was a weeklong summer program of National Inventors Hall of Fame Foundation. This popular program focuses on making learning fun and on fostering the spirit of invention amongst participants. The program primarily focuses on children entering grades 1–6.

APPNA was approached by the City of Germantown Tennessee to help with the cost of participation in this program for children from hurricane-affected areas, currently settled in greater Memphis and enrolled in public schools. APPNA paid heed to this call.

Houston Mobile Clinics for Katrina relief efforts[59]

On 9/11/2005 Houston Muslim Physicians with the help of City of Houston organized two mobile clinics at St. Agnes Church in Southeast Houston (TX). The planning for this ambitious idea started on Friday September 2, 2005 when a group of Houston physicians met with the mayor and his health care team. The only agenda was how to help the city to cope with this catastrophic disaster. Within next few days a talented team was assembled and the infrastructure support with mobile clinics to the poorest areas was initiated. There were plenty of volunteers who donated time and money to help this unique effort for the victims. APPNA physicians were on the forefront.

A Thank You Note for Pakistani Doctors

I am pleased to inform you that the Mayor of Houston, TX, Bill White, praised people of Houston, businesses and organizations without naming any single person or business. However, only specific group that was praised by name was Pakistani physicians for their role in hurricane Katrina at a meeting held by Rotary Club of Houston where he gave a keynote speech. I felt so proud of my Pakistani heritage in front of all my fellow Rotarians. Thank you APPNA doctors. (Abdullah Jafri, Houston community activist)[60]

Joplin Tornado Relief Efforts[61, 62, 63]

Joplin, Missouri was ravaged by an F5 tornado on May 22, 2011, causing miles of damage. It affected some of our APPNA members as well in the path causing massive destruction. SWDRC and St. Louis chapter held an emergency meeting and Dr. Manzoor Tariq approved immediate release of 5,000 dollars. Dr. Manzoor Tariq, Dr. Omar Quadri, and Dr. Nadeem Ahmed (SWDRC member) went to Joplin to volunteer and see patients in the hospital. Dr. Naveed Zaidi, a resident of Joplin whose home was damaged by the tornado, coordinated the volunteer clinic. He had requested medications which were needed by many in the shelters. The St. Louis team along with food and other supplies fulfilled this request.

Hurricane Sandy 2012

Millions of Americans were affected in the aftermath of Hurricane Sandy. Several APPNA members and their families in New York and New Jersey were also affected.

As usual APPNA members stepped up and contributed to Hurricane Sandy relief efforts in New York and Jersey Shores. APPNA SWDRC collected over $50,000. APPNA collaborated with ICNA to distribute heaters, food, winter clothing and blankets to hurricane victims in New York. Dr. Abdul Majeed spearheaded this effort. $10,000 was donated to APPNA New Jersey to provide food, shelter and free medical care to hurricane victims in the area.

APPNA Helped in Aftermath of Illinois Tornado Devastation[64]

A tornado of great destructive force struck North Central Illinois on late Thursday April 9, 2015. Not only two lives were lost but a great deal of property damage was sustained by the victims of this natural disaster. The whole town of Fairdale was completely destroyed and town of Rochelle was severely damaged.

APPNA reached out to help the victims. APPNA SWDRC and APPNA Disaster Response/Medical Corp committees assessed the situation and coordinated efforts with leadership of APPNA PPS Illinois. APPNA immediately released $5000 to help the disaster victims and their families. These funds were presented to the Sheriff of Rochelle. Several APPNA Physicians and their families from Illinois were at the Disaster site to help in rehabilitation. Dr. Shahid Rashid, Secretary APPNA also joined the team.

An Eyewitness account of Tornado by Dr. Sohail Khan

"What an eye opener! We had no idea before going to the devastated area what was waiting for us! We registered to help with the cleanup operation through Operation Blessing—In Rochelle Illinois. We were assigned to help clean up a restaurant and a house on outskirts of Rochelle, Illinois. The place was totally desecrated and the surrounding houses were completely demolished. We met the owner of a restaurant Eva, an Albanian Muslim whose father was my patient some 10 years ago and presently a patient of Dr. Sohail Hanif (a cardiologist in Dixon, IL; another team member of ours) recognized us. Another was Sal, a gentleman of Mexican descent, a cook and a waiter at that restaurant who used to live in the restaurant, now homeless and jobless.

When the Tornado came they all took refuge in a hole in the ground—a dried out drain under the restaurant—where they were buried under rubble and were excavated after 3 hours by emergency crew. The team was able to connect with these survivors right away! We could see tears flowing from their eyes and a smile, as if we were their family! We tried to console them and assured them that they will be ok! and helped clean up the debris. Dr. Muhammed Hurnani another team member, a dentist from Rockford had an empty apartment in the area and he arranged for his 3-bedroom apartment for Sal and moved him in the apartment right away. Another member of our team Dr. Nadeem cared for a head trauma patient in coma at St. Anthony Medical Center."

Social Welfare and Awareness Campaigns

APPNA Hayat[65, 66, 67]

This project was initiated in 2007 and was active through 2008. The focus of the project was to increase awareness of "Breast Cancer" among women of South Asian descent in the US. This public awareness campaign of SWDRC established a website with materials in Urdu. SWDRC had a booth at ISNA convention by the volunteers to educate masses about early detection and cure of breast cancer. The campaign also aired their message through GEO TV channel in 2008.

Bone Marrow Registry Drive [68, 69]

When the case of "AG," a young medical student from Khyber Medical College with Aplastic Anemia surfaced and KMC Alumni association first became involved in her care; the social Welfare committee pledged to raise funds following the initiative taken by the KMC alumni. However, while money was a necessity, it became evident that another significant problem had emerged. None of her relatives or friends matched as a donor. Her classmates and medical college alumni launched a concerted effort, but no donor could be found in Pakistan. Finally, a donor was found in USA and funds were collected to provide financial help, but unfortunately, it was too late.

The National Marrow Donor Program (NMDP) was created in 1987 to provide marrow transplants to patients in need. At present, it maintains a registry of 5.3 million HLA typed volunteers for potential marrow donation, but only 55,000 are of South Asian origin. In March of 2007, the Social Welfare committee of APPNA started working with the South Asian Marrow Association of Recruiters (SAMAR) to increase the number of South Asian Donors in USA. SAMAR has recruited more than 50,000 volunteer marrow donors and has facilitated 35 actual transplants. Among the SWDR committee, Dr. Aisha Zafar, Dr. Zaffar Iqbal, and Dr. Rubina Inayat were on the forefront of bone marrow registry drive in APPNA. Dr. Muneer Abidi (MI), Director of Stem Cell Lab and collection facility, Wayne State University, Karmanos Cancer Institute, Detroit, MI, was instrumental in providing essential technical guidance on the project.

Social Welfare and Disaster Relief around the Globe

Iranian Earthquake Relief 2004
In 2004 APPNA responded to the Baiman Earthquake Project, which resulted in a handsome collection of $42,000. It was sent for helping the victims through a charity called Earthquake Relief Fund for Orphans (ERFO). Dr. Nadeem Zafar spearheaded this campaign.

Indonesian Tsunami 2004
The December 26, 2004 *Indian Ocean tsunami* was caused by an earthquake that is thought to have had the energy of 23,000 Hiroshima-type atomic bombs. More than 250,000 people were presumed dead in a single day is the most devastating tsunami in modern times, traveled 375 miles (600 km) in a mere 75 min. That's 300 miles (480 km) per hour, leaving more than 1.7 million homeless affecting 18 countries.

The social media activism via APPNA listserv was instrumental in creating awareness of Indian Ocean Tsunami in 2004. Dr. Nadeem Zafar was on the forefront among many others. SWDR committee got activated and APPNA raised $155,250 for tsunami relief fund.[70] Dr. Afzal Arain (CA) of APPNA served in medical relief at Banda Aceh, Indonesia. The Give-Light Foundation of California opened an orphanage in Banda Aceh that was co-sponsored by APPNA funds. About $40,000 were given to Hidaya Foundation (USA) for joint projects in tsunami affected areas. APPNA fall Council 2005 also approved another $40,000 for supporting Hidaya Foundation proposal for building a hospital in Banda Aceh.[71]

APPNA's Response to Indonesian Earthquake 2008

As a response to the earthquake in Indonesia, an emergency conference call of SWDR committee was called on Tuesday, May 30, 2008. It was decided that previously collected funds for tsunami relief, some of which were transferred to Hidaya Foundation for building a hospital there but were unused at that time, be redirected for immediate relief in the new earthquake area. APPNA's total contribution was around $80,000.

APPNA Haiti Earthquake 2010

The SWDRC collected around $15,000 for the victims and dispatched a team of doctors to the affected area. We contributed to the relief and rehab phases of this disaster. The first responders' team consisted of five persons: Babar K. Rao, MD, FAAD (New York), Khalid Rao MD (MI) Jose Luis Cruz, MD (Dominican Republic) Omar Noor, MS3, (George Washington University) Sean Shafi, MS2, (UNIBE—Universidad Iberoamericana).

Dr. Babar Rao shared his experience: *"The experience of just being within Port-au-Prince was humbling in itself. The degree of destitution was just incomprehensible: people everywhere you look with no food, no water, and no place to sleep or even spend their days out of the harsh sun, and open wounds in need of immediate care. The most jarring concept is that there is no end in sight to this transient state. These people are not waiting for an insurance payment to replace their belongings. There are no relatives to rely on for help because their entire families are facing the same obstacles, if they are even alive. There is no government to rely on for the same reason.*

We offered our help wherever we saw the need; we provided medical services, but we also distributed water and supplies with the rest of the volunteers. It was clear that the need for goods and manpower was not met immediately—the intense level of aid that was being provided will have to be maintained long-term before this city is habitable again."

APPNA Medical Mission to Nepal Earthquake 2015[72]

Dr. Babar Rao with an elderly lady at a relief camp in Nepal following earthquake in 2015

A 7.8 Richter scale magnitude earthquake shook Nepal on April 25, 2015. APPNA members responded and a team of volunteers consisting of Dr. Afzal Arain (surgeon), Dr. Qamar Zaman (PK) (a pediatrician), Dr. Ali (pediatrician), Dr. Babar Rao (dermatologist), and Mr. Wasim Momin (ICU nurse) was formed along with two local doctors and a nurse: Dr. S Sherpa, Dr. N Sherpa, and Ms. Shrestha whose participation was crucial. The team visited three different villages, all within a two-hour drive from Kathmandu; Bungamati, Pahadiya, and Thapa.

The APPNA team provided medical care for around 1,000 patients across these three villages and in tent city. Most of the patients needed acute care for fevers, pain, wound care and anxiety. There were children lining up for healthcare without parents, as well as elderly who walked long distances to get to these clinics. Patan Hospital in Kathmandu was also visited and the team met and spent time with various specialists.

The team met with the local Rotary Club and its President-Elect Ms. Sita. During this meeting, they explained what they were doing for the current crisis in Nepal and asked if APPNA could help them in building shelters and houses in a nearby village (Lele). For this purpose, $ 16,270 was raised and through Dr. Afzal Arain who had volunteered there, these funds were given to Rotary Club for construction of temporary shelters for the victims of this earthquake. A total amount of about $30,000 was spent on Nepal earthquake project.

APPNA Medical Corps (AMC) 2015[73]

Dr. Mubasher Rana, APPNA President 2015, initiated APPNA Medical Corps to create a permanent body of physicians dedicated to worldwide disaster relief. Dr. Asaf Qadeer (TX) and Dr. Shahid Rashid (TX) were appointed as Chair and Co-Chair, respectively. This medical corps is the result of efforts initiated in 2010 and 2012 that tended to separate the Disaster Relief part from Social Welfare and Disaster Relief Committee (SWDRC).[74]

To participate in medical relief and other charitable activities especially in Pakistan and in North America is one of the six point APPNA objectives for which this organization was founded.[75] The mission of APPNA Medical Corps is to provide global assistance to victims of manmade and natural disasters irrespective of race, religion, creed and political conviction, guided by the principles of medical ethics. *"The scope of AMC is limited at present due to our limited experience, resources, and manpower available at the present time,"* Dr. Rana expressed and he predicted, *"Our history of dedication to deliver at the time of need for disasters gives us hope to make AMC known as frontline medical relief organization in the years to come."*

The goal of Medical Corps is to build a strong organizational structure with standing operating procedures and creation of readily available manpower and material resources. Building these resources is a huge undertaking and will require a lot of funding along with preparation for the logistical challenges that have to be dealt with speed, focus, and determination to reach the neediest in a disaster affected area.[76]

Under the auspices of APPNA medical Corps, APPNA physicians and volunteers completed a successful medical mission to Coban, Guatemala in July, 2016. The team comprised of Dr. Zeenat Safdar (pulmonologist), Dr. Mir Ali (pediatrician), Jane Winning, RN (Rotarian and organizer of this mission) and 3 teenagers/ young adult volunteers: Amal (Medical student), Sidra and Waqar (high schoolers). The mission was set up at the request of a school for indigent children and young adults who do not have access to the Guatemalese medical care and services as they are Nicaraguans settled in Guatemala.

Dr. Zeenat Safdar wrote: "Some of the school kids and adults that we saw had never seen a physician before and were very nervous- sweating with dilated pupils. We did general physical exams, saw/treated > 250 patients ages 1 yr. to 80 years. Cases we saw included walking pneumonias, bronchitis, asthma, UTI, Otitis media/ externa, hydrocephalus and others. Many kids with complaints of headaches actually had poor vision and needed eye glasses. One couple age 79 and 80 with limited ambulatory capabilities had to be driven for more than 2 hours to get to this clinic. This was both an exciting and rewarding experience for the team. The young volunteers found this experience not only rewarding but came back with an awareness of suffering and poverty that exists in this world and zeal to make a difference."

One of the young volunteers, Sidra who wants to pursue a career in medicine wrote: "My recent experience in Guatemala was indescribable-- it was so much more than I could have even imagined going into my first mission trip overseas. I can't describe the sense of fulfillment I felt when I saw a child walk out of the doctor's office smiling, waving Adios to me. The kids were always happier after they left the doctor's office."

Conclusion:

This chapter recounts the charitable and disaster relief work done by APPNA in our resolve to helping the destitute and those who are less fortunate. These are the glimpses of courage and generosity shown by the members of APPNA over the years. Interspersed between these major events, are the countless moments and selfless sacrifices of individual members, their families, and volunteers from all walks of life, who joined hands in the service for humanity. Dr. Nasim Ashraf, past president of APPNA, during an interview with the author in 2011 expressed his view on APPNA's role on philanthropy, *"the very "raison d'être" of organizations like APPNA is to do charitable work and look out for the interest of its membership. Given that it's the largest and most organized professional organization of Pakistani expats in the world, it has a higher "calling." In order to affect public policy with the aim of promoting "poor-friendly" government policies, APPNA should always strive to foster alliances and partnerships with other likeminded organizations, as well as the government both here in the U.S. and in Pakistan. Only then would our efforts succeed in creating better opportunities for the disenfranchised and APPNA would achieve its true potential."*[77]

End Notes:

1 The present form of the chapter would have not been possible without direct input from the following members and contributors: Wasique Mirza, M. Shahid Yousuf, Aisha Zafar, Nasir Gondal, Mubasher Rana, Abdul Majeed, Maqbool Arshad, Shahid Sheikh, Sajjad Savul A.R. Piracha, Nadeem Kazi, Sabir Ali Khan, Zainab B. Alam, and M. Aslam Malik.
2 APPNA Constitution and Bylaws; Appendix C, 2014
3 www.brainyquote.com/quotes/authors/m/muhammad_ali_jinnah.html
4 APPNA Newsletter 16:1, Spring 2006, page 6
5 APPNA Journal 6:3, Summer/Fall 2005, page 11
6 Ibid, page 14
7 Ibid, page 7
8 Ibid, page 14
9 Ibid, page 10
10 . APPNA Newsletter, 15:2, Winter 2005, page 44
11 Ibid, page 23
12 Ibid, page 6
13 Ibid, page 26
14 Ibid, page 38
15 Ibid
16 APPNA Newsletter, 16:1, Spring 2006, page 25
17 APPNA Newsletter, 15:2, Winter 2005, page 21, page 37
18 APPNA Journal, 9:1, Summer, 2007, page 21
19 APPNA Newsletter, 15:2, Winter 2005, page 29
20 Ibid, page 21
21 APPNA Journal, 9:2, Winter, 2007, page 6
22 APPNA Journal 10:2, Winter, 2008, page 21
23 APPNA Newsletter, 15:2, Winter 2005, page 2
24 APPNA Newsletter, 16:1, Spring 2006, page 13
25 APPNA 18:1, Spring 2008, page 9
26 APPNA Newsletter, 8:1, Summer 2006, page 3
27 APPNA Newsletter, 8:2, Winter 2006, page 6
28 APPNA Journal, 9:1, Summer, 2007, page 21
29 APPNA Newsletter, 15:2, Winter 2005, page 34
30 Ibid, page 36
31 APPNA Journal, 10:2, Winter 2008, pages, 5, 18, and 21
32 APPNA Newsletter, 17:1, Fall 2007
33 APPNA Journal, 12:2, Winter, 2010, page 14
34 A report by Dr. Salma Tanweer, communication with Dr. Nasir Gondal via email
35 APPNA Newsletter, 13:1, Summer 2011, page 25
36 APPNA Newsletter, 22:2, Spring, 2012, page 17
37 Dr. Mubasher Rana, personal communication
38 APPNA Journal, 25:3, Nov. 2015, page 7
39 APPNA Journal 6:3, Winter 2005
40 APPNA Journal, 9:2, Winter, 2007, page 7 and 27
41 APPNA Journal, 11:2, Winter, 2009, page 15
42 APPNA Journal, 10:1, Summer, 2008, page 16

43   APPNA Journal, 11:2, Winter, 2009, page 15
44   Report submitted by Dr. Shahid Sheikh via email for *APPNA Qissa II*
45   . Report by Dr. Babar K. Rao, APPNA Summer 2013, page 60
46   APPNA Institute of Public Health segment is based on the report submitted by Dr. Sabir Ali Khan
47   APPNA Journal, 25:3, Nov. 2015, page 47
48   The Hepatitis C report was contributed by Dr. Maqbool Arshad for *Qissa II*
49   APPNA Journal, 10:2, Winter 2008, page 37
50   APPNA Journal, 25:3, Nov. 2015, page 15
51   References: www.endpolio.com.pk (Last accessed 10/14/15)
     http://www.polioeradication.org/content/publications/advocacy_guide.pdf
52   Report submitted by Dr. Abdul Majeed for *Qissa II*
53   APPNA Journal, 11:2, Winter, 2009, page 15
54   Report submitted by Dr. Sajjad Savul for *Qissa II*
55   APPNA Journal, 11:2, Winter, 2009, page 15
56   *APPNA Qissa*, Literary Circle of Toledo, Ohio, 2004
57   APPNA Journal 6:3, Summer/Fall 2005, page 54
58   Treasurer's Report by Dr. Shahid Usmani, Spring 2006
59   Ibid, page 54–55
60   APPNA Journal, 6:3, Summer/Fall 2005, page 55
61   APPNA Journal, 13:1, Summer, 2011, SWDR report
62   APPNA Newsletter, 21:2, Fall, 2011, SWDR report
63   APPNA Journal, 13:2, Winter, 2011, SWDR report
64   e-Newsletter to APPNA membership, April 2015
65   APPNA Journal, 9:2, Winter 2007, SWDR report
66   APPNA Newsletter, 18:1, Spring 2008, SWDR report
67   APPNA Journal 10:1, Summer 2008, SWDR report
68   APPNA Journal, 9:2, Winter 2007, page 29
69   APPNA Journal, 13:1, Summer 2011, page 32
70   Treasurer's Report by Dr. Shahid Usmani, Spring 2006
71   APPNA Newsletter, 16:1, Spring 2006, page 20
72   APPNA Journal, 25:3, Nov. 2015, page 11
73   Ibid, page 33
74   APPNA Journal, 12:2, Winter 2010, page 15
75   APPNA Constitution and Bylaws; Objectives page 5, 2014
76   APPNA Journal, 25:3, Nov. 2015, page 33
77   APPNA Journal, 13:2, Winter 2011, page 13

3

FROM APPNA SEHAT TO HUMAN DEVELOPMENT FOUNDATION

APPNA SEHAT[1]—the Crown Jewel of APPNA

A Synopsis of its Evolution[1]

In the early 1980's, APPNA gave many newly arrived immigrant physicians the sense of community they yearned for. However, APPNA's creation was premised on charitable ideals, and the founding fathers did not lose sight of it. Since its inception, APPNA started making significant contributions to various health care projects in Pakistan, but it took a leap of faith in October 1987[2], when it unanimously endorsed the idea of a health improvement project funded and managed by APPNA. Dr. Nasim Ashraf made the presentation that led to the creation of APPNA SEHAT (Scientific, Educational, Health and Administrative Training) two years later.

Dr. Nasim Ashraf, one of the youngest leaders of APPNA at the time, along with a renowned health and development expert, Dr. Frederick Shaw, conducted a feasibility study in Pakistan, which focused on grass-roots empowerment utilizing health education and administrative training. He then refined the proposal for an initial two-year pilot project, the Village Improvement Model (VIM)[3]. In 1989, the preventive health care

---

1   Dr. Omar T. Atiq wrote this part of the chapter for *APPNA Qissa II*. Dr. Atiq chaired APPNA SEHAT Committee in 2001–2002. He served APPNA as its 25th President in 2004. He was awarded the APPNA Gold Medal in 2014.

project was launched in some of the poorest villages of Mardan, Sahiwal, Murree and Badin. Interventions to provide clean drinking water, sanitation, immunization of women and children and growth monitoring and counseling were selected based on the major causes of morbidity and mortality. The program oversight was provided by the APPNA SEHAT committee, which initially included Drs. Nasim Ashraf (Chairman), Khalid Riaz (Secretary/Treasurer), Waheed Akbar, Zaheer Ahmed and Murtaza Arain. Later, many other dedicated members served on the committee, as well.

The project was a phenomenal success. Independent assessments showed that 95% of targeted children had been fully immunized, 90% of women of childbearing age were immunized against tetanus, and 100% of targeted women had been taught proper procedures to tie umbilical cords and to make oral rehydration solutions. All villages had functioning health committees. The success of the concept of APPNA SEHAT opened doors for funding from international donors, and in 1992, APPNA SEHAT embarked on replicating its achievements with three subsequent "Village Improvement Projects, I–III." APPNA SEHAT served around 150,000 people in over 90 villages towards the late 1990s, with an average cost of $1.1 per beneficiary.[4]

APPNA SEHAT interventions reduced the infant mortality rate by 45%, maternal mortality was decreased from 5 to 0.7 per 1000 live births, and the population growth rate dropped by 59%. Moderate to severe child malnutrition rates decreased by more than 55% while family planning and antenatal care rates increased by several folds in the APPNA SEHAT villages. Over time, the health care expenditure decreased significantly in the APPNA SEHAT villages. The women's participation increased and so did the overall wellbeing of the targeted population as measured by social and economic activity, though the latter was not formally measured.[5]

APPNA SEHAT continued its growth trajectory in Pakistan with committed leadership and overwhelming membership support. In 1995, based on the poor Human Development Index (HDI)[6] ranking of Pakistan, the APPNA President, Dr. Mushtaq Sharif, appointed a Human Development Task Force, comprising Dr. Nasim Ashraf, Dr. Khalid Riaz, Dr. Zeenat Anwar, Dr. Waheed Akbar, Dr. Shahnaz Khan and Dr. Omar Atiq. The Task Force generated recommendations for a Community Development program focused on primary health care, mass literacy and poverty eradication in Pakistan.[7] After considerable deliberations and consultations, APPNA launched an autonomous entity, the Human Development Foundation of North America (HDFNA), in July 1997. APPNA President Dr. Shaukat Khan rolled out the red carpet for the inaugural function of HDF. It was a gift to the people of Pakistan on the occasion of Pakistan's 50th independence anniversary. The resolution establishing HDFNA recognized the need to expand the scope of activities from APPNA SEHAT's primary health care project to include primary education and poverty alleviation, as well as understanding of the importance of collaboration with like-minded people and organizations.[8] Dr. Mahbub ul Haq gave the keynote address at the inaugural session of HDFNA. The new foundation was cosponsored by APPNA, Society for International HELP (SIH) (President Dr. Khalid Riaz), an Illinois based community organization, and the Noor Foundation (President Mr. Akram Chaudhry (NJ).

In 1998, the HDFNA board was led by two past APPNA presidents, Dr. Nasim Ashraf and Dr. M. Khalid Riaz. The HDF board, comprising many APPNA members, approved HDFNA's vision, mission and goals to "launch a non-political movement for a social change and community empowerment through mass literacy, enhanced quality of education, universal primary health care, and a grassroots economic development." In 1999, HDFNA added the Education and Economic Development components to the existing APPNA SEHAT program and an integrated project began. Since then, HDFNA has methodically expanded its project sites, programs, collaborations, and affiliations. It has streamlined its governance and operations to align them with its evolving mission and goals. Over time, it has ventured into disaster relief operations as well as partnered in curative health care projects.[9] HDFNA has been an active participant in information exchange and capacity building in its areas of interest. It has also been working towards attaining scale and sustainability.

APPNA SEHAT and HDFNA continued to provide much needed services to hundreds of thousands of Pakistanis due to the selfless dedication of scores of APPNA members and others. The results were gratifying and outcome was much beyond initial expectations. However, it was becoming clear that adoption of the programs at the national level with active government involvement would be necessary to deliver the benefits to a wide enough spectrum of the country to make any significant difference in its Human Development Index. These prescriptive concepts, programs and potential gains were presented to various government functionaries, provincial and national leaders for consideration and adoption, but despite promising words, no curative action was forthcoming.

In the year 2000, a task force of HDFNA consisting of Dr. Nasim Ashraf, Dr. Shahnaz Khan, Dr. Zaheer Ahmed and others met Pakistani President General Pervez Musharraf during his visit to New York and advocated for a nationwide human development program. Later, Dr. Nasim Ashraf visited Pakistan and presented the idea to the President and his cabinet. The President accepted the plan and asked Dr. Ashraf to help implement it in Pakistan. In 2001, the Government of Pakistan established the Task Force on Human Development to conduct a study on the issue at hand. Dr. Ashraf chaired the task force with two other HDF directors (Mussadiq Malik and Khalid Riaz) as its members. The key findings of the Task Force were that there was inadequate capacity, lack of competency, and managerial efficiency within the public and private sector delivery systems. The community participation was dismal and it had no decision-making rights. Moreover, the gaps in service delivery, quality, and financing were evident.

In 2002, the Government of Pakistan established the National Commission for Human Development (NCHD) as a statutory autonomous body mandated to support and augment human development efforts in Pakistan. Simultaneously, a private, independent, and not for profit, entity called the Pakistan Human Development Fund (PHDF) was created to mobilize resources from around the world to support NCHD activities. The Government of Pakistan contributed a sizeable sum to its endowment fund. The creation of NCHD and PHDF was based on the premise that HDFNA leadership will move to Pakistan to help deliver on their mission of 'human development' in Pakistan. It sounded a remarkable opportunity to partner with and utilize private and government resources to realize the HDFNA dream. Dr. Nasim Ashraf and Dr. Mussadiq Malik took the challenge and moved to Pakistan. The rest of HDFNA leadership led by Dr. Khalid Riaz and Dr. Shahnaz Khan decided to continue with HDF in North America and to execute its work through non-governmental organization (NGO), HDF-Pakistan.

NCHD envisioned a fully literate society where the education of all children up to the secondary level was ensured. Its mission was to support the Pakistan government by filling implementation gaps and improving public sector delivery mechanisms to achieve that vision. This unique public-private partnership model eventually covered all of the districts in Pakistan. It worked diligently to increase the enrollment of children in schools by establishing over 15,000 feeder schools every year in areas where there were no schools. It collaborated with local education departments for capacity building and trained over 130,000 teachers in the country. In the academic year 2011–2012, it enrolled 2.2 million children, doubling the enrollment since 2002–03, when program was started. It also established 164,190 adult literacy centers throughout the country with 3.84 million adults becoming literate, out of which 95% were females.[10] These were some of the many achievements of NCHD/PHDF over the ensuing years. Unfortunately, with the transition to a new government in Pakistan in 2013, the emphasis on human development and the support to NCHD slowly withered away. Dr. Ashraf was replaced and the NCHD program suffered the same fate as other public institutions, becoming a nest of nepotism, corruption, and inefficiency. NCHD is still standing, having delivered the proof of concept, with the Supreme Court of Pakistan having backed its purposeful creation.

Although APPNA SEHAT and HDFNA were not officially linked to NCHD/PHDF, the vision, mission and achievements of NCHD/PHDF can be directly attributed to those of APPNA, and are indeed widely recognized. With the departure of Dr. Ashraf to Pakistan in 2001 to help create and lead NCHD, Dr. Omar T. Atiq was appointed chair of the APPNA SEHAT committee, and Dr. Shahnaz Khan joined Dr. Khalid Riaz as co-chair of HDFNA. APPNA SEHAT was expanded to include 200,000 people, and efforts were initiated to graduate students from villages that had been adequately trained in targeted health care interventions, so that other villages could be brought on board. Efforts were also made to streamline the relationship between APPNA SEHAT and HDFNA for a more collaborative partnership. In addition, APPNA SEHAT and NCHD began mutual cooperation for the greater good, as well.

In 2003, the committee was totally revamped with Dr. Zaheer Ahmad's appointment as its chair. There were some issues that surfaced because of the autonomous status of HDFNA and its overlapping governance with APPNA SEHAT. Unfortunately, the new committee failed to adequately perform and sustain its function. After the initial boost in funding at the summer meeting banquet in 2003, its funding also dried up later. In retrospect, that was the beginning of the end of APPNA SEHAT. The following year, a concerted effort was made to revitalize APPNA SEHAT. Dr. Hassan Bukhari was appointed as the chair of the committee. He promptly visited the program sites, aggressively raised funds, and tried to get the program back on track. He succeeded to a great extent and the program did well for the next couple of years. However, the general APPNA membership had moved on perhaps to deal with urgent needs of disaster relief in the aftermath of 2005 earthquake in Pakistan. The subsequent APPNA leadership had little attachment to the struggles and triumphs that had glued the earlier leadership and membership to APPNA SEHAT. Dr. Bukhari continued to nourish the program the best he could over the next several years with assistance from a few committed supporters. Nevertheless, in 2009, with mounting apathy in APPNA towards APPNA SEHAT, the curtain was finally drawn on this recipient of the American College of Physicians Richard and Hinda Rosenthal Award for its novel, cost effective, health care delivery model. Dr. Bukhari continued to privately run the program from 2009 onwards under "APP KI SEHAT" by the funding from his private trust, Hassan and Talat Bukhari Foundation. This venture, however, came to an end with the passing of Dr. Bukhari in 2015.[11]

So, why did APPNA walk away from APPNA SEHAT? It is a complex issue with many explanations, some of which have been alluded to earlier. Unequivocally, APPNA allowed APPNA SEHAT to evolve into a more comprehensive program, HDFNA, but it failed to complete the transformation because of its remorse over the loss of control of HDFNA. The situation became more complex with the establishment of NCHD and Dr. Nasim Ashraf's departure from leadership of both APPNA SEHAT and HDFNA. The events occurring in 2003 were the final straw that broke the camel's back. It was APPNA SEHAT's preeminence in APPNA that carried it for five more years, before APPNA realized and accepted that SEHAT had delivered on its promise long ago, and that it shall continue to do so for a long time to come without being tethered to it. So, APPNA SEHAT voyaged from being a topic of discussion in APPNA meetings to permeating its soul, leaving everlasting memories of common cause, dedication, friendship, struggle, service, achievement and charity.

The Human Development Foundation

We dream of a Pakistan where Every child must attend school,
Primary healthcare is for all Clean drinking water is not a
luxury, and Communities are vibrant and self-sustaining.

To realize this dream, APPNA visionaries embarked on a journey in 1997 with a sheer energy of passion and a single-minded determination; they were joined by many more professionals and businessmen of Pakistani descent to become a part of the movement called Human Development Foundation (HDF). The Human Development Foundation, a US based 501(C)3 not-for-profit organization, has become the platform for the Pakistani expatriates to bring about a change: "HDF is a vanguard example of Pakistanis in and out of Pakistan...who have decided that it is not only that they can do something, but that they must," observed Professor Adil Najam.[12]

According to HDF Chair BOD, Dr. Atiya Khan, the organization's core strength is its holistic model of development that constitutes an integrated set of development interventions. These provide a strong basis for comprehensive engagement and partnership with the local communities. The HDF's holistic model focuses on five components that they call, Power of Five. These include, Primary Healthcare, Education & Literacy, Social Mobilization, Economic Development, and Sustainable Environment.

The HDF has impacted the lives of hundreds and thousands of people in Pakistan. Briefly, over one million people benefited from HDF's Holistic Model and Partnerships. At present (2015), HDF has 287 Village Development Organizations (VDO's). Around 10,000 children are enrolled in the HDF schools every year. The infant mortality decreased from 85/1000 to 23/1000 live births in the villages served by the HDF. The 11,243 persons participated in the Technical/Vocational skills program. Eight hundred and sixty-two (862) potable drinking water projects were completed.

"The HDF vision is to ensure a wide public participation in national decision-making—whereby public spending is re-directed to significantly increase investments in education, primary and preventive health care, and grassroots economic development. The culture of dependence on foreign aid and loans must be curtailed so that social and economic entrepreneurs are given the space to create a vibrant and just society—A society where ready access to justice for all is ensured, constitutional supremacy and rule of law is established, and the independence of judiciary and media is respected," stated Dr. Naheed Qayyum in an article published in 2008.[13] The statement above reflects on the crisis of governance and corruption that plagues the under developed societies in countries like Pakistan. It is direct reflection on the Humane Governance Index (HGI). The term HGI was coined by the (late) Dr. Mahbub ul Haq, a Pakistani Economist, whose vision inspired APPNA leaders to start HDF.[14] Dr. Haq passed away in 1998, a year after the founding of HDF. A book on the work of Dr. Haq was published after his death in 1999.[15]

In 2015, HDF Pakistan embarked on its "Inflection Point Strategy," which involves transforming the entire organization to prepare it for the next decade with younger leadership and fresh ideas. "We have also part-nered with Sustainable Development Policy Institute (SDPI), a leading think tank in Pakistan" said Dr. Khalid Riaz, the Chair HDF Pakistan. This partnership would enable HDF to learn from worldwide best prac-tices and develop strategic alliances with other likeminded organizations to develop more effective poverty alleviation programs. Finally, it has also adopted the Sustainable Development Goals of the United Nations. HDF is set to embark on the journey to develop sustainable SMART villages, compliant with SDGs in Pakistan.[16]

End notes:

1   Service to homeland: APPNA provides Vital Health Care to Pakistan, in
     APPNA Qissa, 2004, 31–55
2   APPNA Executive Council meeting minutes, October 3, 1987
3   APPNA Executive Council meeting minutes, June 25, 1988
4   APPNA Newsletter, Fall 1990
5   APPNAIYET 1989–2000
6   hdr.undp.org The Human Development Index (HDI) is a summary measure
     of average achievement in key dimensions of human development: a long
     and healthy life, being knowledgeable and have a decent standard of living.
     The HDI is the geometric mean of normalized indices for each of the three
     dimensions.

7   APPNA Newsletter, October 1995
8   APPNA Executive Council meeting minutes, July 3, 1997
9   *APPNA QISSA* 2004, p 47–50
10 NCHD Presentation 2014
11 Dr. Talat Bukhari, personal communication.
12 Naheed M. Qayyum (IL) (KEMC 77), a lifetime member of APPNA, is a member of Board of Directors of Human Development Foundation. The excerpt is taken from her article published in Summer Convention Journal, 2008, 46
13 Ibid, 47
14 Human Development Foundation of North America: Past, Present, and Future by Dr. Shaukat H. Khan, APPNA Journal, 4:1, Summer 2002, 20
15 Human Development in South Asia, The Crisis of Governance, Oxford University Press, 1999
16 The information is contributed by Dr. M. Khalid Riaz, Chairperson, HDF-Pakistan.

4

APPNA CATERS TO YOUNG PHYSICIANS FROM PAKISTAN

"In order to move others deeply we must deliberately allow ourselves to be carried away beyond the bounds of our normal sensibility." Joseph Conrad (1857–1924)[1]

Background:

The passion for advocating for the rights of foreign medical graduates' dates back to the early years of APPNA's founding. In 1987, APPNA took the lead on the issues of Foreign Medical Graduates (FMG) and formed an Alliance of FMGs. This alliance evolved into the International Association of American Physicians (IAAP) in 1988. The struggle of the IAAP for the rights of FMGs (1983–1996) resulted in numerous remarkable accomplishments.

In July 1984, APPNA appealed to the American Medical Association (AMA) on the FMG's issues. The Executive Council unanimously passed a resolution asking the AMA to establish a mechanism by which qualified foreign medical graduates are given equal chance to compete with American medical graduates for entry-level programs in postgraduate education.[2] The effective lobbying with congress eliminated the amendment to the Budget Reconciliation Bill in 1986 that proposed elimination of all funding for FMG training in the US. The AMA yielded to the advocacy efforts of the IAAP and created a section for International Medical Graduates (IMGs), to address the issues of foreign trained physicians in organized medicine in 1989. Also in 1989, major bills were passed in the Senate as well as in the Congress that brought IMGs at par with US medical graduates; once a physician was licensed in the US, there would be no distinction as to where that physician received medical training. In 1992, the Health Professional Reauthorization Act was passed resulting in the establishment of the National Council on Medical Licensure; allowing the Council to make recommendations to the US Department of Health and Human Services on how to insure non-discriminatory medical licensing practices. The greatest victory was called the Solarez/Kennedy/Simon bill for its major sponsors, which finally put to rest the issues of Medicare and Medicaid funding for the training of international medical graduates. The bill mandated that residency programs receiving federal funds could not discriminate based upon the country of origin and medical school graduation.[3]

APPNA Welcomes Young Physicians:
Medicine is a world-wide guild of professionals of like mind and traditions.

The profession in truth is a sort of guild or brotherhood, any member of which can take up his calling in any part of the world and find brethren whose language and methods and whose aims and ways are identical with his own. —Sir William Osler[4]

In March 1990, APPNA's executive council created a new membership category called Physicians-in Training (P.I.T.) Section at a reduced membership rate of 25% of the regular annual fee. This was the first of several steps that the Association took in recognition of our own young physicians as future of APPNA.[5] In 1996, the executive council approved the establishment of the Physicians in Training Resource Center at APPNA's central office.[6] The P.I.T. Section was represented in APPNA's executive council by a nominee of the President each year. This P.I.T. Section phased out in 2007 after the standing Committee on Young Physicians (CYP) had taken charge of physicians-in-training issues from 2004 onwards.

APPNA Organizes Young Physicians Coaching Seminars:

As the second wave of physicians began to settle down in the US, their involvement in APPNA grew both in the local chapters and in the alumni associations from mid-1990 onwards. These physicians then took charge of helping the incoming young physicians by mentoring and coaching them according to their specific needs. The NYC Chapter was on the forefront of this organized effort through APPNA's platform. On August 6, 2000, the first Young Doctors' Seminar was held at the LaGuardia Marriott in New York City. The Seminar was Directed by Dr. Mahmood Alam, who was on the faculty of S.U.N.Y. Downstate Medical Center and the President of the NY Chapter at that time. This much appreciated activity focusing on Young Physicians coaching then became a yearly activity of the NYC chapter. Similar activities were also initiated by some other chapters and different alumni associations. These activities remain a major focus of mentoring young physicians by CYP over the years.[7]

APPNA Young Physicians Movement Starts in 2003:[8]

The recent history of the Committee on Young Physicians (CYP) dates back to the immediate post-9/11 era when an alarming number of the young physicians got their visas refused. Most of them had secured residency training jobs in the US and their visa issuance was placed on hold pending their security clearance. Starting-off as an Ad hoc committee in 2003, the CYP was officially given the status of a standing committee of APPNA in 2004.[9] The CYP has now become an effective platform that caters to young physician's needs. APPNA CYP continues to take pride in helping young physicians by provision of wide range of services for their guidance and support. CYP activities include but are not limited to:

    a)   Holding educational seminars and one-on-one mentorship sessions

    b)   Assistance in securing electives and clinical observership rotations

c) Coaching in securing residency positions and assistance in post-match scramble
d) Research competitions in collaboration with RESA Committee
e) Provision of residential accommodation in numerous cities
f) Offering scholarships and soft loans for the needy medical students and young physicians
g) Facilitating visas: The CYP has been working very closely with Advocacy Committee on the visa and security clearance issues for more than a decade (2003–2015)

CYP Connects with Young Physicians through Electronic Media:

Soon after the creation of the CYP, the APPNA website was used effectively to connect with young physicians. However, a separate website called www.ypprc.org was launched in 2005, a link for which was available on the APPNA.org homepage. The young physicians could register and apply for help on visa-related issues on the website. From 2006 onwards, the CYP started to play a broader role in other activities beneficial to young doctors besides visa clearance. The website was instrumental in connecting effectively with the young physicians regardless of their current country of residence. They were now better prepared to travel to the US for future training. In 2007, CYP devised a program titled 'Do's and Don'ts of Residency.' The program focused on awareness about cultural differences, work ethics, and healthy peer relations.

After realizing the enormous impact of electronic communication, a new interactive website www.cyponline.net was launched in 2009. The committee continued their efforts that year, which were started four year ago in helping the young physicians during the post-match scramble. More than 200 applicants registered at the website, while 50 volunteers registered to assist them. CYP also strengthened its efforts to help the young physicians currently in the USA. In 2011, Manzoor Tariq, Tariq Alam, Asra Hashmi, Afnan R. Tariq, Rubina Inayat, and Shamail S. Tariq published a handbook titled 'A Guide to US Residency.' This resource was made available on the website and provided information on USMLE, interview skills, and seeking residency in IMG friendly programs.

Another website update was made in 2012 to include new programs and information for residency applicants. Then, in 2014 an online system was set-up for remote research mentoring for the interested young physicians The website cyponline.net was again updated in 2015. Many features including residency match lists of Pakistani-Descent Residents and Program Directors; a list of CYP mentors for US clinical experience and other educational material were incorporated. CYP utilized its list of mentors as well as the online application system developed by an Ad hoc Committee for Electives and Clinical Observership to help young physicians gain US clinical experience. Numerous alumni associations, DOGANA, NANA, JSMUAANA, and PPS (Chicago Chapter) also offer online assistance to young physicians to find electives and clinical shadowing.

Mentorship Program:

The first one-on-one mentoring program was organized at the APPNA summer meeting on July 8, 2006 in Chicago. The mentoring program was jointly organized by the Research Education and Scientific Affairs Committee (RESA) and CYP. "A mentor is someone who cares and who helps," as noted by the Co-Chair of RESA Rizwan Naeem, who helped to organize the mentorship program along with Raza Dilawari (Chair RESA), Rubina Inayat (Chair CYP), and Rizwan Khalid (President PIT section). The major goal of the mentoring program that was conceived during this session was to create a pooled database of researchers in the medical sciences, program directors and practicing physicians who could provide guidance to young physicians and medical students in their career development.

APPNA mentors with young physicians after a session at summer meeting 2007

As Dr. Busharat Ahmad (MI), past chair of the IMG section of AMA and one of the lead mentors of the program said, *"there is no single formula for good mentoring. Mentoring styles are as varied as human relationships. Having a formal mentoring program in place is an effective way to guide talented young physicians and it helps to ensure that APPNA will continue to lead as a professional, educational, and charity organization in the future."* Another mentor Dr. Farrukh Malik wrote, *"My time was well worth meeting the two young physicians, Faisal from North Carolina and Sameer from Karachi. The enthusiasm was mutual and sincere. I believe such an exposure is very informative for the young physicians not exposed to US medicine and its intricacies."* Dr. Ghazala Mazhar, a young physician who attended the program also expressed her views via an email, *"I don't think the value of mentoring can be overstated. It was wonderful having a resource for advice and feedback. All I can say is that this was the most valuable program APPNA did during the meeting."*[10]

The mentorship program has become an important activity that is being carried out at different APPNA meetings and continues to nurture the needs of young physicians' professional development and encourages them to attain their fullest potential leading to a successful career.

Career Counseling Seminars:

APPNA efforts to help and guide young physicians and medical students took a leap forward in 2006 during the presidency of Dr. Rashid Piracha. During that time, Dr. Adeel Butt, Program Director of the International Scholars Program at the University of Pittsburgh School of Medicine was instrumental in shaping an organized effort on career counseling, which had been an APPNA priority for long time. This could only happen with the collaborative efforts of the RESA and the CYP committees as well as many dedicated APPNA members like Dr. Rubina Inayat, Dr. Faisal Cheema, Dr. Rizwan Naeem, Dr. Mohammad Haseeb, and Dr. Rizwan Khalid. In 2006 alone, three career counseling seminars were held at New York, California and at the Chicago summer meeting, respectively. Another three were also held during the APPNA winter meeting in December 2006 at KEMU Lahore, DUHS Karachi and RMC Rawalpindi, respectively. Besides the accomplished faculty from the US and Pakistan, Stephen Seeling, vice president for operations for the ECFMG was the special invitee, who also spoke at all the three seminars in Pakistan.

As Dr. Butt reported in the Winter 2006 APPNA Journal, *"We continued to expand the tradition started four years ago (2002) with a stand-alone lecture on career counseling at Aga Khan University, which was attended by 250 students and young graduates. This has now expanded over the years to become a comprehensive seminar on career choices both in Pakistan and in North America."*[11]

Dr. Adeel Butt and Dr. Faisal Cheema are conducting a career counselling seminar in Lahore, Pakistan 2008

One-On-one counselling of young physicians

After a decade of hard work, the CYP continues to offer career counseling seminars and research competitions which are held every year. In 2015, Dr. Rizwan Khalid (NY) directed a successful coaching seminar, which was held during the APPNA Spring meeting on May 2, 2015 in Crystal City, VA. Later on, Dr. Khalid additionally organized a Research Seminar during the APPNA summer meeting on August 15, 2015 in Orlando, FL. RESA and CYP continue to work closely to promote the educational activities for young physicians.

Reflections on Pakistan[12]

Stephen Seeling was the former Vice President of Operations for the Educational Commission for Foreign Medical Graduates (ECFMG). In 2006, Dr. A. R. Piracha had asked Mr. Seeling to assist in resolving the delayed visa issuance at ECFMG level. Mr. Seeling was happy to help APPNA for the cause of young physicians. Subsequently, he was invited by Dr. Adeel Butt to speak at various Career Counseling Seminars in Pakistan. Here he describes the memories of his first visit to Pakistan:

Steven Seeeling, Vice President for Operations at ECFMG, addressing at an APPNA meeting

"Beyond the wonderful food and the spectacular sites, it is the Pakistani people I will never forget. I was invited by APPNA to participate in a series of seminars for medical students and young physicians at several medical schools in Pakistan. I left Philadelphia for Pakistan on December 14, 2006, excited but unsure of what would come. I knew that I would be speaking at medical schools in Lahore (King Edward Medical College), Karachi (Dow University of Health Sciences), and Islamabad (Rawalpindi Medical College), and had a good sense of what the audiences would want to know. I had done the obligatory research on the geography, politics, and culture of Pakistan. And, of course, I had heard the admonitions to 'be safe and be careful.' But I was not prepared for the overwhelming graciousness and hospitality of the people I met during my week-long stay. And of all the people I met, it is the medical students and young physicians who will always stay with me.[13]

Months after the trip, the scenes are still vivid: a packed house of over 300 medical students (about half women, half men) at King Edward Medical College (founded 1860) in a large, dark-wooded, balconied hall that felt like Oxford. Polite but incisive questions about ECFMG, USMLE, and graduate medical education in the United States—this was a group that required you to bring your "A" game. The memory of the medical student, who insisted on carrying my briefcase. I declined and his professor approached. In a gracious tone, he asked me to accede to the student's request, explaining, "It will make him feel useful; it is the Asian way. "Walking through the nearly empty medical library at Aga Khan University at 5:30 pm, only to see two students separately studying prep materials for the USMLE. At Dow University in Karachi, talking with students after the session had broken up, and getting e-mails upon my return home, thanking me for giving up some of my lunch hour to answer their questions. At Rawalpindi Medical College, students asking me for my autograph— really! In one case, giving me a rupee bill to sign. (I said I would sign only if the young man would spend it immediately.)

There were others. Seeing a Philadelphia cheese steak "with Philadelphia cheese" on the menu of the restaurant in my Lahore hotel; driving to the Pakistani-Indian border at dusk to view the choreographed lowering of the Pakistani and Indian flags; eating at a KFC in Lahore (chicken and fries both good) staffed by individuals with speaking/hearing disabilities; visiting the Faisal Mosque in Islamabad, which accommodates

100,000 worshippers; attending and being very impressed by the due process and intellectual rigor of a meeting of the Disciplinary Committee of the Pakistani Medical and Dental Council.

None of this would have been possible without APPNA. The career counseling seminars organized by APPNA were universally outstanding. The information was timely and the presenters were not reluctant to provide the kind of practical candid advice the audience needed to hear. Before attending the APPNA seminars, for example, I had never heard anyone emphasize the importance, while interviewing, of being professional in dealing with support personnel at the residency program. On a personal level, it was APPNA's invitation to participate that gave me a set of experiences I will never forget. But for me, it will always come back to the students and young physicians, and their hunger for information about opportunities in the United States and entry into postgraduate training here. There is a tremendous amount of information on the Internet, and it is often wrong. The students that I met in Pakistan, and many thousands throughout the world who we will never meet, look to APPNA and ECFMG for accurate, objective information. They rely on us. That is something we should all pledge never to forget."

APPNA and New Accreditation Standards for Foreign Medical Colleges by ECFMG

In September 2010, ECFMG announced that, effective in 2023, physicians applying for ECFMG Certification will be required to graduate from a medical school that has been appropriately accredited. Since that announcement, a process for recognizing the agencies that accredit medical schools has been developed. This process will allow medical schools accredited by recognized agencies and their graduates to meet ECFMG's accreditation requirement.[14]

As soon as a process for recognition of medical school accrediting agencies was made available by ECFMG in early 2015, the APPNA LPOC (Liaison with Professional Organizations Committee) under the leadership of Ayesha Najib (AZ) started working with PMDC (Pakistan Medical and Dental Council) and LCME (Liaison Committee on Medical Education) to help Pakistani Medical Colleges satisfy these upcoming new accreditation requirements. A seminar during the APPNA Spring meeting 2015 in Crystal City, VA was held, where the Director of LCME Dr. Dan Hunt and

Dr. Masood Hameed President of PMDC (Pakistan Medical and Dental Council) were speakers. Dr. Hunt briefed the audience about upcoming changes in the Medical School Accreditation required by ECFMG and answered the audience's questions. Dr. Masood Hameed joined via video-conference and gave an account of the work PMDC is doing to meet this requirement.

This new accreditation requirement by ECFMG for medical schools was given top priority by APPNA for the sake of future physicians coming to the US for residency training. APPNA has pledged to work with PMDC and other organizations to educate all the medical schools in Pakistan in order to prepare them to meet the required accreditation credentials in a timely manner.

Research Seminars for Physicians-in-Training (PIT) and Students:

On July 2, 2005, history was made at the APPNA Summer Convention. For the first time ever, fourteen physicians in training were selected on merit to deliver four oral and eight poster presentations during APPNA's continued medical education (CME) program. This research competition was organized by the RESA committee and the Physicians-In-Training section. Primetime slots were provided for oral presentations during the Saturday morning CME session. A highly qualified abstract review committee was appointed that selected 12 abstracts out of 31 submissions.[15]

Similarly, a second P.I.T. research seminar was held the next year on July 8, 2006 at the CME meeting during the Summer APPNA Convention held at Chicago, IL. A total of 47 abstracts were received including one from Pakistan and one from England. Eleven abstracts were chosen for oral and poster presentations by a committee of 5 faculty members. Cash awards and certificates of achievements were given to the winning presenters. The RESA committee and the P.I.T. section put in enormous efforts to hold these seminars. The role of Raza Dilawari, Rizwan Khalid, Rizwan Naeem, Adeel Butt, Faisal Cheema and Tehseen Mozaffer among others was instrumental in organizing these highly successful educational seminars.[16]

Adeel Butt and Faisal Cheema took the research seminars to the next level and held them in Rawalpindi and Lahore during the winter meetings of 2006 and 2008 in Pakistan, respectively. It was indeed a labor intensive step that they carried on their shoulders in order to enhance research interest in future physicians from Pakistan. Dr. Butt reported in 2006 that they received 50 high quality abstracts and 20 were selected on merit for presentations due to time constraints. As Dr. Butt noted, "we hope that the students and physicians in training from Pakistan would be able to present their original research and be recognized and encouraged for their hard work, original ideas and contribution to the advancement of medical knowledge."[17] In 2008, a research seminar was successfully held during the summer meeting. An online portal was also developed for submission of research abstracts to be presented at the winter meeting in Lahore, Pakistan. The accepted abstracts were published in a special supplement of Journal of Pakistan Medical Association (JPMA).[18]

APPNA and Post-Match Scramble:

Traditionally, the residency match week was called 'Post-Match Scramble.' The process was chaotic. The unmatched applicants used to desperately approach the unfilled programs. In 2005, the CYP initiated a post-match scramble program in order to assist the unmatched young physicians by using its contacts and forwarding their resumes to different program directors for this uphill task. The co-chair of the CYP in 2005, Rubina Inayat, reported "More than 35 Residency applicants registered via our website and the team utilized all its resources to help the applicants find a post-match position."[19] Since then, the CYP assisted the unmatched young physicians by using its contacts. However, in 2012, the post-match scramble was changed into 'Supplemental Offer and Acceptance Program (SOAP).' It is a standardized and uniform process whereby unmatched applicants apply to unfilled programs through the Electronic Residency Application Service (ERAS®). The CYP continues to remain active, and provides general guidance to the unmatched young physicians.

APPNA establishes Temporary Housing for Young Physicians:

In 2009, under the leadership of Rashid Piracha and Rubina Inayat, the CYP proudly launched a new 'APPNA House' project to provide temporary accommodation of young physicians at a rental facility in the Bronx, NY. It could accommodate at least 15 residents at one time. The residents would pay nominal rent and shared the grocery cost, while one senior resident was appointed the "house in-charge." The APPNA NY House was expanded in 2010, and could now accommodate 20 residents at a time. The APPNA NY House project was continued in 2011–2012 and a second female one bedroom-apartment was added. In 2013, the APPNA NY house was moved from Bronx to a better and safer neighborhood in Queens, NY. The APPNA NY Chapter has been monitoring the activities at the house with financial support from Central APPNA to subsidize the cost.

The APPNA House in Detroit, MI was launched in 2012. Four apartments (3 males, and 1 female) were acquired by Dr. Majid Aized (MI). KEMCAANA, Woman Physicians of APPNA, Dr. Nasar Qureshi (NJ), and Dr. Muhammad Suleman (LA) were among the sponsors of this effort. Dr. Shahid Yousuf (MI) wrote in the APPNA Journal 2013, *"She is the first doctor of her family to have come to the USA. She heard of Detroit APPNA House while residing in Virginia. Another female doctor who had previously resided there told her about it. She corresponded by email and was soon booking her ticket to Detroit. Her father was so concerned about her safety and wellbeing that he asked her sister who resides in Canada to come to Detroit and pick her right from the airport and take her to APPNA House. Within two weeks of her arrival, Dr. Majid Aized, had arranged her externship."*

The financial burden (over $60,000 per year) of New York and Detroit Houses maintenance on central APPNA was completely taken off, Dr. Shahzad Iqbal, Chair of the CYP 2015 reported.[20] Both houses were placed on a self-sustaining model and the New York House application and payments were made available online.

PPS/APPNA house was founded in December of 2014. This property was purchased by PPS chapter for providing temporary housing for job seeking Pakistani physicians replicating same approach that was successfully practiced in New York and Detroit. The resident physicians at this house are mentored for job seeking. They also receive assistance in obtaining electives and observership positions.

In addition, an Iqbalians House in Philadelphia was established by (Allama Iqbal Medical College Alumni Association of North America (AIMCAANA). Since 2009, the Iqbalians House has served hundreds of young physicians and has indirectly helped them in getting into residency training programs.

In 2011, a Doctors House in Philadelphia was also established by the King Edward Medical College Alumni Association of North America

(KEMCAANA) during the term of Dr. Tariq Jamil (NY) as KEMCAANA President. It is a 5-bedroom house located in the Upper Darby section of Philadelphia. Dr. Masood Akbar (PA) purchased a house in Philadelphia and KEMCAANA leased it for students and young physicians' that were coming to the United States for Clinical skill testing and residency interviews.

APPNA Establishes a Scholarship Endowment Fund for Medical Students:[21]

The Scholarship Endowment Program was unanimously approved during the APPNA Executive Council 2013 Spring Meeting in New York. It all started with a fellow physician who wished to remain anonymous and pledged to match up to $1,000,000 of funds donated to the APPNA Scholarship Endowment Fund. This fund would provide scholarships to deserving medical students receiving their medical education in Pakistan; an excellent opportunity to repay our debt to our *alma maters*.

The salient features of the management of the fund are briefly listed:

- APPNA Scholarship Committee will maintain sub-accounts for each participating alumni association that represent its Pakistani Medical College.
- The number of scholarships for each medical college is dependent on the contributions of that institution's alumni.
- All monies collected will be deposited and subsequently invested in a newly established and specific APPNA Scholarship Account. The scholarship will be paid out of the income and appreciation of the fund, allowing it to remain perpetual.
- A minimum of $10,000.00 is required in the sub-account to receive one scholarship.

The APPNA Scholarship Project has made great strides since its inception in 2013. The contributions have exceeded two million dollars, including the matching grant of one million. The total value of funds in the APPNA Scholarship Endowment Accounts, which are invested with Stephens Inc., a member of New York Stock Exchange, were $1,989,956.17 as of December 31, 2015.[22] As Dr. Masood Akbar, chair of APPNA scholarship committee explains, *"The pledge from our colleague was very generous and selfless but its success hinged entirely on the generosity of the participating Alumni Associations...(and)...We accepted the challenge and raised over* **ONE**

MILLION DOLLARS to support the bright young men and women studying Medicine in Pakistan."

Loan Program *(Qarz-e-Hasana)*

The CYP introduced a loan program *(Qarz-e-Hasana)* in 2015 for the deserving young physicians from Pakistan who were interested in pursuing post-graduate medical training in the United States. The loan is awarded to the needy and deserving candidates annually based on an established criteria including but not limited to academic excellence and financial hardship. The recipient receives up to $5,000 to facilitate for USMLE examinations, travel for clinical skill testing as well as the interviewing process for the residency programs in the US. Similar efforts to lend monitory support for the indigent young physicians were also carried out in 2006 and 2013.

Unsung Heroes helping Young Physicians

It will be unfair to conclude this chapter without mentioning the contributions of countless "unsung heroes" whose dedicated work would never be recognized. These ambassadors of goodwill continue to help young physicians selflessly. Numerous physicians, either in their private offices or at hospitals, provide opportunities for job seeking Pakistani doctors to work as observers (shadowing) or do research electives.

Among them are indeed numerous APPNA members and leaders as well. Two of them, Dr. Faisal Cheema and Dr. Adeel Butt, are also known for their active role in mentorship of young doctors. Dr. Cheema managed to provide meaningful research electives to dozens of young physicians for over a decade at Columbia Presbyterian in NYC where he was a research scientist. This research exposure paved the way to obtaining residency position for numerous candidates. Similarly, Dr. Butt was able to help several deserving young physicians into the internal medicine residency program at University of Pittsburg, PA, where he was the Program Director of the International Scholars Program.

It's also worth mentioning one such unsung hero who passed away in 2015. Mr. Akram Chaudhry, an entrepreneur from New Jersey, who was among the founders of PAK-PAC and also served as its president (1996–1998).[23] He offered his help during the visa delay crises in 2003. He hosted a Sunday afternoon dinner at his home in North Jersey, where the guest of honor was New York Senator, Chuck Schumer, who came along with his wife. During the informal meeting at the feast, Mr. Chaudhary, introduced his guests to Senator Schumer. Dr. Asim Malik and Dr. Mahmood Alam were among them. They were asked by Mr. Chaudhry to brief the Senator on the issue of visa delays of young physicians who were not able to join their residency programs. A few days later, Senator Schumer's office called Dr. Asim Malik if he could provide names of the doctors who got residency positions in New York and were not able to join due to delays in security clearance. Three names were given and those three young physicians were able to join their training programs within two weeks with the personal intervention of Senator Schumer.

Conclusion:

"In order to move others deeply we must deliberately allow ourselves to be carried away beyond the bounds of our normal sensibility,"—Joseph Conrad's poignant words are on par with APPNA's resolve in catering to young physicians from Pakistan. APPNA's assistance to these doctors recounted in this chapter along with its efforts on the advocacy for these physicians are the demonstration of APPNA's commitment to guide, educate, assist and uplift these individuals seeking residency training and post graduate medical education. The assistance in the placement of these doctors in the residency training programs goes a long way in establishing a greater Pakistani American community in the long run. This volunteerism plays a broader role in serving the society and these deliberations have indeed gone beyond the bounds of normal sensibility of APPNA workers. Indeed, the selfless APPNA volunteers' resilience and dedicated efforts were instrumental in providing successful assistance to these doctors from Pakistan in the adverse post 9/11 environment.

End Notes:

1   See: www.britannica.com/biography/Joseph-Conrad
2   Minutes of APPNA Executive Council, July 14, 1984
3   *APPNA Qissa*, A history of Association of Pakistani Physicians of North America, 1978–2003; Political Activism and the FMG Issue, page 18–28, 2004.
4   Sir William Osler, Chauvinism in Medicine, in Aequanimitas, 267.

5   Minutes of APPNA Executive Council, October 9, 1992

6   Minutes of APPNA Executive Council, August 1, 1996

7   APPNA Journal, 5:2, Winter 2003, page 16.

8   Dr. Shahzad Iqbal, Chair CYP 2015, has contributed to the year-to-year history of CYP 2003–2015

9   Minutes of APPNA Fall Executive Council meeting, 2004

10   APPNA Journal, 8:2, Fall 2006, page 41

11   APPNA Journal, 8:3, Winter 2006, page 40–41

12   APPNA Journal 9:1, Summer 2007, page 35–36; Reflections on Pakistan by Stephen Seeing

13   Ibid

14   See: http://www.ecfmg.org/news/2015/02/13/process-recognition-medical-school-accrediting-agencies-now-available/

15   APPNA Journal 6:3, Summer/Fall 2005, page 26–29

16   APPNA Journal, 8:2, Fall 2006, page 40

17   APPNA Journal, 9:1, Summer 2007, page 33

18   APPNA Journal, 10:2, Winter 2008, page 9

19   APPNA Newsletter, 16:1, Spring 2006, page 15

20   APPNA Journal/Newsletter, 25:3, 2015, page 47

21   Dr. M. Masood Akbar, Chair APPNA Scholarship (Ad hoc) Committee 2015, contributed to this report

22   APPNA.org reported under APPNA Scholarship Fund, January 2016

23   Mr. Akram Chaudhry was a community leader who always led by example in serving the community when it was needed the most. He was also one of the founding members of Human Development Foundation (HDF) and merged his own, Noor Foundation, with HDF at the time of its inception in 1997. He was among the only two non-physicians known in APPNA as being the Life-time (paid) members. The other being Hank Bashore (TX), the manager of APPNA lifetime Investment Fund.

5

APPNA ADVOCACY FOR YOUNG PHYSICIANS, CIVIL LIBERTIES, AND SOCIAL JUSTICE[1]

ADVOCACY IN POST SEPTEMBER 11, 2001 (9/11) ERA

Immediately following the 9/11 attacks, APPNA denounced the horrific acts of terror in which, close to 3,000 innocent civilians died. On the evening of 9/11/2001, then President Dr. Riaz M. Chaudhry called a joint tele-conference of officers and the Chair of Board of Trustees, and the following resolution was passed.[1]

"The Association of Pakistani Physicians of North America strongly condemns the atrocious and brutal acts of terrorism on September 11. We deeply mourn the unprecedented loss of lives in the terrorist attack on New York City (NYC) and Washington. Nothing justifies the immoral and inhumane act that affected so many innocent lives. We can assure everyone that APPNA stands together with the people of the United States in this time of terror. We urge the United States Government to act quickly in apprehension and punishment of the perpetrators."

---

1   Dr. Nasir Gondal contributed to this chapter especially in the section on social justice. Dr. Gondal was the Co-Chair of APPNA Task force on Young Physicians created in 2003. Later, he was appointed as the founding member of newly established APPNA Advocacy Committee in 2004.
He has also served as the Co-Chair of this committee in 2006.

Copies of the resolution were sent to 27 senators and 42 congress representatives who were deemed friendly with Pakistan. It was also sent to the US President, Secretary of State, Secretary of Defense, the National Security Advisor, the Governor of New York, and the Mayor of NYC.[2]

Shocked by the enormity of the events, first response of APPNA and its members were to show support and solidarity with their adopted homeland, America. APPNA Disaster Management Committee under Dr. Saud Anwar along with the New York (NY) Chapter launched APPNA NY Crisis Management Center on September 18, 2001 in Franklin Square NY. Riaz A. Chaudhry was NY Chapter President. This effort received much positive attention in the media, and showed APPNA's concern for those affected by the terrorist acts. The venue of fall meeting of APPNA that year was changed from Florida to NYC to express support. It was held on November 10 at LaGuardia Marriott where 9/11 heroes were honored and $35,000 were raised and donated to American Red Cross.

For the Pakistani American Physicians and APPNA, there was concern, pain and confusion. The imagery of terror so close to home in their adopted homeland was very shocking. There was disbelief that it could be done by people claiming to be followers of Islam. It was soon followed by the concern for backlash, which did take place. It took place in many ways at different places.

Soon after the 9/11 event, there was an increased scrutiny of Pakistanis living in US, especially in main urban areas where many were rounded up. Most of them would be undocumented immigrants and were eventually deported. APPNA's chapters in major cities like New York did partner with many local organizations and worked closely with the Pakistan Consulate to help detained Pakistanis in their legal and social issues.

Locally in NYC, a coalition of various Pakistani organizations was put together under the APPNA, NY Chapter leadership in 2002. The coalition was called FAPA, Federation of Pakistani American Associations. FAPA was composed of more than ten organizations with a rotating presidency of six months by each organization starting with APPNA NYC under Dr. Faheem Butt. It worked in close collaboration with various nonprofit organizations in New York working on the detainees and undocumented Pakistanis. It arranged for financial and legal help for the detainees. In 2002 National Security Entry Exit Registration System (NSEER) was implemented. This 'Special Registration' called on all male foreign nationals of 25 countries including Pakistan to get re-registered and undergo a lengthy interrogation. FAPA was actively involved in helping these Pakistanis in their legal aid.

In the summer of 2002, APPNA helped to organize a Pakistan-American Summit in Washington, DC, to show its support for the USA. Other organizers included the Pakistan American Congress and PAK-PAC. Some 60 members attended in what was considered the first step in establishing a presence in Washington for Pakistani Americans. The summit focused on the members' concerns about national and international issues as a community. The participants emphasized their American identity, notwithstanding their Pakistani background. Members of Congress and members of the White House administration were also invited.[3]

It took some time to appreciate the effects of 9/11 on the lives, responsibilities, rights and privileges of Pakistani Americans. The hurriedly passed Patriot Act not only adversely affected Pakistani nationals living in the USA but also those trying to enter USA for higher education, earning a livelihood or for immigration purposes.

Effects of increased scrutiny of visa applications from Pakistani physicians applying for US residencies was first noticed in 2003, more than a year after the 9/11. Many Aga Khan University graduates matched for residencies were delayed or denied visa to enter USA. That jeopardized their jobs and training as they would not be able to start on time. Through the email listserv of APPNA members it was realized that numerous graduates from other medical colleges were also facing similar situation. This email activism started by Faisal Cheema (AKU) and Zafar Iqbal (DMC) led to the formation of a task force. An emergency telephone conference call was held on June 29, 2003. Raana Akbar APPNA President appointed a Taskforce for Visa and Licensure Issues. Asim Malik (KEMC) and Nasir Gondal (RMC) were appointed Chair and Co-chair, respectively. The members of the Taskforce were Mahmood Alam (AIMC), Sajid Chaudhry (AIMC), Zaffar Iqbal (DMC), Waheed Akbar (KEMC), Faisal Cheema (AKU), Saud Anwar (AKU), Busharat Ahmad (DMC), Saeed Akhtar (SMC), Omar Atiq (KMC), Javed Suleman (SMC), Adnan Khan (DMC), and Nadeem Zafar (DMC). It was felt that the US lawmakers be made aware of the situation and educated about its urgency. A Day on the Hill, first of its kind was organized on September 24, 2003. Waheed Akbar was the team leader. A young entrepreneur, Asad Malik (MI), helped a great deal in putting together the event. A workshop was held in the morning followed by visits to the offices of about 40 lawmakers. The purpose of meeting with lawmakers was three folds: 1) to educate legislators about the issue of visa denials and security clearance, 2) to emphasize the adverse impact of this policy on the US urban healthcare, and 3) to ask for their support for helping physicians of their constituencies.[4]

The objectives of the taskforce were to increase awareness of the problem of visa issuance and security clearance. A campaign of advertisements and letters to editors in newspapers of Pakistan to reach out to the young physicians was undertaken. It helped in raising awareness among those physicians seeking residencies in US. The petitions signed by 327 individuals were sent to Secretary of State Colin Powell and another 296 to Secretary of Homeland Security Tom Ridge. Individually signed letters were sent; 539 to various Senators and 175 letters to various congress representatives. Dr. Saeed Akhtar in Islamabad made several trips to US Embassy for that purpose.[5]

By the end of the year 2003, 77% of all the Pakistani physicians with Visa problems who had contacted APPNA received clearance and were able to join their residencies. This was considered a significant achievement, which could not have happened without the endless work of the Taskforce that made liaison with the State Department, US Embassy in Pakistan and lobbying through various Congressmen and Senators. All the Directors of the residency programs were approached requesting them to grant extension by allowing some grace time for joining the residencies beyond July 1. Many of them entertained the request favorably.

The year 2004 was a watershed moment for APPNA's advocacy efforts. A forum on advocacy was organized by Dr. Nasir Gondal and Dr. M. Saud Anwar at the spring APPNA meeting, which was held in March at NYC. The APPNA Summer Meeting that year was changed from Detroit to Washington DC with the purpose of holding an advocacy day. The theme of the year "Liberty, Freedom and Justice — Preservation of Civil Rights" was adopted by the president, Dr. Omar Atiq. The Advocacy Day on the Hill was held on June 10, 2004 in the Russell Senate Hall. Many senators including the newly elected junior senator from New York Hillary Clinton, Blanche Lincoln (D-AR), Arlen Specter (PA), Tom Carper (D-DE), Lincoln Chafee (D-RI), Tom Harkin (D-IL), and Tim Johnson (D-SD) attended. They all spoke about the need to help physicians and young doctors.[6] It was preceded by a briefing by ACLU, CAIR and National Immigration Forum. APPNA members were briefed on how to lobby. About 100 APPNA members participated in visiting congregational offices for CLARA and SAFE Act lobbying. Later there was a Symposium on Civil Rights. Participant organizations included Democracy Now (Amy Goodman), National Immigration Forum, NAACP, CAIR, and ACLU. In December 2004, members of the Committee for Young Physicians, including Dr. Rubina Inayat, Dr. Adeel Butt and Dr. AR Piracha met with U. S. Ambassador Ryan Crocker, in Islamabad to discuss the issue of discrimination and racial profiling that was being practiced.[7]

This activism of APPNA on behalf of its members and Pakistani Physicians in general needed a standing committee. In 2004, President Omar Atiq created two new standing committees in APPNA. One was Committee on Young Physicians (CYP) to tackle the issues faced by the new trainees and applicants to the residency programs. The second was the Advocacy, Legislative, and Governmental Affairs Committee with a wide area of work including holding an Annual Day on the Hill to lobby for the issues of importance to Pakistani Physicians in particular and to Pakistani Americans in general. The members of the first advocacy committee were Hussain Malik, Abdul R Piracha, Omar Atiq, Nasir Gondal, and Saud Anwar.

Advocacy and Legislative Affairs Committee was to be a liaison between APPNA and other political action groups including PAK-PAC and other organizations of Pakistani Diaspora.

Since then, mostly every year APPNA has held its Annual Day on the Hill in Washington, either along with its meetings or as a separate event. The emphasis on different concerns has shifted from year to year but the J1 Visa issues and security clearance of young physicians have been the main focus of the advocacy meetings.[8]

Advocacy efforts were further enhanced in 2005 and a direct liaison was established with the US Embassy in Islamabad to help facilitate the Visa and Security issues of young physicians. A meeting was arranged between APPNA officers and US Department of State through CAIR for expediting the security clearance for new physicians. Advocacy efforts were focused on US Pakistan relations that year and a related seminar was held in conjunction with the Spring Meeting in Washington, DC. A meeting was also held in the Pakistan Embassy Washington where possibilities were explored on finding common ground for helping the physicians. Moreover, a Day on the Hill was held on November 17, 2005 with collaboration of several other organizations to lobby the congress for $1 billion in humanitarian aid for the Pakistan/Kashmir earthquake victims. A bill to approve this was passed by the US congress.[9]

These efforts got a boost in 2006 under the leadership of A. Rashid Piracha. It was another year where advocacy efforts were definitely advanced. A successful advocacy day was held in Rayburn Building 2325 in Washington on April 6. It was held in collaboration of CAIR, ACLU, PAK-PAC, PAL-C Pac, and American Organization of Muslim Lawyers. The objective was to secure support for the Senate Bill 2138 End Racial Profiling Act (ERPA), help the Muslim Charities with funds earmarked for earthquake 2005 relief and to express concern about National Security Agency's (NSA) Wiretapping Program. More than 50 lawmakers' offices were visited for lobbying. Fifteen congress representatives spoke at the event which was well covered in the media. The next day, April 7, there was a meeting with the Department of Homeland Security, arranged through PAKPAC. Furthermore, in order to enable upcoming leadership of APPNA trained in public speaking and advocacy effectively, a Leadership Training Program was conducted by Ibrahim Hooper and Arsalan Iftikhar of CAIR in conjunction with Continued Medical Education (CME) program in the Spring Meeting held in Washington, DC.[10]

APPNA Advocacy team meets with Senator Obama (D-IL) on young doctors visa delay issues (2006). (L to R) Mahmood Alam, Rubina Inayat, Barack H. Obama, M. Saud Anwar, and Faiyaz Hussain

The collaborative efforts of the committee on Young Physicians (CYP) and Advocacy Committee started to bear its fruit in 2006. The 92% resident physicians arrived on time that year. In year 2005, 74% of the Pakistani young physicians were able to join their residency programs on time as compared to only 26% and 62% in years 2003 and 2004, respectively.

However, the total number of Pakistani physicians securing J1 visa positions dropped 37% in year 2005. Dr. Piracha and Dr. Rizwan Khalid also arranged a meeting through Dr. Busharat Ahmad and briefed AMA's IMG section on the visa delay issues of Pakistani doctors in 2006. The delay in joining the training programs by Pakistani origin physicians due to tardy process of security clearance was obviously putting these candidates in jeopardy since the program directors had no shortage of competitive candidates from other countries.[11]

It was felt in 2007 that in the coming years, Pakistani American community would benefit with prompt help available through a professional civil rights organization, which can be called upon by any APPNA member in time of urgent need. After soliciting various proposals from civil rights and advocacy organizations, President Nadeem Kazi signed a contract with the Muslim Advocates, a nonprofit organization of Muslim lawyers headed by Farhana Khera.[12,13] APPNA also worked with Institute of Social Policy and Understanding (ISPU) and Muslims Public Affairs Council (MPAC).

The advocacy efforts continued in 2008. The theme for that year was Empowering Community through Activism and Solidarity. President Mahmood Alam sent a letter to all the US Senators and Congress Representatives expressing APPNA's concern regarding profiling and infringement of the civil liberties of Pakistani-Americans. Along with the Annual Summer Convention of APPNA, there was an advocacy day on June 26, 2008 in the Capital Building HC5. It was in collaboration with PAK-PAC, Muslim Advocates and the Center for Voter Advocacy. Among others it was attended by Senator Joe Biden who was the Chair of the Senate Foreign Relations Committee at that time and was in the process to sponsor the Biden Lugar bill, which was later passed as Kerry Lugar bill since Joe Biden left the Senate to be the Vice Presidential candidate with Barack Obama. Later, in the afternoon a meeting was held with the State Department. APPNA's voice was also echoed at the U.S. Senate Judiciary Committee's subcommittee on the Constitution, Civil and Property Rights at a hearing on "Laptop searches and other violations of privacy faced by Americans returning from abroad. On June 25, 2008, Farhana Khera, executive director of Muslim Advocates, testified before that committee chaired by Senator Russ Feingold. A special message by the Democratic Party presidential candidate Barack Obama on this subject, was read during the Saturday Banquet June 28, 2008.[14]

APPNA leadership continued to meet with US officials at the Islamabad Embassy, the State Department, and the Department of

Homeland Security to expedite specific individual cases of visa delays that
were known to APPNA. A website was developed that had a link at the
APPNA website in order to allow physicians in Pakistan to register on the
website and submit their individual issues and problems so that advocacy
committee could address their cases specifically the issue of obtaining
security clearance. The proactive role of the advocacy committee in 2008
paved the way of excellent working relationship between Dr. A. Rashid
PIracha (chair) and Ms. Furuta-Toy, the Director of Public Liaison and
Visa Services at the Department of State in Washington, DC. APPNA was
allowed to send lists of applicants to her. She used to review those cases
individually and was able to expedite and obtain security clearance for
many young physicians. whose jobs were jeopardized due to visa problem.

The theme of the Advocacy Day in 2009 was lobbying for the
Enhanced Partnership with Pakistan Act (aka) Kerry Lugar Bill and the visa
issues. Zia Moiz Ahmad was the chair of the committee and Saud Anwar
and Zahid Imran played vital role that year.

By 2011 a newer generation of APPNA activists took the helm. Zaffar
Iqbal was the chair of the advocacy committee under President Manzoor
Tariq. The visa issue and security clearance had become more complicated
and there was a need to push for more congressional support on these issues.
On June 5, 2011, the committee members met with officials at State Dept.
and US Homeland Security representative. Later that year on December
6, there was a successful Advocacy Day held where these issues were raised.
Largest number of congressmen attended APPNA Day on the Hill.[15,16] In
2012, Manzoor Tariq as the Chair of Advocacy committee, continued to
enhance the efforts and a direct link was established with the AF-PAK *(a
highly controversial neologism used within US foreign policy circles to designate
Afghanistan and Pakistan as a single theater of operations)* representatives.

In order to move from ad hoc arrangements every year APPNA
President Javed Suleman and Advocacy Chair Talha Siddiqui in 2013 felt
that there should be an increased and organized contact with the congressional offices as well as continuity of dialogue year after year. These efforts
culminated in hiring a lobbyist firm. Ari Mittleman, who had been a congressional staffer and was working for a lobbying firm. This firms signed
contract with APPNA in 2013. This arrangement had its benefits at a cost.
The Day on the Hill in 2013 was to lobby for HR 2428; to provide incen-
tives to physicians to practice in rural and medically underserved communities, and for other purposes.[17]

The advocacy efforts of APPNA reached a new high point under the leadership of President Asif Rehman and Chair Advocacy AR Piracha in 2014. The Day on the Hill was successful in raising the issue; all the young physicians who approached APPNA for visa clearance help were able to get their visas and started residency training on time.[18, 19]

It was realized that APPNA has to find a way to deal with the ever-changing officials at State Dept., US Embassy in Islamabad, and Homeland Security. It was important to lobby for a bill which will make it incumbent upon the State Dept. to approve a special process for three months, from April to June, to expedite the visa process and security clearance of young physicians from Pakistan hired for residency training that starts on July 1 every year. This was promoted vigorously by APPNA and bipartisan sponsorship was achieved through the offices of the Democratic Congresswoman Grace Meng of New York and Republican Congressman Tom Emmer of Minnesota. They jointly co-sponsored the HR 1920 and 1921 GRAD Act (Grand Residency to Additional Doctors). Introduced in House (04/21/2015), this bill directed the Secretary of State to:

- Designate a Department of State officer or employee whose sole responsibility during the months of March, April, May, June, and any other period of time determined by the Secretary, shall be to facilitate the expedited review of J-visa applications of aliens applying for U.S. admission to participate in a graduate medical education or training program; and
- Provide appropriate Foreign Service officers with training related to medical graduates and medical graduate programs in the countries in which they are serving.[20]

In 2015 the day on the Hill was held on April 30. More than 30 offices were reached and the theme was to get the support for the Meng Emmer GRAD Act as mentioned above. As there was a change in Congress after the midterm elections, the GRAD Act had to be reintroduced.[21] Later, on May 15, 2015, this bill was referred to the subcommittee on Immigration and Border Security.

Broadly speaking, every year, APPNA's advocacy efforts have become more focused with professional assistance of a lobbyist. This happened despite the yearly changing of guards in APPNA, which at times puts extra burden and complexity on the organization to find consistency and continuity with different leadership goals for each year. The question is often asked about the benchmark of success in APPNA's advocacy efforts over the last decade? In 2003, when the issue of visa delays surfaced, only 26% of those who had the residency contracts could get in to join their training on time and maximum of 77% could make it later during the year with fierce efforts by APPNA. During the last few years, the success rate is 100%.[22] The introduction of H.R. 1921 is a testament to the tenacity of APPNA members and the increasing number of socially conscientious activists amongst them. Much more can be done and could have been done. But the progress and the consistent direction of the advocacy efforts assure that APPNA advocacy on young physicians' issue, which started in 2003, continues to make progress every year despite onerous and burdensome US policies regarding the entry of bright Pakistani physicians seeking higher education and training in the US.

APPNA and Issues of Profiling and Civil Liberties in America

APPNA sought to address the issue of profiling and curtailment of civil liberties of its members under the USA PATRIOT Act[23] since 2001. Numerous APPNA members reported their experiences of humiliating questioning they faced by the authorities upon arrival at the airports after a foreign travel to either Pakistan or to Middle Eastern countries. Moreover, being an organization of Pakistani descent physicians, APPNA itself anticipated higher scrutiny by the state and federal agencies. APPNA acted to develop and implement policy and procedures of best practices in its financial transactions and spending of charitable donations for our work in Pakistan in collaboration with other non-profit organizations. The awareness of APPNA leadership across the board and rigorous scrutiny by the Council has been successful in doing what was right for the Association.

The issue of working with other civil rights organizations has been rather complex and for the same reason controversial. Many APPNA members, in their personal capacity, work with different organizations that have emerged as champions of civil liberties for Muslims in the post 9/11 era. One such organization is Council on American-Islamic Relations (CAIR). In 2006, President A. R. Piracha worked with CAIR when issues of civil liberties were at the height of discussion. Next year in 2007, President Nadeem Kazi took a more cautious course on APPNA's behalf. He signed a number of memoranda of understanding (MOU) with different organizations in promoting APPNA's stand on civil liberties, lobbying with lawmakers, and working on philanthropic ventures. These memoranda of understanding were reviewed by the attorneys before APPNA signed on them. The memoranda were signed with "Muslim Advocates" (MA) and Muslim Public Action Committee (MPAC) for civil liberties, with PAK-PAC on lobbying for Pakistan, with HDFNA on charitable work in Pakistan, and with Institute for Social Policy and Understanding (ISPU), an independent, nonpartisan research organization specializing in addressing the most pressing challenges facing the American Muslim community and in bridging the information gap between the American Muslim community and the wider society. One of ISPU's research was supported by APPNA. It was entitled, *"A Window into American Muslim Physicians: Civic Engagement and Community Participation—Their Diversity, Contributions and Challenges."* It was published in 2012[24]

The Council approved a contribution of $100,000 to Muslim Advocates (MA) to fight for APPNA members' rights in USA and advise us on a case by case basis if any of our members face profiling.[25] This action was approved during fall meeting in 2007 and first of the four yearly installments of $25,000 were given to MA. MA had a matching grant of $100K from Ford Foundation. The MA successfully halted the "mapping" or massive data and intelligence gathering plan by Los Angeles Police Department (LAPD). MA also produced an educational DVD on Racial Profiling, which has been widely distributed in our community and its premier viewing happened during the APPNA summer meeting of 2008 at Washington DC. Furthermore, Zahid Imran, a psychiatrist from Baton Rouge, LA and Salam al-Maryati, executive director of MPAC met with US Department of Defense to discuss the psychological needs of prisoners at Guantanamo Bay. A joint statement was issued by APPNA, MPAC, and US Defense Department that was posted on APPNA website.[26]

APPNA's members and intellectuals alike, are engaged in what affects us as a people in this global village on earth. APPNA Journal, an official publication of the Association, has been replete with editorials and articles which reflect on current geopolitical situation and issues of civil liberties since 9/11 tragedy. APPNA members actively participate on all the avenues of social media. Any relevant event occurring anywhere in the world becomes a point of discussion within hours. Our members become readily engaged in issues like, human rights, plight of minorities, women issues, radicalization of our faith, terrorism, Islamophobia, and lately home grown terrorism that impacts significantly our lives in our adopted home and the country of our children's birth. APPNA and its affiliates have been working with US authorities to help filling the gap between the two countries. Numerous messages from the US lawmakers and leaders on foreign affairs published in APPNA meeting magazines over the last decade are testimonials of APPNA's vital role in promoting understanding and cooperation.

APPNA and Social Justice in Pakistan

By the year 2000, the next exodus of Pakistani physicians who reached the US shores in the 80's and 90's had completed their post graduate training and had settled. They started to attend APPNA events and showed interest albeit ambivalence towards organization's policies by some of them. They were similar to the earlier generation in many ways but at the same time emphasized a different set of priorities and interest to APPNA. Growing up in an increasingly stifling environment in Pakistan, many were more conscientious and involved in the social and political issues back home compared to their predecessors.

This new infusion of membership in APPNA's ranks helped the formation of new and the resurgence of old alumni organizations as well as the creation of new local chapters. At the same time, there was more yearning for a democratic and transparent process in APPNA, and a desire to be involved in social and political issues both in the US and in Pakistan.

"Mr. President, we are helped in that quest (of civil rights) by your policies and actions in Pakistan. When we demand justice and fair play in our adopted homeland (America), it helps to have a just and fair society in our motherland (Pakistan). When we demand due process and equality before law, for all citizens in the United States, it helps to have the same in Pakistan. When we demand protection for the rights of the Muslim minority in America, it is helpful to have the rights of minorities secured here (Pakistan)."[27]

The above statement is an excerpt from APPNA President Omar Atiq's speech delivered at a reception in the presence of chief guest, President of Pakistan Gen. Pervez Musharraf. This took place at the winter APPNA meeting held jointly with Khyber Medical College convocation at Peshawar in December of 2004. Dr. Atiq's statement was in contrast to the speeches given at that time during the annual PAK-PAC dinners in Islamabad where glorification of the military rule was usually witnessed year after year without any mention of issues pertaining to the common people of Pakistan. The founders of APPNA had expressed at numerous occasions that APPNA tended to work with the government officials in Pakistan on the issues of common interest without siding with political parties let alone supporting a military rule.[28] The hosting of General Zia ul Haq or his representatives at APPNA meetings and collaborating with the military regime during the 1980's, even for assisting on issues of healthcare and education were perceived by some as legitimizing dictatorship. However, this practice was significantly curtailed during General Musharaf's regime. APPNA and its Alumni Associations focused on the educational endeavors and philanthropy by working with either medical professional organizations or through the administration at the medical colleges. This shift in emphasis was made possible due to a process of organizational maturation and acquisition of a status of respect and clout by APPNA.

In 2003 and 2004, the Social Welfare and Disaster Relief Committee (SWDRC) of APPNA under the leadership of past President, Dr. Javed Akhtar, got involved in the issue of women imprisoned in Pakistan under the "Hudood Ordinance." An initiative was taken by Justice retired Nasir Aslam Zahid from Karachi who single handedly worked for providing the legal help for those women; majority of them being incarcerated due to lack of legal representation. Mr. Zahid was invited to the 2003 APPNA summer meeting in Orlando, Florida where he spoke as the chief guest at the SWDRC held seminar. About $14,000 were raised. Drs. Ahmad and Naheed Hilal from Alleghany, New York made the single largest donation for the cause. Subsequently, Dr. Yasmeen Rashid, President of Pakistan Medical Association (PMA), Punjab, from Lahore joined the struggle. APPNA also donated $10,000 in 2004 in support of providing justice for incarcerated women. Numerous attorneys were hired by the organization of retired Justice Zahid to help those women out of incarceration; many of them with their small children.[29,30]

APPNA as a Big Tent

While APPNA itself remains apolitical and steers a centrist course towards charitable and educational endeavors, its meetings provide space to address social issues like minority rights, journalist killings, targeted killings of physicians, women rights, security issues stemming from terrorist activities, and the restoration of justice and democracy. Many organizations comprised predominantly of Pakistani American Physicians have found space through APPNA's platform. Moreover, APPNA annual conventions and other meetings regularly hold "Social Forums" organized by its various Alumni Associations with focus on social and political issues in Pakistan.

Prominent politicians and social justice leaders travel to these meetings to have their voices heard by APPNA members and through them, by the Pakistani American diaspora at large.

Evolving avenues of communications have significantly helped the interaction and networking of APPNA members. In December 1999, Adeel Butt utilized the internet to put together an email list of members as an informal forum for online discussion, which got attention of hundreds of members within a short period of time.[31] Another listserv started by Mansoor Hussain and Raana Akbar, (circa 2002), created a new platform where APPNA members exchanged views and coordinated their efforts in areas of mutual interest. Later, when the official list ceased to exist, APPNA members converged on private lists managed by APPNA members. The foremost amongst them are yahoo group's Apnalist and Globemedic managed by Shahid Latif and Amin Karim, respectively. Both lists are mostly populated by APPNA members but have non-APPNA participants as well. Later the emergence of social media in other forms provided expanded access for members to communicate. This communication has been vital for many of APPNA activities including issues of social justice in Pakistan. A Social Forum event was started by DOGANA at APPNA summer convention in 2003 by Zia M. Ahmad. Later many other alumni associations either partnered with DOGANA or held their own social fora, addressing various issues of social justice in Pakistan. Numerous physician-based independent organizations emerged out of these activities and they drew their strength from APPNA members. A few organizations with socially conscious agendas owe their existence to APPNA. Examples include the Asian Americans Network Against Abuse of Human Rights (ANAA) in 2005, Association of Pakistani American Physicians for Justice and Democracy (APPJD) and Doctors for Democracy and Justice (DFD) in 2007.

In 2002 it was reported in Herald Karachi by Reema Abbasi that two young girls Saima, 20 and Shama 17 were gang raped. Amna Buttar (FJMC) and Zaffar Iqbal (DMC) spearheaded a campaign of collecting 300 signatures in Summer Meeting 2002 in New York. During the meeting, a conference call was held which was attended by the attorney of the victims amongst others via telephone. These efforts of APPNA members led to the formation of the APPNA Ad hoc Committee for Suffering of Violence against Women in Pakistan. This committee eventually evolved into an independent organization Asian Americans Network against Abuse of Human Rights (ANAA). ANAA was headed by Amna Buttar with a vision of progressive and enlightened Pakistan where there is no room for discrimination and injustice. On July 2, 2005, ANAA held its first symposium during the summer APPNA meeting in Houston, TX. The topic was "Violence against Women in South Asia—the ground reality in Pakistan."[32] Along a similarly tragic line, in 2005, Shazia Khalid, a Pakistani physician was allegedly gang raped in Sui Baluchistan. This issue was taken up by many APPNA members. When General Pervez Musharraf visited USA in 2006, many APPNA members rallied outside Roosevelt Hotel in New York to protest on his inflammatory remarks on gang rape.

In 2007, the Chief Justice of Pakistan, Iftikhar M. Chaudhry, was removed unjustifiably according to some. He was once seen as a part of pro-government judiciary, partially responsible for the legitimization of military rule in 2000. However, he achieved iconic status overnight when removed by President Musharraf. He stood his ground. His detention triggered a movement for the establishment of a democratic rule in Pakistan. Started by the lawyers, the movement was soon joined by the civil society. It motivated many APPNA members to react. APPNA planned to create a taskforce for the purpose. There was a debate in APPNA rank and file about its direct participation in political campaigns. During this argument a legal opinion was sought by the then President Nadeem Kazi. APPNA's stance as a 501(C) 3 organization was considered to fall outside of APPNA's charter. Concerned APPNA members passionate about the issue, formed an independent organization; the Association of Pakistani American Physicians for Justice and Democracy (APPJD). Mahjabeen Islam wrote an article in APPNA Journal titled, "APPNA choked by its own charter" expressing the frustration of members who wanted to join the popular movement in Pakistan. APPNA had to stay within the confines of its well-defined status.[33] Later in the year when the state of emergency was declared in November 2007, APPNA activists from New York and northeast US along with many other organizations held an emergency rally outside Pakistan Consulate in New York.

APPJD liaised with other Pakistani organizations under an umbrella of Coalition for the Restoration of Justice and Democracy (CRDP). Many APPNA members including Omar Atiq, Mohammad Taqi, Ashraf Toor, Faheem Butt, Zahid Imran and Amna Buttar visited Pakistan and participated in the movement for the restoration of the chief justice, in their private capacity. Prominent leaders of the Lawyer's movement participated in seminars held during APPNA Summer Convention in 2008.

The Lawyer's movement attained significant recognition worldwide. The Medal of Freedom honors the accomplishments of those individuals who have struggled to defend the legal system's fundamental obligation to liberty, justice and equality. The Medal of Freedom is the highest honor the Harvard Law School Association has to offer, and in 2007, it was offered to Pakistani Chief Justice Iftikhar M. Chaudhry. Mr. Chaudhry was put on the same platform as the former South African President Nelson Mandela, a world-renowned Nobel laureate who struggled for freedom and equality against all odds.[34] The Chief Justice was also honored by APPNA's President Mahmood Alam in a reception hosted by DFD in New York City in 2008. Zahid Imran and Muhammad Taqi of APPJD and Abdul Majeed and Qazi Kamal Haider of DFD had been actively involved in this movement.

United Social Forum 2009:
"Swat—Paradise lost or Heaven gained?"

Beginning in 2009, Pakistan saw one of the largest displacements of individuals in country's 62-year history. These heartbreaking events were occurring predominantly in Swat valley, which is also known as a Paradise on earth. The valley begets this name not only because of lush green pastures, fruit laden orchards, snow-capped mountains, and the gushing waters of Swat river; but also because of the simplicity and hospitality of its people and a rich culture.[35] In 2009, the Taliban took over large parts of Malakand division in Khyber Pakhtunkhwa (KPK) province. Subsequent military action led to the exodus of almost three million internally displaced persons (IDP) to various areas of KPK. It was the time when numerous members of APPNA from KPK expressed their concern about the situation and initiated awareness and fundraising to help the IDP. The fundraising was later carried on by the SWDR committee.

Dr. Amjad Hussain, past president of APPNA, took the initiative of holding a social forum at APPNA summer meeting about the situation and proposed the title, "Swat, a Paradise lost or Heaven gained." APPNA activists like Mohammad Taqi (KMC), Suhail Siddiqui (SMC), Zahid Imran (QMC), Rizwan Naeem (SMC), Talha Siddiqui (DOW), and Sophia Janjua (RMC) got involved soon after the announcement. The DOGANA President, Muslim Jami, felt the need for unity on this issue of major national geopolitical situation. A broad based committee was formed and the traditional Dow Social Forum was transformed into the first ever "United Social Forum" of APPNA. Jamil Farooqi was appointed the Chair of this united social forum that took place on July 3, 2009 at San Francisco, Marriott. Amjad Hussain moderated the jam-packed forum in which following panelists participated apart from Ms. Maleeha Lodhi, who also attended the forum. Dr. Babar Awan, MNA (PPP), Mr. Javed Hashmi, MNA (PML-N), Dr. Farooq Sattar, MNA (MQM), Dr. Pervez Hoodbhoy, (Educationist), Mr. Shuja Nawaz, (Political analyst, author), Mr. Haji M. Adeel, Senator (ANP), Mr. Sajjad Burki, (PTI), and Dr. M. Iqbal Khalil, (Jamaat-e-Islami). In his brief speech, President APPNA, Syed Samad, emphasized the importance of democracy, independent judiciary, and rule of law in Pakistan.[36] In 2011 at the APPNA annual meeting in St Louis, the memory of slain journalists was immortalized in the name of Hyat Ullah Khan Award. APPJD started this award for courage in Journalism. It was given to Omar Cheema and Babar Wali.

In 2013, two seminars on social justice were held under the Advocacy Committee. The seminar on targeted physician killing in Pakistan was held in NYC at APPNA spring meeting. Mohammad Taqi, Rizwan Naeem, Beena Sarwar, and Mrs. Isphahani were among the organizers. The second seminar titled "Death of Religious Freedom in Pakistan, An End to Jinnah's Legacy," was held at Orlando, Florida during the APPNA summer convention. DOGANA and SMCAANA joined hands with the Advocacy Committee to arrange this very informative seminar.[37]

Physician Killings in Pakistan[38]

ہم جو تاریک راہوں میں مارے گئے

Since the late 1980's there has been killing of physicians in Pakistan. Many of the first killings were in southern Punjab and later it spread to Sindh and then to what is now Khyber Pakhtunkhwa. While in the beginning, some murders appeared random or were perceived as criminal acts to obtain ransom; it turned out to be a systematic plan to destabilize peace and harmony. Being members of middle class, physicians enjoy considerable respect and deference. Targeting them, along with other professionals like lawyers, artists, community activists and civil servants sends a chilling message to the public at large. It promotes the feeling of helplessness and being defenseless. The majority of the physicians killed were members or perceived to be members of the Shia community. Some physicians of targeted killings were Ahmadi, while a small number of Sunnis have also been the victims. Some of the slain physicians were American citizens as well.

Many physicians especially from minority sects left Pakistan for theirs and their families' safety. Some of them are members of APPNA and have compelling tales to tell.

Initially, there was some ambivalence by APPNA and many of its members in taking a position on this issue. There had been heated debates about it. Then in May 2002, Dr. Safdar Zaidi was killed in Karachi on his way home from his clinic. He was a nephrologist, who was trained at Rush University, Chicago and later moved to Phoenix, Arizona. He was an APPNA member, and a previous National Student Federation activist. He had decided to go back to serve his family and community. By that time physician killing was almost a daily tragedy and more than 80 physicians, mostly Shia, had been killed.

A group of physicians had a protest walk in St. Louis
at the APPNA summer meeting in 2011

Mohammad Suleman, APPNA President 2002, took personal interest. He called a council meeting and within a few months was able to have a meeting with the Pakistani Ambassador in US, Maleeha Lodhi. Spearheaded by Mansoor Abidi and other Dow graduates, the movement had participants from other medical colleges including Zahid Imran, Naveed Iqbal and Babar Cheema. It involved aggressive letter writing campaign and placing large supportive advertisements in Pakistani newspapers. The Chair Board of Trustees, Aslam Malik, wrote a very passionate letter. Some physician representatives including Naveed Iqbal, traveled to Pakistan to show support and solidarity, and met with the Federal Ministry, and collaborated with PMA. In the same year 2002, DOGANA's annual banquet theme was physicians' killings. Khalil Shibli and Umar Daraz traveled from UK and highlighted the issue of the systematic killing of minority physicians in Pakistan. This vociferous and effective stand of APPNA in the US and in Pakistan was perhaps instrumental in having some arrests related to the killings. For a long time, it seemed that the issue of physician killing had stopped, showing that perhaps raising voice and having a concerted effort by APPNA and its members did produce results and some lives were saved!

However, the vicious acts of targeted killing did not stop. Almost every year there had been physician killings and in 2012 and 2014 the numbers jumped up again. In 2013 Ali Haider, an ophthalmologist along with his son Murtaza were killed while dropping Murtaza at school. Then, in 2014, another Pakistani American Physician Dr. Mehdi Ali Qamar, an Ohio based cardiologist and belonging to Ahmadi sect was killed in cold blood. He went to Pakistan to provide free cardiac procedures at a hospital of his community. An Ad hoc Committee was created by President Asif Rehman in 2014 and Muslim Jami was appointed its chair. A letter in protest of physician killings was sent to prime minister of Pakistan, Mian Nawaz Sharif. There was a demonstration during the Annual Meeting in Washington DC in August 2014. Many physicians wore red ribbons and T shirts. Naseem Shekhani wore it while receiving award for his services during APPNA banquet. President Asif Rehman showcased it in his speech and a documentary on physicians' killing was shown during the meeting. The issue was taken to US Congress and various Congressmen were briefed on this issue. An APPNA delegation also visited the Pakistani ambassador to register their protest against inaction of the Pakistani Government and their failure to even acknowledge the cold blooded murder of Dr. Mehdi Ali Qamar. APPNA members in various cities organized protests including New York City and Houston.[39]

APPNA 2014

Asif M. Rehman, MD
President

Mubasher E. Rana, MD
President-Elect

Asaf R. Qadeer, MD
Secretary

Shahid Rashid, MD
Treasurer

Javed Suleman, MD
Immediate Post President

Association of Physicians of Pakistani Descent of North America

6414 South Cass Avenue Westmont, IL. 60559   P: (630) 968-8585   F: (630) 968-8677   W: www.appna.org

June 18, 2014

To: The Right Honorable Mian Nawaz Sharif
Prime Minister of Pakistan

Sir,

We the undersigned Pakistani-American doctors wish to protest the Pakistan government's inaction with regard to the increasingly frequent assassinations of our colleagues in Pakistan.
In the larger context, we wish to register our strong condemnation of target killings physicians, journalists, moderate liberal thinkers, professionals, intellectuals, and the endangered minorities occurring in Pakistan to generate anarchy and create a climate of fear. The recent murder of Dr. Qamar Mehdi is but a continuation of the repeated attacks on doctors in Pakistan. By failing to prosecute the criminals involved, the State is implicitly condoning such massacres. We urge the authorities to fulfill their obligations and establish rule of law and take swift action against the perpetrators.

We wish to remind that murderous crimes have reached unthinkable levels. In most cases, those culpable openly and proudly take responsibility for their actions, even while exhorting their followers to more senseless killing.

We demand that the government immediately take the following steps:

1. Investigate these reprehensible killings and prosecute the killers;
2. In the case of Dr. Mehdi the government of Pakistan and its authorities have yet to acknowledge that a murder took place. We demand an end to this apathy;
3. Provide protection of witnesses and security of judges so that the trials take place in a secure environment;
4. Arrest and try in court the leaders of defunct organizations such as Sipah-e-Sahaba, Lashkar-e-Jhangvi, and other militant outfits, which openly vilify Shias, Ahmedis and other minorities;
5. Ban and tackle the threats posed by these organizations in an effective manner so that they are not allowed to simply continue operations under different names;
6. Enforce legislation, which makes it illegal to encourage violence against any and all ethnic or religious groups and strictly instruct police to shut down any gathering where such hate-speech occurs;
7. Implement the existing laws on hate speech that justifies violence.

We hold that the current situation is headed for a catastrophic breakdown of society and God forbid a situation of possible civil war unless your government takes prompt action. As a professional group that cares for the country of our origin and association, we urge you to take immediate and effective action. Enough blood has already been spilled.

Respectfully yours,

Muslim Jami, MD
Chair, Ad Hoc Committee on Social Justice

Asif M. Rehman, MD
President

The available list of physicians killed by sectarian violence is included in the Appendices of this book. Some of the perpetrators of this violence have been convicted and eventually faced the death sentence when the moratorium on death penalty was lifted in 2015.

APPNA and PAK-PAC[40]

Under its charter, APPNA cannot participate in political activities. Due to this limitation, Pakistani American Political Action Committee (PAK-PAC) was created during the presidency of Arif Toor in 1989. PAK-PAC was registered with Federal Elections Commission to lobby in support of Pakistani issues in the US. Despite having its ups and downs, PAK-PAC has survived and keeps working on the mission for which it was established more than 25 years ago. In 2011, the first president of PAK-PAC, Nasim Ashraf, reflected on the founding of PAK-PAC. *"As the Pakistani-American community was coming of age and APPNA was also getting stronger between 1980–1990, political activism and lobbying for Pakistani causes became more and more prevalent. Again, APPNA took the leadership role in setting up a separate entity called PAK-PAC in 1989. But I would like to tell you also about an oft-forgotten contribution that APPNA made to the very survival and livelihoods of foreign medical graduates before even PAK-PAC was officially registered. In the mid-eighties, quite a few states started to question the need and role of foreign medical graduates (FMGs). Reciprocity in licensing and eligibility for Medicare and Medicaid funding for FMGs was in jeopardy. At the annual meeting of APPNA held in Washington, D.C in 1985, we invited representatives from all the major organizations of FMG's and forged an Alliance of Foreign Medical Graduates comprising the Indian Medical Graduates Association of US, the Islamic Medical Association, the International Medical Graduates (representing fifth pathway students) and two other organizations besides APPNA. Dr. Ikram Khan was the APPNA president at that time. A former U.S. Senator was hired to lobby for the "right of every licensed physician, irrespective of their medical school, to practice freely in every state of the Union and that no discriminatory laws are enacted by any state contrary to above." This Alliance achieved its purpose when the late Senator Ted Kennedy had a law enacted in 1992 to protect the rights of FMGs. It was APPNA's brainchild to bring all the organizations together. PAK-PAC, in my opinion, has led the way for advocacy and political activism not only for physicians, but for the Pakistani American community in general. While other organizations, such as Pakistan American Congress, also played a major role in lobbying for Pakistan, PAK-PAC remained as the sole federally registered political action committee. Again, it was APPNA and its membership that was the driving force behind PAK-PAC. It is up to the APPNA leadership to decide what PAC could serve its cause better. There are many accomplishments of PAK-PAC but the passage of the Brown Amendment has been the most notable."*[41]

Dr. Mohammed Suleman, who has also been involved with PAK-PAC since its inception and served PAK-PAC as its president in 2010–2011 sheds light on the circumstances when Pressler's Amendment was introduced and PAK-PAC's efforts led to the passing of Brown Amendment in the 1990's. *"It is a long story, briefly; at the end of the cold war United States downgraded her relationship with Pakistan on the ground that the new global environment did not warrant the old strategic partnership. In 1990 economic and military sanctions were imposed on Pakistan under the Pressler Amendment. A country specific law was proposed that singled out only one nation on the nuclear issue, while other nations in the same category were not impacted. One consequence of the Pressler amendment was the US decision to withhold Pakistan military equipment contracted prior to 1990. It was worth 1.2 billion dollars at that time even though Pakistan had paid for the equipment. Also in 1992 and 1993 there was very well coordinated effort by certain political groups to have the country of Pakistan declared a terrorist state? PAK-PAC continued to help educate the members of the congress to avert that threat and restored the relationship. In 1995 Brown amendment helped ease the Pressler amendment by removing from the purview of Pressler Amendment all non-military assistance. Meanwhile, PAK-PAC continued to educate Senator Larry Pressler on his misguided views about Pakistan. Later on, Mr. Tim Johnson defeated Senator Pressler from South Dakota. Even the former CIA Director, James Woolsely, had discussed the role of the Pakistani American Community in this particular election."*[42]

PAK-PAC has been active in the post 9/11 era. It has helped APPNA in the visa and security clearance issues of young physicians over several years. It has issued statements and took positions on various issues pertaining to the Pakistani-American community in US. During the congressional hearing initiated by representative Peter King (R-NY) in 2011, PAK-PAC took the stand. *"PAK-PAC believes that the King hearings are creating a false narrative with the use of collective guilt. First—naturalized Muslims in the United States are Americans first—period. Second—hundreds of Muslims died on 9/11—we were all attacked. Congressman Ellison talked about Mohammed Salman Hamdani, a Muslim-American paramedic who lost his life on 9/11 trying to save victims. Third—the largest single source of initial information on planned terrorist attacks by Muslims in the United States involved tips from the American Muslim community itself.—the very community that Congressman King is singling out. Fourth, it is correct that Faisal Shehzad (a Pakistani-descent citizen), the Time Square Bomber was an American Muslim—but so was Alioune Niass, the street vendor who first alerted authorities to the smoking car in the middle of Time Square, while Faisal Shehzad was mentioned by many at the hearings, efforts of Alioune Niass went unnoticed."*[43]

APPNA's relationship with PAK-PAC has not always been steady. APPNA distanced itself from PAK-PAC due to its perceived support of President General Pervez Musharraf's military rule and dictatorship in Pakistan. In December 2002 the sitting president of APPNA declined to participate at a Dinner Meeting of PAK-PAC in which President General Musharraf was invited as chief guest. Instead, Treasurer elect was asked to represent APPNA while President elect, the second person in the hierarchy of APPNA leadership was not. Another reason for the discord between APPNA and PAK-PAC during the decade of 2000 was PAK-PAC's alleged involvement in APPNA's internal politics. Some of the PAK-PAC leaders, allegedly, extended open support for APPNA presidential candidates of their choice. This so-called political mistake backfired. It is said that PAK-PAC supported candidates did not win in APPNA and, elected presidents opposed by PAK-PAC did not keep the much needed relationship.

Since 2010 onwards, mostly due to the leadership of Dr. Muhammad Suleman, past president of both APPNA and PAK-PAC, the distance between PAK-PAC and APPNA has started to recede. More recently, during the strategic planning meeting of APPNA at Orlando, FL, in January 2015, the current President of PAK-PAC, Riffat Chughtai, immediate past President Dr. Salman Malik, and Dr. Muhammad Suleman extended their support for assisting APPNA on lobbying with lawmakers and helping with advocacy for young physicians' issues. Mrs. Chughtai made a presentation on PAK-PAC's new vision to work in the United States with lawmakers in order to support Pakistan in combating terrorism at the height of the present geopolitical situation, which threatens Pakistan's own security and sovereignty. (A report on PAKPAC provided by Riffat Chughtai and Irfan Malik (former executive director of PAK-PAC) is included in the Appendices of this book).

ENDNOTES

1   Minutes of APPNA Executive Council November 10, 2001
2   APPNA *Qissa,* Chapter 5, page 86
3   Ibid
4   APPNA Newsletter, 14:1, Spring 2004, page 12
5   APPNA Journal Vol 5:1, Fall 2003 pages 9 and 35
6   APPNA Journal Vol 6:2, Winter 2004 pages 29 and 39
7   APPNA Newsletter Vol 15:1, Spring 2005, page 7
8   APPNA Newsletter Vol 15:2 Winter 2005 page 2
9   Ibid
10 APPNA Newsletter Vol 16:1 Spring 2006 page 2 and 14
11 Ibid, page 15
12 APPNA Journal Vol 9:1 Summer 2007 page 7
13 APPNA Journal Vol 9:2 Winter 2007 page 6
14 APPNA Journal Vol 10:1 Summer 2008 page 11
15 APPNA Newsletter Vol 21:2 Fall 2011
16 APPNA Journal Vol 13:2 Winter 2011
17 36th Annual APPNA Convention publication, Advocacy Committee report
    page 65
18 APPNA Newsletter Vol 24:2 page 24–25
19 See: https://www.congress.gov/, search for H.R. 2484, HR1921
20 Ibid
21 APPNA e-Newsletter Vol 6, May 2015
22 Committee on Advocacy, Legislative, and Governmental Affairs of APPNA,
    report by A.R. Piracha, 2014
23 www.justice.gov/.../ll/highlights.htm
24 A Window into American Muslim Physicians: Civic Engagement and
    Community Participation—W. Abu-Ras, L.D. Laird & F. Senzai, 2012
    (www.ISPU.org)
25 APPNA Journal 9:2, Winter 2007, page 6
26 Ibid
27 APPNA Journal 6:2, Winter 2004, page 7
28 APPNA *Qissa*, Chapter 4, page 59
29 APPNA Journal 5:2, Winter 2003, page 26
30 APPNA Journal 6:2, Winter 2004, page 23
31 APPNA *Qissa*, Appendix VII, page 294
32 APPNA Journal 6:3, Summer/Fall 2005, page 48
33 APPNA Journal 9:1, Summer 2007, page 14
34 APPNA Journal 10:2, Winter 2008, Zainab Alam, page 35
35 APPNA Newsletter, 19:2, Fall 2009, page 40
36 Ibid
37 Special Summer Meeting Journal, 2013, page 65
38 This segment on physicians Killing in Pakistan was contributed by Dr. Nasir
    Gondal, who is indebted to Dr. Zaffar Iqbal, Dr. Muhamaad Taqi, Dr.
    Zahid Irman, Dr. Mansoor Abidi, Dr. Naveed Iqbal, Dr. Nadeem Kazi, and
    Dr. Muhammad Suleman for their input.
39 APPNA (Magazine) Newsletter, 24:2, August 2014, page 28
40 *APPNA Qissa*, A history of APPNA, 2004, page 81
41 APPNA Journal, 13:2, Winter 2011, page 14
42 APPNA Journal, 13:1, Summer 2011, page 24
43 Ibid, page 16

6

APPNA ON ADVANCEMENT OF MEDICAL EDUCATION

The Roles of RESA, MERIT, and Telemedicine Committees

Introduction

To foster scientific development and education in the field of medicine and delivery of better health care for all is one of the fundamental premises on which APPNA was founded. APPNA being an organization of Pakistani descent physicians in North America further resolved to encourage medical education and delivery of better health care in Pakistan specifically by arranging donations of medical literature, medical supplies, and by arranging lecture tours, medical conferences, and seminars in Pakistan.[1] The founders of APPNA were poised to deliver on the premise of educational advancement in healthcare. The first national symposium of APPNA entitled "Health Care in Pakistan" was held on September 15, 1979 in Detroit, MI.[2] "Meeting was great a success. The total number of attendees as well as the caliber of presentations was quite unexpected. I am quite convinced that given the time this organization could play an important role in shaping the future of health care in Pakistan," stated Dr. S. Amjad Hussain (OH) in a letter to Dr. Zaheer Ahmad (MI).[3]

In subsequent year, President Kamil Muzzafar organized APPNA's first scientific meeting entitled "Healthcare and Advances in Medicine and Surgery," on December 17, 1980 in Karachi, Pakistan. In the program,

Dr. Iftikhar Salahuddin, the conference chair, stated the objectives of the conference. "This conference is based on the belief that medicine is a shared legacy of all mankind and is conceived with the idea of repatriating, if for a brief period, the country's literati. It is a forum for presentation of scientific papers and exchange of views. Topics on health care are germane to our present state of affairs. It is however not our intention to come home and point a finger at our infirmities, nor to censure our system. Rather, we hope to explore avenues where Pakistanis abroad can contribute in providing health care with dignity to our elderly, or infirm and our helpless. Most importantly it is an occasion not only to teach, but learn; not only to express but to listen; not only to see, but to experience our country; and it is an opportunity, above all, to proclaim that in spirit and conviction we stand by our country."[4] In the above statement, Dr. Salahuddin has laid down the principles of APPNA's engagement for the promotion of education and delivery of healthcare in Pakistan. Ever since, during the annual winter meetings in Pakistan, APPNA has focused on the premise of medical education and advancement of healthcare its founders had envisioned.

The Research, Education, and Scientific Affairs (RESA) Committee:

RESA committee has been a standing committee of APPNA from the very beginning. It is responsible for overseeing all major research, educational and scientific affairs activities of the organization. The committee is primarily responsible for organizing scientific sessions and educational programs at all the APPNA meetings. These include provision of Continued Medical Education (CME) programs in North America, Pakistan, and at other International Meetings. RESA committee has also been a resource for CME programs held at various chapters and alumni associations.[5]

Over the last three decades, RESA committee has been delivering high quality programs with cutting edge topics and state of the art lectures to its members. APPNA received its accreditation by Accreditation Council for Continuing Medical Education (ACCME in April 2001 after three-year-long hard work of the Association spearheaded by Drs. Juzar Ali and Raza Dilawari.[6] The committee has established a network of physicians whose dedication and hard work have made it possible to develop CME programs that have been consistently rated very good-to-excellent by the attendees. RESA committee has been instrumental in developing young doctors research seminars and mentorship programs in collaboration with the Committee on Young Physicians since 2005. The web-based programming for CME has also been embraced by the RESA committee. The first web-cast of CME program was launched on the CME lectures delivered at the summer meeting in Chicago (2006) with the effort of host committee CME chair, Dr. Arif Agha.[7]

RESA committee members planning for CME program under the leadership of late Dr. Raza Dilawari. circa 2006-2007

The (late)Dr. Raza Dilawari's unparalleled contributions to RESA committee are highly commendable. He chaired the committee for several years; 2004–2007 and in 2010. He received APPNA Lifetime Achievement Award for his relentless services to APPNA and academic medicine before his passing in 2011. He was a great teacher. He left his legacy by mentoring so many younger physicians that are asset to RESA committee in the years to come. His reports as RESA chair were always very insightful. "*Several challenges are facing our program. CME remains under-funded. We have not been able to raise sufficient funds from commercial support. In my opinion, the lack of a permanent committee of people committed to raising funds on the ongoing basis is a major reason,*" Dr. Dilawari shared his frustration in a report to APPNA Newsletter.[8]

There are several other physicians whose leadership have contributed towards the success of RESA committee. Dr. Shabbir H. Safdar (MO) was APPNA President in 1999. He served RESA in the nineties and also chaired the committee in 2008. In his report on RESA he had proposed creating a semi-autonomous CME secretariat at APPNA office to offer seamless CME programs in the US and abroad. He also concurred with Dr. Dilawari on procuring adequate funding for the program.[9] Dr. Adeel Butt (PA) was RESA chair in 2009 who also had a decade of services to RESA related activities to his credit. Dr. Tariq Jamil led the committee in 2011 to advance its mission. Dr. Jamil and Dr. Ayaz Samdani (Chair RESA 2012) contributed towards preparing APPNA for reaccreditation with ACCME.[10] Dr. Rizwan Naeem was appointed chair of RESA by President Javed Suleman in 2013. Dr. Naeem also served in the capacity of RESA co-chair as well as the chair of several CME meetings in the past. Dr. Mohammad Jahanzeb (FL) and Dr. Jawad Hasnain (MD) served RESA committee chairs in 2014 and 2015, respectively. Dr. Raheel R. Khan took the challenge of chairing RESA in 2016. There are indeed dozens of educationists, researchers, and physicians who have served on RESA committee over the years. The dedication of these unsung heroes has always been the success factor in APPNA.

APPNA—MERIT:[1]

MERIT is the Medical Education & Research International Training & Transfer-of-Technology Committee of APPNA. It was conceptualized in 2006 and established in 2007 in order to improve medical education at undergraduate and post-graduate level, especially in Pakistan's pubic medical teaching institutions. APPNA President Nadeem Kazi appointed Dr. Naheed Usmani as the committee chair in 2007. MERIT achieved the status of a standing committee of APPNA in 2008.[11] MERIT has become one of the exemplary successes of APPNA, first under Dr. Usmani's leadership (2007–2011) and then under Dr. Babar Rao's leadership (2012–2016).

APPNA MERIT undertook a number of initiatives in pursuit of its mission, from creation of a visiting faculty program for Pakistan, to symposia on modernizing undergraduate medical curriculum, weekly e-teaching

---

1   Dr. Naheed Usmani was the founding Chair of MERIT and served from 2007–2011. She has contributed a synopsis on the work of MERIT since its inception to 2011 for *APPNA Qissa II*. It is included in the Appendices of this book. Dr. Babar Rao put together the work by MERIT under his leadership from 2012–16.

Grand Rounds for post-graduate trainees, helping establish CPSP-approved new specialty areas and fellowship programs, and creating specialty-specific networks for collaboration among APPNA specialists and with their counterparts in Pakistan.

(Lt. to Rt.) Dr. Mahjabeen Islam, Dr. Naheed Usmani and
Dr. Nadeem Kazi at APPNA winter meeting in Karachi, 2007.

The Visiting Faculty Initiative was envisioned as a year around program that placed APPNA specialists in assignment throughout the year in Pakistan's medical universities. APPNA MERIT established formal collaboration with Pakistan government's **Visiting Expatriate Pakistani Consultants** program and the **Higher Education Commission** so consultants could visit under their auspices, making APPNA's contribution to medical education improvements in Pakistan very visible to the GOP. The program continues at the alumni level, with well-established visiting faculty programs at DUHS and KEMU, however, no further applications could be processed from 2011 onwards in absence of APPNA central office support for the MERIT program. In the Fall of 2007, **APPNA SUKOON** (APPNA Palliative & Hospice Care Educational Program) was launched in Pakistan to educate medical institutions and increase the awareness in the lay public about the new areas of palliative medicine and hospice care. MERIT scholars visited different medical teaching institutions in Pakistan and taught individually or in symposia the core curriculum of palliative care. SUKOON also sought to educate Pakistan government health departments about the vital importance of morphine and derivatives and ensuring their easy availability for relief of pain and suffering for the ailing. In November 2011, APPNA faculty joined with INCTR and participated in a Palliative Care Seminar held at SKMCH.

In 2008, MERIT launched the Specialty-Specific MERITnets, to mobilize APPNA specialists to help create Centers of Excellence in post-graduate training in specific specialty areas in Pakistani medical institutions. MERITnets enabled APPNA specialists in a particular specialty to collaborate on-line, meet together at Specialty-specific conferences, work with their Pakistani counterparts on book chapters and articles, and present at specialty-specific conferences in Pakistan.

MERIT also helped develop fellowship programs in new specialty areas currently lacking in Pakistan: Critical Care Medicine, Emergency Medicine, and Pediatric Hematology Oncology. This collaboration included establishment of training standards, curriculum, visiting training faculty and finally examiners for certification of trainees. College of Physicians and Surgeons of Pakistan (CPSP) accepted APPNA MERIT contributions and approved Critical Care and Pediatric Hematology/Oncology as new CPSP Specialties, during Dr. Usmani's MERIT tenure.

MERIT also held a colloquium at KEMU on undergraduate medical curriculum reform in 2008, which served as a catalyst for implementing a modern curriculum that is now being introduced across the country.

In 2009, APPNA MERIT e-teaching was conceptualized and was tested in the summer meeting of live Grand Rounds in Neurology for Pakistan, beamed to medical universities and colleges via internet-based videoconferencing. Faculty and post-graduate trainees attended in hundreds in major Pakistan cities. In 2010, live broadcasted Grand Rounds became regular, beamed twice a week, and were attended by faculty and post-graduate trainees in over 16 medical universities and colleges across Pakistan. The grand rounds were recorded and a video library was developed that was available for physicians to review at www.appnamerit.com.

Dr. Babar Rao, who had been involved in APPNA MERIT since its inception, was appointed the Chair of the MERIT Program in 2012. He was told to make MERIT financially self-sufficient and his team was able to collect $60,000 in 2012 to continue MERIT's work. The committee decided to use a commercially available service, WebEx, and with economical IT support was able to run the MERIT Program with only $10,000 per year. In 2015, about 30 Medical Schools were participating in lectures and this number is increasing steadily.

In 2014, CPSP approved the Child Psychiatry Fellowship (FCPS) in Pakistan, based on the contributions of APPNA MERIT Psychiatrists, along with their colleagues in Pakistan, and UK. The program is based on the US model of the 2-year fellowship in child psychiatry that is offered after finishing training in general psychiatry for 4 years. This fellowship is expected to start in 3 major universities in the country in 2015. APPNA MERIT will continue to play a major role in education and training of these fellows in the years to come.

APPNA MERIT visits at the Regional Office of the College of Physicians and Surgeons of Pakistan in Lahore, 2008. From left to right (standing), Prof. S.M. Awais, Dr. Amina Ahmed, Dr. Sohail Ahmed, Dr. Masood Akbar, Dr. Tanveer Zuberi, Commander Saeed and Miss Nadia. (sitting) Dr. Mubasher Rana, Dr. M. Hasseb, Dr. Naheed Usmani, Prof. Khalid Gondal, Dr. Mahmood Alam, and Prof. Hafiz I. Ahmad.

One major reason of successful MERIT program was this committee's unequivocal support by all the sitting presidents of APPNA regardless of their political affiliation. *"The continued support of all the committee members and all specialty chairs for their help was instrumental for making this program successful. The program will continue to expand,"* stated MERIT chair Dr. Babar Rao, (2012–2016).

APPNA Telemedicine:[2]

Dr. Mubasher Rana, President APPNA 2015 asked Dr. Naheed Usmani to lead a Telemedicine committee in December of 2014. A core group of hardworking APPNA physicians was put together. Its initial task was to develop the Vision and the Mission statements of this newly created ad hoc committee.

Vision: To improve health care quality and access to specialist medical care for underserved populations in Pakistan.

Mission: To set up Internet based consultations between specialists in North America and referring doctors from Pakistan in order to improve patient care through recommendations for latest treatments and timely access to specialist knowledge. Via this telemedicine service, also educate Pakistani physicians on the principles of evidence-based medicine as practiced in USA.

The committee decided that APPNA needed to focus on a telemedicine initiative (physician-to-physician consultations) rather than on a Telehealth project (direct patient to US based consultant services), that would have presented with both logistical as well as physician malpractice coverage issues.

The Telemedicine Committee has enrolled more than 200 US consultants who responded to the blast email request to recruit volunteers. The committee initially selected National Rural Support Program (NRSP), a nonprofit rural support NGO that serves 2.4 million poor households with the goal of serving the underserved population. NRSP identified the initial 2 hospitals in Sargodha district: Surgicare hospital and Sadiq Hospital. For urban setting, the Indus Hospital in Korangi, Karachi was selected given its reputation of rendering excellent care free of cost. All these entities agreed to participate in the pilot. Using APPNA MERIT Grand rounds series, Dr. Usmani reviewed APPNA Telemedicine project on July 5, 2015. The participants included Dr. Sarwar from Sadiq Hospital, Dr. Shafiq from Surgicare Hospital and Dr. Atiya Rehman, Indus Hospital, along with young doctors and students from KEMU, DUHS and Rawalpindi Medical College.

---

2   Dr. Naheed Usmani contributed to this report on Telemedicine.

There was a lot of excitement generated by this lecture. APPNA's target was to make this service available to all hospitals and clinics in Pakistan after the testing pilot phase.

APPNA was offered the use of a telemedicine internet-based system from Axim Systems as well as support of their IT team, totally free of cost in July, 2015. From July to September, with the full engineering support, the Committee was able to develop and customize this APPNA Telemedicine web portal. Telemedicine Committee proceeded to conduct a pilot with King Edwards Medical University with KEMCAANA's support. Mr. Rashid Javed, director of KEMCAANA computer lab using APPNA virtual conferencing support, was trained. Prof Irshad Hussain, East Medical Unit 1 and his junior physicians were added. Dr. Bilal sent a complicated case of a young man with disseminated fungemia from Pakistan, which was referred to Dr. Sajid Chaudhry, an APPNA infectious disease specialist who rendered a second opinion. Thus APPNA Telemedicine was born!

In December 2015, APPNA Telemedicine committee presented the initiative all over Pakistan (Islamabad, Rawalpindi, Lahore and Karachi). The presentation was welcomed by 12 medical institutions and the Family Medicine Association on their annual function. By Summer 2016, APPNA Telemedicine had enrolled 23 teaching medical institutions, 3 NGOs and multiple small clinics and hospitals.

In April, 2016, Mr. Todd Shea of CDRS (Comprehensive Disaster Response Services) asked APPNA Telemedicine to help his physician and healthcare workers working at Swat Mother and Child Health Center with their patient population. The Swat clinic has become an enthusiastic user of the APPNA Telemedicine service. As of August, 2016, APPNA Telemedicine had received more than 100 consultations from Swat in just 4 months. APPNA consultants responded to these second-opinion requests, spanning Pediatrics, Nephrology, Obs/Gyn, Neurology, ENT, Cardiology, Diabetes, Pulmonology, Oncology, and Orthopedics. According to Mr. Shea, his physician and staff are very happy and find the opinions rendered very useful, resulting in changes in therapy in 90% of the cases. "*APPNA physicians are now actively giving second opinions using the web portal. 2016 has been a year of tremendous growth and logistical challenges, as the potential for this intervention is huge,*" reported DR. Naheed Usmani, Chair Telemedicine, 2016.

APPNA Tele-Health Project in Mardan, Pakistan

In the middle of the troubled areas of Pakistan with all the geopolitical turmoil, Tele-Health project in Mardan has been an oasis in a wilderness. It all started in the aftermath of earthquake in Pakistan (2005). APPNA was a partner to provide state of the art telehealth to this rural hospital with the collaboration of Atif Mumtaz an IT student from Stanford University, UM trust in Mardan, and National University of Science and Technology (NUST) in Islamabad. This hospital is successfully running services on a regular basis in rural Mardan District of Pakistan (in the village of Zahidabad, Khyber Pakhtoonkhaw (KPK), which is about 200 km North of Islamabad).

A state of the art dedicated internet access via VSAT provides a satellite based internet facility which makes this hospital and town totally connected to Wi-Fi. All medical records are electronic. They have cell phone based follow-ups for reminders regarding immunizations, lab results, and follow-up visit. Stanford grant was followed up with procuring a multi-year competitive grant for capacity building of lady health workers in rural Mardan via use of ICT-based telemedicine from USA National Academy of Science (NAS). APPNA launched this ground-breaking project with the help of this grant in 2009.[12] *"Our goal is to build capacity of Lady Health Visitors (LHVs) of rural Pakistan through teaching them the use of Information and Communication Technologies (ICT). This grant highlights a new paradigm as to how organizations like APPNA can work with US funding agencies to provide help and promote medical education in Pakistan,"* stated Dr. Rizwan Naeem in his report to APPNA Journal.[13]

Endnotes:

1   APPNA Constitution and Bylaws, 2014, Aims and objectives, 5.
2   The Founding of APPNA, chapter 1, *APPNA Qissa*, 2004, 6–7.
3   Ibid, 8
4   Ibid, 9–10
5   APPNA Constitution and Bylaws, 2014, Appendix C, Committees, 31.
6   The Maturing of an Organization, chapter 4, *APPNA Qissa*, 2004, 71.
7   APPNA Journal, 8:3, Winter 2006, a report on CME by RESA, 42

8   APPNA Newsletter, 16:1, Spring 2006, Report of RESA Committee:
     Supporting the Mission of APPNA, 11
9   APPNA Journal, 10:1, Summer 2008, 19
10   APPNA Journal, 13:1, Summer 2011, 27
11   Minutes of APPNA Fall meeting, 2008.
12   In 2010, APPNA graduated Tele-Health project in Mardan, which continues
     to serve independently.
13   APPNA Journal, 11:2, Winter 2009, 34—Dr. Rizwan Naeem was PI for
     a grant from USAID and NUST for a Tele-healthcare based hospital and
     training project in Mardan, Pakistan

7

CHAPTER ACTIVISM IN APPNA

A group photo of participants of APPNA fall meeting in 2009
at Niagara Falls, Canada hosted by Canada Chapter

Introduction

APPNA's regional chapters have emerged as centers of dynamic activity in recent years. These local organizations provide a platform that brings Pakistani-American physicians together and establishes APPNA at the grassroots level. APPNA requires at least 25 active members from a region to apply for chapter status. A proposed chapter needs to have a set of bylaws that regulate its activities. Then the chapter can come into existence after an evaluation by the President-elect and a formal approval by APPNA's executive council.

In 2015, APPNA had 33 local chapters, most becoming active in the last 20 years. Each chapter has a seat at APPNA's Council. Initially, this council was made up of alumni presidents and councilors; representatives from nine geographically defined regions in North America. These Regional Councilors did represent the regions but not necessarily the regional chapters. This practice continued until 2005 when a 2004 amendment to the bylaws took effect, replacing the regional councilors with the presidents of each local chapter. This democratically elected chapter leadership and its representation in the council provides the basis for grassroots approval of all decisions made by the council.

Activities at the chapter level lend support to building a better Pakistani American community in a variety of ways. Typically, chapter activities range from annual dinners, *Eid* festivities, picnics, CME programs, seminars on social issues, and business meetings. APPNA chapters also serve the purpose of organizing the Pakistani diaspora in North America by supporting the needs and activities of their local societies. Numerous APPNA members have served as ambassadors for their communities in this time of profiling and intensified security. Chapters activities also include advocacy efforts with political representatives, helping young physicians with housing, mentorship seminars, electives and observerships. Chapters take pride in organizing National Healthcare Days and in establishing and maintaining free medical clinics in their neighborhoods. The chapters are encouraged to have their own 501c3 status so that they can better maintain their accounts and support local fundraising efforts for charitable causes.

Those opposed to the formation of regional chapters had expressed concern that these local groups would become "organizations within the organization." They felt that the Chapters' independent actions would overshadow APPNA activities organized by the central leadership; and that local leadership would make policy statements that were not approved by the APPNA Council. The supporters of chapter activism are proud to have involvement at the local level. They feel that their endeavors compliment those organized by central APPNA. *"I have been a life member of APPNA for a long time but could not manage to go to the meetings until we had a local chapter,"* said Dr. Shaukat Chaudhary, President New Jersey Chapter (2004) of APPNA at the annual dinner.[1]

Chapter activism began during the first decade of 2000 when the second wave of Pakistani-descent physicians was beginning to get involved in their local communities around North America. The following section provides highlights of the chapter activities. The narrative provided is based on the reports collected for *APPNA Qissa* or from the chapter reports published in APPNA Newsletters/Journals over the last several years.

The Alabama Chapter:[2]

The Alabama Chapter was founded in 2007 by Dr. Ehtsham Haq and Dr. Samia Moizuddin, with support from many others. It has become one of the most vibrant chapters. Typically, the APPNA Alabama Chapter does not only act as a group of physicians but is also part of the local community, says Dr. Haq. The Alabama Chapter has arranged Eid Melas, AMA Category 1 CME programs (Chair Dr. Khurram Bashir) twice a year, and musical entertainment.

Alabama Chapter Clinic at work. Among other workers, Dr. Ehtsham Haq is pictured.

The APPNA Alabama Chapter and Birmingham Islamic Society (BIS) started a joint venture of a free clinic in Birmingham, Alabama, called the Red Crescent Clinic of Alabama (RCCA). In 2015 under the leadership of then President Dr. Mubasher Rana, APPNA donated $15,000 to support equipment and supplies for the clinic. Waseem Sadiq Ali played a key role both in the inception of the Alabama Chapter and the free clinic.

This clinic is providing medical services to the local communities without any charge. The APPNA physicians are the key volunteers who provide the free services. Dr. Samia Moizuddin, Dr. Talha Malik, Dr. Rabia Zaman, Dr. Zakir Khan, Dr. Mina Khan, Dr. Zakir Qureshi, and Dr. Ehtsham Haq among others give their time and money to support this noble cause. Student volunteers include Alabama Chapter Youth Chair, Numair Ehtsham, who was among the first volunteer students to contribute his time since the inception of the free clinic in 2012. He represented the Youth at the APPNA Advocacy meeting in Huntsville, Alabama in 2015 in order to gain support from Congressman Mo Brooks for GRAD ACT/HR 1921. Dr. Maqbool Patel and Adil Patel provide state of the art technical support for the free clinic.

Arizona Chapter:

In the summer of 2002, a handful physicians of Pakistani origin residing in Arizona decided to form the APPNA—AZ chapter. Since then, the chapter has grown to about 100 members. The Chapter has been involved in many charitable activities, both locally and in Pakistan. After the devastating earthquake in northern Pakistan in 2005, the Arizona chapter raised over $100,000 to rebuild the most affected areas and contributed in the building of the APPNA Village. The chapter has also been running two free clinics, one each in Phoenix and Tucson. The Arizona chapter has also been quite active in the local community—partnering with organizations such as the Pakistan Information Cultural Organization (PICO) to build bridges and form a working relationship with various public offices and interfaith groups. The chapter members have been presenting CME lectures in local professional organizations. Moreover, free educational health seminars are organized for the community to provide them with a better understanding of various illnesses and their prevention.

The following physicians served the Chapter as Presidents from 2002–2016—Nadeem Kazi, Yousuf Khan, Akhtar Hamidi, Azam Khan, Asim Khawaja, Taqi Azam, Azhar Jaan, Faran Bashir, Nusrum Iqbal, Habib Khan, and Maqbool Halepota.

Northern California Chapter:[3]

Dr. Afzal Arian (CA) proposed the idea of forming a northern California chapter in 1998 at the APPNA summer meeting in Los Angeles. Dr. Mubasher Rana (CA) served as the first president of the chapter. The first chapter meeting was held in 1999 at Wyndham Garden Hotel in Pleasanton, CA and was attended by more than 50 physicians with their families.

The chapter continues to hold a yearly medical camp on Pakistan Independence Day in San Francisco which has helped thousands of attendees. After the disastrous 2005 earthquake in Pakistan, Dr. Tehmina Khan and Dr. Afzal Arian visited Pakistan and helped victims in the relief effort. A fundraising event was also held for earthquake victims. In 2007, the chapter again held a fundraising event for the cyclone disaster in Baluchistan Pakistan.

In July, 2009, the APPNA summer meeting was held in San Francisco. It was chaired by Dr. Mubasher Rana whose leadership with the help of twelve subcommittees and hundreds of selfless volunteers made it a memorable event. In 2010, a National Health Care (NHC) Day was held for the first time on June 4 and was organized by Dr. Sabir Khan (CA). Since then NHC Day has been held every year at 2–3 locations in Northern CA.

In 2011, Chapter President Dr. Shahid Abbasi, ran a Bone Marrow Registry Drive under the direction of central APPNA. A fundraising dinner for Pakistan flood victims was also held in 2011, where $14,000.00 was collected. A young physicians' forum was organized by Dr. Aifra Ahmed. Several residency program directors attended and guided aspiring physicians with their residency application and the interview process. Similar programs have been held several times in subsequent years.

In 2012, a food drive was organized under the leadership of Dr., Sabir Khan. A free clinic was also established in Vallejo that same year and continues to serve the indigent population of the area. In 2015, the Spring meeting was held in association with the JSMU Alumni retreat. Dr. Sabir Khan, President of the JSMU Alumni and Dr. Muniza Muzzafar, chapter president were the co-organizers. In the same year APPNA president Dr. Rana had the APPNA fall meeting at the historic Fairmont Hotel in San Francisco. The chapter under the leadership of Dr. Munir Javed contributed to make this meeting a great success. Polio eradication efforts in Pakistan were highlighted at the meeting and Dr. Larry Brilliant was the keynote speaker at the Saturday night banquet. Shaykh Hamza Yusuf, founder of Zaytuna College was the chief guest.

Since its inception, Dr. Mubasher Rana, Dr. Atab Naz, Dr. Aslam Barra, Dr. Zubeda Seyal, Dr. Shaukat Shah, Dr. Fayaz Asghar, Dr. Saadia Khan, Dr. Zulfiqar Ali, Dr. Munir Javed, Dr. Shahid Abbasi, Dr. Sabir Khan, Dr. Tanvir Sattar, Dr. Noorulain Aqeel and Dr. Muniza Muzaffar have been presidents of the chapter.

The Canadian Chapter:[4]

The Canadian chapter of APPNA was formerly approved as a component society during the 2008 Fall council meeting. Dr. Arshad Saeed who led this effort of forming the Canadian chapter was appointed as its founding president. However, Canadian representation in APPNA has existed from the beginning. In fact, an APPNA executive council meeting in Toronto was held in 1998 during the presidency of Dr. Durdana Gilani (CA).

The Canadian chapter hosted a very successful fall meeting of APPNA from September 25 to September 27, 2009 at Niagara Falls with the help of the up-state New York Chapter. APPNA members from all over North America got together in Niagara Falls, Ontario for this historic meeting. The meeting was also attended by a large number of Canadian physicians, members of Ontario parliament and local elected officials. The keynote speech was given by Dr. Nancy H. Nielsen, MD, PHD, President, American Medical Association. President APPNA 2009, Syed A. Samad presided over the meeting.

The second Annual Dinner of the Canadian Chapter was held in Mississauga at the Apollo Convention Centre on May 23, 2015. It was a well-organized event and approximately 270 people attended. The meeting also served to liaison with food bank groups in the Greater Toronto area. The SANSAR, an organization committed to promoting cardiovascular health for South Asians through community awareness, education and research also collaborated. The event was organized by the Executive Council, Drs. Humaira Ali President, Dr. Naheed Chaudhry and Dr. Mahjabeen Ahmad.

North Carolina Chapter:[5]

The APPNA North Carolina Chapter was founded in 2002. Dr. Waheed Bajwa (NC) was its first president. The NC Chapter was a major contributor to the APPNA 2005 Kashmir Earthquake Fund. The second president, Dr. Khalid Aziz, was also a key figure in the iniation of many key projects, including the APPNA Diabetes Initiative. The APPNA Diabetes Initiative hosts free quarterly seminars that educate the public about diabetes prevention and treatment. The Diabetes Initiative also conducts seminars for physicians in Pakistan discussing cutting edge developments in the field of Diabetes Mellitus. The APPNA Free Clinic is held every Thursday afternoon and treats uninsured patients. The APPNA Free Food Program feeds more than 150 indigents at a time.

In 2010, the NC Chapter collected $120,000 for the APPNA Pakistan Flood Relief Fund, which made the chapter the second highest contributor to that fund. The NC chapter was also a major contributor to the APPNA Burn Center in Rawalpindi, Munirabad Housing Project in southern Punjab, and the Somalia Funds.

"We pride ourselves on being a close knit group. We put strong emphasis on actively recruiting new membership, with special focus on young physicians. In addition, we are working to provide more networking opportunities, social events, and charitable endeavors," Dr. Amjad Bhatti (President) and Dr. Sohail Sarwar (President-elect) reported in 2015.

The Greater Cincinnati Chapter:[6]
This chapter was approved as a component society of APPNA in 2006. Dr. Farooq Mirza and Dr. Rashid Khan were on the forefront of its inception. The Chapter has reinvigorated itself recently and is becoming an integral part of the community in Greater Cincinnati.

The Greater Cincinnati Chapter was one of the major contributors for the clean water project of APPNA in Pakistan. The leadership is also highly involved in young doctor's mentorship and training. Dr. Saeed has been instrumental in providing an observership program through Cincinnati Children's Hospital for the past many years, resulting in numerous young doctors to get residencies. *"There is no doubt we have very dynamic, motivated community and as our chapter continues to grow, we expect to see more great things happening in our community,"* said Dr. Muhammad Afzal, president 2015. He further reported *"We conducted our very well attended first educational symposium in May 2015 on the unique topic of advances in nutritional therapeutics and nationally known speaker enticed the audience with remarkable new discoveries on how nutrition can help in Alzheimer's disease and cancer.*

The Connecticut Chapter:[7]
Dr. Atique Mirza and his wife Dr. Faryal Mirza, with the help of Dr. Saud Anwar and his wife Yusra Anis-Anwar, presented the idea of forming an official organization to provide a platform in Connecticut to local physicians of Pakistani origin in 2003–2004. The first executive committee was

announced on April 13, 2005. Atique Azam Mirza, Rizwan Khalid, and Lalarukh Mufti were elected as president, secretary, and treasurer, respectively. Dr. Atique Mirza remained president of Connecticut Association of Pakistani Physicians (CAPP) for the first few years in order to stabilize its infrastructure.

Once CAAP was recognized as a component society of APPNA in July of 2005, it was renamed CT APPNA. Since its inception, Drs. Inam Kureshi, Muhammad Afzal Memon, Salman Zafar, Momina Salman and Faryal Mirza have served as Presidents of the organization.

Dr. Atiq Mirza reported, "The CT APPNA chapter is thriving and has become an integral part of the community in Connecticut. The annual Pakistan Day event has now become a tradition. It is usually held at the end of August to celebrate the independence of Pakistan. The children are often highlighted in our programs by participating in talent shows. We have an ongoing charity and humanitarian programs for migrants in collaboration with Catholic Charities. The chapter's membership is involved in mentoring young doctors and assisting them in obtaining clinical observerships through St. Francis Hospital. This program has helped numerous young doctors get residencies in the USA. There is a dynamic, motivated team and as the chapter grows and matures, we expect to see great things happen in future."

The CT chapter helped the local Nepali community during the tough time of the Nepal earthquake and partnered with APPNA and the Helping Hands organization to provide rescue efforts. The chapter also held multiple youth events with USPAK foundation; a Washington D.C. based organization for youth mentorship and empowerment.

Pakistan-Descent Physician Society (PPS) Illinois:[8]

PPS is one of the two the oldest chapters of APPNA (the other being the Washington/Maryland/ Virginia chapter[9]). The account given below is based on the excerpts from a PPS history article written by one of its founders, Dr. Nasir Rana.

After pondering over the idea of organizing a medical society for Pakistani physicians, PPS was conceived by Drs. Rana and Mushtaq Sharif. Three more physicians (the late Mushtaq Khan, Tariq Ghani and Khalid Riaz) were recruited, and the group came to be known as the "Gang of Five." Mrs. Tanveer Khan was nominated as the Women's Auxiliary president along with several members at large.

It is in this spirit of camaraderie that PPS, a Chicago chapter of APPNA has consistently been in the forefront whenever a need arises for worthwhile causes. For that matter, any cause involving Pakistan or human catastrophes both natural and man-made sans Frontiers'. We are always there with APPNA or without APPNA to bring our collective resources and our humanity for the Pakistan flood relief, floods in Bangladesh, human sufferings in Bosnia, 9/11 tragedies, or recent tornadoes in Missouri, Shaukat Khanum cancer hospital appeal, APPNA Sehat, Al-Shifa eye hospital appeals, HDF or NCHDF, tsunami relief, earthquake relief or Katrina or establishment of CHAPS as a pilot project for community based health awareness programs. Recently (in 2008) PPS and its membership helped APPNA to launch a model health center at the central office. It is staffed with our member physicians and headed by one of our own, Dr. Imtiaz Arain. We, the PPS and its membership always rise to challenges and come together as one strong family, one voice in unison and move in one direction with élan. Whole of Chicago works with one objective to assist those who need our help, comfort those who are in need of comfort and educate those who lack education.

The following past presidents of APPNA came from the area represented in the PPS chapter. Dr. Kamil Muzaffar (1980–81), Dr. Mohammad Murtaza Arain (1988–89), Dr. Mushtaq A. Khan (1991–92), Dr. M. Khalid Riaz (1993–94), and Dr. Mushtaq Sharif (1996).

Dr. Hasina Javed, president PPS 2015 briefly reflects on the recent chapter activity, "*PPS/APPNA house (a temporary low cost residence for Pakistani physicians seeking residency training and research opportunities) was founded in December of 2014 (through the untiring efforts of Dr. Sohail Khan and his dedicated team). The project is standing strong after surviving the initial six months of growing pains. This is a huge undertaking but with the grace of God and the ongoing support of the membership we are headed in the right direction. A simple registration (electronic) system for both APPNA house and observership program is working well. PPS Illinois is leading the way for other similar programs. We want to thank all the preceptors who are mentoring the young Pakistani Physicians. Training sessions are also provided at the house to assist the Physicians in their clinical skills exams. PPS/APPNA Health Clinic continues to serve our indigent population with new extended hours and additional staff.*"

South Florida Chapter:[10]

The initial meeting of area Pakistani descent physicians was called in February 2005. Dr. Iftikhar Hanif was chosen as the first President and Dr. Iqbal Zafar Hamid was named as the Secretary of the chapter. A two-year term was agreed upon.

This chapter donated $68,000 for 2005 earthquake funds. Another philanthropic project has been the One Rupee School which was supported for several years. A health clinic in Miami, named UHI clinic has been supported by the contribution of our members. Most of the physicians working in the clinic are APPNA South Florida members.

APPNA South Florida chapter has always cherished our youth and for that reason, right from the beginning, we started to conduct Youth Debates. The children from elementary school to college freshman participate in these yearly debates. We have seen our children grow and become good speakers and debaters. The Medical Lecture series, organized by Dr. Mazhar Majid and Bazgha Majid, has been a great success. A large number of physicians attend and benefit from these educational meetings.

APPNA South Florida had the privilege to organize the 2010 APPNA fall meeting in Miami which was a great success and another Spring meeting is scheduled for May 2016. The 2015 leadership includes President Dr. Mian Ahmed Hasan, Secretary Dr. Aliya Asad and Treasurer Dr. Shahid Rhandhawa. The past presidents of APPNA South Florida are Dr. Iftikhar Hanif, Dr. Iqbal Zafar Hamid, Dr. Rahat Abbas, Dr. Syed Javed Hashmi and Dr. Danyal Khan. Dr. Zafar Hamid is now elected secretary of national APPNA after serving his term as treasurer in 2015.

The Nevada Chapter:[11]

The Nevada chapter of APPNA (NVC-APPNA) was founded in 2002. Dr. Farooq Abdullah served as its founding President. Since then, the chapter continues to grow both in number and stature.

In 2012, the chapter hosted the national APPNA spring meeting, which was well attended by over 350 participants many of whom flew in from across the country. The White House's legislative affairs Chief, Mr. Rob Nabors, was the guest of honor along with many local and national politicians. In the summer of 2012, the chapter hosted a visit by the former Pakistani Ambassador Dr. Maleeha Lodhi. This was a meet and greet with the local community and the Worlds Affairs Council. Many of the social and political challenges faced by Pakistan were discussed in detail at the dinner. NVC-APPNA was actively involved in making an interfaith connection with the Sikh community immediately after the Wisconsin tragedy with visits by the office bearers to the local *gurdwaras*.

In January of 2013, NVC-APPNA hosted a Sandy Relief "Glam-Sham" as a fund raiser for the victims of hurricane Sandy. NVC-APPNA continues its involvement in the philanthropic work including free medical clinics, the APPNA health day, the APPNA food drive and fund raising for various events.

New Jersey Chapter:[12]

The New Jersey Chapter has experienced a tremendous growth since its founding in 2003. About thirty (30) physicians from all over New Jersey gathered on a Sunday afternoon in winter at the appeal of Dr. Mahmood Alam to discuss the chapter's formation. Dr. Mahmood Alam was appointed its founding secretary and Dr. Shaukat Chaudhrey its president. The true test of the chapter unfolded when Pakistan was hit by the worst earthquake of her history in 2005. Under the presidency of Dr. Avais Masud, the organization was successful in collecting a significant number of funds ($200,000) and in kind donations for the earthquake victims.

New Jersey APPNA doctors and volunteers feel pride in
serving at free medical clinic every sunday 9-12pm

In 2008, APPNA president, Dr. Mahmood Alam, held the fall meeting of APPNA in new Brunsick, New Jersey. The meeting was a real boost for the chapter and successfully brought Pakistani-descent physicians together to work for the growing community.

The NJ APPNA Sunday Free Clinic was started with the efforts of Dr. Farooq Rehman, Dr. Iqbal Jafri and Dr. Mohammad Zubair in 2011. Dr. Saira Zubair has been managing the clinic with the help of volunteers every Sunday since its inception. JFK Medical Center, Edison, NJ provides the clinic space, a nurse coordinator, and necessary supplies. The commitment and dedication of the volunteers has made the program a real success. The physicians are helping the indigent without regard to race, nationality, financial status or ethnicity.

In 2013 with the tireless efforts of Dr. Rabia Awan, APPNA GHUR (home) was established for young female physicians who needed temporary residence after arriving from Pakistan; a good project that could not be sustained beyond 2015.

A number of women leaders have led the chapter as presidents— Dr. Shahnaz Akhtar, Dr. Shahida Abbas, Dr. Rabia Awan, Dr. Yasmeen Chaudhry, and Dr. Razia Awan. Dr. Nasar Qureshi, president APPNA 2016 also served this chapter as president in 2007. He made significant contributions including creating a women's forum. Dr. Mohammad Zubair, a past president of the chapter, has served the chapter since its inception. He was instrumental in obtaining an independent 501-c-3 IRS status for the chapter and establishing an endowment investment fund for APPNA-NJ as chair of the chapter's BOT in 2014. Dr. Zafar Jamil, Dr. Muhammad Siddique, and Dr. Nadeem Haque have also served as chapter presidents.

New York Chapter:

The New York City (NYC) Chapter includes members from New York City, Long Island, Westchester County and neighboring areas of upstate NY. APPNA meetings were initially started in NYC by Dr. Tariq Javed. In 1997, the chapter was re-vitalized into a vibrant democratic organization. Dr. Asim Malik took the lead to become the first elected president of this Chapter in a most significant general body meeting held at LaGuardia Marriott in March 1997. It was presided over by the APPNA President Dr. Shaukat Khan. Many physicians travelled long distances to attend historic event. Among them was Dr. Saeed Bajwa—a renowned Neuro-surgeon and past Secretary of central APPNA—who traveled all the way from Binghamton, NY to attend. Dr. Abdul Rehman and Dr. Izhar Haque wrote the Bylaws for the chapter. Dr. Mahmood Alam, Dr. Faheem Butt, Dr. Nasir Gondal, Dr. Zoha Gondal, Dr. Sarwar Ghuman, (late) Dr. Kalbe Abbas Gardezi, Dr. Madiha Javed, Dr. M. Mazhar Haque, Dr. Naghmna Haque, Dr. Inam Haq, Dr. Salman Zafar, Dr. Shamim Salman, (late) Dr. Asad Ali, Dr. Syed Javed Ahmad, Dr. Tariq Javed, Dr. Aftab Chaudhri, Dr. Farida Chaudhri, Dr. Isma Habib, and Dr. Rashid Chaudhry were among 119 physicians who were present at the meeting.

NYC Chapter (Lt. to Rt.) Nasir Gondal, Salman Zafar, Mohammad Aslam, M. Mazhar Haque, Qazi K Haider, Sarwar Ghumman, Abdul Majeed, Asif Rehman, and Iqbal Jangda

The NYC Chapter has been a very active chapter of APPNA. It has catered to the needs of young physicians since its inception. The tradition of holding formal young physicians' coaching seminars in APPNA was started here in 2000. In fact, numerous New York based physicians were part of the Young Physicians' Taskforce that was created in 2003 to address the visa delays and security clearance issue of physicians from Pakistan. Among them, Nasir Gondal, Asim Malik, Faisal Cheema, and Mahmood Alam took the lead. The chapter has also been instrumental in supporting the New York APPNA House, which was established in 2009. APPNA House provides temporary residence for young job seeking Pakistani physicians.

The members of this chapter have always responded to the call for help in both natural disasters and manmade crises. The NYC Chapter was involved from the very first day in the aftermath of the September 11, 2001 terrorist attacks in NYC (see details in chapter on Advocacy).

The physicians from this area were also at the forefront of volunteering during Pakistan earthquake in 2005. Numerous physicians from NYC went to Pakistan to serve in the disaster relief efforts. Moreover, the Mansehra Rehabilitation Project was sponsored by the generous donations of more than $200,000 from the NYC chapter. The efforts of Dr. M. Mazhar Haque, Dr. Qazi K. Haider, Dr. Abdul Majeed, Dr. Faheem Butt, Dr. Riaz A. Chaudhry, Dr. Iqbal Jangda, Dr. Asim Malik, Dr. Pervaiz Qureshi, Dr. Abdul Qadir, Dr. Salman Zafar, Dr. Muhammad Hamid, Dr. Ahsan Nazir, Dr. Mohammad Aslam, Dr. Nasir and Zoha Gondal, Dr. Javed Suleman, Dr. Asif Rehman, and many others were instrumental in this fundraising.

Past APPNA presidents, Dr. Mahmood Alam (2008), Dr. Javed Suleman (2013), and Dr. Asif Rehman (2014) first served this chapter in various capacities before assuming leadership role in central APPNA.

The Upstate New York / PA Chapter:

After being established in 1997, the Upsate NY and PAs chapter's dream of an APPNA Free Clinic finally became a reality on May 7, 2005. It was opened at the Ernie Davis Family Center/Economic Opportunity Plan in Elmira, New York. The project of EOP/APPNA Free Wellness Clinic was led by Dr. Mushtaq Sheikh and Mrs. Bushra Sheikh, and was supported by Dr. Ashraf Sabahat (President 2005), Dr. Zahid Asgher, Dr. Naeem Parvez, Dr. Abdul Qadir and Dr. Najeeb Rehman. Mrs. Andrea Ogunwumi, the Executive Director of the EOP/Ernie Davis Family Center was instrumental in putting the plan together and providing the clinic space. The inaugural ceremony was attended by State Senator, George Winner, Mayor of Elmira, William O'Brien II, and APPNA President, Dr. Hussain Malik. This is perhaps the very first clinic of APPNA which continues to provide primary healthcare to the indigent population over the last 10 years. The Clinic has brought a good name to the Pakistani American Community and Pakistani American Physicians. The Governor of New York, David Paterson also acknowledged this service in his letter by praising the efforts in 2008. Corning Glass/EOP recognized the dedication and devotion of Dr. Mushtaq Sheikh by award-ing him the Distinguished Citizen Award.

The APPNA-Ohio Chapter:[13]

APPNA-Ohio was started in 2002 and now it is about a 140 members strong chapter of APPNA. This chapter has completed many short term and long term humanitarian projects over the years. A few of the projects are as follows.

Mehdi Qamar Memorial Medical Supplies for Poor Project (started 2011): In collaboration with outreach at Nationwide Children Hospital and Medwish (Cleveland), APPNA-Ohio has developed a network to send medical supplies to needy hospitals in Pakistan that are used free of charge for poor patients. The forty foot containers full of medical supplies are sent every year to Pakistan. The recipients include but are not limited to the Sind institute of Urological Transplant (SIUT) which is the largest free Renal Transplant Center in Asia under Dr. Adeeb Rizvi.

Pediatric/Neonatal ICU project: APPNA-Ohio in collaboration with PMCAANA and APPNA-SWDRC, started a project in 2011 to upgrade Pediatric ICU and Neonatal ICU at Punjab Medical College (PMC) in Faisalabad Pakistan. The fundraising collected over $200,000 and was able to establish PICU/NICU at PMC. The PMC Alumni (PMCAANA) coor-dinated the training of young physicians, nurses and respiratory therapists on PICU care including ventilator management. Now it is a thriving and fully functional tertiary care PICU/NICU which is self-sustaining, pro-vides care free of charge to the children in need and by doing so has helped save thousands of children ever since.

Khpal kor (Hamara Ghar) School project: APPNA-Ohio is helping this school by raising funds for them to improve education in Pakistan. Khpal kor is an English medium school for girls and boys in Mingora, Swat. All children are orphans. They excelled in high school and many have finished college. The three of them are also on the Pakistan gymnastics team. These children are orphans because of the unfortunate killings due to the geopo-litical situation in the area and also due to natural disasters like floods. The school has a huge number of children on its waiting list. It is recognized by KPK board of secondary education. Other organizations involved are USAID, UNICEF, KPK government and the Malala trust.

The Greater St. Louis, Missouri Chapter:

The Greater St. Louis, MO, chapter is growing with leaps and bounds with every passing year. This chapter has been working hand-in-hand with Central APPNA in all its noteworthy endeavors. Among other local projects, the APPNA supported free clinic is a much appreciated program. Two of the past presidents of APPNA, Dr. Shabbir H. Safdar, and Dr. Manzoor Tariq are part of the extended greater St. Louis community. St. Louis is also home to many founding members of APPNA. One of the key meetings during the founding of the Association was held at the residence of Dr. Sadiq Mohyuddin in St. Louis. Dr. Ishaq Chisti, an ophthalmologist, was honored with an APPNA Gold Medal Award in 2012 for his meritorious services for APPNA over the last three decades.

Landmark inauguration of APPNA St. Louis Chapter Clinic in 2011

One of the key components of the Spring Meeting (2015) agenda was the "Future Physicians Workshop," President of the Chapter, Dr. Hasan A.H. Ahmed, reports, *"This activity allowed medical students and in-training physicians to share their experiences with one another. High school and undergraduate students also had the chance to interact with them for advice, motivation, and support in how to pursue a career in the medical field. This workshop was very successful and more than 60 attendee benefited from this activity.*

During spring meeting, we invited residency program directors Dr. Leon Robison and Dr. Fred Balis as guest speakers. Their contributions to the cause of foreign medical graduates were recognized. Dr. Beth Ward was our key note speaker. She presented a robust clinical update on sleep apnea. Her presentation was followed by a very interactive question and answer session.

Spring meeting attendance of 450 plus was (probably) the largest gathering of any of the component chapters of APPNA in USA. The winter meeting is dedicated to "Women Physicians of APPNA-STL." We will be celebrating and recognizing the achievements of our female colleagues. We will recognize our women physicians that have taken a leading role in academics and community service."

Washington DC, Maryland, Virginia Chapter (DMV):

The DMV is recognized as the first local APPNA chapter founded in North America. In the early 1990s many Pakistani-American physicians moved to the Washington D.C. area. Dr. Hamid Qureshi, Dr. Pervez I. Shah, and Dr. Nisar Chaudhry were among those who are considered among the founders. Due to the chapter's geographical juxta-position with the nation's capital, the members of this chapter have always played a significant role in assisting APPNA by lobbying with legislators for the cause of international physicians and the Pakistani-American Community. APPNA has held five of its last twelve annual summer meetings in Washington D.C. These summer conventions were held in 2004, 2008, 2012, 2014, and 2016 with very successful attendance and programming. Dr. Zahid Butt (2004 and 2012), Dr. Hameed Peracha (2008 and 2014), and Dr. Talha Siddiqui (2016) were the chairs of these meetings whose leadership with the help of dozens of volunteers resulted in great outcomes.

The following physicians have served as presidents of the chapter since 2001: Dr. Hameed Peracha. Dr. Mubashar Chowdhry, Dr. Mohammad Akbar, Dr. Tariq Mahmood, Dr. Sohail Qarni, Dr. Mubarak Khan, Dr. Rashid Nayyar, Dr. Samia Waseem, Dr. Naseem Lughmani, and Dr. Waseem Ul Haq.

Other Chapter Activities in 2015

Florida APPNA Chapter President 2015, Dr. Ayaz Shah, shared the following activities,

> *"Among many other things, we are presently striving to introduce the new generation into chapter activities, as we believe that the future of APPNA stems not only from new physicians arriving from overseas; our future lies right here with our kids who are already holding enormous roles in their communities, making a difference in the world through education, charity, social activities, and even politics. We are sure that through the incorporation of these young, bright and fruitful new minds, our chapter and APPNA will sustain extensive growth in the near future.*
>
> *We will continue to support and guide Pakistani medical graduates who are in Florida for residency interviews. In order to stay relevant with our members in Florida, we are anticipating combining our meeting in September with another local Pakistani organization. Our goal in the coming years is to increase our membership, help with running free clinics, and numerous other measures to help our Pakistani community."*

APPNA Heartland Chapter, Kansas City (MO)

The heartland Chapter reached out to less fortunate in their neighborhood during the holy month of Ramadan.[14] What started as a Food Pantry in Memphis, Tennessee developed into a National Food Drive of APPNA at 15 locations across the United States. More than 50,000 meals were served to community members in need. *"That means tonight somebody's going to have a meal because of something that they've done for us. They made that association and have chosen Harvesters to help fulfil their commitment to feed the hungry in the community,"* said Harvesters Chief Resource Officer Joaana Sbelien in response to a gift on 5,000 meals by APPNA Heartland Chapter to the Harvesters in Kansas City, MO.

Minnesota Chapter

Dr. Bushra Dar was the 2015 president of the **Minnesota Association of Pakistani Physicians (MAPP)**, which was established in the fall of 2010. She reported, *"We are still in initial phases and hoping to continue to grow. In the last few years we have organized 3 major events including CME seminar,* *a fashion show and a benefit dinner for Human Development Foundation (HDF). We held our second very successful fundraising Iftar dinner for HDF on June 19, 2015. The chapter has recruited several new members and leaders to infuse new energy in this organization this year and hope to continue to grow. MAPP board and members plan to continue to be involved in free health clinics within the Twin Cities, MN, and will partner with APPNA to organize local events in our area for National Health Care Day."*

North Texas Chapter
Dr. Mohammad Zaim Nawaz, who was 2015 President of North Texas Chapter stated, *"Our chapter is based out of Dallas, Texas and serves over 500 physicians of Pakistani descent in our area. Our mission, as always, has been to uphold ethical and moral values, engage in social and professional activities, support educational and intellectual pursuits, upgrade medical care and thus glorify our Association."*

APPNA PUN, is a new Delaware Valley tristate chapter of APPNA that represents the contiguous counties of Pennsylvania, southern New Jersey, and Upper Delaware. This was one of two chapters founded in 2014. The other was the San Antonio Chapter in Texas.

Dr. Sarwat Iqbal, who co-founded the PUN chapter along with Dr. Sajjad Savul, Dr. Haroon Durrani, and others reported, *"Our main mission and long term goal is to help and guide our youth in becoming people of character and integrity; who are humble and tolerant. We want them to be successful in all fields of life and help their young friends with academic, internship, and job opportunities through network and unity and make allies and supporters. So they can live without fear, in peace and with pride. We participate in all projects that APPNA does and do those at local level like APPNA FREE CLINICS."*

Other APPNA Chapters as of 2015
- Arkansas Chapter
- Southern California Chapter
- New England Chapter (APPNE)
- Kentucky and Indiana Chapter
- Michigan Chapter

- Oklahoma Chapter
- South Central Pennsylvania Chapter
- San Antonio Chapter (TX)
- Southern Chapter
- North East Tennessee Chapter
- South Texas Chapter
- South Central Texas Chapter
- Wisconsin Chapter
- Virginia Chapter (Richmond)

APPNA Free Clinics:

Since 2008, APPNA Clinic located at the APPNA central office in Westmont, IL has been serving residents of Westmont and surrounding communities on every Saturday morning to noon. The APPNA clinic services are provided across gender, racial, religious, ethnic and socioeconomic lines. The clinic patients seek individualized but comprehensive healthcare, which the Clinic is able to provide free of charge. For a variety of reasons, APPNA Clinic patients find comfort in seeking treatment there; perhaps they find their needs are met at a free clinic with care, passion, dignity and with full measure of respect.

The clinic staff includes physicians, students and a phlebotomist, all of whom donate their time on a volunteer basis. According to Clinic Chair Dr. Imtiaz Arain, *"the goal is to offer healthcare beyond screenings and occasional vaccinations. APPNA Clinic tends to offer a comprehensive primary care with physical evaluation and treatment, prescription medications and on-site blood draws. More specialized care, including social services, patient counseling, and ophthalmology services, are also available."*

Besides the clinic mentioned above, which was inaugurated by Dr. Mahmood Alam in October 2008, numerous other clinics have been initiated by local chapters across the United States in the last seven years. Some of these clinics are highlighted previously with their chapter's activities. Most clinics are run on the week-ends by volunteer staff and physicians. Different models of clinics have been adopted according to local needs and the available support system. Some of them are stand alone and independently run like the one at APPNA offices in Westmont, IL, where laboratory work and diagnostic testing is provided by local healthcare facilities. Other models include clinics that are run in collaboration with Islamic Centers and other non-profit organizations. A few are established in medical offices where facilities and staff are provided for by physician practices without charge.

The Long Range Planning Committee of APPNA appointed a task force on APPNA Clinics in 2015. Dr. Imtiaz Arain, a member of the Board of Trustees was appointed as its Team Leader. This task force will examine the prospects and working of the free clinics in America.

APPNA National Healthcare Day, a project conceived and instituted by Dr. Nasar Qureshi and Dr. Azam Kundi, has been organized by all the active chapters of APPNA since 2010. Several APPNA chapters across the United States and Canada hold free clinics and provide free flu vaccinations for the needy of their communities. The APPNA National Healthcare Day attracts local politicians and the press, alike. The activity is usually covered in local print and electronic media. There is a strong desire to serve our adopted homeland by the membership and Pakistani-physicians along with their families and friends enthusiastically volunteering.

APPNA Chapter Initiative[15]

In 2005, the APPNA Chapter Initiative was started by some members and was led by Dr. Shahid Sheikh, the president of the Ohio chapter at Columbus at that time. Dr. Sheikh proposed that APPNA chapters should have more recognition by APPNA and that one evening at the APPNA summer meeting should be celebrated as "Chapter Night." He was able to garner support from the following chapter presidents: Ashraf Sabahat of Upstate New York, M. Yaqoob Shaikh of South Texas, Naheed Usmani of New England, Aftab Ahmed of Kentucky/Indiana, Nadeem Zafar of Mid-South, and Busharat Ahmad of Michigan. This group held a meeting on July 3, 2005 during the Summer Convention in Houston and the Executive Committee was asked to participate. The need for the regulation of chapter activities was recognized. Subsequently, Dr. Shahid Sheikh published a report on this in the APPNA Summer/Fall Journal. Chapter night has invariably been organized since 2009 on the Wednesday evening of the Summer Convention. This activity is usually a social gathering with a diner and entertainment. The official business pertaining to chapter activities is conducted at the Council Meeting where chapters along with alumni associations are recognized as component societies of APPNA.

**THE EXECUITVE COUNCIL OF NEW YORK CHAPTER
ASSOCIATION OF PHYSICIANS OF PAKISTANI – DESCENT OF NOTH
AMERICA
NYC-APPNA**

Cordially Invites to

COMMUNITY EMPOWERMENT SEMINAR

On Sunday April 10, 2005
5:00 PM – 9:00 PM

ADRIA-RAMADA
220-33 Northern Blvd., Queens, NY
718-631-5900

SEMINAR DIRECTOR
Mahmood Alam, MD

Co-Directors
Asifur Rehman, MD
Iqbal Jangda, MD

Seminar Co-Chairs
M. M. Haque, MD, President NYC-APPNA
Qazi K Haider, MD, President-elect NYC-APPNA

PROGRAM

Obtaining Visas & Security Clearance, an Up-date
A. R. Piracha, MD, President-elect APPNA

LEGISLATIVE DIPLOMACY & PHYSICAINS
Suad Anwer, MD, Secretary, PAK-PAC

NEGOTIATING THE IMMIGRATION MAZE
Stephen Perlitsh, Esq. Attorney-at-Law

EMPOWERING MUSLIM WOMEN
Working at the grass root level
Rubina Niaz, Esq.

SOUTH ASIAN HEALTH INITIATIVE & APPNA
Shazia N. Anam, MPH

Dinner will be served

A snapshot of Chapter Activities in APPNA

The Regulation of Chapter Activities under Central APPNA[16]

The previous information on chapter related activities showcases APPNA's involvement and support of their local communities. This profound service to community is what has made APPNA a grassroots movement. APPNA was started in 1978 as an ethnic organization of Pakistani descent physicians residing in North America. As the Chapters started to grow not only in number but also in influence both inside and outside of APPNA, issues of the regulation of chapter activities and compliance with the 501C3 charter surfaced about a decade ago. The leadership of APPNA felt,

"While it is of utmost importance that the component societies have their independent profile and run their own affairs according to their membership desires, it is equally important to appreciate that the affiliation with APPNA is APPNA's privilege. The component societies have to conform to a uniform and centrally adopted framework while engaging in APPNA related work. It is APPNA's responsibility to train, educate and assist the local leadership of component societies in organizational work.[17]

An Ad hoc committee was appointed in 2011 by President Manzoor Tariq to examine the relationship between the central office and component societies (CS). Dr. Nasir Gondal chaired the committee. The committee members were Mahmood Alam, Imtiaz Arain, Omar Atiq, M. Khalid Riaz, and Saima Zafar (Ex-Officio as President Elect).

The committee was formed to enhance the relationship between the central office and component societies (CS).

The main objectives of this committee were as follows:

1. To ensure compliance between APPNA and its component societies.

2. To help maintain APPNA & its component societies' nonprofit status and, if possible, look for avenues to register the societies separately in the states they exist.

3. To provide conflict resolution between component societies & central APPNA and among component societies.

4. To assist the President-Elect with the component society verification process.

The following issues were identified by the committee and their solutions were recommended as follows:[18]

1. **Compliance on timely financial reporting from component societies to APPNA offices:**

    This had been a major problem that has invariably led to delays in the compilation of APPNA's financial statements, which resulted in the revocation of APPNA's registration by the State of Illinois a few times. Solution: The component societies were encouraged and offered professional help by central APPNA to register themselves with their state as a 501 C-3 organization affiliated with APPNA as the parent body. This solution has worked. Many CS are now registered as non-profit organizations in numerous states. The newer chapters and smaller alumni associations that were not independently registered are required to comply with reporting of their financial statements to APPNA office no later than March 31 each year.

    In 2012, Dr. Saima Zafar (President) and Dr. Arif Agha (Chair Office Management Committee) were able to further streamline the accounting of APPNA at the central offices in a major overhaul of the office staff. That was achieved by the hiring of a new book keeper and the creation of paperless computer based methodology to close the gap of non-compliance at various levels. Ms. Jennifer Wozniak, JD was promoted as administrator of APPNA. Dr. Zafar who sat on the ad hoc committee while she was president elect and therefore gained insight on dealing with the component societies in 2011. She had great success in implementing APPNA policies with CS during her presidency in 2012.

    In 2014, Dr. Mubasher Rana as President Elect instituted an online recertification process for the component societies. This service has streamlined and made it easier for the component societies to submit their compliance and financial reports to APPNA.

2. **Uniform Bylaws that govern the Component societies.** Complete compliance with the parent organization's constitution, bylaws and policies and procedures was lacking. In the Spring

Council Meeting, 2011, *"The committee unanimously recommended that the requirements and the guidelines outlined in the organization's bylaws and the previously approved policies and procedures, be implemented with immediate effect."* Solution: A uniform template for the CS Bylaws was created in early 2012 and was made available to all the CS. A copy of the existing Bylaws was obtained from the CS's and a remedy was suggested in cases of discrepancy between the parent organization and the CS.

3. **Representation in Council (Proxy)**: Another important issue was the representation of component societies at the council meetings. It was noted that many times individuals without authority were representing the CS's when an officer was unable to attend the meeting. At other times, some familiar faces were seen repeatedly to represent component societies. Solution: It was resolved that, *"The delegation of representation of component society in Council meetings through proxy should follow a set process, only elected officers with decreasing hierarchical position should represent the component societies. It should not be the discretion of the president of the CS to nominate anyone to represent in case president was not able to attend. The meeting and teleconference rules should be stricter; only the next person in line of authority should be allowed to represent the component society. For example, if the President is not available, president elect should attend and represent the CS."*

4. **Role of Central APPNA as final arbitrator in locally irresolvable component society conflicts:** No provision of conflict resolution policy exists between component societies & central APPNA and within the component societies. Solution: The role of Central APPNA as a final arbitrator in locally irresolvable chapter conflicts needs to be determined. There should be a clear process of conflict resolution in the Bylaws of the CS. There should be a provision to take the matter to APPNA or Ethics and Grievance Committee if conflict could not be resolved at the chapter level. However, these rules should be part of the CS's bylaws.

5. Development of policy and procedure needed that assists President-Elect to do Bylaws mandated fiduciary responsibility with the component societies.

The committee found out that policy and procedures about the relationship of APPNA and its component society did exist since 1996. These policy and procedures were up-dated by Dr. Tariq Cheema in 2007. Since then, a comprehensive package about the relationship between APPNA and component societies (CS) and requirements to be fulfilled is sent to all CS. However, compliance with the policies remains a major issue. The Committee recommended additional points to the Component Societies membership package that highlight the requirements of APPNA. They include:

1. Recognition of APPNA as a parent body with overall governance authority.
2. Membership criterion should be the same for the chapters as for APPNA.
3. Election/officers terms should be in line with APPNA.
4. Financial responsibilities and its timely reporting should be strictly followed.

End Notes:

1   APPNA Journal, 6:2, Winter 2004, page 29, Chapter Activism in APPNA Comes of Age, an article by Mahmood Alam
2   Dr. Ehtsham Haque, founding president of Alabama Chapter contributed to this report
3   Dr. Shahid Abbasi, Past President APPNA Northern California Chapter contributed to this report
4   Dr. Arshad Saeed, the founding president of Canadian chapter contributed to this report
5   Dr. Khalid Aziz, past president of North Carolina Chapter contributed to this report
6   Dr. Muhammad Afzal, president 2015 of Greater Cincinnati chapter contributed to this report
7   Dr. Atique A. Mirza and Dr. Monina Salman, past presidents of CT chapter, contributed to this report

8   Pakistani Descent Physicians Society: A Historical Perspective by Nasir Rana, MD, MPH—Life Member PPS

9   *APPNA Qissa*, Chapter 4, The Maturing of the Association, 2004.

10   Dr. I. Zafar Hamid, founding secretary of South Florida Chapter contributed to this report

11   Dr. Rizwan Qazi, president Nevada chapter 2013, contributed to this report

12   Dr. Razia Awan, president APPNA-NJ contributed to this report

13   Dr. Shahid Sheikh, past president Ohio Chapter, contributed to this report

14   APPNA Journal 14:2, Winter 2012, 12

15   APPNA Journal 6:3, Summer/Fall 2005, page 46

16   APPNA Newsletter, 21:1, Spring 2011, page 8

17   APPNA Newsletter, 21:2, Fall 2011, page 17

18   Ad hoc Committee for Relationship between Center and Component Societies; Report Fall Meeting 2011 by Dr. Nasir Gondal

8

DEMOCRATIC APPNA: A SYNOPSIS OF ITS ELECTORAL REFORMS

Introduction

The continuum of democratic process by holding elections every year is a hallmark of APPNA that is unparalleled amongst the expatriate Pakistani societies throughout the world. The elections are not only held at the national level; they are also a requirement for all the component societies that are represented in APPNA Council. Electoral politics always face issues of voter recruitment and voter suppression regardless if they are the elections of a country or of a comparatively small organization like APPNA. The credibility of the fairness in the system is often questioned across the board when a difference of a few votes is encountered in fiercely contested elections. This chapter is a synopsis of electoral reforms in APPNA that evolved in the last three decades to make APPNA a strong democratic institution.

APPNA's code of election conduct has a long history that started with the elections held in 1987. A closely contested election was decided by few votes and demands for a fairer and more transparent system followed. The first code of election ethics was approved at the spring executive council meeting held in April 1988. This 9-point code of ethics was prepared by the Ethics and Grievance Committee headed by Dr. Zaheer Ahmad (MI) in the backdrop of the complaint launched by contestants who lost 1987 elections by few votes.[1] Although this code proposed good practices on the ethical conduct of the contestants, the flaws inherent to the election policy and procedures required amendments in the APPNA Bylaws. In subsequent years, other complaints about election procedures were also surfaced. Dr. Mushtaq Sheikh (NY) and Dr. Tariq B. Iftikhar were candidates in the 1998 elections. They had seriously questioned the impartiality of APPNA office and the officers who performed the oversight in the election process, which they believed was rigged.

Landmark Changes in the Electoral Process of APPNA:

It is imperative to identify the issues pertaining to the elections from a historical perspective and then see how the organization tried to fix it. APPNA has, over the years, tried to define itself in the process of finding answers to a number of procedural questions.

Procedural Issue #1: **Who should oversee the elections?** In the 1994 Bylaws, Chapter 10 (Election), section 3 says: *"The Secretary, after recording the receipt of the ballot and verification of the standing of the member in the Association, will hand over the unopened ballot to the chairman of the Nominating/Election Committee for tabulation."*[2] The impartiality of the secretary of the Association who may also be a candidate for president elect could not be defended. There was indeed an inherent bias seen in this procedure and was the point of contention as stated above. **Remedy: In 1999, APPNA made a landmark decision to outsource the election procedural oversight to Election Services Corporation based in New York.** That company conducted the elections for 15 years in accordance with APPNA bylaws while upholding the legal requirements of sending and receiving mail-in-ballots from 2000–2014. Dr. Riaz M. Chaudhry (LA) as the secretary of the association in 1999 took this initiative and is credited for this change. Dr. Shabbir Safdar (MO) was the President. Although, this single step established a transparent election procedure at a cost, it did not address other issues pertaining to election process.

Procedural Issue #2: **Who is qualified to vote?** This issue has been a major source of contention and has loomed in APPNA for over a decade. It remains a point of debate in APPNA circles despite numerous remedies sought through constitutional amendments over the years. Until 2004, the membership eligibility as defined in the bylaws included the following: *"a physician must hold a valid permanent license in North America or in the country where he/she is practicing, or in Pakistan,."*[3] The eligibility of physicians outside of North America to become the voting members did not fit well with the contested elections in APPNA in the mid-1990s. At occasions, supporters of some of the presidential candidates during 1998–2002 did take advantage of this clause. This practice was considered by many to be an abuse of the system.

Remedy: Dr. Mohammad Suleman took the initiative of making the governance of APPNA more transparent by proposing a number of constitutional amendments even before he became the president in 2002. **The removal of the clause allowing for APPNA membership outside of North America was part of the amendments, which were approved in 2004.** Another important 2004 change pertinent to voter eligibility is also worth mentioning. The Physicians-in-Training members were always welcomed to become APPNA members without paying any membership dues. This option of membership without paying dues given to the resident physicians who could also vote bore a lot of criticism. The critics had cited numerous occasions of voting abuse by the candidates who had access to residents in training. **The amendments done in 2004 took away their right to vote unless they paid full annual dues.**[4] Furthermore**, the duty of membership verification was also reassigned to the president elect in 2004.** It was based on the assumption that having no vested interest in the elections, the president elect would perform this duty with utmost impartiality.

2006 Election Controversy: The election for the president elect's position between Dr. Alam and Dr. Munir in 2006 was decided by a margin of only 4 votes in favor of Dr. Alam. A recount done at the same meeting of Nominating and Election Committee (N&EC) made no difference. According to APPNA Bylaws a simple plurality in voting is required to declare a winner. The option for a runoff election could only be exercised if there is a tie vote.[5] Dr. Zeelaf Munir contested the results and chose to seek judicial recourse for her contention despite an appeal by the Chair of Ethics and Grievance Committee that promised her a fair hearing within the organization.[6] *Munir v. APPNA* was filed in September 2006 in the Circuit Court of Cook County, Chancery Division. Dr. Munir's grievance with APPNA was based on her contention that her complaint was not entertained at the right time within the organization to her satisfaction and she had challenged the fairness in election process.

During this process of litigation, a motion by the plaintiff for temporary restraining order stopping Dr. Alam to assume the position of President elect on January 1, 2007 was denied.[7] Subsequently, President APPNA Dr. Nadeem Kazi, Executive Director Dr. Tariq Cheema, and Office Manager Denise Bert were summoned for depositions. The plaintiff's attorney pursued President Nadeem Kazi during his deposition to obtain the statement that APPNA will hold another election amongst the two presidential candidates if it is proven that four or more ineligible members voted in the elections held in 2006.[8]

The voter eligibility clause in APPNA bylaws states, "To be eligible for active membership in the Association or in any of its component societies, *a physician must hold an un-revoked license in North America and/ or be involved in Academics, Medical Research, or management in any field of Health care in North America, and comply with all the provisions of the Bylaws of their society and this Association (Bylaws sec. 13.6.2.*" The Judge overturned the APPNA presidential election of 2006 based on the fact that four APPNA non-licensed members voted whose membership eligibility could not be satisfied within the provision of criteria mentioned above.

APPNA held a new election based on the court order in the fall of 2007.[9] The court also required APPNA to provide a completely re-verified list of voters prior to holding the fresh elections. The total number of eligible voters decreased by 76 in 2007 as compared to 2006 due to arduous verification process. The elections were conducted under the most scrupulous rules ever observed in APPNA history. The ballots were counted on December 1, 2007 at a special meeting held for this purpose at Chicago IL. Both candidates were invited by the N&E committee to agree and have a final sign off on the rules before ballots were opened. The results of the counting were unprecedented and both candidates were tied securing 612 votes each.[10]

The Drop Scene of Election 2006:

There was less than one month left for the president of APPNA 2008 to take office after December 1, announcement of tied elections. A runoff election was required. Practically it takes 3–4 months to complete an election process in APPNA and there was an impasse. Neither candidates nor the membership had the heart to go through this mentally and physically challenging exercise again. The custodians of the organization asked both candidates to come up with an amicable solution that ends the fiasco and brings much needed unity in the divided organization.

After two weeks of discussions, both candidates were successful in ending the impasse for the sake of organization to move on. On December 20, 2007, Dr. Zeelaf Munir wrote a letter to the membership expressing her withdrawal as a candidate for presidency allowing Dr. Mahmood Alam to assume the office of President APPNA 2008. She wrote, *"After all the work you have done to understand the issues and vote according to your conscience, we have arrived at a standstill. And according to our constitution we should have to vote again. As always, I stand ready to fight for a strong APPNA.... I still believe with all my heart that I am the best candidate to lead APPNA. I still maintain that the way to strengthen APPNA is through a culture of accountability and transparency, upholding democratic values and a robust constitution. However, as this year comes to a close and APPNA is left rudderless and bereft of consistent leadership for 2008, it is equally important that we bring stability to the organization that we love. That is why I decided, with great sadness, in the larger interest of the organization, to withdraw as a candidate for the President of APPNA-2008."*[11]

Dr. Munir ran for presidency of APPNA again in 2008, and won with a wide margin to become the 31st president of APPNA.

The role of Nominating and Election Committee (N&EC) has been limited to overseeing the elections after nominations are received from the aspiring candidates that they secure themselves. However, the founders of the association had a perceived role of N&EC as primarily of preparing a slate of nominations with the option to entertain nominations from the general membership if someone desires to be on the ballot and is not nominated by the N&EC.[12] This theme, however, has not worked ever since the elections are contested in APPNA. The president's nominated N&EC has often been perceived to lack impartiality needed and the respect that committee deserves. Therefore, N&EC has not been able to establish a credible role on nominating and counseling the prospective candidates in the present culture of APPNA politics. So far, ferociously contested elections were only averted by the personal understanding of aspiring candidates when they made wise decisions to let one candidate go and the other waited a year or two while complimenting each other in serving the association. One such example is the understanding that was developed between

Dr. Shaukat H. Khan (PA) and Dr. Durdana Gilani (CA). Both served the organization in tandem in 1997 and 1998, respectively.[13]

More recently in 2015, Dr. Raheel R. Khan (VA) has made a case for more proactive role of N&EC in an article published in APPNA Journal titled, making a case to choose APPNA's future leaders.[14] Dr. Khan has suggested to creating a Leadership Selection Council (LSC) that works under N&EC and is represented by all the alumni associations affiliated with APPNA. Then, he proposed to seek nominations from the general membership. These nominees present themselves in person with their credentials to the LSC. Eventually, the LSC by a process of elimination selects only two candidates as the nominees of the N&EC to be put on the ballot for elections. Dr. Khan concluded, "Adopting this process should help level the playing field and encourage good, talented members to seek leadership role in the Association, irrespective of the voting strength of their alumni. With only two candidates contesting, the elected officer will likely be elected by the solid majority of the voting membership."

Elections Reforms Beyond 2007:

An ad hoc committee on election reforms was appointed in 2007 by Dr. Nadeem Kazi. Dr. S. Amjad Hussain (OH) Chaired this five-member committee. Other members were Dr. Aslam Malik (TX), Dr. Khalid Riaz (IL), Dr. S. Sultan Ahmed (NJ), and Dr. Irfan ul Haq (NJ). The election code of conduct in APPNA had gone through numerous revisions since 1988. In 1994, past president Dr. Mushtaq Khan wrote an election policy that was incorporated into bylaws.[15] Ten years later, a 13-point revised code of conduct was signed on October 2, 2004 by the president Omar Atiq, president-elect Hussain Malik, and secretary Zeelaf Munir. The code of conduct proposed in 2007 had all the provisions of the code signed in 2004 with the addition of some professional ethics, which were very much needed in the growing culture of lavished spending and aggressive marketing by the aspiring candidates. Commercials in public media were banned. APPNA members were given the option to be on the "no call," "no mail," or "no fax" list to avoid any kind of intrusive campaigning. The negativity against any candidate was forbidden. The penalties for disobeying the rules were also proposed with mechanism of launching a complaint that could go from N&EC to E&GC and finally to BOT. Furthermore, *"all candidates shall agree that upon conclusion of APPNA procedures for dispute resolution the decision arrived by APPNA shall be FINAL and shall not be subject to any recourse outside APPNA whether judicial or extra-judicial in any state of union."*[16] This election reform bill, which was prepared by the ad hoc committee in 2007, was taken up by the Nominating & Election committee (N&EC) of 2008. The N&EC revised the document and proposed minor changes. The Election code of conduct was finally approved at the spring council meeting in March 2008 at Louisville, KY.[17] Nevertheless, the enforcement of these rules remain a challenge for the organization.

Voter Verification Dispute of 2009:

Although, the election code of conduct of 2007–2008 set the new ethical standards that were sought at the height of the court mandated re-election of 2007. Ironically, it did not address the issue of the non-physician members' eligibility to vote and the ethical issue of vote buying. Both of these issues resurfaced again in 2009. The voter verification issue became contentious between the Chair of membership committee and the President Elect. Both had different interpretations of bylaws clause on the eligibility of non-licensed members. Moreover, verification of eligibility especially on new member applicants could not be completed on time. This rigorous policy of document verification was adopted in APPNA after the court decision in 2007. The BOT had to intervene and pleaded for more collegial work between the executive director, the president elect, and the chair of the membership committee. Some of the contestants raised the issue of provisional ballots that were issued to numerous members whose verification was still pending and vehemently opposed to include their votes in the counting. It caused so much trouble that the N&EC could not hold Election Meeting to count the ballots at the 2009 Summer Convention as mandated by our bylaws. Eventually, the APPNA executive committee sought legal opinion. The attorney issued a statement on July 27, 2009 to address all the contentious issues. While, the attorney proposed the best solution under the circumstances, she strongly recommended amending the bylaws in order to remove redundancy in the roles of president elect and the chair of membership committee in membership verification. The attorney also suggested counting all those provisional ballots as long as their verification was completed on the day of counting.[18]

Constitution and Bylaws (CABL) Committee Proposes a Renewed Policy on Voter Eligibility in 2009:

The interpretation of the provision of non-licensed physicians involved in Academics, Medical Research, or management in any field of Health care in North America to be the active members remained an issue of interpretation in APPNA despite previous remedies. The CABL committee in 2009 elaborated on the issue of non-physicians' eligibility and tried to define the scope of terms "Academics," "Medical Research," and "Management." The committee Chair, Asif Rehman (NY), presented its recommendations at the fall council meeting in 2009 that generated an intense discussion. Mufiz Chauhan (AR) who was also the part of CABL committee, passionately made arguments in favor of proposed changes. Other participants were Mahmood Alam (NJ), Riaz M. Chaudhry (LA), Arif Muslim (NY), and Mohammad Haseeb (MO). The CABL committee proposed guidelines on the interpretation of non-licensed physicians were adopted.[19] The committee proposed that "Research" should be authenticated by the institutional review board or similar authority and academic position should be at the level of a faculty position to be considered for active membership in APPNA. Moreover, a manager of doctor's office or of a clinical laboratory does not come under the purview of "Management in Healthcare field."

The Impact of Ratification of Amendments to Bylaws in 2012 on Election Policy:

President Saima Zafar (IA) is credited for securing the approval of amendments to the Bylaws by the general body in 2012. The tenacity of Dr. Mohammad Suleman (LA) as the chair of CABL committee was instrumental in completing this process. These amendments were approved by the Council in 2006 and 2007 pending ratification by an affirmative vote of more than 50% of active membership. Omar Atiq (AR) and Nasar Qureshi (NJ) were the chairs of the CABL committee in 2006 and 2007, respectively. Both had played a significant role in putting together the changes pertinent to the improved governance of the Association.[20]

According to the changes in the Bylaws effective January 1, 2013, the election schedule was moved from summer to fall seeking the nominations three months prior to fall council meeting, which moved the election season to start after the summer annual convention. Since 2013, APPNA started holding presidential debates, a feature that is very much appreciated by the membership. Now, APPNA secretary and treasurer could focus more on organizational work rather than campaigning for their next election that used to start in early spring according to the old election schedule. Another change in the bylaws was the assignment of membership confirmation to executive committee taking it away from the responsibilities of the president elect. It was felt that a committee of five members could do a better job than one person when dealing with the oft-contentious issue of membership verification.

More Election Reforms through the Bylaws Amendments in 2014:

APPNA President Asif Rehman, (NY) appointed Mahmood Alam (NJ) chair of the CABL committee in 2014 to amend the bylaws in order to accommodate Council approved changes, which he had suggested in the fall of 2009 as the chair of the CABL committee. The CABL Committee had seven different alumni represented and work started at a fast pace. It was another landmark year in APPNA in which new changes were incorporated to further improve the election policy and procedures. It was also first time in APPNA history that proposed amendments were discussed in CABL at four sessions, presented to council twice, and after council approval ratification by the general body was achieved within the same year. The changes pertaining to elections in the Bylaws were the following:

- All annual dues-paying members are eligible to vote provided they are current members and had at least 1 paid membership in the Association during the last 2 years preceding the elections. *(This was a fiercely debated decision taken to curb the "seasonal" annual paid membership in APPNA that was primarily sought by the aspiring candidates for increasing their voters bank)*
- The members of the Association shall cast their votes by secret ballot either by mail or electronic media conducted by an authentic election agency approved by APPNA Council.
- All nominees for the election of the officers of the Association shall have served for at least one year on the Council as the President of a recognized component society. Any past officer of

central APPNA is also eligible to run for any office in future.

Any member whose dues are not received by the central office by July 7 will be considered in arrears and will not be eligible to vote in the elections that year.

In 2015, there were additional important changes instituted in the election Code of Conduct to limit the period of campaigning and to discourage violation of the code of conduct. These were:[21]

- Any violation of the election code of conduct by a candidate will be communicated to the membership.
- The formal election campaign could only be started after the APPNA Summer meeting. For example, a candidate cannot send campaign emails or postcards/letters prior to the summer meeting. Similarly, social media campaigns and phone calls by candidates are also not permitted before the formal start date of campaigning.
- Candidates are not allowed to present themselves at any component society meetings prior to the formal campaign start date.

First elections via electronic balloting in 2015:

Bylaws amendment in 2014 paved the way to electronic voting that happened in the very next elections in 2015. This was the final landmark achievement pertaining to APPNA elections in a decade. It was probably the most significant step since outsourcing of election procedure in the year 2000. Dr. Mubasher Rana took the challenge as president and assigned Sohail Khan (IL), who had experience of spearheading DOGANA electronic balloting, along with Sajjad Savul (NJ), Chair N&EC to arrange and oversee the first electronic elections in APPNA.

The mail in balloting had serious issues over the years. Although apparently a simple procedure if you follow the instructions, it had an embarrassingly high rate of ballot rejection based on errors of omission by the voters. A review of 15 years of mail-in-ballot practice reveals inherent flaws leading to rejection of 8%-10% ballots received by the election company. The lack of signing the outer envelope and not using the secret ballot envelope were the two most common errors that out rightly removed those ballot from counting. The voter's signature on the outer envelope was required as an attestation that it was from the intended voter who voted, non-else.

The use of secret envelope was needed to keep the privacy of the voter so nobody would ever know who voted for which candidate. Now let us analyze the outcome of election results in the last one decade in the backdrop of information of high percentage of ballot rejection. The 5 out of 10 presidential elections in APPNA during 2004–2013 were decided by less than 50 votes. In fact, 3 of them were decided with 10 or less votes difference. This difference is less than 1% of total votes counted. Whereas, the errors in mail-in-voting resulted in up to 10% votes rejected. Theoretically, losing candidate could have won if all ballots were counted. The counter argument is that it could have also increased the margin of winning candidate. Furthermore, electronic balloting significantly increased the rate of return of ballots from roughly 70% by mail-in-ballots to 85% with electronic ballots and cost less than 50% compared to mail-in-ballots.[22] Therefore, this small step taken by the leadership has proven to be a big leap for the organization. This bold act of sweeping change from mail-in-ballots to exclusively electronic ballots had its own critics thought out the election season. However, the seamless procedure of electronic ballot has proven the critics wrong. The electronic elections survey reflects excellent satisfaction of the voting members. Most APPNA leaders and past members of the N&EC committee would agree that the impact of electronic voting on the election process in APPNA surpasses all the other logistic changes that were ever done in the past two decades.

Nomination and Election Committee 2006
(Lt to Rt) (standing) Aftab Ahmad, Mufiz Chauhan, Farooq Mirza, Mohammad Suleman (Chair), Ahsan Rashid, Raza hassan and Ishaq Chisti
(Sitting) candidates representatives, Naureen Zafar and Nasir Gondal

End Notes:

1   *APPNA Qissa* (2004), The Maturing of an Organization, 63
2   Constitution and Bylaws of APPNA, 1994, 21
3   Ibid, 12
4   Constitution and Bylaws of APPNA, 2004, 13
5   Constitution and Bylaws of APPNA, 2004, 24
6   Letters from Zeelaf Munir, E&GC chair, Dr. Latafat Hamzavi, Chair BOT 2006, Dr. Shabbir H. Safdar, on file in APPNA archives
7   Circuit Court of Cook County, IL, Case No. 06 CH 17770
8   Munir v. APPNA, Deposition of Nadeem Kazi, a public record available at the Circuit Court of Cook County, IL, Case No. 06 CH 17770
9   Individual membership files on record in APPNA offices.
10 Final Results—December 1, 2007—APPNA Election, copy on file
11 Zeelaf Munir's letter to membership, December 2007, copy on file.
12 APPNA Journal, 14:1, Summer 2012, *APPNA Qissa*—APPNA Qazia, an article by S. Amjad Hussain, 19
13 Dr. Shaukat H. Khan told this historical story in a bus full of APPNA members to a trip to Sedona, AZ, in 2002.
14 APPNA Journal, 25:3, 2015, 24
15 Document on file, in the Archives of APPNA, July 22, 1994 and re-typed February 25, 1997
16 Report on Election Reform Committee (APPNA, copy on file, December 12, 2007
17 Minutes of the Spring council meeting, March 2008
18 Legal opinion by Rebecca Boyd-Obraski at Nagle & Higgins, P.C. Attorneys & Law, letter on file, July 27, 2009
19 Minute of Fall Council meeting held at Niagara Falls Canada, September 26–27, 2009
20 Council approved changes in Bylaws 2006 and 2007, documents on file.
21 The revised election Code of Conduct, 2015, copy on file.
22 The report of Nominating and Election Committee Chair Sajjad Savul, 2015

9

ORGANIZATION BUILDING: CHALLENGES AND OPPORTUNITIES

Introduction: All organizations face challenges. The successful ones are those that turn these challenges into opportunities. The leaders and active members in any organization are the ones that identify the challenges and morph them into part of the growth and advancement of the organization. APPNA has faced many challenges, trials, and tribulations since its inception. The maturing of the organization with its earlier challenges in the initial 25 years were eloquently discussed by the authors of *APPNA Qissa* (1978–2003).[1] Since its inception, most of the presidents of APPNA have written about these issues that were discussed by the organization at various levels. These fora included the General Body, Council, and Board of Trustee meetings. The annual Strategic Planning Retreat was another forum held numerous times (2004–2015) at the beginning of the year. A review of published messages from APPNA presidents gives us the glimpses of what concerned our leaders about the organization.

The 2002 President, Mohammad Suleman, in that years' Fall newsletter expressed, *"It is my earnest desire to streamline the APPNA working and make all the necessary changes in the document of our governance. This year's election has once again shown the need and importance of bringing necessary changes."*[2] Raana Akbar president 2003 reflected, *"There are two particular constitutional problems that can be particularly troublesome for APPNA. The definition of a member must include provision of licensure for all members except those who are in activities pertaining to research. Chapters must have some linkage with individual representation and geographical representation.... I will endeavor to improve the work of central office... It is no longer enough to live in this country in secluded islands of segregated culture. We as an organization must stop reminiscing and take part in organized medicine. APPNA is in a process of applying for delegate status in AMA House of Delegates."*[3]

The President of 2004 Omar Atiq, in his report to Newsletter talked about the Association Development expressing: *"All the participants (Strategic Planning Conference January 24–25 in Dallas) agreed that professional management of APPNA with appropriate staff and resources, including an executive director is imperative for the organization to advance to next level. Once in place, these resources will facilitate improved governance, regulatory compliance, and long term strategic planning."*[4] In 2005, President Hussain Malik felt that the APPNA Charitable Foundation is the answer to all the issues of fundraising that we need for APPNA *Sehat*, Free Clinics, social welfare projects, and educational scholarships.[5] Moreover, as president elect in 2004, Dr. Malik had conducted an opinion poll survey asking members their input in running the organization. Although response rate was only 5%, membership's opinion was counted in making future plans.[6] Dr. Piracha, president 2006 eluded, *"Items on my agenda include increasing the membership and internal reorganization of the office. I strongly believe that at this time younger members of the organization should take charge and lead it to a greater future."*[7]

As president in 2007 Nadeem Kazi, hoped: *"Our executive director is going to help integrate all the facets of this voluntary organization into a cohesive entity. We have been working on rationalizing APPNA's policy and procedures to run the organization more effectively."*[8] Then in 2008, President Mahmood Alam shared his vision in a newsletter *"The greatest asset of APPNA is the voluntary force of our members whose enthusiasm to work for the common goals will promote this year's theme, "Empowering Community through Activism and Solidarity."* He later continued to write that, *"the scope of this work is enormous, and our limited resources require organization building and resource development to further expand the horizons of our work."*[9] Syed A. Samad, president 2009, after a retreat in Little Rock, *AR, said, "Emphasis continues to be on improved governance, fiscal discipline, increase in membership, and liaison with other professional organizations in US and Pakistan."*[10]

As President in 2010, Zeelaf Munir, had the following to share: *"We could use this moment between the old APPNA and the new APPNA to act out all of our slights and perceived injuries—character assassination is a thrilling and oft—employed blood-sport in APPNA's history—but let us return to the guiding question: Will this practice carry APPNA into the future, or will it undercut its growth? Instead, we chose and urge everyone to channel all our energies in constructive and creative ways. Let us focus on the institution of APPNA, on the health of the organization. "First do no harm" applies as much to this noble institution as it does to our patients. This should be the legacy of our collective efforts, and not ego-driven short termed objectives. Inshallah, APPNA will be here long after we are gone, serving the needs of future generations."*[11]

The 2011 President Manzoor Tariq reported the outcome of the strategic planning meeting held on February 5–6, 2011 at St. Louis, MO: *"Everyone's voice was heard and their suggestions and comments were integrated into a collaborative Mission, Vision, and Goals of APPNA. We formed a Strategic Planning Oversight and Implementation Ad-hoc Committee to ensure that the suggestions made at the Strategic Planning Meeting are implemented and put into action. This committee consists of four subcommittees, each focusing on the top four goals of APPNA as determined by voting at the meeting: The Transparency and Accountability Enhancement Committee, the Leadership Development Committee, the Office Administration Committee, and the Membership Increase and Retention Committee. These committees are working to ensure the meeting's goals became a reality."*[12]

"We remain committed to our theme for 2012 to Enlighten, Empower and Excel," said the then President Saima Zafar and added, *"One of our key goals this year is supporting our young physicians in primarily three areas: nurture and support young physicians through networking for electives; expand their housing options to add subsidized housing for young physicians in Michigan; facilitating the visa process so they can join their residency on time."*[13] President in 2013, Javed Suleman, said, *"Transparency and accountability in all functioning of APPNA are our guiding lights. Inclusion and diversification are the approach. By lowering the Life Time and Annual Dues for 2013 by 40%, we have opened the doors wider for new members to enter and join our ranks. My team's goal is to steer APPNA in the direction where mutual respect, positive attitude and productive working atmosphere prevails."*[14]

President of APPNA in 2014, Asif Rehman, focused on two important initiatives that were important for organization building; the formation and launching of APPNA Foundation and constitutional amendments to streamline election reforms.[15] Then President Mubasher Rana, outlining the theme of 2015 said; *"APPNA First" is based on the firm believe that as long as we put APPNA before our personal interests, we can achieve whatever we strive for.*[16] While focusing on improved governance in APPNA, he appointed President Elect Nasar Qureshi to lead the taskforce in 2015. Dr. Rana argued, *"Times have changed and so should we.—A complete reevaluation of APPNA's governance structure is needed to build an organization of the future which will serve its membership for many years to come."* Dr. Nasar Qureshi, President 2016 stated, *"There is no doubt in my mind and those of many an APPNA member, that APPNA is at an inflection point. The organization has grown, gathered momentum and achieved a lot. It is up to us, that we use this point in the journey of APPNA, to ensure a vibrant and dynamic growth. To achieve that, we will have to, as any organization should, take inventory of our strengths and weaknesses and make a plan for the future."*[17]

All of the above statements underscore the issues that APPNA faced and the leadership proposed the solutions to strengthen the organization for the advancement of its goals. This chapter seeks to examine how APPNA faired in addressing the issues identified and succeeded in turning these challenges into opportunities. (Election reforms are discussed separately in the chapter, Democratic APPNA)

Challenges at the APPNA Office:

Organization building cannot be achieved without effective management and the oversight of any organization. APPNA is no exception. The role of the Office Management Committee has been pivotal in this regards. The present APPNA office building was purchased in 1992 at Westmont, Illinois. The (late) Dr. Mushtaq Khan (IL) was the president and is credited for acquiring the building and establishing central APPNA office at the present location. The OMC has always helped to manage the APPNA office with 2–3 membered staff that served the purpose for two decades 1992–2012. Dr. Mushtaq Khan and Dr. Mushtaq Sharif, both past presidents of APPNA and residents of Chicago area, have contributed a lot in the management of APPNA offices especially during the decade of 1992–2002. They created standard operating procedures (SOP) for the governance of office. Dr. Sharif had been an icon of institutional memory for APPNA for years. He would go into the APPNA office and get any document out from the paper archives if needed for reference purposes. Dr. Iltifat A. Alavi (IL) also made significant contributions to the office management and oversight. His selfless dedication for the organization, besides office management and being Chair of the CABL committee, earned him the APPNA Gold medal award in 2002. He is among the only few members of APPNA who achieved this distinction without being a past president of APPNA.

As the organization grew in size and stature, the effective role of the APPNA central office to orchestrate its operations came under intense debate. It resulted in the conceptual approval of an executive director in 1998.[18] The complexities of operations of APPNA have grown a lot during the last 15 years (2001–2015), which were beyond the ability and capacity of the two to three membered staff. The Executive Committee (EC) of APPNA is charged with running the day-to-day affairs of the organizations. However, with APPNA being a national organization, its officers often reside elsewhere in the country. Moreover, the yearly change of officers vitiates against continuity in developing a longitudinal oversight of work at APPNA offices. The effective oversight by OMC could also be guaranteed only if members appointed to this committee staggered over the years. During the decade of 2001–2010 several changes were instituted to improve the central office in order to better serve the membership that grew from 1,000 to 3,000 during that period. The hiring of an executive director for a process-based management of APPNA offices was deemed necessary.

Hiring an Executive Director for APPNA:

The Executive Council (EC) in 1999 came up with job description of an Executive Director (ED) that was very much desirable to streamline the ever-increasing and demanding work at the APPNA office.[19,20] The ED job description had the following salient features. ED provides leadership and policy guidance for the organization and directs all operations being conducted at the Central Office. The duties included to implement the policy decisions and directives of the Executive Council and to ensure adherence to the Standard Operating Procedures (SOP) and the Bylaws of APPNA. The ED reports regularly to the President of APPNA and ensures that the Executive Council is fully informed of all the activities at the Central Office. The ED also helps prepare annual budget for the Central

Office by the Treasurer. The ED hires, supervises, and evaluates the office staff. ED does periodic updates of the office policy and procedure manual and insures effective communications by the office including proper operation of emails and website maintenance. Moreover, the ED insures proper bookkeeping, preparation of quarterly financial statements by the accountant, and regulatory compliance required by the state of Illinois for non-profit charitable organizations.

During the period of 2000–2003, several attempts were made to hire an ED that fulfils the proposed job description but the salary of $100–125,000 for a qualified and experienced person was prohibitive at that time. Eventually, President Omar Atiq (AR) was able to manage hiring Mr. Michael Thompson, Ph.D. in the fall of 2004. Mr. Thompson had retired as the ED of a national professional medical society after eighteen (18) years of service. Initially, Mr. Thompson was hired as a consultant while level of his involvement and his compensation was being discussed. He appeared to sync in with APPNA very well. As a consultant to APPNA, he wrote a report entitled, "the Roadmap to the Future" that was presented in the November special Council Meeting, 2004. Here is a glimpse of what he thought about APPNA: *"The very foundation of APPNA is its emphasis on the volunteer support and activity of the membership. APPNA is a perfect example of how democracy and inspired, visionary leadership can work hand-in-hand to take an organization such as APPNA to the next levels of efficiency, purpose and influence."*[21]

Unfortunately, he resigned from APPNA in 2005 within few months of his appointment. In his letter to the president and the EC, he expressed his dismay, *"It is with sadness that I am sending to you my resignation as a consultant to APPNA. I have found that my skills, background, and experience have not been utilized in the last six (6) months. The ethical issues that continue to be raised—whether about India trip or the upcoming Houston meeting—are so foreign to my sense of right or wrong and my reputation and work in the medical nonprofit arena, that I feel compelled to formally terminate my relationship to the association without further notice."*[22] President Hussain Malik immediately responded to his letter and cited cost prohibition in hiring him as ED, *"All of us including myself have expressed my gratitude to you for your services to APPNA in a relatively short period of time. We have mutually discussed several times that you are too expensive for APPNA at* *the present time, i.e. $96,000 per year for 48 weeks working 2 days a week or $240,000 working 5 days a week.*"[23]

In all fairness, most APPNA leaders who were active at that time would agree that Mr. Thompson's appointment was the right decision at the wrong time. APPNA had encountered the worst "infighting" due to mistrust among the leadership. The salary for hiring a qualified and experienced ED had been an issue in APPNA. It was suggested at the time of hiring the ED in the fall of 2004 that annual membership dues could be increased to $250 to meet the administrative expenses and payroll. However, decision on its implementation was tabled.[24] Nevertheless, the process-based management of any organization would pay for its hired executives to successfully run operations.[25]

President Rashid Piracha (WV) took over the office of APPNA president in 2006 and hired Tariq Cheema as APPNA's ED. Dr. Cheema was a non-licensed physician who earned his medical degree from Turkey. He was the Executive Director of a non-profit organization, Doctors Worldwide, prior to joining APPNA. His hiring resulted in decreased reliance on the OMC for oversight of APPNA offices. APPNA Presidents mostly relied on his supervision of 2 fulltime and 2 part-time staff members. His services were instrumental during the APPNA's involvement in earthquake related rehabilitation activities in Northern Pakistan (2005–2007) and in Baluchistan earthquake in 2008. It goes to Dr. Cheema's credit that he hired Sidra Tul Muntaha in 2007. Sidra, a pharmacist by training played an important role in helping with membership and meeting services. Moreover, her much needed assistance with ACCME related documentation was commendable. Dr. Tariq Cheema is also credited for re-writing all the Standard Policy and Procedure documents, Operating Agreements, and numerous Memoranda of Understanding with affiliate organizations under the leadership of President Nadeem Kazi in 2007. The ED also had to put in a lot of time and efforts during the two law suits in which organization was involved (Munir vs. APPNA in 2006–2007, and DBN vs. APPNA in 2009). Dr. Tariq Cheema was also instrumental in acquiring and renovating the building next to APPNA office (2007–2008) and in establishing the Free Clinic in the new building.

Dr. Cheema definitely brought a discipline in APPNA office which led to improved performance with his administrative role. However, his role as executive director and the salary of $80,000 at start and $95,000 at his departure (albeit without fringe benefits or any over time) for that position was always debated in the EC meetings. Dr. Cheema who always worked very closely with the sitting president and did submit to wishes of the presidents in carrying out the work that at times was not approved either by the EC or the Council. On the other hand, he did not have any protection as the whistle blower that an ideal organization would offer. In 2010, President Zeelaf Munir had appointed an ad hoc committee to evaluate the job of ED and its role in APPNA management. Dr. Tariq Cheema's input was also sought. However, Dr. Cheema chose to resign even before the recommendations of the committee were presented to EC.[26]

The reaffirmed Role of OMC in 2010 and beyond:

The departure of Tariq Cheema in 2010 reaffirmed the need for the role of OMC especially for proactive oversight. President Zeelaf Munir (DE) appointed Dr. Mushtaq Sherif (IL) as the chair of OMC who could fulfill that role due to his long standing experience with APPNA office management. The next year in 2011, another stalwart of APPNA from Chicago, Dr. Imtiaz Arain was appointed as the Chair of OMC by President Manzoor Tariq. By this time, the organization had learnt that an executive director is not a silver bullet that would address the long wish list of requests that the organization could afford to have financially or otherwise. The organizational culture at APPNA remains president-dominated and will not change until a concerted effort is made to improve a rule-abiding governance.[27] Meanwhile, it was felt that we need an effective executive who could organize the work at APPNA office as an administrator rather than hiring an ED. This idea brought in Ms. Jennifer Wosniak, J.D., who was hired as APPNA administrator on June 18, 2011. Ms. Wosniak's hiring was the beginning of a complete revamping of APPNA secretariat with qualified staff that could provide the proper assistance our membership deserved.[28]

A Quiet Revolution Comes to APPNA Office 2011–2012:

APPNA needed a team of dedicated workers with visionary leaders to bring the central office up to the mark with process-based management and this team is worth mentioning. It included: Dr. Imtiaz Arain (Chair 2011) Dr. Arif Agha (Chair 2012), Dr. Mansoor Alam (Chair 2013, 2015 and 2016), Dr. Javed Imam, Dr. Aftab Khan (Chair 2014), Dr. M. Sohail Khan, Dr. Sajid Mehmood, Dr. Aisha Zafar, and Dr. M. Ishaq Memon.

It took more than two years of dedicated work by this team to change the work ethics by hiring qualified staff. The electronic and physical transformation of the APPNA office that paved the way for an organized APPNA secretariat was then carried out. This history would be incomplete without mention of its salient features:

- Jennifer Wozniak had the full support of President Manzoor Tariq and President Elect Saima Zafar, Chair OMC Imtiaz Arain, and other members to take helm of the affairs as administrator in 2011. It led to reassignment of duties with job description.
- Dr. Arif Agha had a new vision for office with two primary goals for 2012. Making APPNA office paperless and redesign the entire office to corporate standards.[29]
- **Qualified Staff:** The OMC of 2012, in a major culture changing move, let the three members of old staff go (2 with only high school level education) and replaced them with the new, highly educated staff with JD (Jennifer Wozniak), MBA (Nicholas Suh) and BBA qualifications with less payroll expense to APPNA. Moreover, non-certified overpaid accountant was replaced with licensed CPA. A new external audit firm was also retained at 40% lesser cost. Karolina Strack was hired as administrative assistant in 2015 and has been a valuable addition to the staff.
- **APPNA goes Green:**[30] Working with Hasan Tariq of IQVIS Technologies, Dr. Arif Agha developed e-APPNA. It was the most salient feature of central office revolution. APPNA virtually became paperless using the web based technology. The self-service members' portal extended numerous membership friendly options from membership renewals to signing up for meetings and making donations via secure PayPal option. Database driven management is the key to online event registration by members since nearly 50% of APPNA activities revolve around domestic or international meetings. CME related activity had significant enhancement for the participants and speakers alike. CME programs were placed online with the facility to obtain instant CME certificates. ACCME related documentation was made effective to improve compliance. The key inclusion to the staff for this service was Nicholas Suh by Dr. Agha and his team. Mr. Suh had an MBA degree, had worked with IBM and in the field of technol-

ogy for many years. He took over the newly developed e-APPNA and advanced it further.

- **Office and Clinic Renovation:**[31] At the 2012 Spring Meeting in Las Vegas, Dr. Agha presented the need to remodel APPNA central office and the Clinic. The council overwhelmingly approved the renovation budget contingent upon proceeds from the Summer 2012 Meeting. The remodeling work started in December of 2012. Dr. Agha led the renovation project beyond his term till it was completed. APPNA's new office is equipped with corporate style reception area, state-of-the-art conference room, and technological facilities to web stream meetings. High-tech audio-visual equipment allows the facility to video-conferencing between the EC and APPNA staff. A small executive kitchenette adds form to function. The clinic is renovated to match any private medical office. The Clinic renovation made it ADA compliant facility with addition of two, gender specific handicap accessible rest rooms.

This major overhaul at the APPNA Offices in Chicago was completed in April of 2013. Its impact on organizational health, productivity, and outlook could only be appreciated if someone had thoroughly known APPNA as an organization and visited the APPNA office before and after the renovations were completed. This being said, it is not buildings that make institutions. It is the positive attitude and behavior of the staff and organizers that build institutions. The institution-building at the APPNA office has indeed transformed the way new APPNA has emerged over the last few years. An article by the mastermind behind this transformation, Dr. Arif Agha (IL), titled "Reflections on New APPNA" is available online and is a historically relevant read for those who may be interested.[32]

Fiscal Discipline and Regulatory Compliance: Mr. Zahir Qazmi (IL) served as a part time accountant for the organization from 1992 to 2006. APPNA had issues of compliance with regulatory government requirement as a Tax-exempt organization. In 2006, an in-house accountant was hired for book keeping, tracking the financial reports from the component societies, and for preparation of financial statements.

The Social Welfare and Disaster Relief committee of APPNA adopted a more proactive role during the period from 2005–2015 (see chapter titled,

Giving back to Community). Obviously, these commitments required enhanced secretarial support that needed substantial amount in over-time payments to the staff. In 2006, a proposal by the secretary, Mahmood Alam (NJ), was approved at the Spring Council Meeting. He proposed to with-hold 5% of all funds collected for any disaster relief to offset the admin-istrative cost at APPNA office.[33] Dr. Alam said that 5% will be the only overhead for charitable donations. He argued, "it is far less than any other ethnic non-profit organizations spend on administrative cost, which is typ-ically 10%–15%." The motion was approved.[34] As the work load at APPNA office grew, the administrative overhead could not be supported by the membership dues alone. To that effect, President 2012, Dr. Saima Zafar proposed to collect credit card transaction fee from the members instead of organization absorbing the cost. The decision made by the EC added another $30–40,000 in revenues each year for the organization. APPNA International Meetings have also been contributing to revenue generation for office overhead expenses. The average profit from each international trip is about $20,000 after all the expenses are met.[35] APPNA is now having 2–3 international trips a year. The summer meetings are also consistently making profits in the last several years. However, that profit often helps to offset the losses at other meetings specially the winter meetings in Pakistan. On the other hand, intermittent reduction in annual membership dues has always resulted in decrease in revenues that are very much needed to meet the increasing cost of office management in APPNA.

ACCME Accreditation and its Sustenance:

Accreditation Council for Continuing Medical Education (ACCME) granted APPNA accreditation in 2001 after a three-year-long effort.[36] The ACCME accreditation stipulates timely documentation for CME related activity. This additional work not only required assistance of a qualified per-sonnel; it also put an extra strain on already limited capacity of office staff to handle the workload. In the initial years after accreditation was achieved, Dr. Shabbir Safdar (MO), hired a local administrative secretary, Helen Allen, to take care of the CME work in St. Louis, MO. This arrangement could work only as long as Dr. Safdar was the RESA chair. The focus and priorities in APPNA change every year with the change of guard. This kind of arrangement was also sought by Dr. Raza Dilawari (TN) who chaired RESA for several years. Sidra Tul Muntaha worked as part-time CME coordinator and kept the ball rolling. The task of filing proper documentation remained an uphill and complicated task for the association. APPNA is not *per se* a typical medical organization. APPNA is an organization of ethnic medical professionals whose focus is also on social/charitable work and standing against the political and social forces that would discriminate against international physicians.[37] Moreover, APPNA is unique in the way that CME programs are carried out at numerous national and international locations throughout the year remote from the central office. This complexity of providing CME according to the standard set by ACCME requires much efficient and dedicated staffing, which APPNA always struggled to provide. The review of RESA chairs reports over the past several years reveals that the lack of proper management and secretarial assistance had always been their concern despite offering CME programs that were consistently rated good by the attendees. APPNA's CME program was put under probation by ACCME in 2007 and in 2011 that APPNA managed to survive. It was reported in the 2016 Spring Meeting that APPNA lost its accreditation by ACCME in December 2015 and a decision to re-apply was made.[38] It was also debated in the meeting that if the work ethics of APPNA for proper CME documentation remains an issue over the years then it may be better to outsource this activity as APPNA did successfully in the past before the accreditation was granted by ACCME in 2001.

APPNA Meetings:

APPNA meetings organized by central APPNA have evolved into well-organized mini conventions over the years. The quality of the programs has improved both in contents and presentation. The membership related services in terms of ease of registration, hotel accommodations, provision of ancillary services at the meeting venue, and CME programs are all well-organized and much appreciated. However, other than scientifically evaluating the CME programs as required by ACCME, the organization has lagged behind in conducting the customer satisfaction survey after each meeting. The tradition of APPNA Meeting Chairs presenting their reports to the Council has also been curtailed in the recent years. However, the concern of members about ever increasing cost to APPNA families to attend its summer convention has been brought up in the General Body Meeting.

The overall success of the meetings is the product of the untiring volunteer work of the local host committees along with the hard work of central APPNA staff and leadership that goes without saying. The international meetings are similarly very popular and have successfully maintained the interest of the members who have consistently enjoyed these tours over the years. The one person that could be singled out for his superb performance and professionalism is APPNA's Event Manager, Mr. Tipu Ahmad. Tipu has always delivered working with each new leadership year after year. The preassigned seats at the banquets that started in 2009 is one of the many disciplines that Tipu has helped to achieve.

The Growth and Retention of Membership in APPNA:

There are perhaps more than 15,000 Pakistani-descent physicians in North America. Roughly, ½ of them are in APPNA database. Active APPNA membership has steadily grown over the years and had reached the 3,500 mark in 2014. This number includes both life-time members and annual dues paying members. Yet, only 25% of Pakistani-descent physicians in North America are active members. These numbers may appear low but are still better than American Association of Physicians of Indian origin (AAPI) as well as the largest American doctor's organization, American Medical Association (AMA). The issue of the best way to increase active membership in APPNA has been an enigma that has no straight answer.[39] How can we make APPNA attractive and relevant to Pakistani-American physicians despite APPNA's three-decade-long hard work to assist young physicians as soon as they arrive in this country? It may just be the general apathy of physicians towards joining any professional organization. The answer lies in the priorities one would establish. Most physicians join their specialty professional organizations while paying annual dues in the range of $500–$850. It is debated that paying dues should not be prohibitive for those potential members that find APPNA to be a representative organization and is relevant to Pakistani-American physicians. The question of relevancy is even more complex for the second generation US born-and-raised Pakistani-descent physicians and it remains one of the challenges that APPNA faces today.

In the last 10 years (2006–2015), special efforts were made by the leadership to attract more active members into the association by decreasing membership dues. This trend was started by Dr. AR Piracha in 2006. Dr. Manzoor Tariq in 2011 and Dr. Javed Suleman in 2013 followed the trend. Although membership increased in 2006 and 2011, it is hard to prove that it was exclusively due to the decrease in membership fee from $125 to $100. There was a definite increase in membership due to a sweeping 40% reduction in dues in 2013. This decision resulted in annual membership at $75. Accordingly, potential members could become lifetime-members by paying only $1,150. This sale for life-time membership brought in a large number of physicians. There has been a definite decrease in annual membership due to large influx of life-time members in 2013 from the potential members' pool. Moreover, a two-year membership requirement for voting members approved in 2014 has also decreased the number of annual members made at the time of elections. The statistics have shown that before 2013, on average APPNA had about 1200 Life-time members and over 1700 annual members. In 2015, there were about 2,000 Life-time members and about 1200 annual members. The decisions to cut the membership dues and two-year requirement for voting members have cost the organization a decrease in annual revenue of about $60,000.[40] The proponent of membership dues reduction argue that strength lies in numbers. They argue that reduction in dues brings in more members whose participation in the organization would generate the revenues for this predominantly charitable organization. The critics of dues reduction, on the other hand, find it counterintuitive to the growth of organization. They argue that we pay far more in membership dues to our professional organizations—why not to APPNA? The proponents of membership dues increase in APPNA advocate that organizational capacity to maintain the payroll, let alone the hiring of new staff to run the organization, is not possible with the present fee schedule. Hence, the hiring of a qualified executive director remains elusive.

APPNA's Role in Organized Medicine:

Dr. Busharat Ahmad, recipient of APPNA lifetime achievement award, has always been an advocate of participation in organized medicine. In his own words he expressed: *"I began the fight, first on the county level, in Marquette, then later at the national level with the help of organized medicine. I found this to be the most effective means to fight the discrimination against IMG's (International Medical Graduates). I established special IMG sections in the Michigan State Medical Society (MSMS). Medical societies in other states established similar IMG sections. In the American Medical Association (AMA), with the help of other state medical societies, state and national legislatures, regulatory agencies and the US Congress.*" When Dr. Syed Nadeem Ahsan asked him about his most gratifying experience during an interview, Dr. Ahmad replied, "Winning the battle for equality for International Medical Graduates."[41] Numerous other APPNA members have also been involved in State Medical Societies. Dr. Abdur Rehman (NY), Dr. Waheed Akbar and (late) Dr. Raana Akbar (MI), Dr. Arif Muslim (NY), Dr. Mushtaq Sheikh (NY), Dr. Hamayun Chaudhry (NY), Dr. Omar Atiq, (AR), Dr. Ayaz Samdani (WI), and Dr. Muhammad Suleman (LA) are the few known to the author.

APPNA became a provisional member of Specialty and Service Society (SSS) of the AMA in 2003 during the presidency of Dr. Raana Akbar, who had always wished that APPNA could also be seated in the AMA House of Delegates (HOD).[42] The AMA requires that 33% of active members of any medical organization need to be the members of AMA to have a representation in HOD. This is a percentage that APPNA could never achieve. Nevertheless, Dr. Waheed Akbar represented APPNA in the SSS of AMA in 2003 and subsequently for several years. As he reflected in an APPNA Journal: "*Every time (I attend SSS at AMA), two things catch my attention. The first is the relative lack of the IMG presence, especially Pakistani-American, in organized medicine. The second, which I find impressive, is the hard and diligent work of AMA delegates for bringing the concerns of practicing physician to the leadership of organized medicine, and finding ways to resolve them.*"[43] Dr. Waheed Akbar also reported AMA resolution number 236, which was introduced in 2005 by the IMG section and was adopted by the HOD for expeditious security clearance and visa processing of IMG physicians, particularly from Pakistan. The AMA bills H-255.971 and D-255.993 were also passed in support of the Conrad-30 program that authorizes J-1 visa waivers for IMG's.[44]

The Turmoil of 2005: Power of a Picture

In 2005, a group of 250 APPNA physicians along with their families went for a trip to India from March 7–17, 2005. The main objective of the trip besides visiting historical places was, as President Hussain Malik put it—APPNA Building Bridges People to People to promote goodwill among the people of both countries.[45] The organizing committee included Dr. Shaukat Khan (PA) as Chair, and Dr. Rizwan Naeem (TX) and Dr. Nisar Chaudhry (MD) were Co-Chairs. Dr. Chaudhry, was instrumental in obtaining Indian visas for Pakistani-descent physicians with American Passports. Dr. Naeem facilitated a memorable trip through a relative, Dr. Najma Heptullah, who was a member of Indian Parliament at that time. Dr. Naeem is also credited for organizing a great CME program. The trip was rated excellent by its participants.

After the trip was over, a controversy surfaced about giving plaques to Indian politicians from APPNA platform. It started with a picture posted by M. Shahid Yusuf (MI), in which Mr. Advani was being awarded a plaque by APPNA. APPNA related group e-lists were flooded with expression of free speech by dissenting members. These members vehemently expressed their disapproval of giving a plaque of recognition to Indian politician, Mr. LK Advani. Mr. Advani had been accused of masterminding the demolition of historic Babari Mosque in Ayodhya (Faizabad) India, in 1992. Hundreds of Muslims were killed during the riots which ensued.[46] In the midst of mounting campaign against him, President Malik apologized and accepted full responsibility of this "mistake" in a letter he wrote to the membership.[47]

The Debacle at the Spring Council Meeting, April 30–May 1, 2005:

By the time of Spring Council Meeting in 2005, criticism against the India trip grew. Besides incensed issue of giving plaque to Mr. Advani, Dr. Hussain Malik's decision to adopt two villages in India by APPNA where APPNA *Sehat* style basic healthcare and education would be offered at a cost of $40,000 came under intense scrutiny. The critics of this presidential decision argued that president had no authority to spend more than $10,000 without approval from BOT unless project is budgeted and approved by the Council.

In the Spring Council Meeting, some of the council members demanded that the President-Elect should preside over the meeting during the hearing of complaints against president Malik. Dr. Malik's appointed parliamentarian had to step down under intense pressure. The scuffling on the India issue resulted in the abrupt ending of the meeting when three out of five officers walked out in protest, leading to an impasse. The meeting was reconvened with the intervention of BOT chair Jafar Shah (IL) and secretary Shabbir Safdar (MO). The Council eventually passed a resolution noting that any financial spending decisions by the president in future would require approval by the Council. Dr. Malik was also advised to follow the bylaws that require the president to manage day-to-day affairs of the Association in consultation with the Executive Committee (EC).

Meanwhile, another issue surfaced on the conduct of the president in May, 2005. It was found out that the President Malik has also signed an open ended entertainment contract with Digital Broadcast Network (DBN). This contract gave DBN the exclusive right to provide entertainment for APPNA banquets with the right of first refusal if APPNA decided to contract with any other vendor for that purpose. The contract also allowed DBN to videotape all APPNA events and could air them on the ARY television network. The signing of this contract by the president without approval for the EC was another issue that did not follow the due process and led to filling of another complaint to E&GC by a group of APPNA members who felt presidential decisions were detrimental to the organization.

Ethics & Grievance Committee (E&GC) takes Action:

The issues noted above resulted in complaints filed against the president to the Ethics and Grievance Committee (E&GC) and BOT after the spring Council Meeting was over.[48]

The E&GC investigated the matter and its chair Dr. Busharat Ahmad (MI) presented the report at a special Council Meeting held at the summer convention on July 1, 2005. The E&GC reprimanded Dr. Malik for overstepping his authority as president in making decisions pertaining to India trip without consulting the executive committee. There was a demand for his resignation in the Council. In response to E&GC report, Dr. Malik apologized for his mistakes and offered to pay from his own pocket the money he had promised for adoption of villages in India. He said, "I have made some unpopular decisions, which I felt would enhance APPNA's image in promoting people to people theme between India and Pakistan. However, I would not resign from presidency under political pressure of my opponents." Eventually, a motion was passed to take this matter to general body (GB) meeting for further discussion and action.

General Body Meeting 2005:

There was an emotionally charged atmosphere in the 2005 GB meeting and discussion ensued after the quorum was established. The GB appointed

Dr. Khalid Riaz (IL) as parliamentarian. A motion for the removal of Dr. Malik as president was passed by a majority vote.[49] It was not entertained by Dr. Riaz, who cited that provision of removal of an APPNA officer does not exist in the Constitution and Bylaws of APPNA. Besides harsh criticism by opponents in GB, Dr. Malik also had his supporters that vouched for his sincerity with the organization. Among them, Dr. Shaukat Khan, pleaded mercy and respect for the president. He defended Dr. Malik and told the GB that plaques were made in India by one of the local organizers with inscription of thanks to the Indian leaders for their hospitality, nothing else.[50]

Eventually, a motion was carried to approve the following recommendations of E&GC.[51]

Dr. Hussain Malik was reprimanded and was requested to resign. The following conditions were imposed on him if he chooses to continue as president.

- Dr. Malik should pledge to seek approval from the council for his future actions. This should be monitored closely by the Board of Trustees.
- Dr. Malik should be required to submit full disclosure of all events surrounding the trip to India to the Board of Trustees.

The E&GC also made recommendations to making new rules by the Association in order to recall an officer in future who does not follow the policy and procedures of APPNA.

- Board of Trustees should be granted additional power to intervene if a member or officer is engaged in the acts of utterances which violates APPNA's Constitution or are contrary to the collective will of the Executive Council or General Body. These powers may include temporary suspension of rights and privileges of such an officer or member.
- Remedies against non-compliance; if a member or officer fails to abide by the requirements imposed by the Council, Board of Trustees or General Body, the sanctions could include; censor, suspension and/or dismissal of the rights of the officer or even APPNA membership.
- Since there is no clause for impeachment or removal of an officer in the APPNA Constitution and Bylaws, the Board of Trustees should ask the APPNA Committee on Constitution and Bylaws

to come up with an amendment to include those actions.

Moving Forward with Harmony and Unity of Purpose:

The events of the first half of the year in 2005 were unprecedented and were quite traumatic for the organization especially for President Hussain Malik. The first indication of restoration of harmony among the officers while BOT investigating the issues pertaining to India trip and DBN contract, was the letter from BOT Chair M. Jafar Shah (IL) to the Council members on August 30, 2005.[52] The trustees expressed their satisfaction on the cooperation they received from Dr. Malik. The board also unequivocally indicated that Dr. Malik remains the president of the organization until the end of his term. The board concluded, "Matters related to India trip involve plaques, village sponsorship and full disclosure by the president. Dr. Hussain Malik has complied by making full disclosures as to who arranged the trip, who was involved, who traveled to India either at subsidized rate or on complimentary basis. Dr. Shah reported, "to the satisfaction of the BOT, the president has answered these questions and as it is known, he has apologized and taken full responsibility." Dr. Malik will personally raise funds in order to fulfill the monetary obligations to the promised adoption of villages in India. The board also recognized the complexities involved in regards to APPNA contract with Digital Broadcast Network (DBN) and recommended to end the contract through negotiations as soon as possible.[53]

In the subsequent months during his presidency, Dr. Malik conducted himself in compliance with BOT directives and followed the organizational rules of making decisions in consultation with EC. Furthermore, he kept his promise and deposited $24,000 from his own pocket to sponsor a village in India before his presidency ended. The idea of starting basic healthcare model in an Indian village came to an end when it was realized that no local support is available to carry out such a project. The part of Dr. Malik's donation ($11,000) was eventually given to Federation of Aligarh Alumni Association (FAAA). The FAAA was active in Uttar Pradesh for polio eradication at that time. Hussain Malik's dream for helping the poor across the border came true when Polio was eradicated in India for which he had made a personal contribution. Dr. Malik felt vindicated when APPNA was given President Zakir Hussain Community Recognition Award for its contribution to help eradicate polio in India at the annual convention of FAAA in August 2008.[54]

APPNA Foundation:

Dr. Hussain Malik presented the initial concept of APPNA charitable foundation at the January 29 planning meeting of the Council in 2005. The Bylaws of the foundation were also approved. Dr. Malik envisioned, "it (the foundation) will be an umbrella organization for all APPNA Charitable projects like APPNA Sehat, Free Clinics, and Educational Scholarships."[55] A fundraiser for this nascent foundation was also held on July 4 at the Houston meeting. Dr. Ahmed Sayeed led the effort along with other members of host committee and raised about $70,000.[56] Unfortunately, further progress on the foundation could not be made in the organization during 2006–2007.

In 2008, President Mahmood Alam made an effort to revive the foundation and urged its founder Dr. Hussain Malik to present it for approval in the 2008 Spring Council Meeting. It turned out that the APPNA Council was not ready to take the concept of this foundation to next level and the item was tabled for further discussion in future. The critics of APPNA Charitable Foundation had expressed two major concerns. Firstly, they asked, why create a new charitable organization for fundraising for APPNA projects when APPNA itself enjoys 501c3 status? Instead, an endowment fund could be created within APPNA to fund charitable causes, the critics suggested. Secondly, some members feared that the pursuit of leadership of such foundation within APPNA may be divisive and counterproductive.[57]

In 2014, there was a renewed interest in launching the APPNA Foundation. President Asif Rehman appointed Naseem Sheikhani (MO) to chair a three-member committee on establishing the foundation that included Nasir Gondal (NY) and Ahsan Rasheed (CA). The vision for creating an endowment fund for APPNA was invigorated. APPNA Foundation was registered in April and received approval for 501c3 status from the IRS in September 2014. The foundation aims to support charitable and humanitarian projects, promote literacy, and to promote health education through APPNA sponsored programs through a structured and dedicated organization that is committed to raising funds for the Pakistani-American diaspora.

The foundation faced two setbacks in 2015. Firstly, Naseem Sheikhani resigned as its Executive Director to pursue his bid for APPNA presidency. Secondly, a new concept of charitable fundraising was introduced as the "Qatra Fund" led by Mahjabeen Islam (OH). Dr. Islam proposed that small monthly donations in the range of $50–$100 would be more appealing to the thousands of Pakistani-American physicians that could raise substantial amount to support projects under SWDR committee and other philanthropic ventures. The APPNA Foundation's supporters perceived introduction of "Qatra Fund" as an impediment to their efforts of fundraising through the foundation that was activated just a year ago. President Mubasher Rana defended his position by arguing that APPNA Foundation is an endowment for long term investment for charitable work. Whereas, with the Qatra Fund—Qatra, small drops of water could make an ocean, and is a concept based on small recurrent donations that could cumulate into huge fund. Only time will tell how these two excellent ideas for fundraising running parallel would fair at the charitable market place in APPNA.

APPNA and Pakistan Politics:

The presence of politicians from Pakistan at APPNA meetings has always generated intense debate among APPNA members. Some of them profess to be aligned and would not hesitate to boo a political leader that does not belong to the party of their liking. Therefore, the trend to honor Pakistani politicians at the annual banquets has declined in recent years and no politician from Pakistan has been invited at APPNA banquet since 2009.

Nevertheless, what happens in Pakistan affects Pakistani-Americans emotionally or otherwise. The summer APPNA convention is one such occasion where Pakistani politicians as well as those involved in the advocacy for social justice are generally welcomed and attracts large crowds. These gatherings are either organized by alumni associations or other non-APPNA organizations led by APPNA members.

The summer convention in 2008 at Washington DC attracted many Pakistani politicians. There was a popular uprising against General Musharraf's government by the lawyers' movement spearheaded by the deposed Chief Justice, M. Iftikhar Chaudhary. The Association of Pakistani Physicians for Justice and Democracy (APPJD), and Doctors for Democracy (DFD)—a New York based group, both comprised of

APPNA members, organized an event during the convention, which was well-attended. The ambassador of Pakistan to the US was also invited in addition to the representatives of major political parties. Honorable Wajih Uddin, the supreme court justice of Pakistan, was one of the guest speakers at the gathering. In the event Mr. Ambassador was booed by a physician during his speech. Ambassador Haqani felt humiliated. This unfortunate incidence was exploited by numerous Urdu newspapers in which APPNA was labelled as aligned with anti-Musharraf movement.

APPNA-Affliated Organizations

As the organization was growing in early 1990s and onwards, the need for an organized inclusion of the APPNA family grew at a rapid pace. The social and youth fora were added to organize women and children of APPNA members.[58] These fora were later on replaced with three major groups, APPNA Alliance, SAYA, and CAPPNA. APPNA Alliance emerged as the affiliate organization of the spouses of APPNA members that has been dominated by women leaders. Subsequent to the creation of APPNA Alliance, the social forum continued to serve as the platform for the singles of APPNA family. Its activity was initially limited to the Annual APPNA meeting where singles were provided an opportunity to socialize and probably look for their potential future partners. The social forum's activities were taken over by Young Professionals Network (YPN) in 2008. YPN was organized by Naheed Arshad, an APPNA Alliance member from Wisconsin, whose focus was entirely on bringing the young professionals together for finding their life partners from a common heritage. This program has been very successful and expanded over the years.

Initially, the Children of Association of Pakistani Physicians of North America (CAPPNA) was formed to organize the children of APPNA under one banner and the Youth Advisory Committee was formed to oversee and to advise on the activities of this group.[59] Soon it was realized that all youth does not fit into one group. The Society of Young Adults (SAYA) was then created to have youth between the ages of 18–28 in one group and CAPPNA's membership was then limited to the age group of 12–17, a group that always needed adult supervision and guidance. Similarly, physicians-in-training were placed under one umbrella and membership to this future group of physicians has been limited to newly arriving Pakistani physicians enrolled in residency training programs. Another group, the

North American Medical Alumni (NAMA), was created for graduates of North American schools who were of Pakistani heritage.[60]

APPNA Alliance

APPNA Alliance has emerged as the most visible affiliate organization of APPNA. Alliance has been provided with an assigned night at the APPNA summer meetings since its inception. Alliance holds its annual dinner on Thursday nights—a highly celebrated family dinner night—where everyone, young or old is invited. This program showcases the activities of this energetic group of women whose aspiration to focus on APPNA as a family is highly appreciated. Alliance has contributed a lot in the philanthropic endeavors of APPNA and its affiliated organizations. One of the consistent beneficiaries of Alliance is the Human Development Foundation (HDF), which started with sponsorship of a Community Health Center at Lahore by HDF. Alliance president in 2005, Bushra Sheikh (NY) was instrumental in this collaboration.[61] The Alliance also passionately supported the earthquake related APPNA work, which was spearheaded by Alliance president Sajida Arain (IL) in 2006.[62] Alliance president, Hamida Tariq (MO) in 2007 further promoted the philanthropy and raised funds for the projects like HDF and APPNA Sehat. Mrs. Hamida Tariq also strengthened the financials of Alliance by raising substantial funds and making lifetime members.

In 2008, Alliance president Mrs. Mehreen Atiq (AR) proposed to streamline activities by adopting new policy and procedures in order to strengthen APPNA Alliance at the grassroots level. She also arranged extensive Alliance programming for the Summer Convention in 2008. It included seminars on domestic violence, business and entrepreneurship, and family life in Islam, besides having a great entertaining family night banquet featuring the famous Pakistani orator, Zia Mohiuddin.[63] Alliance also continued the tradition of giving to the charities by donating $20,000 in 2008. Next year, in 2009, president Rukhsana Mahmood (TX) advanced the progress by emphasizing philanthropy and family in APPNA.

Mrs. Samrina Haseeb assumed the role of Alliance president twice, in 2010 and 2014, respectively. In 2010, she produced the first Alliance magazine, "Jewel Notes" to highlight alliance activities. Samrina was also instrumental in organizing a fundraiser for HDF in St. Louis (MO) on March 28, 2010 and helped raise $130,000 for an HDF project in Pakistan. The theme for the 2010 Summer Alliance meeting was "Restoring the Hope, Empowering the Women." The meeting's main focus was women's health awareness with particular attention to the remote areas of Pakistan. The keynote speaker, Faryal Gohar, an internationally known women's rights activist, presented the plight of women's health in Pakistan.

Rania Asif (AZ) was the Alliance president in 2011. She said, "Alliance is a social organization with a purpose. This year we are trying to raise awareness on women's health issues."[64] In 2012, Fatima Elahi (TX) moved the agenda of APPNA Family forward. In 2013, Alliance had another dynamic president, Hajra Shani Kazi (AZ). The theme of alliance that year was, "Think globally, Act locally." Her focus was on the children being raised as second generation Pakistani-Americans. As she said in her message as Alliance president, "I compare my children with my own childhood and ask, myself, who has it better? My children who live in a world where the words Muslim, Pakistan, and Islam are a household name coined to terrorism or the childhood where I was the unknown in the US? She then answered the question herself, "actually both worlds of these two generations were good and bad. It's all about what we do with any given situation. We can't change the past but we can change what is going on today for our children."[65]

In 2014, the theme for Alliance was "Lighting the Way for Future Generations" according to Samrina Haseeb in a report she submitted specially for *APPNA Qissa*. The focus was the underprivileged children and orphans in Pakistan. The keynote speaker was Alex Kronemer, the CEO of Unity Production Foundation. The father-son team of Babar Suleman and 17-year-old Haris Suleman was highlighted for their adventurous spirits and commitment to education of children in Pakistan. "They left for a journey around the world in 30 days to promote the cause for education in a single engine plane from Plainfield, Indiana, USA. They were raising funds for The Citizens Foundation Schools. On the final leg of their journey their plane crashed in the Pacific Ocean! May Allah bless their souls and reward them for their endeavor to help others," stated Mrs. Haseeb in her report. The Alliance President was Jabeen Bukhari (MI) in 2015, who continued the mission of the Alliance in letter and spirit and relayed the torch to Farah Haider to lead in 2016.

SAYA and CAPPNA

The activities of SAYA and CAPPNA are usually linked to the APPNA Summer Convention. These youth groups go back to their routine life after having fun with other young people of Pakistani-descent from similar family backgrounds. Both organizations are usually assisted by the host committee as well as the sitting president to have programming of their liking. The review of the published reports about SAYA in APPNA news-letters over the years gives some insight to their thought process. They are proud Americans of Pakistani-descent and are always eager to help those who are less fortunate and needy. They try to develop their own world at APPNA meeting to have good time and socialize. Besides their own programs, they can usually be found in the hallways and other areas outside of APPNA banquet programs where they find a sense of camaraderie among each other.

SAYA Volunteers

One of the striking features of the youth program at APPNA summer meetings is the "Debate Program" that has been organized by longtime APPNA stalwart, Dr. Salim Afridi (FL). It started in 2003 at Orlando (FL) meeting. The topic was "Islam's survival is in its Liberal Revival" and pro and con arguments were sought from the debaters. Similarly, debates were also held in subsequent years with fascinating topics. Some examples are "Do you think Death Penalty should be implemented as a form of punishment?" (2004); "The current Islamic Institutions have failed the American Muslims" (2007); "Should the future of Pakistan be of concern to Pakistan-American youth?" (2008); "Is Internet a blessing or a curse?" (2013); and "Should there be limits to Freedom of Expression?" (2015). The winners receive cash prizes. The judges use a scoring system based on speaker's appropriateness on attire, time, content, and delivery of speech.

WAPPNA and APPNA Women and Children Affair Committee

Women Physicians of APPNA (WAPPNA) is an affiliate organization that focuses on women issues especially the plight of women in Pakistan. WAPPNA has partnered with several human rights organizations to raise the awareness about women issues since its inception in 2010. Drs. Humeraa Qamar, Shaheen Mian, Naheed Chaudhry, and Sarwat Iqbal have served WAPPNA in leadership positions. *"Our mission is to empower oppressed and underprivileged women and children in the world by providing resources, education, and training to be self-sufficient and contribute to society with honor and live with respect,"* stated Dr. Sarwat Iqbal in a report to APPNA journal.[66]

Women and Children Affaires (Ad hoc) Committee has its lone star leader, Dr. Lubna Naeem, who has been passionately advocating for women and children's health in APPNA since 2013. Her main focus is twofold; Childhood obesity and Breast Cancer Awareness Campaigns. Dr. Naeem has singlehandedly led the educational campaigns to promote healthy eating in children in the schools and elsewhere in the community. She has successfully arranged—Healthy Living Walks—at APPNA summer meetings in 2015 and 2016.

APPNA—NAMA (North American Medical Association) The Rise and Fall of NAMA

Association of Pakistani Physicians of North America (APPNA) adopted its new name, Association of Physicians of Pakistani-descent of North

America (keeping the same acronym) on November 19, 2004, when the revised constitution was ratified by the general membership.[67] This change was a reflection on the mind set of APPNA leadership to gear it towards a future North American organization that is embraced by our second generation that grew up here and graduated from North American medical schools. These young physicians were given a platform in APPNA to network under NAMA in 1997.[68] Most of them were exposed to APPNA as children participating with their parents. After initial enthusiasm, this group's interest in joining and participating with APPNA as its component society has dissipated over time. Unfortunately, NAMA lost its status as one of the component society of APPNA in 2015 after inactivity on the part of NAMA over the past several years.

The lack of NAMA's participation in APPNA is a major concern. In 2015, the Long Range Planning Committee (LRPC) appointed a Task Force to look into the reasons behind the perceived lack of interest by North American physicians. Some members fear that without NAMA, APPNA may not be able to sustain as a relevant organization in North America. Therefore, it was desirable to take action. In order to start a meaningful discussion on the issue in 2015, LRPC decided to first conduct a root cause analysis. A mass email questionnaire was sent to more than three thousand members on March 6, 2015. Answers to the following questions were sought in a straw poll. About forty members cared to respond.[69]

1. Is the current APPNA social culture a misfit environment for second-generation physicians?—Responses: Yes 76%, No 24%

2. Does the diverse group of physicians (NAMA) who have graduated from different medical schools have nothing else in common but heritage?—Responses: Yes 68%, No 32%

3. Would it be better to provide programs of interest to second-generation physicians to work for the community at large under APPNA rather than isolating them in a group?—Responses: Yes 88%, No 12%

4. Does the change in the governance of APPNA that incorporates the second generation and makes it attractive for them to play leadership role would work?—Responses: Yes 80%, No 20%

5. APPNA has no medical student section. Would it be helpful to attract the future physicians by giving them student membership

and involving them in charitable work like Free Medical Clinics and APPNA Medical corps?—Responses: Yes 90%, No 10%.

6. **The Reasons behind the apparent lack of NAMA's interest in APPNA:** In your opinion, what are the three major reasons that led to NAMA's disqualification as a component society of APPNA? In response to this question, more than thirty (30) members chose to express their opinion. A representative narrative of most of the comments is summarized below.

Dr. Attaullah Arain (IL), a senior member of APPNA said, "It is important for them (NAMA) to remain connected to their roots. APPNA is a good way to connect with their land of origin, and they should recommend ways how APPNA could serve them better." Dr. Ahmad Saeed Khan (AZ), another senior physician felt, "these are very different people who grew up in different culture and they think differently than their parents. Their interest is very different too. They may not find a fulfilling experience in current APPNA." Dr. Rashid Hanif, (MD) said, "APPNA is seen as a social organization with its focus in issues related to Pakistan only. That limits the options for these physicians. (Also) The way 'uncles' run organization is probably another reason for their lack of interest."

Dr. Humayun Chaudhry, DO (NY), an academic physician and the President of Federation of State Medical Boards shared the following, "Second-generation physicians need to be shown value for their membership and participation. They will typically not join for the sake of joining or networking. APPNA needs to demonstrate added value beyond CME (which they can get anywhere, including online) and entertainment programs (which they can attend on their own). The second-generation physicians also do not see value in many of the vendors in the exhibit hall, who offer clothing and jewelry that can be obtained elsewhere more affordably. They are (also) turned off by the aggressive and relentless campaigning of physicians seeking higher office, and by the occasional displays of incivility at membership meetings."

Dr. Fatima Hassan (MI) said, "APPNA meetings are the avenues where physicians get together and socialize. Unfortunately, these meetings do not attract AMGs (American graduates). One reason could be lack of structure and focus on socialization only. Another reason is lack of marketing of

APPNA activities catering to local communities as well as charitable activities across the world......"

Dr. Mona Karim insightfully expressed, "I was active in NAMA in late 90s/early 2000s while in medical school and training. I think there are several reasons it has not been attractive to American graduates. Firstly, most of us don't primarily identify as Pakistani. Those who are more religious are usually heavily involved in ISNA or other Islamic organizations rather than ethnic ones. Those who are more cultural have many friends who are Indian/Bangladeshi etc. and broadly identify as South Asian/desi. Secondly, the culture of APPNA can be very cliquish and gossipy. I only went to APPNA meetings with my parents but on my own, never felt comfortable there...Thirdly, the social events at APPNA are geared toward a native Pakistani audience. Many of us are not familiar with current Pakistani singers or have little use for buying expensive "joras" if we are not attending many Pakistani events. It was fine to go with our parents while we were young and meet some of their friends' children there. But all my friends stopped going once they had jobs and were independent of their parents... Also, APPNA got a reputation as a matchmaking venue, so once many of us were married, it made no sense to attend anymore."

Dr. A Khan commented, "NAMA doctors do not have alumni structure like old Pakistani doctors. They do not know each other like older cohorts from various med schools in Pakistan.

There is no kinship or camaraderie among them. They are just too busy in studies and residencies. They are just like other young Americans, lost and confused and alien to Pakistani crappy culture of poor religious understanding on the part of archaic parents."

Dr. Azhar Majeed (CA), another North American graduate said, "The politics our 'uncles' play is prohibitive. We don't belong to any of the APPNA Pakistani medical alumnus. Many of us young physicians have large student debt and are self-made. We live in large cities. We are not the wealthy APPNA docs of small towns who have nothing better to do than gossip and hear music programs once a year. We are starting our careers and families. We are American Muslims involved in Muslim American fabric of America." Dr. N. Shams, shared, "APPNA is too focused on Pakistan (and) is a social club for first generation Pakistanis." Dr. Farhat Osman (OH) said, "Young North American graduates have many other obligations. Belonging to APPNA is not their priority. APPNA is committed to improving conditions in Pakistan which they cannot relate to. American graduates have huge loans to pay off and this becomes their priority." Dr. Ghazala Kazi (MD) optimistically said, "These young people are busy in establishing their professional and personal lives and don't have time for these activities. They will return." Dr. Zahida Siddiqui, shared, "My children actually love it. I think it must be that they (American graduates) are just starting up in life and don't have time yet."

Re-Engaging NAMA

A straw poll led by the task force on NAMA asked: "What is the most important advice would you give to attract second-generation physicians?" It was the last and 7th question of the Straw Poll that task force on NAMA conducted. The responses were very insightful.

Dr. Erum N Ilyas said, "I have attended APPNA meetings since the early 1980s (parents are Naseem Khan, MD and Khurram Hanif, MD). NAMA seemed to rise and fall in this time period. My husband and I attempted to attend NAMA 4 years ago (2011) and the meeting had been cancelled due to lack of interest. We, of course, still attend APPNA (regardless of NAMA) and look forward to it every year but I think a revitalization of NAMA may be truly possible recognizing that now is the time to attract the attention of the 2nd generation of physicians that are now ready to give back. APPNA sells itself—it is easy to convince our friends to attend now that our children are older and looking for social outlets while we are looking for opportunities to enrich them culturally and academically."

Dr. Fatima Hassan, being one of the North American graduates, offered solutions. "Bring AMGs in leadership positions to attract others and develop trust. Do not separate them out and cut them and leave them on their own. We need to change ourselves. We should not expect them to change and sing Pakistani anthem with us when none of us know a single verse of American anthem. Cut down on show off rich cultural parade at annual meetings and focus on healthy, constructive activities involving all age groups and variety of physicians. I don't mean to say that there should not be any social and cultural activities but these should not be the sole focus of the meeting. I think in coming years there will be less and less number of Pakistani physicians coming to USA. We will need AMGs to keep this name alive."

Dr. Nadeem Kazi (AZ) commented, "APPNA never offered anything which is interesting to the American Pakistani graduates. Start engaging them in a leadership position. They may want local American artist for the annual conventions. Start local program(s) through their alumni (Medical schools) to engage them in local social project(s). Involve them in committees as chair and co-chair." Dr. Ahmad Saeed Khan (AZ) suggested, "Involvement in fulfilling experience (charitable work in USA and Pakistan). Getting them involved in activities, which they may find fulfilling, fun and enjoyable. Giving them opportunities to develop their own projects and programs. Giving them leadership role as much as possible." Dr. Ariba Khan recommended, "they should be involved in activities with APPNA and not isolated as NAMA. they should have a representation in APPNA leadership."

Dr. Mujtaba Qazi (MO), a north American graduate and an established ophthalmologist, who has been contributing to the mainstream APPNA and served as St. Louis (MO) chapter president (besides serving on numerous committees) has valuably suggested: "Automatically include medical students as NAMA members, waiving APPNA /NAMA membership fee. Use Pakistani Student Associations or MSAs in Medical Schools to identify members, using Free Medical Clinics and APPNA Medical Corps as activities to promote for participation." He further shared his feeling that sounds like a speech for his fellow NAMA members, "As first and second-generation physicians of Pakistani heritage, we are seeking a professional organization that will offer opportunities: (1) to expose our children to our Pakistani heritage and culture; (2) for us to provide medical services and expertise to our local community and to Pakistan. With respect to the latter, there are multiple opportunities for service through APPNA, including through the various philanthropic projects organized by APPNA members, by volunteering in the APPNA Medical Corps, and by participating in medical education and training at medical institutions in Pakistan. APPNA provides a professional platform to develop a network, including among sub-specialties, for transfer of skills and technologies. We are only beginning to scratch the surface of these opportunities for: telemedicine, educational seminars in Pakistan, assistance and advocacy for Pakistani medical students seeking research, residency and fellowship positions in North America, development of volunteer positions and programs for Pakistani-American college or medical students, expansion of APPNA free clinics as off-shoots of APPNA local chapters, and the development of second-generation Pakistani-American physicians and professionals who can serve as an interface between the Pakistani-American community and American businesses, professionals, and politicians."

Dr. Mona Karim shared, "The main attraction for the second generation will be the ability to do charity work both locally and in Pakistan. There is a strong desire among the second generation to do good for the poor and unfortunate. I agree you should attract future physicians with student membership and involvement in charity work. Even though I have not attended an APPNA meeting in over 10 years, I have regularly given money towards APPNA's charitable work. This is what will interest the second generation the most." Dr. Azhar Majeed pleaded, "Involve us! Don't treat us as lower than you because we didn't go to KE or Dow. We want to come to Pakistan to visit and volunteer at nonprofit clinics and help."

Dr. Humayun Chaudhry, recommended to the NAMA group to "Get involved and get engaged with APPNA to meet and network with new colleagues of your own background (who also graduated from medical schools in North America) with similar interests. APPNA will need to provide leadership roles for NAMA graduates, who can be given funds and shown appreciation to promote activities that they vote to support."

There were some short and sweet suggestions as well, including the following: "Find a way that the younger generation could claim any sort of ownership for this forum" (Anjum Qureshi); "There is no need for a separate section for young physicians" (Ghazala Kazi); "Involve them in politics and media outreach" (Zahida Siddiqui); "waiving membership charges for few years after graduation and then sliding scale type of dues payable (also) providing them with low interest loans for studies" (Farhat Osman); "No in-fighting, No corruption, and straightforwardness" (Nisar Ahmed); and last but not least, "If we want APPNA to survive, the future is with NAMA" (Dr. Naeem Khan, IL).

End Notes:

1   Inside APPNA: The Maturing of an Organization, *APPNA Qissa*, Literary
    Circle of Toledo, OH, 2004, 57–78.
2   APPNA Newsletter, 12:2, Fall 2002, 1
3   Ibid, 2
4   APPNA Newsletter, 14:1, Spring 2004, 1
5   APPNA Newsletter, 15:1, Spring 2005, 1
6   APPNA Membership Survey, document on file, 2003–2004
7   APPNA Newsletter, 16:1, Spring 2006, 3
8   APPNA Journal, 9:1, Summer 2007, 6
9   APPNA Newsletter, 18:1, Spring 2008, 1
10 APPNA Newsletter, 19:1, Spring 2009, 7
11 APPNA Journal, 12:2, Winter 2010, 5
12 APPNA Journal, 13:1, Summer 2011, 6
13 APPNA Journal, 14:1, Summer 2012, 5
14 APPNA Newsletter electronic version, Spring 2013,
15 Minutes of the Spring Council Meeting, 2014
16 APPNA Newsletter, 25:3, Fall 2015, 3
17 APPNA President's Message, Summer 2016
18 The Maturing of an Organization, *APPNA Qissa*, chapter 4, 70
19 Ibid
20 APPNA Journal, 5:2, Winter 2003, OMC report by Iltifat Alavi
21 APPNA Journal, 6:2, Winter 2004, 12–13
22 Michael Thompson, email letter to APPNA EC, June 18, 2005, copy on file
    in APPNA archives
23 Hussain Malik, response to resignation letter from Mr. Thompson, copy on
    file in APPNA archives
24 Minutes of the special council meeting November 20, 2004, held at Hyatt
    Regency, Rosemont, IL.
25 Quality Management of Building Design (ISBN 978-7506-1225-8), by Tim
    Cornick at the University of Reading.
26 The 2010 recommendations of the Ad-hoc committee on ED and the
    resignation letter of Dr. Tariq Cheema, copies on file in APPNA archives
27 Minutes of the special council meeting November 20, 2004, held at Hyatt
    Regency, Rosemont, IL.
28 APPNA Journal 13:2, Winter 2011, OMC report, 9–10
29 APPNA Journal 14:1, Summer 2012, OMC report, 30–31
30 APPNA Fall Meeting Journal, October, 19–21, 2012, 9
31 APPNA Journal, 14:2, Winter 2012, OMC report, 9
32 APPNA Summer Meeting Journal, 2013, 48, 49
33 APPNA Newsletter, 16:1, Spring 2006, treasurer's report, 6.
34 Minutes of Spring Council Meeting, April 6–7, 2006
35 Tipu Ahmad, international meeting organizer, personal communication
36 The Maturing of an Organization, *APPNA Qissa*, chapter 4, 71
37 Roadmap to future, Executive Summary by Michael G. Thompson, Ph.D.,
    2004
38 The Minutes of APPNA Spring council meeting, May 7, 2016

39   The future of APPNA by Tanveer Imam, APPNA Newsletter, January 2012, 1

40   The annual financial analysis (2015) by Dr. Mubasher Rana, personal communication

41   APPNA Journal, 12:2, Winter 2010, A profile in Dedication, Dr. Basharat Ahmad, Interview by Nadeem Ahsan, 29

42   APPNAN Journal 5:2, Winter 2003, 22–23.

43   APPNA Journal, 8:1, Summer 2006, 27–29.

44   IBID

45   APPNA Newsletter—Message from the President—15:1, Spring 2005, 1

46   Soundvision.com—India—What is the Babri Mosque Issue? Abdul Malik Mujahid

47   Hussain Maliks letter to membership, April 22, 2005, copy on file

48   The grievance was filed to the Ethics and Grievance Committee (E&GC) by Nasir Gondal (NY), Mahjabeen Islam (OH) and Nadeem Ahsan (NJ) on May 3, 2005 in which the plaintiffs expressed their concern about the conduct of President Dr. Malik with regards to adoption of the villages in India, document on file in APPNA archives.

49   Minutes of general body meeting July 2–3, 2005 held at Houston, TX.

50   Ibid

51   Ibid

52   The letter from Chair BOT, M. Jafar Shah, August 30, 2005; on file in Archives of APPNA

53   APPNA reached an agreement over two lawsuits filed by Digital Broadcast Network (DBN) in 2007. These lawsuits were dropped under the terms of the settlement, DBN provided entertainment services during the summer and Fall APPNA meetings in 2009.

54   APPNA Journal, 10:2, Winter 2008, 37

55   APPNA Newsletter—Message from the President—15:1, Spring 2005, 1

56   APPNA Journal, 6:3, Fall 2005, 62–63

57   APPNA Journal, 10:1, Summer 2008, 7

58   APPNA Constitution and Bylaws, 2004, 34, 36

59   *APPNA Qissa*, 2004, in chapter 4 page 74

60   APPNA Newsletter, 7:2, 1997, 18.

61   APPNA Journal, 6:3, Fall/Winter 2005, 60

62   APPNA Newsletter, 16:1, Spring 2006, 21

63   APPNA Newsletter, 18:1, Spring 2008, 16

64   APPNA Journal, 13:1, Summer 2011, 29

65   APPNA Alliance Publication, Summer 2013. Hajra Shani Kazi was raised in St. Louis (MO). She like most of us has raised 2 children with her husband Nadeem Kazi. Her concerns about our children are widely shared by the Pakistani-descent mothers across the board.

66   WAPPNA report in APPNA Journal 25:3, 2015

67   President's Report in APPNA Journal, 6:4, Winter 2004

68   APPNA Newsletter, 7:2, May 1997, 18.

69   www.dictionary.com/browse/straw--poll; an unofficial poll to determine the opinion of a group or public on some issue

10

THE FUTURE OF APPNA

"Although predicting is perilous, not predicting is even more perilous. It leaves us unprepared to the changes going on right under our noses, confronts us with recurrent surprises and makes us reactors instead of agents of change."—Jerome Kassirer[1]

Roadmap to the Future

The late APPNA President Raana Akbar poignantly stated in 2006: **"APPNA sets a successful precedent for the future in the context of a flourishing, secular, democratic organization of mostly Muslim Americans.** Since it is the only organization of its nature and record in the Diaspora, it assumes a greater importance than its size would presume. Even though it is an organization that is supposed to represent physicians it ends up representing all Pakistani Americans. As such APPNA leadership is under a pressure of various kinds. First, APPNA has the responsibility of representing immigrants, a people who have had the collective experience of a majority Muslim culture in the country of their birth and now have the second collective experience of being beleaguered minority undergoing frequent harassment in the country of their adoption. APPNA's leadership must understand both these experiences—independently and as they coexist—and synthesize them to develop a strategy to withstand the pressures of the present circumstance. **The confidence of our past must be brought in to build fortitude in the community, to help us endure, survive, and resist the present and what may perhaps lie in the future."**[2]

Her powerful words pave a roadmap for APPNA's future. The contents of this book are testament to the fact that APPNA has neither lost sight of its role as an ethnic professional medical organization nor as the leading organization of the Pakistani-American community at large. The challenge is, how do we enhance our organizational strength to maximize the impact of our work? The effective handling of internal challenges would have a profound impact on the external pressures APPNA faces. Where will APPNA be in the next 10 years? It is not difficult to predict. The answer lies in answering a more important question, namely, where would APPNA like to be in the next 10 years? Once Malcolm X said, "Future belongs to those who prepare for it today." A roadmap built with consensus will determine APPNA's destiny.

APPNA—Building a Signature North American Organization

APPNA has now reached the point where significant changes in its governance are needed to make it a signature North American organization that both meets present day challenges and leads the organization into a sustainable future. This stage is often called an infection point[3] in business strategies and denotes a turning point or a game changer. Michael Thompson, PhD, had worked for APPNA for few months (2004–2005) in a capacity of a consultant. He wrote a report on APPNA's strengths and weakness and made recommendations on how to lead into the future.[4] He noted, "What holds APPNA together is not a common medical/surgical specialty, but strong ethnic, religious, and cultural ties that transcend the host culture of western life style, language and diversity." He also pointed out that "the founders of APPNA began the Association using a western medical association model imposed on a South Asian cultural mindset. That has left the Association with a unique and somewhat cumbersome organizational structure."

Organizational building cannot be achieved without building trust, and this trust should exist as the glue that holds APPNA officers together for the common good of the society they serve. In her 2006 article, Dr. Akbar also commented: "Faced with a daunting task, APPNA's leaders must understand the basic principle of organizational development. A leader must understand that his/her presidency is not the know all, be all and end all, that he/she is a part of the greater whole, his/her term is one year, and that he/she must continue the work of his/her predecessor and leave a legacy for his/her successor. Unfortunately, APPNA leaders tend to start each year with clean slate, which is problematic. The solution is not in increasing the duration of the term but to continue to work as an ongoing team."[5]

Improved Governance in APPNA:

The continuity of work is as important as the continuity of patient care that all physicians are required to do for better outcomes. In 2015, by revitalizing the Long Range Planning Committee (LRPC), the issue of APPNA's governance was given a top priority. This seven-member committee includes the president elect, president, and immediate past president and one nominee from each of them. In addition, one Board of Trustees (BOT) member is also represented. This committee structure with all of the stake-holders being represented is deemed paramount to the development of successful long-range planning and to promote much-needed culture of harmony among APPNA officers. Furthermore, the LRPC felt that the elected leaders will have the opportunity to conceive long-term projects of their interest early enough to have them discussed by this committee with due diligence before the final approval by the APPNA Council. Once approved, these projects will have longitudinal oversight by the LRPC. It is hoped that the assigned role of LRPC in 2015 will be respected by all the future leaders of APPNA in order to develop well founded projects in the years to come. The highest potential of APPNA may then be achieved.

The failure of full implementation of existing APPNA rules is another aspect of poor governance. "When rules exist but only some of the time, the political process falls into disarray," noted renowned Pakistani economist, Dr. Mahbubul Haq who also pointed out that "most governance failures in South Asia are failures of implementation."[6] A cultural change in APPNA is needed where everyone is respected and leaders work together under the checks and balances imposed by the bylaws and standard operative procedures. That most needed trait of following the rules and working together for unity of purpose amongst the officers is not always witnessed in APPNA. It has been proposed that the BOT should be involved in more robust oversight and that BOT be authorized to intervene if rules are not followed. This change in the authority of BOT requires a constitutional amendment—a small step of amending the Bylaws could be a leap forward for APPNA. In fact, APPNA consultant Dr. Thompson advocated for major changes in the Bylaws while addressing the growth of the organization, "The Association has tended—as all organizations do—to grow with no real idea of the impact of new committees on the budgets, overlapping responsibilities and personal areas of authority and even power. The Bylaws need to be strengthened in such a way as to provide for the flexibility needed to respond quickly to sudden needs, but to prevent areas of power and/or control outside of the administration of the organization for developing."[7] APPNA needs to cultivate a culture of transparency and accountability to strengthen its organizational capacity. This capacity building appears to be a rate limiting step in the kinetics of APPNA. The membership should elect those leaders who would be catalysts of change instead of mere reactors to the situations we face.

Will APPNA be Relevant in the Future?

This question has been asked time and again in the post 9/11 era. Many members have expressed their fear that continued influx of doctors from Pakistan may decline significantly overtime. How will APPNA survive if this fear becomes a reality? The good news, however, is that may not happen in the foreseeable future. A review of Educational Commission of Foreign Medical Graduates (ECFMG) data on ECFMG certification over the last 25 years reveal that there has not been any decline in Pakistani medical school graduates coming to the US for residency training on yearly basis despite the road blocks imposed by new security clearance rules.[8] Pakistan is only second to India in ECFMG certification. The share of both countries in the total residency slots in the US for India and Pakistan is little over 10% and 7%, respectively.

APPNA, as an organization exists as a unit of many relationships. One relationship is that of its ties to Pakistan, another is that of its role in the United States. As noted earlier, the future of APPNA has sometimes been said to be resting on the future Pakistani-descent physicians in the United States. For instance, in a recent survey done on the lack of participation of North American graduates of Pakistani-descent (NAMA) in APPNA, Dr. Naeem Khan (IL) said, "If we want APPNA to survive, the future is with NAMA." NAMA's lack of meaningful engagement and participation in APPNA activities has been a challenge that required immediate attention of the leadership. It has become evident over the past several years that NAMA lost its interest as a group to participate in APPNA. Therefore, a taskforce on NAMA was initiated by the long range planning committee (LRPC) in 2015.

The highlights of the opinion poll on NAMA are summarized here for future reference. 88% of the responders agreed to provide programs of interest to second-generation physicians to work for the community at large under APPNA rather than isolating them in a separate group. 80% stated yes to changing the governance of APPNA in a way that would make it attractive for second generation physicians to play a leadership role in APPNA. And 90% said yes to engaging medical students as members and to involving them in charitable work like free medical clinics and APPNA Medical Corps. A similar plea to attract and include medical students in APPNA was proposed by Asima Ahmad in 2008—when the Society of Future Physicians was approved by APPNA Council.[9] This proposed work on medical students was never taken up by the incoming leaders and it remains a window of opportunity for APPNA if any aspiring leader would like to take action in future.

APPNA and Pakistan:

Aspects of wellbeing of Pakistanis have been a top priority in APPNA and will remain so in the future. Both volumes of APPNA *Qissa* are replete with the roles organization played in educational, philanthropic, charitable, and disaster relief activities in Pakistan. APPNA has been working through its partners even in the areas where geopolitical situation is perceived prohibitive due to the current circumstances. APPNA's vision was to enhance the impact of its APPNA SEHAT program by adding literacy improvement and poverty alleviation to a very successful basic healthcare model in rural Pakistan. The Human Development Foundation (HDF) was born in 1997 to convert this vision into a reality by offering a holistic model to uplift the poor people of Pakistan. A lot more could be achieved in the future if both organizations work together with a shared vision for Pakistan.

APPNA MERIT and Telemedicine educational programs are being effectively managed by the committee members working with institutions that benefit from these programs. More recently in 2016, APPNA has signed a memorandum of understanding with USAID to assist in medical work that organization does in Pakistan. APPNA's role is more of providing professional help for the programs that are funded by USAID. APPNA may also be able to enhance the impact of its work in Pakistan through creating the Commissions on Education and Social Welfare in future. Clearly, APPNA has retained strong cultural, educational and charitable ties to Pakistan, and this is an effort that we can only see as continuing in the future.

APPNA and North America:

In a commencement address, Dr. S. Amjad Hussain stated that "Immigrants to a different culture follow one of the three paths while trying to adjust to a new life in a strange land. Some of them live in the past surrounded by comforting sounds and smells of a land they left behind. They live virtually in a physical ghetto. This is a common narrative of most first generation immigrants. Then there are those on the other extreme who soon after their arrival dive into the avant-garde culture of host country a culture that is strange and alien to even some Americans. They emerge from this cultural baptism as new persons, cleansed of their past. Unfortunately, such baptism does not change the color of their skin, facial features, or foreign accent. There is however a third choice, a difficult one and that is to integrate with host society and act as a bridge of understanding and a voice of reason between the two disparate worlds."[10]

It may seem obvious that vibrant immigrant groups like Pakistanis who are proud of their heritage would choose the third option for their integration into American society. Dr. Shahid Shafi shared his feelings on the integration in an article published in an APPNA Newsletter, titled "The Unfinished Odyssey of Pakistani Physicians" by expressing, "I often wonder why we're not integrated in our local community. I know for sure that is not indifference, because we Pakistanis are a passionate people. We can spend hours discussing the most recent happening in Pakistan but we don't apply this same energy to participate in a local school board meeting. We will get up at 2 a.m. to watch a world cup cricket game between Pakistan and India but we won't spend few hours coaching a little league soccer team in our town. We drive for hours to spend an evening with another "desi" family but we won't often invite our "gora" neighbors to a dinner at our home. We will donate money to Edhi but not to the local soup kitchen or homeless shelter. We won't go to a town hall meeting of mayoral candidates for our town. We won't know our elected representatives. We won't rally for our local charities. We don't help with local watch dog groups. We don't raise money for the firefighters, police, and EMS of our towns."[11] Dr. Shafi made his compelling argument to Pakistani descent physicians to get involved in the local communities and should not remain invisible living in a segregated culture of their own.

Islamophobia and the Geopolitical Climate in the United States

Many may tie the future of APPNA with the future of Pakistani-Americans in the United States. Should the immigration policies for Pakistani physicians intending to immigrate to the US become tougher, the future of our organization faces a great risk. Should anti-Muslim bigotry grow, future generations of Pakistani-Americans may be less likely to show pride in their ethnic background and culture. Truly, the expression, "9/11—A day that never ends" is dually haunting for people like Pakistani-Americans. Nearly 3,000 innocent citizens were killed in the unprecedented events of terror that day, which were carried out by those claiming to be Muslim.

APPNA has denounced each and every incidence of violence and terrorism in the US and around the world in the most vociferous way since the 9/11 attacks. Many media outlets continue to portray all Muslims as suspects and a cycle of backlash continues even 15 years after the incidents. In such a climate, Pakistani-Americans have no choice but to build a bridge of understanding in their adopted homeland. The voices of reason have been muffled in the atmosphere of Islamophobia leading to violence against Muslims and the people who look like them, mostly bearded turban wearing Sikhs. Unfortunately, acts of violence did not stop at 9/11 and continue to happen in the United States and elsewhere. The trauma of each event carried by the "Muslims" fuels the incidents of backlash in which innocent Muslims are targeted.

Moving Forward with Compassion and Love

Presently, our world is full of violence and sectarian atrocities. APPNA has a huge responsibility to step up its role as an ambassador of the Pakistani community to denounce deplorable acts of terror regardless of the perpetrators. A physician, as a healer in any society who treats ailments afflicting their patients regardless of their faith or ethnicity, could play a role in healing the trauma of ethnic and racial violence. Likewise, Pakistani physicians could play a greater role in fighting the hate crimes and brutality against any community. APPNA chapters are well positioned to deliver a great deal in that promise of promoting peace in their neighborhoods by dispelling the rising myth that "all Muslims are terrorists." At the recent Strategic Planning Meeting in February of 2016, President Nasar Qureshi shared his vision to expand the role of APPNA's standing Committee on Advocacy, Legislative, and Governmental Affairs. Dr. Qureshi proposed to having two members from each chapter to participate in the Advocacy Committee to kick-start the work of defending Pakistani-American's civil liberties beyond our present scope of work in helping young physicians' from Pakistan in their visa and security clearance issues.[12] Engaging with and working along-side respective local communities as full stake holders is also incumbent on us if we wish to be respected as citizens of this country.

On December 2, 2015, 14 people were killed and 22 were seriously injured in a terrorist attack at the Inland Regional Center in San Bernardino, California, which consisted of a mass shooting and an attempted bomb-ing. A young couple of Pakistani ethnicity was implicated and both were also killed by the law enforcement. A Pakistani-American neurologist from the neighborhood in Pomona CA, Faisal Qazi, immediately led the fund-raising efforts to help the bereaved families. The LA Times reported, "In just four days, the Muslims United for San Bernardino campaign has raised more than $100,000 from more than 1,000 donors across the country, including in Florida, Michigan, Ohio and Tennessee. The money will be disbursed through San Bernardino County and the United Way to assist victims' families with funeral expenses and other needs…"[13] The commu-nity was in fact able to raise more than 200,000 for the affected American families.[14]

Another example of compassion for and solidarity with the victims of terror was witnessed after the violent attack at an Orlando night club on June 12, 2016. APPNA denounced this horrific act of terror in which 49 people were massacred and 53 were injured by a lone "Muslim" gun-man. A few days later, on June 19, APPNA also held a vigil in support of innocent victims of hate in Orlando's Lake Eola Park. For Pakistani physicians and their families to show this kind of compassion and love towards these victims of violence are an example of what goes a long way in healing the wounds of hate crimes and to curb prejudice against minori-ties and Muslims in American society. As Maya Angelou once said, "Love recognizes no barriers. It jumps hurdles, leaps fences, penetrates walls to arrive at its destination full of hope."

APPNA and Civil Rights of Pakistani-Americans

Mr. Khizr Khan, a Pakistani-American lawyer, made an appearance along with his wife Ghazala Khan on the final day of Democratic National Convention (DNC) on July 28, 2016. Both are Gold Star parents of a US military captain, Humayun Khan who valiantly lost his live in Iraq while protecting his fellow soldiers in 2004. He was awarded Bronze Star Medal and Purple Heart for his bravery and sacrifice for the country. At the DNC, Mr. Khizr Khan made the strongest case for American Muslims being patriot citizens in an effort to dispel Anti-Muslim rhetoric in a most compassionate way by telling the story of his son who sacrificed his life for his country.[15]

Subsequently on August 8, 2016, Mr. Khizr and Mrs. Ghazala Khan were the special guests at the APPNA Annual Banquet at the National Gaylord Resort near Washington, D.C. Most APPNA members felt Khan family and the sacrifice of their son, Humayun, gave them a ray of hope in the darkness of racism and anti-immigrant stance that all minorities are facing with the rise of bigoted rhetoric of "I want my country back," and "make America great again." Mr. Khizr Khan also spent more than three hours with APPNA youth in a room packed to capacity. Mr. Khan was helpful in addressing the concerns of US born children who may be the victims of discrimination and hate crimes in the years to come. However, perhaps more importantly, Mr. Khan, unabashedly both Muslim, and an American of Pakistani ethnicity, shows us that hope remains in the future of Muslims and Pakistanis in America. Such hope is encouraging towards the future of APPNA as well.

Conclusion: APPNA has accomplished a lot in the last 38 years. APPNA will continue to play its pivotal role in philanthropic and educational activities. More importantly it will continue to shape the future of Pakistanis in North America. A stronger APPNA in the US will have more valuable impact on the wellbeing of Pakistan. Nevertheless, by no means has APPNA reached its full potential. Improved governance and meaningful involvement of NAMA will indeed strengthen the organization and ensure its progress in future. Moreover, we will need to involve our colleagues in academics and research more effectively in the organization. We have yet to fully utilize this important resource to help our young physicians and promote research projects. APPNA has grown big enough that we need professionals to run the organization. We will need to strengthen our office staff to provide proper oversight and continuity of our projects. We also need to find additional sources of revenue by partnering and fortifying our relationship with foundations to collaborate in our charitable activities. In addition, we need a robust and effective grant application program. All this can be accomplished and much more. There is no doubt the best days of APPNA are yet to come.

End Notes:

1   Jerome P. Kassirer is Distinguished Professor at Tufts University School of Medicine and Adjunct Professor of Medicine and Bioethics at Case Western Reserve University in Cleveland, Ohio. He was Editor-in-Chief of New England Journal of Medicine for more than 8 years.
2   Representations of Leadership—by Raana Akbar, APPNA Journal, 8:2, Winter 2006, 14–15
3   https://www.khanacademy.org/.../points...inflection...
4   Roadmap to the Future, Executive Summary by Michael G. Thompson, PhD, available in the archives of APPNA.
5   Representations of Leadership—by Raana Akbar, APPNA Journal, 8:2, Winter 2006, 14–15
6   Human Development in South Asia—The Crisis of Governance, Oxford University Press, 1999
7   Roadmap to the Future, Executive Summary by Michael G. Thompson, PhD, available in the archives of APPNA
8   www.ecfmg.org —Top five countries based on aggregate data over a 25-year period. *Data current as of January 26, 2016.*
9   APPNA Journal, 10:2, Winter 2008, APPNA Medical Student Section, 22
10   APPNA Journal, 9:1, Summer 2007, 7
11   APPNA Newsletter, 19:1, Spring 2009, 43
12   Minutes of the Strategic Planning Meeting February 20, 2016
13   The LA Times, December 8, 2015.
14   Personal Communication with Dr. Faisal Qazi
15   www.cnn.com/.../dnc-convention-khizr-khan-father-of-us-mus...

11

APPNA Affiliated
Alumni Associations

Historical Perspective

The graduates of King Edward Medical College were the first to initiate an effort to organize an alumni group in the Unites States even before APPNA was founded. In 1978, the graduates of the six older Colleges-King Edward, Dow, Fatimah Jinnah, Nishtar, Khyber, and Liaqat-were involved in the founding of APPNA.[1] The alumni associations of these colleges formed and joined APPNA in the organization's early years. In the 1990's graduates of relatively newer medical colleges from Pakistan followed the trend and organized themselves into alumni associations. These include: Allama Iqbal, Rawalpindi, Sindh, Quaid-e-Azam, and Aga Khan. In 2008, the alumni of Punjab Medical College, Faisalabad, and, five years later, the alumni of Baqai Medical College, Karachi, joined APPNA as component societies.

The North American Medical Association (NAMA) was formed due to growing impetus for the inclusion of medical graduates of American and Canadian medical schools in APPNA. Most of these graduates were exposed to APPNA due to their parents' affiliation with the organization. NAMA was given the recognized "Alumni" status by APPNA in 2002.[2] Even though they were not graduates of a single medical school, they organized themselves into one organization being Pakistani-descent physicians. Unfortunately, NAMA's interest in APPNA related activities dissipated slowly over the last few years. NAMA lost its status as a component society of APPNA in 2015.[3] A detailed analysis of the rise and fall of NAMA and its future is discussed in the chapter titled "Organization Building" of this book.

In recent years, a significant number of Pakistani-descent physicians, that have graduated from Caribbean medical colleges, have gotten involved in APPNA. This group also organized themselves into an "Alumni" association and they became a recognized component society of APPNA in 2011.

In addition, according to APPNA's Bylaws, dentists were always qualified to be active members of APPNA along with physicians.[4] As their numbers and participation grew in APPNA, they aspired to form their own specialty group, called "Dental APPNA." It was recognized as an affiliate of APPNA in 2008.

The advancement of education and medical care remains the major focus of the North American Alumni Associations of Pakistani medical colleges. Their affiliation with APPNA as component societies of the association strengthens APPNA and deepens its influence to support philanthropic ventures while maintaining the cordial relations with faculty and administration at Pakistani medical colleges. The Alumni Associations bring a strength to APPNA that translates into the broader wellbeing of our communities both here in the United States and in Pakistan. The reports from different Alumni Associations in this chapter reflect on these activities. These reports are historic testaments to the activism of volunteers that continues to transpire into remarkable achievements.

Endnotes

1   APPNA Alumni in *APPNA Qissa* page 91, 2004
2   Abid, page 149
3   Minutes of APPNA Spring Council meeting, 2015
4   APPNA Constitution and Bylaws, adopted in 1986, page 12

Allama Iqbal Medical College Alumni Association of North America (AIMCAANA)

Allama Iqbal Medical College Alumni Association of North America (AIMCAANA) was established in 1997 with Dr. Atique Azam Mirza as the founding President. Dr. Mirza continued to serve as president for the next three years. A new team of officers was elected at the APPNA summer meeting held at Atlanta, GA in 2000. Dr. Jalil Khan from Flower Mound, TX, and Dr. Mahmood Alam, from New York were elected as President and President Elect, respectively. Since then, it has progressed to become one of the most vibrant alumni associations of APPNA. AIMCAANA continues to promote and support the concerns of young medical graduates and those of its alma mater, AIMC.

Since its inception, AIMCAANA has been blessed with the services of many selfless members who have not only helped with the growth of the alumni but who have also served APPNA and its chapters in various capacities. Dr. Mahmood Alam, an Iqbalian with the longest history of service to APPNA, served as its president in 2008. Dr. Sajid Chaudhary has also served APPNA in various positions. He was APPNA Secretary in 2008 and was later elected to serve as President in 2017.

Dr. Sajid Chaudhary has been a stalwart supporter of AIMCAANA since its inception (serving as president in 2003 and executive director since 2009). He has played a pivotal role in the revitalization of the alumni under the invigorating leaderships of Dr. Muhammad Babar Cheema in 2008, Dr. Rizwan Akhtar in 2009, and Dr. Tahir Latif in 2010.

In 2008, AIMCAANA underwent multifaceted dynamic changes to meet the demands of expanding membership. The AIMCAANA bylaws revision was initiated and subsequently completed in 2009. AIMCAANA became the first alumni association of APPNA to conduct its election via mail ballot to give ownership to membership through a transparent process.

Dr. Chaudhry started an electronic email group, Iqbaliansalumni@
yahoo.gruop.com that initiated electronic communication with Iqbalians
in 2003. Subsequently in 2008, more emphasis was given to enhance communication with members, including the updating of the AIMCAANA
website and the creation of a blast email system with 800 subscribers. The
first edition of the newsletter, AIMCAANA CONNECTION, was also
published. An endowment fund was established and $50,000 was contrib-
uted by generous Iqbalians.

AIMCAANA (left to right) Dr. Tahir Latif, Dr. Saad Usmani, Dr. Shahram Malik,
Dr. Raza Khan, Dr. Sajid Chaudhary, Dr. Babar Cheema, Dr. Monim

AIMCAANA has also begun to bring awareness to social justice issues
in Pakistan by offering thought provoking discussions and solutions at the
Social Forums. It started in 2008 with the visit of Barrister Aitzaz Ahsan,
who was then leader of the lawyer's movement in Pakistan. These Social
Forums continued with discussions on numerous contemporary issues
like combatting extremism, the future of Baluchistan, the conditions of
journalists in Pakistan and the targeted killings of physicians. At the 2015
annual meeting, AIMCAANA organized a workshop highlighting healthcare fraud and abuse.

In 2008 a Citizens Committee was formed in Pakistan to oversee the philanthropic initiatives of AIMCAANA in Pakistan and was comprised of citizens residing close to the college campus. This Citizens Committee eventually transformed into a registered body as the Pakistani-American Iqbalians Welfare Society (PAIWS) in 2014. PAIWS now acts as AIMCAANA's philanthropic partner in Pakistan. Mr. Aslam Khan (a.k.a. Uncle Aslam), retired Vice President of IDP Bank, has served as coordinator of Citizens' Committee and PAIWS since 2008. He has selflessly played a vital role in the completion of AIMCAANA projects along with other members including Nazeer Choudhary, Dr. Mansab Ali, Abid Rasheed, Muhammad Saleem and well-known journalist Suhail Warraich. In 2014, AIMCAANA successfully filed and obtained its independent 501c3 registration in the United States.

AIMCAANA projects:
Jinnah Allama Iqbal Institute of Diabetes and Endocrinology (JAIDE):
Since 2009, JAIDE continues to serve thousands of diabetic patients at this recognized post-graduate endocrinology fellowship-training center. It was started with the help of Principal AIMC Professor Dr. Javed Akram in 2009. It was expanded with the construction of JAIDE II to meet increased demand and was inaugurated in November 2015.

Iqbalian House in Philadelphia:
This house provides temporary residence to recent graduates of AIMC who are pursuing their careers in the USA. Since 2009, Iqbalian House has served hundreds of young physicians and has indirectly helped them in getting into residency training programs.

Scholarship/Qarz-e-Hasna:
Scholarships and funding is provided to medical students and recent graduates of AIMC who require financial assistance. It has been in operation since 2009.

Cancer Treatment:
AIMCAANA sponsors an out-patient chemotherapy infusion area that has been serving thousands of poor patients at Jinnah hospital since 2010. Its expansion is planned.

Assistance in Building Repairs:

Several structural improvements in the Gynecology ward, Jinnah hospital reading room, and the Dental department were carried out in 2011.

Zakat Funds:

Financial assistance has been available to poor patients at Jinnah hospital to obtain life saving medications through a transparent process. This was started in 2013.

AIMCAANA's success as a vibrant alumni association has been due to the involvement of our young Iqbalians. They have demonstrated commitment and support for its initiatives and have assumed leadership roles within the organization. AIMCAANA members take great pride in being an integral part of our alumni association and this is the driving force behind all of our successful endeavors over the years. We continue to be resolute in our belief; *Iqbalian once, Iqbalian forever.*

Dr. Mumahhamd Babar Cheema contributed to this report.

Aga Khan University Alumni Association of North America (AKUAANA)

The alumni of Aga Khan University in North America established an organization in 1993. The first reunion was held in 1994 at the Cosmos Club in Washington D.C. The "AKU Alumni Association of North America" (as it was called then) operated for all AKU alumni of the School of Medicine.

The second reunion was held in 1996 and the third in 1997 in Houston where other alumni took over management of the association. The association continued to function as an informal group while a parallel group developed under the auspices of the Association of Physicians of Pakistani Descent of North America (APPNA).

In 1999, APPNA leadership invited AKU alumni to organize their reunion during the APPNA Fall Meeting held in September in New York. APPNA was eager to bring the AKU alumni association under its umbrella as it had done with other alumni associations of major Pakistani medical schools. A formal resolution was introduced at the APPNA meeting held in New Orleans and AKU was formally inducted as a component society of APPNA in 2000 with full voting rights.

The organization participated in mentorship programs, immigration assistance, research and counseling programs, identifying class representatives as well as re-invigorating the AKUNAMA (Aga Khan University Newsletter and Magazine for Alumni).

AKUAANA members continue to contribute to their alma mater and to Pakistan. Over the course of the last 25 years, contributions have been made in philanthropy, exchange programs, research development, education and student support. Various alumni have returned to Karachi to give lectures, provide best practice guidelines and collaborate on projects in public health, critical care, emergency medicine, pediatrics and surgery. Large philanthropic gifts were donated by the classes of 1988, 1989 and 1990 for their 25th year anniversaries. Other classes have also contributed anonymously to Aga Khan University and have developed mechanisms to help with student loans and educational development.

Besides supporting AKU directly, alumni continue to provide leadership in Pakistan by developing links with other NGOs such as The Citizens Foundation (TCF), Developments in Literacy (DIL), Hunar Foundation and the Indus Hospital. Natural disasters have unfortunately affected Pakistan and alumni have quickly assisted providing material, financial and medical assistance.

AKU alumni have been recognized by APPNA as academic leaders in North America and across the globe. AKUAANA and APPNA are thus partnering to leverage the alumni to promote APPNA's education mission.

In 2015 the organization adopted our mission and vision to broadly encompass and guide our growth. We look forward to serving the needs of alumni and our communities in Pakistan and America.

Mission:

Represent the social, academic and philanthropic interests of the AKU Medical School Alumni in North America whilst connecting alumni, spouses and their families.

Vision:

To develop a dedicated alumni organization that works together to improve our members continued success in North America and globally.

Our Values:

We believe that giving back to society is our most important responsibility. We will do so by connecting alumni with each other and the University to build traditions, foster academic leadership, provide philanthropic options and serve the diverse needs of our community.

Our Strategy:

The organization will promote:
1. Community engagement
2. Philanthropic engagement
3. Academic engagement
4. Political engagement
5. Alma Mater Engagement

Dr. Faisal G. Qureshi, president AKUAANA 2015, contributed to this report.

Dental APPNA

Dental APPNA is one of the newest members of the APPNA family. The force behind its establishment was APPNA physician and activist, Dr Sarwat Iqbal, whose efforts brought to attention the need for dentists to organize within the association. In 2008, Dr Iqbal and a group of Philadelphia based dentists founded Dental APPNA, seeking to bring together Pakistani descent dentists residing in North America. The first executive committee in 2009 consisted of: President: Javaid Iqbal DDS, President-Elect: Mian Khalid Iqbal DDS, Secretary: Abdul Sami Janjua DDS, and Treasurer: Mubarak Malik DDS.

Dental APPNA's stated goals are to provide care for underserved communities in North America and Pakistan, to provide continuing education for members, and to organize Pakistani descent dentists to network professionally.

From its start, Dental APPNA has been involved in charitable activities in Pakistan. In 2010, during Dr. Sami Janjua's presidency, it partnered with Shine Humanity to work in a charity hospital in rural Kashmir. Used equipment and supplies from the U.S. were donated to the dental clinic at the hospital. In the early nineties, Dr. Tahir Paul, a pediatric dentist and 2011 Dental APPNA President, had helped to establish a dental clinic at the SOS village in Lahore in order to provide oral health care for the orphans at the institution. In 2011, Dr. Afshan Haque had the opportunity to serve at this clinic for three months. She was able to provide routine restorations, cleanings, root canals and crowns for the children.

Dental APPNA luncheons at the APPNA summer conferences have been successful in bringing together Pakistani dentists from around the country. Dr. Tahir Paul, Dr. Khalid Almas, a periodontist and Dr. Naheed Usmani, an oncologist, were among the first guest speakers to provide informative lectures during these meetings.

Under Dr. Afshan Haque's leadership in 2012, Dental APPNA partnered with Remote Area Medical (RAM), sending a team of dentists to rural Tennessee. Dr. Haque, Dr. Aliya Khan and Dr. Lubna Alam spent the weekend providing dental care and oral hygiene instruction to residents of this underserved community. Restorations, extractions and prophylaxis were performed for over 600 patients.[1]

That same year, for the first time, Dental APPNA provided PACE certified credit hours for attendees. The Academy of General Dentistry (AGD) chapter of Washington DC sponsored the meeting, and its president, Dr. John Drumm was in attendance. Dr. Faisal Quereshy, Associate Professor of Oral Maxillofacial Surgery at Case Western Reserve University provided the two-hour accredited lecture.

The founding members continue to contribute to the growth of the association. Dr. Mohammad Arshad, an active member since its formation, has become the backbone of the group. He is dedicated to promoting Dental APPNA, and through his efforts there has been a steady increase in its membership. The attendance at the summer meetings increased from a handful of members in 2008 to close to forty attendees in 2012.

In 2013, Dr. Mohammad Arshad was elected President of Dental APPNA. Along with Dr. Aliya Khan and Dr. Mubarak Ali Malik, he participated in a half day clinic sponsored by Henry Shine Dental Supply Company at Temple University. By registering more than 25 lifetime members, Dr. Arshad also secured Dental APPNA's place as a permanent chapter of APPNA. That year, the Dental APPNA Constitution and Bylaws was formulated and the term for elected officers was increased to two years. At the 2013 summer convention, Dr. Arshad and his team (Dr. Quereshy and Dr. Aliya Khan) arranged for the first Dental APPNA Alumni Dinner. In addition, four hours of continuing education credits were provided to the participants. Also at this meeting, Dr. Quereshy bridged the fields of medicine and dentistry by giving a CME lecture to both physicians and dentists at the APPNA general session.

In 2014, Dr. Arshad and his executive committee continued their efforts to providing a quality summer program and to increase membership. Dr. Faisal Quereshy, Dr. Najia Usman, an endodontist, and Dr. Dean Nadeem Ahmad, a periodontist were the guest lecturers. Twenty dental students were sponsored to attend the meeting.

Dr. Dean Nadeem Ahmad was elected as Dental APPNA President for 2015. He and his executive committee (Secretary Dr. Salman Malik, and Treasurer Dr. Shahida Qazi) are continuing to work for the growth of the organization. They arranged a successful meeting at the 2015 Orlando summer convention. Dr. Mamnoon Siddiqui, an Orthodontist, Dr. Usman and Dr. Almas were the speakers for the educational session.

Dental APPNA offers guidance and assistance to graduates of US and Pakistani dental schools. Its plans include increasing active membership, creating a directory for networking and referral and establishing local chapters so that members can meet regularly. As it continues its work in charity and education, Dental APPNA is rapidly emerging as an important member of the APPNA family.

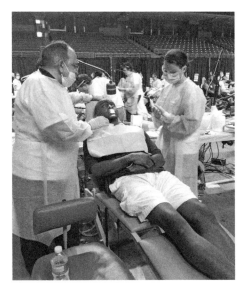

Dr. Mohammad Arshad doing voluntary work on a dental patient at
Liacouras Center, Temple University, Philadelphia, PA - June 1, 2013

Dr. Lubna Alam contributed to this report.

End Note:

1   APPNA Journal, 14:1; 2012, Dental APPNA, We Welcome Those Interested
     to Join, Afshan Haque, DDS, page 13

Dow Graduate Association of North America (DOGANA)

The Dynamic and Vibrant Group of People as Ever.

The Dow Alumni community is unique among Pakistani institutions as it gives the same sense of alumni camaraderie that is visible and felt in many United States institutions. Since the formation of the Dow Graduate Association in Pakistan, Dow alumni have been thriving in all corners of the globe.

The Dow Graduate Association of North America (DOGANA)was established by a small and humble gathering in 1983, and it has grown to become the largest alumni association of APPNA. Its story speaks volumes. Beginning with the creation of the Dow Alumni Website in 1993, the first website of any Pakistani institution, Dow alumni have had a most comprehensive presence on the internet and social media. Dowites are keeping the tradition of social and political activism alive.

Since 2004, DOGANA has achieved many milestones. It is the largest alumni association within APPNA with its total membership reaching 850 and its APPNA membership reaching between 650–750. It has played an ever-increasing role in shaping APPNA activities. It has worked side by side with other alumni to bring social forums to the forefront of APPNA summer conventions. DOGANA also set a trend by becoming the first alumni to establish electronic balloting for APPNA elections. One of its most notable accomplishments is the silver jubilee class project of "Giving Back to Dow."

The Tradition of 'Giving Back to Alma Mater"

The Dow Class of 1976, on their 25th anniversary, embarked on a mission of fundraising with the sole purpose of "Giving back to Dow" and its patients. Teams of dedicated Dowites were established in North America and in Pakistan. This class project, served as a model for subsequent classes to follow, and since then every class of Dow, on its Silver Jubilee anniversary, has given back to Dow and Civil Hospital (CHK). This is a self-sustaining project with the sole purpose of helping underprivileged patients receive the best care at Dow and CHK. Below is a list of projects the Dow graduating classes have donated since the tradition began with the class of 1976 in 2001.

A group of Dow graduates with Farid Qazi and Talha
Siddiqi at APPNA summer meeting, 2016

1976: The Emergency Casualty Theaters—***Donated in 2001***
1977: The Renovate & Equip OBGYN Unit at CHK—***Donated in 2002***
1978: The Surgical Unit, OT—***Donated in 2003***
1979: The Upgrade & Equip Radiology Department at CHK—
Donated in 2004
1980: The Diabetic Eye Center—***Donated in 2005***
1981: The Upgrade and Equip Trauma and ICU at CHK—
Donated in 2006
1982: The 10-Bed New ICU at CHK—***Donated in 2007***
1983: The Upgrade and Equip Pathology Laboratory at CHK—
Donated in 2008

1984: The Gynea OT Project at CHK—***Donated in 2009***
1985: Digitalization of Radiology Department at CHK—
  Donated in 2010
1986: The Pediatric ICU at CHK—***Donated in 2011***
1987: Monies provided for projects at Indus Hospital and CHK—
  Donated in 2012
1988: Establish an Endowment for PWA, upgrades to Arag auditorium
  and Colorectal Center (surgical unit 6) at CHK—***Donated in 2013***
1989: (Batch 1): Upgraded blood screening instrumentation for PWA at
  CHK—***Donated in 2014***
1989: *(Batch 2): Pediatric Outpatient unit at CHK:* **Donated in 2014**
1990: The Post-graduate surgical skills laboratory at CHK—
  Donated in 2015

The Dow Endowment Fund, The enDOW

In addition to the silver jubilee projects, the Dow alumni community has established a comprehensive endowment fund for Dow Medical College and Civil Hospital Karachi. The purpose of this is to provide continuous and sustainable support for the alma mater. Dow alumni generously support this cause, and it has matured into a fully functioning independent 501c3 entity where all alumni contribute on a regular basis.

The Tradition of Innovations and Pioneering Spirit in Dow Alumni

The Dow Alumni community has been at the forefront of many innovations and pioneering projects. It was the first to establish an internet presence in 1993 and the first to establish the annual alumni retreat in the spring of 2005. The first ever APPNA *Presidential Debate* was also organized by DOGANA in 2013. The *Loan Program* (need based) was established for Dow graduates appearing for the USMLE. The *Merit Scholarship* for final year students and the *Research Scholarship* for medical students are some of the projects recently started by DOGANA.

DOGANA Presidents.

The DOGANA leadership has contributed significantly to the growing community of Dow Alumni. DOGANA has the distinction of being the first alumni association to establish its election process entirely online with complete transparency.

1982–1983 Inayat S Husain, MD *Arlington Heights, IL*

1983–1984 Ikram Ullah Khan, MD *Las Vegas, NE*

1984–1985 Tariq Zafar, MD *Monroe, MI*

1985–1986 Hafeezur Rehman, MD *St Louis, MO*

1986–1987 Farooq I. Selod, MD *Fort Worth, TX*

1987–1988 Mushtaq A Khan, MD *Joliet, IL*

1988–1989 Parvez Ilyas Shah, MD *Laurel, MD*

1989–1990 Busharat Ahmad, MD *Marquette, MI*

1990–1991 Salim Chowdhrey, MD *Livingston, NJ*

1991–1992 Aziz R Arain, MD *Downers Grove, IL*

1992–1993 Mohammed H. Peracha, MD *Monroe, MI*

1993–1994 Asif M Sheikh, MD *W. Columbia, SC*

1994–1995 Pervaiz Rahman, MD *Gainsville, TX*

1995–1996 Iltifat Alavi, MD *LaGrange, IL*

1996–1997 Manzoor Husain, MD *Oak Brook, IL*

1997–1998 Abdul Rehman, MD *Staten Island, NY*

1998–1999 Arif Azam, MD *Oak Brook, IL*

1999–2000 Kaleem Arshad, MD *LA*

2000–2001 Zeelaf Munir, MD *Rehoboth Beach, DE*

2001–2002 Rizwan A. Karatela, MD *Palm Beach, FL*

2002–2003 Sadeem Mahmood, MD *Little Rock, AR*

2003–2004 Zia Moiz Ahmad, MD *St. Louis, MO*

2005 Syed A. Samad, MD *Pine Bluff, AR*

2006 Ahsan Rashid, MD *Newport Beach, CA*

2007 Farid Qazi, MD *Macon, GA*

2008 M. Nasar Qureshi, MD, PhD *Englewood Cliffs, NJ*

2009 Muslim Jami, MD *Fresno, CA*

2010 Shazia Malik, MD *St. Louis, MO*

2011 Sohail Khan, MD *Chicago, IL*

2012 Talha Siddiqui, MD *Washington, DC*

2013 Sajid Zafar, MD *St. Louis, MO*

2014 Azeem Qureshi, MD *Hershey, PA*

2015 Asif Mohiuddin, MD *Orlando, FL*

2016 Dr. Danish Saeed, MD *Allentown, PA*

Dr. Rizwan A. Karatela & Dr. M. Nasar Qureshi contributed to this report

King Edward Medical College Alumni Association of North America (KEMCAANA)

King Edward Medical College Alumni Association of North America (KEMCAANA) is the oldest Pakistani Physicians' organization in the United States. It was established in 1975, 2 years before APPNA was founded. Its creation, evolution, and its marriage with APPNA have been beautifully described in *APPNA Qissa*, (2004). Its union with APPNA, while keeping its own identity, laid a path for the other Alumni associations to follow. This concept brought unprecedented strength to APPNA, more so than any other compatriot association in the United States.

While APPNA kept pace protecting the interests of Foreign Medical Graduates in the U.S. and improving healthcare in Pakistan, KEMCANNA primarily focused on the transfer of knowledge and assisting students at the King Edward Medical College (KEMC). From 1985 to 2005, the Post Graduate Education (PGE) Fund helped more than 100 KE graduates in post-graduate training. Some of them are now decorated professors (e.g., Dr. M Jahanzeb) while others (e.g., Dr. Faisal Sultan) returned home to head major institutions.

Although the PGE program was tremendously productive, history reflects that KEMCAANA lacked diversity and breadth of projects in its early years. In the post 9/11 era and with the changing healthcare horizon in the U.S., the PGE program lost its strength. This, however, unleashed KEMCAANA's growth into many diverse areas of educational, scientific, humanitarian and charitable projects.

Establishment of KEMCAANA office (2004):

Fundamental to the growth of KEMCAANA was the establishment of KEMCAANA office and deployment of staff at the Alma Mater. In 2002, a computer lab was established under the leadership of Dr. Asim Malik and 40 computers were donated. This facility provided the physical presence of KEMCAANA at the KEMC. The lab became very popular amongst students and faculty. It has acted as a showcase of KEMCAANA services. In 2004, KEMCAANA employed a fulltime manager, Rashid Javed, to run this lab. He has served with passion and dedication. Today, the total staff comprises of 5 employees whose manpower helps to conduct day-to-day business of the association. During 2004, Dr. Mohammad Jahanzeb, the then president, established KEMCAANA's office in the U.S. also with a secretary (Marsha Smith) in Memphis that lasted for 10 years. He also raised $350,000 as an endowment fund to run various KE projects.

KEMC Elevated to a University (2005):

King Edward Medical College (KEMC) was established in 1860 as the Lahore Medical College. On December 21, 1911, Lahore Medical College was renamed King Edward Medical College in Honor of the late King and Emperor, Edward VII (Albert Edward; 9 November 1841–6 May 1910). Its status was elevated to an independent, degree-granting university on May 12, 2005, when it became King Edward Medical University (KEMU). The status brought autonomy to develop its own academic programs, multiple allied academic disciplines, and research and PhD scholars.

KEMCAANA Retreats (2006):

For many years, there was a feeling that the official business and strategic planning of KEMCAANA at the annual summer meeting was subdued by the overwhelming activity of APPNA festivities. A new, independent retreat to focus solely on KEMCAANA projects was proposed by Dr. Jahanzeb in 2004. This proposal became a reality in Dallas, TX in 2006 under the presidency of Dr. Khalid Mahmood. The retreat has been held annually ever since with great success.

Career Counselling Seminar (2006):

With growing Visa issues after 9/11 and the increasing complexity of the ECFMG qualification process, many KEMU students faced challenges to travel to the United States. A landmark career counselling seminar, spearheaded by Dr. Mohammad Haseeb, was held in Lahore to help resolve these difficulties. It included participation from U.S. residency program directors, U.S. Embassy representatives and Stephen Seeling, Vice President for Operations, ECFMG. More than 450 students attended excellent presentations which delved into—practical "do's" and "don'ts" on how "the process" works. Mr. Seeling later wrote in his reflections that "this was a group that required you to bring your "A" game."

Projects and History 2007–09:

In 2007, during the term of Dr. Ijaz Mahmood, the **computer lab** was expanded to boy's and girl's hostels, a new database driven website was created and visa assistance was provided to KE graduates who had obtained residency in the U.S.

In 2008, Dr. Mubasher Rana expanded the scope of KEMCAANA services with special focus on KEMCAANA members. Many members had faced bureaucratic difficulties in getting their credentials verified from KEMU for the U.S. licensure. An online **Document Verification Process** was established facilitated by KEMCAANA's office at the KEMU.

In order to improve the standards of education at the KEMU, Dr. Rana also initiated efforts to institute curriculum reform at the KEMU. A **Seminar on Curriculum Reform** was conducted with the participation of national and international speakers.

Tuition Help from Alumni for New KE Students (**THANKS) Scholarship** was launched in 2008 by Dr. Bashir Chaudhary and his wife Dr. Tesneem Chaudhary with a mission to provide tuition fee to as many students as possible (if not all).

In 2009, Dr. Mohammad Haseeb formalized the **Visiting Faculty Program**. The program coordinates special visits to KEMU / Mayo Hospital for KEMCAANA members going to Pakistan for spending time in teaching, Grand rounds, and introduction of new procedures that can be easily done in Pakistan. In addition to revising the amendments to the constitution and bylaws, he introduced a **New Logo** and **Mission Statement** to KEMCAANA, entitled "Reaching Out, Giving Back and Changing Lives: Through Education, Research and Service." He also launched the Young Investigator Award, of which he still remains a patron. Dr. Haseeb, along with his class of 1980, donated the **Anatomy Learning Center** ($80K) equipped with virtual dissection software with vivid and astonishing details.

Sesquicentennial Anniversary (2010):

2010 was a milestone year marking the sesquicentennial anniversary of the KEMU. With an air of celebration, a lot of activities took place.

Dr. Masood Akbar was the president that year. He had headed the **KEMCAANA scholarship program** for many years. In 2010, the number of need-based scholarships increased to 64 under his leadership. He also procured the **Hamdani Award of Excellence** to be given to an extremely bright student at KEMU to help him or her pursue post-graduate training in US in the amount of $7,000.00 per year. This award was donated by Mr. Jamal Hamdani, a non-physician philanthropist from California, and the son of a late KEMCOLIAN. Mr. Hamdani, who is also a successful IT businessman donated Wi-Fi equipment that provided **campus-wide wireless internet access**.

Unfortunately, the severe floods of 2010 in Pakistan left large masses homeless. In response to the tragic aftermath of the floods, KEMCAANA built a **KEMCAANA Village** in Farooq Abad (Southern Punjab). Drs. Aisha Zafar, Maqbool Arshad and Mubashar Rana spearheaded the project. In the same year, funds were raised to build 100 homes and 50 of them were completed and delivered in 2010. The **Electronic Medical Library** at the Computer Lab for students and staff was also established.

During the winter meeting in 2010 at KEMU, when the chief minister of Punjab pulled out at the last minute from inauguration (due to an emergency trip to Turkey), retired Professor Zafar Haider made an emotional speech expressing criticism that KEMU was not honored on its all-important 150th anniversary by the head of the state or the province.

Projects and History 2011–15:

In 2011, during the term of Dr. Tariq Jamil, **KEMCAANA Doctor's House** in Philadelphia was established. Dr. Masood Akbar purchased a house in Philadelphia and KEMCAANA leased it for students and young physicians' accommodation that were coming to the United States for Clinical skill testing and residency interviews. In this year, funds were also raised for the upgrading of computer labs at KEMU. The general body approved the Constitution and Bylaws amendments.

Dr. Aisha Zafar led the organization in 2012. She connected with the students directly at KEMU to understand their issues and mobilized them to enhance their **social welfare projects**. She started the **adopt a student scholarship**. In addition, she launched 2 **scholarships, in honor of her parents Professor Hayat Zafar and Professor Bilqees Zafar**, which granted $ 5,000 dollars each. The new **Learning Center** with 20 new computers and multimedia facilities was completed in 2012. The **KEMCAANA Foundation** was registered as an NGO in Pakistan.

In 2011, Dr. Maqbool Arshad focused on preventive medicine to counter the epidemic of Hepatitis C in Pakistan. The **Hepatitis C Initiative** is an advocacy program that has carried out a number of programs. This includes holding Hepatitis prevention experts' conferences and publishing their recommendations to be shared with provincial health departments and major hospitals in the country. The Computer Lab faculty room was converted into administrative meeting room. Dr. Arshad also streamlined and initiated direct **reimbursement of awarded scholarships** to the recipients eliminating payments through KEMU administrative staff. Unfortunately, KEMCAANA was a victim of identity theft in 2013 resulting in fraudulent loss of funds from its Bank account (approximately $140K). The Executive Committee pledged to replenish the loss through personal contributions. Kelly Macias was appointed as the new KEMCAANA secretary in Milwaukee, WI after the resignation of Marsha Smith in 2013.

Dr. Ayesha Najib led in 2014 with great enthusiasm. In addition to advancing many existing projects, she launched an **online teaching program** and facilitated **research mentorship** for KEMU faculty via web-ex spearheaded by Dr. Rehan Qayyum. In 2014, **Wi-Fi was also expanded** to Lady Aitchison and Lady Willingdon Hospitals and Dr. Najib renovated the **boy's hostel swimming pool** (with donation from Dr. Athar Ansari)**, the girl's hostel common room** (with donation from Dr. Ijaz Mahmood) **and doctors call rooms** and class rooms at Mayo Hospital. KEMU was registered with **Global Health Learning Opportunities (GHLO)** to facilitate clinical electives in the US for KEMU students. **KEMCAANA Telemedicine Pilot Project** was started in collaboration with Akhuwat and five clinics were started in rural areas.

In 2015, KEMCAANA president Dr. Ahmad Mehdi Malik focused on the creation of an **Endowment Fund for the Indigent Patients** of Mayo Hospital Lahore. At the June 2015 KEMCAANA retreat, the participants generously donated towards the seed money for that fund of US $100,000. The endowment is for the welfare of needy patients at Mayo Hospital. Many other scholarships and loan services were launched in the recent year's e.g., Najmuddin Masood Ansari Post-Graduate Loan ($5k per year; 2013 by Dr. Athar Ansari), Dr. Maqbool Ashraf Post-Graduate Loan ($5k per year; 2014) and Dr. Aisha Zafar Post-Graduate Loan ($5k per year; 2015 by Dr. Fawad Zafar in 2015).

Some of the past presidents of KEMCAANA, (L to R) Khalid
Mahmood, Masood Akbar, Aisha Zafar, Late Hassan Bukhari,
M. Haseeb, Mubasher Rana, Riaz M. Chaudhry

Concluding Remarks:

Serving the alma mater, helping young students and graduates of KEMU,
improving education, awarding scholarships and loans, providing tools and
technology, assisting in post-graduate training, providing housing, helping the less fortunate and those afflicted with disaster are just some of the
"chirags" of this journey. The mission lives on through the following verse:

SHIKWA E ZULMAT E SHAB SE TO KAHEEN BEHTAR THA,
APNE HISE KI KOI SHMA JALATE JAATE

شکوہ ظلمت شب سے تو کہیں بہتر تھا

اپنے حصے کی کوئی شمع جلاتے جاتے

Dr. Arif Agha contributed to this report.

Punjab Medical College Alumni Association of North America (PMCAANA)

PMC Alumni founders Shahid Sheikh, Shahnaz Akhtar, Amjad Ghani
Sheikh with Mahmood Alam and Khawar Ismail, circa 2008

Punjab Medical College Alumni Association of North America (PMCAANA) is relatively new and small in APPNA. We started with four members a few years ago and within the last five years we have increased our association to 130 members strong. Over the last five years we have started and completed multiple projects with teamwork and in collaboration with our medical school faculty (and their NGO EMed) and with the help of medical students at the alma mater. A few of the projects are noted below:

Pediatric/Neonatal ICU project: PMCAANA started a project in 2011 to upgrade PICU/NICU at the medical school in Faisalabad, Pakistan, in collaboration with APPNA-Ohio, SWDR committee of APPNA, General Electronics and Islamic relief. We were able to raise enough funds to purchase 12 ventilators. The education and training of young physicians, nurses and respiratory therapists in PICU/ventilator care was arranged by Dr. Raza Baloch, Chief of pediatrics at Punjab Medical College. The provision of these ventilators to the local teaching hospitals (Allied and DHQ) has helped in developing a fully functional tertiary care at PICU/

NICU, which is fully self-sustaining. PMCAANA continues to monitor PICU/NICU and ventilator functioning and manages repairs over time. Currently we have twelve fully functioning ventilators and even after four years, these are available free of charge to children in need and they have helped to save the lives of hundreds of children every year. Six more ventilators will be sent to the Medical/Surgical ICU to improve its ability to take care of the growing needs of critically ill children.

PMC House: Under the supervision of Dr. Amjad Ghani Sheikh, (Chairman of Medicine at Carthage Hospital, NY) the training, grooming and teaching of young physicians seeking residency positions in the USA was started in 2006. This facility was officially given the name of PMC house in 2013. Now it is a big house and can host 6–10 students at a time with separate sections for men and women. This residence has a fully functioning kitchen that serves at a very nominal charge. Rotations have also been arranged at Carthage Hospital to offer US medical experience. More than 100 students have benefitted. The majority of students were able to get residency after getting US experience from this program. Initially started for PMC graduates, this house is now open to young physicians from all medical schools in Pakistan.

Medical Supplies for the Poor Project (started 2011): PMCAANA in collaboration with the APPNA-Ohio chapter has developed a network to send medical supplies to PMC through EMed to be used free of charge for poor patients. We have sent a few full sized containers (40 feet each) of medical supplies to Faisalabad. We have formed teams on the ground to oversee and monitor distribution. We assess our local inventory at least twice a year to make sure that all of our donated equipment is in proper use. We plan to continue this collaborative venture.

Trauma Care Project (started in 2013): PMCAANA collaborated with APPNA to start BCLS/ACLS courses at PMC with the help of EMed in 2013. Unfortunately, most of the first responders and even hospital-based physicians and nurses are not well trained in BCLS/ATLS/PALS. This project was initiated to provide this education and we were able to start 2 courses of BCLS/ACLS every month in Faisalabad. This project is self-sustaining and ongoing.

Dr. Amjad Ghani Sheikh and Dr. Shahid Sheikh contributed to this report

Rawalpindi Medical College Alumni Association of North America (RMCAANA)

RMCAANA—From Founding to Present—a journey through 17 years

"Never doubt that a small group of thoughtful concerned citizens can change the world. Indeed, it is the only thing that ever has."
MARGARET MEAD

One is reminded of how RMCAANA came into fruition by these inspirational words by Mead. In 1998, a group of young physicians from Rawalpindi Medical College got together and formed the alumni association with the primary mission of giving back to their alma mater and their community. With humble beginning, the alumni had a powerful message. We wanted to establish an alumni association, which could engage in social work, and at the same time mentor young graduates from RMC into residency or research positions.

RMCAANA was formally established and inducted as an Alumni Association of APPNA on July 9, 1998 at the 20th Annual summer meeting of APPNA in Los Angeles, California. Dr. Babar Rao served as RMCANNA's first president. At the present time, RMCAANA is benefiting from the leadership of Dr. Sohail Minhas in 2015. Over the last decade, the membership of RMCAANA has increased, and emphasis has remained strong on its primary mission. RMCAANA is proud to have started the Burn Center at Holy Family Hospital, and more recently, the Dialysis Unit at Holy Family Hospital. These centers serve the indigent population in Rawalpindi, and its surrounding areas, and are completely free. In addition, RMCAANA has also upgraded the medical Library at DHQ and RMC. Additionally, RMC alumni in the US have helped mentor several young RMC graduates into externship, residency and research positions. Last year, RMCAANA, with APPNA's help, established a scholarship fund for deserving students in RMC.

RMCAANA has had a visible presence in APPNA, and the alumni have served APPNA in several committees, including Constitution and Bylaws, SWDRC, Membership, and provided leadership in its MERIT program and in Advocacy Committee. The alumni continue to grow and hopefully will have a larger footprint in APPNA in the near future. RMCAANA is a relatively young alumnus in APPNA. We remain steadfast in the achievement of our mission and goals. The unifying force in RMCAANA remains its commitment to the alma mater, and its social projects. By being consistent and dedicated, RMCAANA has become an inspirational alumnus to many and will continue to lead in an exemplary way.

"Leadership is the capacity to translate vision into reality."
WARREN BENNIS

Dr. Sophia Janjua contributed to this report

Alumni Association of Caribbean Medical Schools (AACMS)

The idea to organize Pakistani descent graduates from Caribbean Medical Schools, that led to the formation of the association, was that of Dr. Riaz A. Chaudhry from Newburg, New York and Shahid F. Usmani from Orlando, Florida. Dr. Nadeem Ahmad from St. Louis, Missouri, and Dr. Naveed Chowhan from Louisville, Kentucky soon joined the effort to find at least twenty-five active members of APPNA so that the association could be approved. It was at the 2011 summer council meeting of APPNA in St. Louis, MO, that AACMS was recognized as a component society of APPNA.[1] It was agreed upon to honor the senior most founding member to be the founding president. Dr. Shahid Usmani served as president 2011–2012. Dr. Riaz Chaudhry, the founding president elect served as president in 2013. Dr. Nadeem Ahmad and Dr. Naveed Chowhan then served as president of AACMS in 2014 and 2015, respectively.

In the 5th year of our existence (2015), we continue to grow in membership and strength. Our members have been actively involved in social and charitable work. They hold positions in leadership roles, professionally and within APPNA. We are the fastest growing chapter of APPNA because our prospective Alumni are mostly U.S. citizens and are preferred by the training program directors over the J1 visa seeking candidates.

We have devised an electronic mailing list for communication. A directory of Caribbean Schools is being added to guide prospective students in making the right decisions in regards to joining a Caribbean Medical School. Our next generation and our own children born in the United States are attending numerous medical schools in the Caribbean. Our goal is to develop a network to assist new graduates in securing residency positions of their choice.

On a personal note, my (Dr. Chowhan's) own son is attending a Caribbean Medical School and is ready to enter his 3rd year this summer (2015). I am hoping his transition into the U.S. Residency Training will be less cumbersome as a second generation American citizen graduating from a Caribbean Medical School than it was for us from Pakistan. We foresee a tremendous growth in our membership in the next few years since Caribbean Medical Schools tend to be the second best choice for our youth growing up in North America. We would be proud to get these graduates into the folds of APPNA!

Dr. Riaz A. Chaudhry and Dr. Naveed Chowhan contributed to this report

End Notes

1   Minutes of APPNA Summer Council Meeting 2011

Nishtar Alumni Association of North America (NANA)

NANA is one of the oldest and most vibrant chapters of APPNA. According to AMA sources, there are over 800 Nishtarians in the United States. As an Alumni association, NANA is trying its best to attract the involvement of all these Nishtarians. It has had some success, but much more can be done to maximize membership.

NANA has strong representation in APPNA. Four of its alumni have had successful terms as President of the association: Dr. M. Aslam Malik (1984–85), Dr. Shabbir H. Safdar (1999), Dr. Abdul Rasheed Piracha (2006) and Dr. Asif Rehman (2014). Nishtarians have chaired and served various committees in the past, and the tradition continues.

NANA has actively raised funds and completed many projects for our Alma Matter in the last few years. This includes supporting a state of the art ER conference room with audiovisual equipment and simulation lab where hundreds of thousands of medical students, house officers, nurses and medical staff have taken ACLS/BLS courses.

NANA also funded the completion of the extension project for the pediatric ward, a three-story building with classrooms on the first floor and an ICU on the second and third floors. This has resulted in a significant increase in the number of ICU beds for the pediatric population. In addition, NANA has also built a new 27 bed ICU building for adults in Nishtar Hospital, which is now fully functional. In 2015, NANA raised over one hundred thousand dollars to fund a new state of the art Endoscopy unit in Nishtar.

NANA was on the front line during the devastation caused by floods in 2012. It raised thousands of dollars for the victims and the rebuilding of their homes.

APPNA's winter meeting for 2014 was held at Nishtar Medical College, Multan. It was a very successful meeting and was well attended by local, national and international delegates.

The Rehmat Khan Memorial Scholarship program currently provides scholarships to over 50 students every year. This number is going to increase in the near future due to availability of more funds from the profits of investment of half a million dollars for a scholarship endowment fund by NANA. This amount of raising half of million dollars was only possible with a matching donation from a great Nishtarian who wants to remain anonymous.

Immediate Past President Dr. Kamran Rao, current President Dr. Safdar Ali and incoming President Dr. Ghulam Mujtaba for 2016 and all other members of the EC are new faces of NANA and have worked very hard. Dr. Abdul Jabbar was instrumental in raising funds for a new Endoscopy unit and is leading the effort for the timely completion of this project.

All Nishtarians, especially the younger generation, are urged to join and help strengthen the association. As alumni we are indebted to pay back our alma mater in any shape or form we can.

Dr. Haroon Durrani contributed to this report.

Fatima Jinnah Medical College Alumni Association of North America

A group of FJMC Alumni

The Fatima Jinnah Medical College Alumni Association of North America (FJMCAANA) has been particularly blessed for having visionary leaders like Dr. Zeenat Anwar, Munawar Chaudhary, Dr. Mussart K. Qadri and Dr. Sarwat Malik who founded the Alumni Association in 1984.

The following have served as Presidents of FJ Alumni Association:

Zeenat Anwar	Shamsa Hassan	Saadia Khan
Mussarat K. Qadri	Batool Sheikh	Naheed Chaudhary
Sarwat Malik	Bushra Qureshi	Shaheen Mian
Shaista Syed	Attiya Salim	Sarwat Iqbal
Surryia Sabir	Shahnaz Khan	Nosheen Mazhar
Attiya Khan	Naureen Zafar	Manzar Shafi
Anjum Sadiq	Amna Bhuttar	Farhat Osman
Ayesha Bajwa	Fauzia Raana	Tabassum Saeed
Munawar Chaudhary	Rubina Inayat	Samina Hijab

Most of the Alumni Presidents have played a significant role in improving the membership, creating and supporting charitable projects and giving back to their alma mater. They have served their organization with utmost dedication. The first CME seminar was arranged at Fatima Jinnah Medical College (FJMC), Lahore by Dr. Sarwat Malik, President 1987. It was a very well attended and successful event. On June 30, 2015 the status of the Medical College was upgraded to Fatima Jinnah Medical University and the current principle was made the Vice Chancellor of the University.

Since its inception our Alumni, now a (501) c 3 Association, has made a lot of contributions to Pakistan and FJMC. The gift of a complete audiology lab was given by Dr. Zeenat Anwar with the help of APPNA in 1985. Along with supporting the creation of our sister organization the Association of Fatima Jinnah Medical college old graduates; we have donated books, journals and equipment to FJMC. Many of our members have returned to give educational seminars at the college; while others have donated funds for different causes such as food for poor patients at the hospital and scholarships for deserving students. Money has been donated to projects such as the Association of Fatima Jinnah Old Graduates (AFJOG)'s hospital wing at Sir Ganga Ram Hospital. Wheel chairs were donated to the emergency ward of Sir Ganga Ram hospital in 2006.

The following are some of our Alumni's philanthropic endeavors that served the alma mater over the years.

1. A scholarship program was created in early 2000 and it is ongoing. The association sponsors 25 scholarships for deserving students every year.

2. An endowment fund was created in order to move towards financial stability of our organization.

3. Ongoing contribution to the AFJOG projects such as Behbood Vocational Centre and towards the Disaster Relief fund and more recently support for the Hepatitis C initiative.

4. Another major contribution was the establishment of an E-Library with provision of 21 new laptops at FJMC in 2009. The library entrance has a plaque bearing "Donated by FJMCAA." The library has premium Web capability with access to medical journals and electronic books. It is connected to various departments of the college and is scheduled to connect with Sir Ganga Ram Teaching Hospital in 2016.

5. Contribution was made to the educational activities at FJMC by offering courses such as ACLS, ATLS, and ALARM. Interactive teaching on the internet via APPNA telemedicine program was also initiated in 2015.

6. We have started a partnership with APPNA scholarship program in 2014. The most attractive incentive about this program is that each participating alumni association's funds are matched by an anonymous donor. We will benefit from the profit earned by the investment of the scholarship endowment fund, which would be used for helping the deserving student.

We hope that there will be more amongst us who will take the mission forward and nurture the organization.

Dr. Rubina Inayat and Dr. Samina Hijab contributed to this report.

Liaquat University of Medical and Health Sciences (LUMHS) Alumni Association

Liaquat Medical College was established in 1951 at the Civil Hospital Building Hyderabad Campus. It was later moved to the current Jamshoro location, which is at the right bank of the Indus river. It is about 100 miles northeast of the port city of Karachi and about 10 miles northwest of the historic city of Hyderabad.

- LUMHS started as a Medical School in 1881 in the historic city of Hyderabad.
- Raised to the status of a Medical College in 1942.
- Named as Liaquat Medical College in 1951.
- Foundation Stone of Jamshoro Campus laid down in 1954.
- Shifting to Jamshoro Campus completed in 1963.
- Raised to the status of Postgraduate Institute in 1989.
- In January 2001, Liaquat Medical College was upgraded to a full-fledged University, named "Liaquat University of Medical & Health Sciences." The former Liaquat Medical College was affiliated with University of Sindh.

Liaquat Medical College was one of the five founding Alumni of APPNA. Liaquat Alumni came into existence in 1982 at Chicago. Dr. Rafiullah, a neurosurgeon from Wisconsin, was elected as its first President. He was a member of the first graduating class of Liaquat. Drs. M. Murtaza Arain, Syed Latafat Humzvi, M. Mahfoozul Haque, M. Afzal Arain, Amanullah Khan Pathan, Nasreen Kazi, Mahmood Ali Qalbani, Izharul Haque, Kimat Gul Khattak, Azra Haque, Abdus Sattar Sheikh, Maria Sabir and Imtiaz Arain have also served as Alumni Presidents. Current leadership (2015) includes Dr. Abdul Majeed as President and Dr. Tahir Sheikh as President-Elect.

Liaquat Alumni has been one of the most active component societies of APPNA. Dr. M. Murtaza Arain, a Liaquatian, served as APPNA's 10th President (1988–89). He provided space free of cost for an APPNA office for several years. Since the beginning, this Alumni has also played a key role in APPNA's Board of Trustees. Many of the Alumni's former Presidents served as members of the Board of Trustees. Currently, Dr. Imtiaz Arain was appointed as a member of the Board of Trustees of APPNA (2015).

In 1994, under the presidency of Dr. Waheed Akbar, LUMHS arranged APPNA's Winter Meeting at its campus in Jamshoro, Pakistan. During this meeting, accommodations were provided to the participants as house guests of the faculty members of Liaquat. Our 2013 Chicago retreat was historic when LUHMS Vice Chancellor came to attend this meeting from Pakistan.

Many of the Alumni members have been actively involved in social services and humanitarian work. In this regard, Drs. Murtaza Arain and Afzal Arain have been at the forefront of these services in Pakistan, USA, and many other countries. This includes food and water supplies to Tharparkar and Balochistan during a severe drought in 1998. They both provided on-ground services during the 2005 earthquake in Pakistan. Dr. Murtaza Arain has been involved in social, advocacy, and community services nationwide as well as in Pakistan. Dr. Afzal Arain has traveled extensively at his own expense and provided medical help in numerous countries that were affected by natural disasters. Thousands of handicapped individuals have benefited from his well-known wheelchair program, which is ongoing in collaboration with Rotary Club. In this regard, the countries worth mentioning include Bosnia, Kosovo, Indonesia, Haiti, Nepal, Afghanistan, and Africa.

Dr. Imtiaz Arain has been the backbone of the first APPNA clinic established in Chicago in 2008. This clinic, while providing medical care for the neediest, has also created an opportunity for externships for young physicians.

The 2005 earthquake in Pakistan was one of the worst natural disasters to hit our motherland. Liaquat Alumni members played a pivotal role in relief efforts. Dr. Abdul Majeed was the main organizer for fundraising under the New York chapter. We were able to help raise close to $300,000. With these donations, Mansehra Rehab Center was adopted and funded for close to three years, where the earthquake victims were rehabilitated.

In 2011, disastrous rains and floods affected rural Sindh areas. Dr. Abdul Majeed, along with Dr. Khalid Memon, raised close to $70,000 for relief efforts. Half of these funds were spent for immediate relief by providing food, water, and shelter. With the other half, about 40 individuals were put to work by providing them with motorcycle rickshaws. These individuals are still supporting their families through this program.

In 2015, Liaquat Alumni President Dr. Abdul Majeed, with the help of Dr. Khalid Memon and many others, started the Thar Water Project and were able to raise over $120,000 in funds under the APPNA banner. These donations were used to provide sweet and clean drinking water to thousands of needy people in the Tharparkar region on a long-term basis. This work included laying down a 7.6 km water pipeline and constructing three water storage reservoirs, each with a capacity of 10,000 gallons, in the remotest areas of the Thar desert. This project also includes installing 50–60 water pumps in different villages, mainly in Diplo Taulka, where the underground water is drinkable.

In summary, LUMHS has been a key and integral component of APPNA. Liaquatians have always worked hard to uplift the communities under the banner of APPNA wherever and whenever needed.

Dr. Abdul Majeed contributed to this report.

Quaid-e-Azam Medical College Alumni Association (QMCAANA)

QMCAA was established during the APPNA annual summer meeting in Chicago in 2001. The relentless efforts of Dr. Syed Zaheer Hassan from Toledo, Ohio were supported by Dr. Manzoor Tariq to make this dream come true. The graduates of Quaid-e-Azam Medical College, Bahawalpur, who were residing in North America came under one Alumni Association with this effort. The founding president Dr. Manzoor Tariq served for the first few years to making QMCAA a viable organization. Dr. Mohammad Ahmed Alvi, who served initially as the secretary/Treasurer became president in 2006. Dr. M. Khawar Ismail, Dr. Dawood Nasir, Dr. Shabbar Hussain, Dr. Massoud Elahi Mian, and Dr. Mohammad Khalid Iqbal followed the path in leading the organization in subsequent years.

There were several projects initiated or adopted by QMCAA that had a very positive impact on our students in Bahawalpur, Pakistan and the graduates from our Alma mater in the US. Our alumni initiated the BLS & ACLS training at the college and dummies were provided by the Alumni. The Annual Winter educational programs/symposia that were started over a decade ago are still being organized. QAMCAANA has the honor of inviting the QMC Principal or his/her designee to APPNA Summer Meetings in the USA on regular basis.

Dr. Manzoor Tariq started invasive cardiac procedures especially coronary balloon angioplasty & stent placement at the Bahawal Victoria Teaching Hospital several years ago. This free of cost service continues at least on a yearly basis to help the needy.

The scholarships program for deserving students at QMC was also started over a decade ago, and continues with the generous donations from our Alumni. In 2014–2015, our Alumni collected a record amount of money from our members to obtain a matching grant offered by APPNA Scholarship Program. Our Alumni collected $140,000, which is a record for our small Alumni Association.

Massoud Elahi Mian with QMC delegates during the
banquet in Bahawalpur, December 2011

Manzoor Tariq and Dawood Nasir with faculty and medical
students at the winter meeting 2011 in Bahawalpur, Pakistan

The APPNA Winter Meeting at Quaid-e-Azam Medical College (QMC) in Bahawalpur, Pakistan was held on December 21–23, 2011. It was the first ever APPNA meeting held at this 41-year-old institution, located in a desert city full of history and culture. Besides local physicians, medical college faculty, medical students, and dignitaries; delegates from the United States, Canada, South Africa, Sweden and Australia also participated in this three-day long winter convention. Over 500 participants attended the inaugural session on December 21, 2011. On December 22, participants enjoyed CME lectures at QMC from renowned Pakistani speakers along with experienced APPNA physicians. Medical students participated in concurrent poster and oral presentations judged by selected APPNA delegates. Dr. Muhammad Mukhtar, Vice Chancellor of the Islamia University of Bahawalpur, presided over the inauguration ceremony. Outside the facilities, many displays and exhibits were displayed, which provided a glimpse of the cultural and social activities of the area. On Friday, December 23, another scientific session was held. Both scientific sessions emphasized research and local experience in the management and treatment of diseases like diabetes mellitus. Hepatitis C, which is an ongoing epidemic in Pakistan, was discussed with emphasis on the prevention of this oft-fatal disease.

A tour of Darbar Mahal, Gulzar Mahal, QMC's facilities, Bahawal Victoria Hospital, and Islamia University's new campus was enjoyed by the ex-patriates, many of whom were first time visitors to Bahawalpur. The APPNA Banquet was a marvelous event held at the Noor Mahal palace followed by entertainment by Shehzad Roy.

This event was extremely meaningful for both the institution and the city. It was a great feeling to see our institution evolve into a major tertiary care center in Bahawalpur. It was also a wonderful opportunity to meet old friends, share delicious cuisine, and visit this historic city that so many of us remember with fondness. We also thank local government officials for their cooperation and support. We acknowledge the partners of the winter meeting that involved all the major institutions of the city; namely Sadiq Public School, the Islamia University, and Quaid-e-Azam Medical College. Their hospitality and partnership with APPNA was greatly appreciated by the participants.

Dr. Manzoor Tariq, Dr. Massoud E. Mian and Dr. Dawood Nasir contributed to this report.

Jinnah Sindh Medical University Alumni Association of North America

SMCAANA now JSMUAANA derives its roots from Sind Medical College (SMC) Karachi; Now Jinnah Sind Medical University Karachi, Pakistan.

SMC is a relatively young medical College, founded in April 1973 as a result of student activism and public demand. It is attached to Jinnah Hospital Karachi for clinical instructions, one of the premier post graduate medical institutions in Pakistan (JPGMC) which also includes the Institute of Cardiovascular disease (ICVD), and National institute of child health (NICH) in Karachi.

The demand for the creation of SMC was initiated by the student action committees formed in Hyderabad and Karachi. These ambitious students were not able to enter any of the two medical colleges in Sindh despite meeting all of the qualifications and securing high marks in higher secondary school Board examination.

These student action committees were represented by Syed Nadeem Ahmed, Zainul Abedin Siddiqui, Khalid Wahid, and Nighat Sultana from Karachi; Lala Rashid, Taufiq Hyder and Shafqat Abbasi from Hyderabad, Sindh. They were at the forefront of student activism.[1] In order to achieve their goals these students had to carry out hunger strikes and go to jail. The authorities relented when the Pakistan Medical Association (PMA) threw in its weight behind the demand for the second medical college in the city of Karachi.

At the time the Sindh government, due to public demand and political pressure, agreed to the establishment of a medical college at the compounds of JPMC, a federally run Government institution in Karachi. It was agreed that half of the students would be admitted from the Karachi Board and half from the Hyderabad Sindh Board.

On April 7, 1973 Sindh Medical College (SMC) was born and inaugurated by then Minister of Health Mr. Abdul Waheed Katpar who promised to make medical education accessible to every able student in the province. The Government of Pakistan subsequently opened six more medical colleges.

SMC was started in an old building of the pediatric ward at JPMC compounds, an army barrack before 1959, when it became part of the Jinnah Postgraduate Medical Centre. Professor Dr. Khwaja Moinuddin Ahmed was appointed as Project Director.[2]

Initially there were only three departments, Anatomy, Physiology and Biochemistry. Some of the physiology experiments were taught by Professor S. M. Rab in Ward 5 and other JPMC faculty members in their respective departments. Professor Khwaja Moinuddin Ahmed, Project director and first principal of the College was instrumental in developing the many facets of student life, including but not limited to social and political activities, the student union, and student drug bank.

Soon after graduation in 1979, the first batch of students had to struggle for the creation of an adequate number of house jobs for new graduates. An agreement was reached between the federal and provincial government for the training of the new graduates of SMC. The first convocation of SMC was held on the JPGMC ground in March, 1979 officiated by then President of Pakistan General Zia ul Haq.

The initial wave of SMC graduates arrived in the US in the early 80s. Some of these early arrivals included Dr. Seed Akhtar, Dr. Faiq Hamidi, Dr. Zafar Ehsan, Dr. Khalil Khatri, Dr. Javed Suleman, Dr. Aftab Ahmed, Dr. Tanvir Rab and Dr. Sabir Khan. The graduates of Sindh Medical College have excelled in all fields of medicine across the globe.

In the late 80's those who settled in the greater New York area started group meetings at Maimonides Hospital in Brooklyn New York, where some of them were in training at the time which resulted in the founding of the Sind Medical College Alumni Association in 1989. In June of 1994 Sind medical College Alumni Association joined APPNA as a component society which was the first expansion of APPNA executive council since its inception.[3] Now, due to its membership, it has become the third largest component society of APPNA.

In order to improve communications between the SMC alumni, the first newsletter was started in 1990 under the editorship of Dr. Rizwan Naeem. Later, a website was created by then president Dr. Mohammad Ali AKA Jal Ka Jadogar (Web magician).

Alumni Highlights:

Life Saver Project: Startup of basic cardiac life support and advanced cardiac life support training program in Pakistan. This was started during the Presidency of Dr. Pervez Mussarat with the help of Dr. Nadeem Kazi, Saeed Akhtar and Moin Fikree. All of them have spent a tremendous amount of their time, money and effort to make this a success. This project was later adopted by APPNA and currently run by Dr. Saeed Akhtar practicing in Pakistan.

Leadership: SMCAANA has been contributing to APPNA in many ways. They have participated as faculty in the APPNA CME programs, coordinating poster sessions during the summer meetings, leading committees as chairs and leading APPNA as Presidents. Dr. Nadeem Kazi was the first SMCIAN elected President by the general membership in 2007 followed by Dr. Javed Suleman in 2013.

During the 2003 summer meeting we shared our experience with the new graduates of Pakistani Medical colleges on how to get residency and other alternative health care careers; this event has become a trend-setter and part of the parcel of each summer meeting and annual retreats since then organized under the umbrella of the Young Physician's Committee.

Education and Research: SMCAANA also lunched SMC education and research Foundation, a nonprofit foundation to help improve education, research and training in the US and Pakistan. The proposed foundation has been under the guidance of Dr. Slahuddin, an interventional cardiologist, and Rizwan Naeem a geneticist associate professor at Baylor College of medicine. This project has been adopted by APPNA under the MERIT program.

The membership has experienced an exponential growth since 2010 when Dr. Iqbal Zafar Hameed took the leadership as President, and Dr. Aftab Ahmed, President 2011, hosted the first Alumni retreat in Chicago. Dr. Mansoor Alam was appointed as first Executive director of Alumni for five years in 2011.

Not for Profit Organization: 501c3 status was achieved during Dr. Syed Azam's presidency in 2013.

2013—Sindh Medical College which had been operating under the Dow University of Health Sciences was given status of university and named as Jinnah Sind Medical University, Karachi. This was a direct result of Dr. Javed Suleman and his team's activism, hard work and dedication to liberate SMC from years of unfair treatment from the DUHS. SMCAANA adopted its name JSMUAANA in 2013.

APPNA Institute of Public Health: Dr. Javed Suleman during his tenure as President of APPNA also lobbied for the creation of an institute of Public health in Karachi and was able to achieve this monumental task with the help of connections in Sindh Government and APPNA membership in USA. IPH has been functioning and providing quality education to students of Public health from the compounds of JSMU.

Constitution and By-Laws: In 2014, Dr. Ata Siddiqui drafted the Constitution and By-laws for the newly formed JSMUAANA during Dr. Yaseen AbuBakr's Presidency in 2014. After several reviews and revisions, it was presented to the General Body on August 14, 2015 by Dr. Sabir Ali Khan, President 2015. It was approved signed and adopted on the same day.

5th Annual Retreat: Since its first retreat in 2011, each president has hosted an annual retreat in a city of their choice which has been well received by the membership. The most recent fifth annual retreat was held in San Francisco hosted by Dr. Sabir Ali Khan, President 2015. These retreats are becoming very popular and proving to be profitable for the organization.

Community Giving: Members of our Alumni are very generous in supporting medical and social causes. JSMU Alums have been very active in disaster reliefs, free clinics, and providing assistance to needy medical students. JSMUAANA has started an endowment fund which is invested in APPNA scholarship fund. We have been providing tuition assistance to needy medical students at SMC each year.

Dr. Sabir Ali Khan, SMC Pioneers graduate 1979, Dr. Syed Hasan Javed, SMC Pioneers graduate 1979, and Dr. Rizwan Naeem, graduate 1984 contributed to this report.

General Body Summer 2015, CABL signing Ceremony,
presided by Dr. Sabir Ali Khan President 2015

End Notes

1   Appna.org/appnahistory
2   http://www.jsmu.edu.pk
3   Appna.org, under APPNA history 1994

The Khyber Medical College Alumni Association of North America (KMCAANA)

The Khyber Medical College Alumni Association of North America (KMCAANA) is one of the first two alumni associations that voted to affiliate with APPNA in 1979. This is a brief account of our alumni since 2004.

During the first half of the last decade, most of our time and effort was spent on humanitarian projects of great magnitude. October 2005 brought one of the worst ever earthquakes to hit Pakistan. It caused extensive destruction in Khyber Pakhtunkhwa (KPK) and Azad Kashmir. More than 80,000 people perished as a result of the quake, while an estimated 4 million others were left homeless. APPNA initiated immediate relief efforts with support from its component societies. The KMCAANA and the Khyber Medical College-Social Welfare Society (KMC-SWS) were proud partners in the relief work.

The year 2009 brought the humanitarian crisis precipitated by the mass exodus of people from Swat due to military operations in the valley. More than a million internally displaced persons (IDPs) left their homes and sought refuge in others parts of KPK. KMCAANA responded to this man-made crisis with vigor. We organized a fund raising effort in concert with APPNA's SWDRC and its affiliates. More than $100,000 was collected within the first ten days. Relief activities on the ground were undertaken once again, by KMC-SWS. Teams of volunteer medical students and doctors visited the camps on a daily basis, providing both medical and humanitarian relief. During the 2009 APPNA Summer meeting, KMCAANA co-hosted a highly attended symposium, "Swat: Paradise Lost or Heaven Gained," along with Dow and other partners.

In the summer of 2010, the flooding of the Indus River led to a natural disaster considered to be one of the worst in Pakistan's history. The floods, which affected approximately 20 million people, destroyed homes, crops, and infrastructure, leaving millions vulnerable to malnutrition and waterborne diseases. KMCAANA was one of the key APPNA component societies that again joined forces with KMC-SWS, carrying relief efforts into

KPK. SWS's relief projects in KPK have earned them the "Best Youth Wing" award by the Pakistan Red Crescent Society, consecutively for over 25 years.

In spite of KMCAANA's involvement in high-scale humanitarian projects, we continue to stay engaged with the administration, faculty and students of Khyber Medical College (KMC). We continue to explore the ways and means to help our alma mater. Alumni members periodically visit KMC and its affiliated hospitals, interacting with students and meeting with the faculty. State of the art clinical lectures are also given to students at KMC.

In 2011, the alumni established a clinical skills lab at the college providing BLS certification and clinical procedures training. The then Governor KPK, Barrister Masood Kausar, inaugurated the clinical skills lab. Many alumni executives were present at the occasion. As part of acknowledgement of the services of KMCAANA for KMC, the academic council of the college named the skills lab after KMCAANA's founding president, Dr. S. Amjad Hussain. Currently, the plan is to upgrade the lab to provide ACLS certification.

On December 16, 2014, our hearts bled for our Peshawar Army Public School (APS) children when seven gunmen conducted an attack killing scores of innocent children and teachers. Several Khyber alumni psychiatrists in the U.S. along with other APPNA psychiatrists and physicians formed the APS Task Force. From this group, psychiatrists went to Peshawar to facilitate mental health assessments, training and treatment. Khyberian psychiatrists held trauma-focused mental health workshops at Lady Reading Hospital to train mental health professionals and teachers. In total, over 150 participants attended these workshops. Clinical supervision for multiple cases was provided. Our members helped with the initial organizational structure of the psycho-trauma center in LRH. Group session modules were designed for APS children for their January, 2015 school return.

KMC Scholarships: KMCAANA sponsors tuition and living expenses for deserving KMC students via annual scholarships. Students go through a detailed application and interview process. KMCAANA provides these scholarships via direct funding to the college and through APPNA's scholarship endowment funds. More recently, a scholarship fund in the name of APS Principal "Tahira Qazi Scholarship Fund" was established through APPNA in 2015.

With the gracious help of APCNA, the pacemaker bank established at Lady Reading Hospital, Peshawar, continues to provide free pacemakers to patients who are unable to afford such lifesaving procedures.

Khpal Kor (***"Hamara Ghar"*** **or "Our Home") Foundation** remains KMCAANA's long term commitment. Khpal Kor is an orphanage established in Swat Valley, providing orphans opportunities and enabling them to become good human beings and productive citizens. Dr. and Mrs. Naeem Khan continue to be our leaders for the Khpal Kor project.

The Khyber Medical College-University of Toledo visiting professor program has been a success for many years now. This program was endowed in 1995 by Dr. S. Amjad Hussain. Under this program, a basic sciences faculty member from KMC is invited to the University of Toledo for three months to work in research and to learn the latest techniques in teaching.

APPNA Gold Medal for Distinguished Service by Khyberians: The 2014 Gold Medal was awarded to Dr. Omar Taimoor Atiq for his distinguished service to APPNA. Dr. Atiq has been an active member of APPNA and KMCAANA since 1985 and has served in various positions. He is a past president of KMCAANA and APPNA. Previous Gold Medal recipients were Dr. Nasim Ashraf in 1993 and Dr. S. Amjad Hussain in 1995.

Dr. S. Amjad Hussain is probably the most shining star of our alumni. His achievements are too many to count. In 2009, The University of Toledo announced the creation of the **S. Amjad Hussain One Million Dollar Endowed Professorship in Thoracic and Cardiovascular Surgery** in recognition of his myriad achievements. The University has also created a Visiting Professorship in History of Medicine and Surgery in his name. More recently, the University of Toledo announced the appointment of Dr. Hussain as an emeritus professor in the College of Literature, Languages and Social Sciences. This is in recognition of Dr. Hussain's long-standing commitment to teaching humanities to medical students.

Young Khyberian Physicians Committee: Formed in early 2015, assists KMC students and graduates with clinical observerships and the residency process. The committee also initiated a qarz-e-hasana scheme for new graduates to help with residency search expenses. Currently, with Dr. S. Amjad Hussain's efforts, a student elective program is underway at the University of Toledo.

Even though we are one of the smaller alumni, our growth in recent years has been tremendous. Our annual dinner meeting held during the

APPNA Summer Convention is probably the best occasion where we connect with each other on a regular basis. In recent years, we have invited KMC principals and faculty as guests of honor. Our traditional Pashto music evening has become a regular feature that brings back tons of memories from the motherland. Continuing our strong bond with Central APPNA, many of our alumni have served and chaired several APPNA committees. Three of our alumni have served as APPNA presidents. Our friendship and teamwork with other chapters and alumni associations continue to grow. KMCAANA would like to thank our APPNA colleagues who always come forward with open hearts to support our projects.

Presidents since 2004:
Roh Afza Afridi 2005–2006
Ifzal Bangash 2007–2008
Mohammad Taqi 2009–2010
Arshad Rehan 2011–2012
Sajjad Savul 2013–2015

Dr. Sajjad Savul contributed to this report.

12

13 YEARS OF LEADERSHIP

Presidential Perspectives (2004–2016)

Introduction

Since its inception, APPNA's Presidents have served the organization with the utmost dedication and sincerity. These men and women, representing different Alumni and diverse political backgrounds, have one thing in common: a shared love for their motherland and a desire to make a difference in the lives of those in Pakistan. The philanthropic philosophy emphasizing giving back to the country of our origin has been present since the creation of the Association in 1978. However, as citizens of our adopted North American homelands, our desire to serve the American community has grown steadily in the period that is covered in this book, *APPNA Qissa II*. Moreover, the post 9/11 era has reshaped an expanded global vision for APPNA, and the organization's leadership has been compelled to address issues that equally affect us in the United States as well as in Pakistan.

Each APPNA president, from 2004 to 2016, the period which this book encapsulates, has contributed a submission about their respective presidency. The template and concept behind the presidential perspectives in this volume has been streamlined to match those written in the first volume of *APPNA Qissa*, (published in 2004) that covered the first 25 years of APPNA history.[1] Each perspective, more or less covers three important areas. The first part is a brief biography of the president and the second part deals with the achievements during the presidential year. In the third part, the presidents reflect on the issues that they deem important for

APPNA and its future. Some presidents found it convenient to combine the 2nd and 3rd parts.

This chapter has thirteen presidential perspectives. Each perspective gives readers a glimpse into the valuable insights and thought processes of these exceptional leaders. The incorporation of these perspectives also comes with some challenges and contestations in terms of historical events and key initiatives. A similar observation was also made by the authors of first volume of *APPNA Qissa*.[2] The hope here is that we look beyond any perceived misgivings about such details, and instead focus on the positive intentions and the greater good presented in these perspectives.

End Notes

1 *APPNA Qissa*, A history of the Association of Pakistani Physicians of North America, S. Amjad Hussain and Barbara Floyd, Literary Circle of Toledo, Ohio, 2004, page 151
2 Ibid, page 151

Omar Taimoor Atiq
25th President, 2004

Dr. Omar T. Atiq has been an active member of APPNA since 1985. He has served on numerous committees, including the APPNA SEHAT Committee, which he chaired from August 2001 to December 2002. Atiq served as the President of the Khyber Medical College Alumni Association in 1993–94 and again in 2002. He was a member of the APPNA Human Development Task Force, and was a founding board member of the Human Development Foundation of North America.

He is a Professor of Medicine and Associate Director of the Winthrop P. Rockefeller Cancer Institute at the University of Arkansas for Medical Sciences in Little Rock, and Director of the Arkansas Cancer Institute in Pine Bluff, Arkansas, where he has been practicing oncology and hematology since 1991.

Dr. Atiq serves on the Board of Governors of the American College of Physicians, and on its Ethics, Professionalism and Human Rights committee, the International Council, and the ACP Services PAC Board. He has served as President, Chairman of Board of Trustees, and Speaker of House of Delegates of the Arkansas Medical Society. He has been Chairman of Medicine and Chief of Medical Staff at the Jefferson Regional Medical Center in Pine Bluff, and has served on its governing Board.

He has served on the Arkansas State Medical Board, Arkansas Tobacco Settlement Commission, Arkansas Task Force on Racial Profiling, Arkansas Rural Medical Practice Student Loan and Scholarship Board, the Medical Education Foundation of Arkansas, and Arkansas Health Workforce Initiative. He was also appointed to the Arkansas State Oversight Committee on Prostate Cancer.

Dr. Atiq was born and raised in Peshawar, Pakistan. After graduating from Cadet College, Hasanabdal and P.A.F. College, Peshawar and receiving the Gold Medal for topping the list in F. Sc in NWFP, he entered Khyber Medical College in 1978. He graduated as the "Best Medical

Graduate" of the University of Peshawar in 1983. He was Literary Secretary of the Student's Union and Editor in Chief of Cenna—the annual College Magazine at KMC in 1981–82.

Dr. Atiq did his residency in Internal Medicine at the Edward Hines Jr. Veterans Administration Hospital and the Foster G. McGaw Hospital of the Loyola University of Chicago in Maywood, Illinois. He was the Chief Resident at the V.A. Hospital from 1987–88. He completed his Medical Oncology/Hematology Fellowship at the Memorial Sloan-Kettering Cancer Center in New York, NY from 1988–91. Dr. Atiq has several publications in peer-reviewed journals and he has co-authored various book chapters in oncology.

Dr. Atiq is the recipient of the APPNA Gold Medal.

APPNA Achievements—2004

- APPNA adopts its new name: **Association of Physicians of Pakistani Descent of North America.**
- Amendments in the **Constitution and Bylaws** are approved and adopted.
- APPNA budget was formally presented and approved by the Council at its first meeting, for the first time.
- **First Executive Director** of APPNA is appointed.
- APPNA **Committee on Advocacy, Government and Legislative Affairs** is established.
- **APPNA Day on the Hill** during the Annual Meeting establishes advocacy as a key objective of the organization.
- A standing **Committee on Young Physicians** is established.
- Young Pakistani Physicians Resource Center (**ypprc.org**) is created.
- Collaboration with national **civil rights** organizations, like ACLU, NAACP, CAIR, NIF, is initiated.
- **Liaison** with Bangladeshi American and Indian American physician associations is established.
- **Strategic Planning** Conference for establishing short and long-term goals for APPNA is held.
- MOUs with HDFNA and PAKPAC were provisionally approved.
- Proposals for **APPNA Charitable Foundation** and **Cytogenetic Laboratory** at the National Institute of Child Health in Karachi were approved.

- **APPNA SEHAT** was revived and placed on a solid footing.
- **APPNA CME** trip to China.
- *APPNA QISSA*, a history of APPNA, was launched.

Perspective:

My affiliation with APPNA began as a medical student in the winter of 1982, when it held its annual meeting at the Khyber Medical College in Peshawar. I became an APPNA member in 1985, at the start of my residency training, and a life member in 1991. APPNA filled my yearning for familiarity and fraternity during those early years besides introducing me to worthy and pragmatic ideas of service and connecting me to likeminded people.

Over the next several years, I observed a rare cadre of members serving APPNA selflessly and dedicating their time and resources with astonishing generosity. It included people like Nasim Ashraf, Arif Toor, Hassan Bukhari, Arif Muslim and Khalid Riaz, to name a few. During that time, I was given cherished opportunities to serve APPNA and its objectives in various capacities, as well. There was no looking back after that.

In 2004, I had the privilege of serving as the 25th President of APPNA. Some of the highlights of the year have already been mentioned. The first 25 years of APPNA saw a steady growth of membership, which has continued. Even though the organization was on a strong democratic footing with yearly turnover of official leadership, the governance and management had started to show signs of fatigue. The bonds that had nurtured APPNA over its initial years exceptionally well needed realignment. Better membership services and newer modes of communication became necessary. The organization had to go beyond the strong personal commitments and relationships of the founding fathers to function efficiently and prosper. Besides, the events following 9/11 had created pressing issues affecting those already here and those who were on the way.

We started the year with a well-organized strategic planning retreat to clearly elucidate APPNA objectives and goals for the year and beyond. Thereafter, various committees and groups were charged with clear mandates to deliver on tangible goals and they did. The first Executive Director was brought on board to streamline management, long overdue amendments in APPNA constitution and bylaws were introduced and approved

to improve governance, along with the change in the name to reflect changing demographics and to be more inclusive. Staggered terms for standing
committees were introduced besides revamping of policies and procedures
to encourage continuity and to discourage the arbitrary use of authority by
the president and other officers.

The urgent and emerging issues of protection of our civil rights and
liberties, as well as minimizing the hindrances in the path of new graduates
from Pakistan were addressed by strategic allocation of resources, deliberately reaching out to policy makers, civil rights organizations and others,
as well as the formation of dedicated standing committees for advocacy
and legislative affairs for young physicians. Those initial efforts have proved
sustainable and rewarding over the past decade.

APPNA SEHAT, the internationally acclaimed program of primary
health care was revived, and efforts were made to rationalize and formalize
relations with affiliated organizations such as HDFNA and PAKPAC.

Unfortunately, some of the initiatives that were started could not be
continued in the subsequent years but the majority flourished; even those
abandoned are getting a second look, such as the APPNA Foundation and
staggered terms for APPNA committees.

Comparing the first 25 years with the last decade of APPNA reveals
that the organization is still evolving with anticipated flashes of tension,
immaturity and impulsivity, and defiance of traditions and norms. The
good news, however, is that its strong democratic traditions have endured
and those in turn, ensure APPNA's continued progress and realization of its
potential, as long as it continues to have a core group of dedicated, selfless
workers like its founders.

G. Hussain Malik
26th President, 2005

Dr. Hussain Malik was born in Sahiwal, a small village in District Sargodha. He lost both of his parents before he was two years old and was raised by his grandmother and his uncles. He was the first member of his family to finish high school. He completed his Pre-Med Education from Govt. College Sargodha and graduated from King Edward Medical College, Lahore in 1969.

He immigrated to the US in 1970. He completed his internship at the Catholic Medical Center of Brooklyn & Queens. He then spent his next five years at Long Island College Hospital/Downstate Medical Center in Brooklyn, New York where he did a one-year residency in General Surgery, a three-year residency in Otolaryngology, Head & Neck Surgery and a one-year Fellowship in Facial Plastic Surgery.

He has been in the practice of Ear, Nose, Throat & Facial Plastic Surgery at Pocono Medical Center in East Stroudsburg, PA since 1976. He has served for five years as Chairman Department of Surgery and is an Associate professor at the Commonwealth Medical College, Scranton, Pennsylvania.

He was appointed a Member of the Council of Trustees for East Stroudsburg University by Governor Tom Ridge and reappointed by Governor Ed Rendell which he served for 16 years.

Dr. Malik's involvement in APPNA started during the Dallas, TX Meeting in 1994, when KEMC class of 1969 celebrated its 25-year class reunion. He served both KEMCAANA and APPNA as Treasurer, Secretary and President. He has also served on the Board of Directors of Human Development Foundation and as a Board Member of PAK-PAC.

APPNA Heights—2005

Annual Summer Convention in Houston:
Under the leadership of Dr. Asaf R. Qadeer, we organized a benchmark, most successful meeting in the history of APPNA. Dr. Farid Murad, a

Nobel laureate in Medicine, was the key note speaker. Young Physicians Research Awards were also started during that meeting. Our net revenues from the meeting were $225,000, more than any previous meeting. This was largely due to revenue generating business expo model and our mutual agreement with ARY Digital who sponsored the whole music program with no cost to APPNA. They also agreed to promote APPNA humanitarian and welfare projects and in return for their access to APPNA members by ARY Digital. Unfortunately, we could not benefit fully from this deal as APPNA Council denied ARY access to our fall and Winter Meetings and to our humanitarian work for earthquake victims in Kashmir/Pakistan. This was shortsightedness on our part because APPNA needs to promote its humanitarian projects to Pakistani and American Communities like IMANA was doing and benefiting from Geo News.

APPNA Foundation

Most professional organizations and educational institutions have foundations. The objective is to have a dedicated group of members who will raise funds to support APPNA projects like Free Clinics in the US and help Pakistani Physicians get into Residency Programs. Our Humanitarian ventures and Social and Welfare Projects needed revenues to expand the horizons of our philanthropy. Unfortunately, it was not carried through the following year despite approval by APPNA Council. Interestingly, APPNA revamped the original concept and it was finally approved in the spring Council meeting of 2014.

Pakistan/Kashmir Earthquake Disaster

It was the worst disaster in the history of Pakistan in which, tens of thousands of people lost their lives. There were more than 3.5 million homeless and 12,000–15,000 disabled or chronically ill. During the **acute phase**, we provided them with food and water, tents, sleeping bags and blankets. During the **sub-acute phase**, our members volunteered their time by working in Field Camps, Field Hospitals, helping MASH unit in Muzaffarabad, and Tertiary Care Centers in Rawalpindi and Islamabad. In collaboration with Pakistan Islamic Medical Association (PIMA), we provided medical care for more than 120,000 patients and performed several thousand surgical procedures. Because of our members' generosity, we raised $1.7 million and donated more than $4 million worth of medicine, medical/surgical supplies and equipment. It was the year when APPNA raised a record amount of funds in the association's history. Several hundred members traveled to Pakistan at their own expense and had the opportunity to serve large numbers of Pakistani/Kashmiri people affected by the earthquake.

AAPI Delegation Visit

American Association of Physicians of Indian origin (AAPI) Delegation, headed by its President attended our Winter Meeting in Rawalpindi. They also visited the earthquake sites and donated funds to help the victims.

Perspective

APPNA Trip to India

During my Presidency, I felt that APPNA could play a larger role in improving the lives of Pakistani Americans in the US and also our countrymen back home. *The greatness of any organization is gauged by its service to humanity.* During the last 60 years, Pakistan has been preoccupied with its conflict with India. Most of its financial resources have been exhausted towards that cause.

I thought, if we could develop people to people contact, maybe we could play a role in improving the relationship between the two countries and thus divert the country's resources towards improving the lives of its people. Towards achieving that end, we organized a Good Will Trip to India in March 2005. The theme of the trip was "Building Bridges, People to People." We were all very excited to visit India but to obtain Indian visas was a monumental task.

With the help of Dr. Nisar Chaudhary and his contacts in Washington D.C, we were able to get Visas for all 250 physicians and their families. Dr. Rizwan Naeem worked extremely hard in arranging our meetings with several Indian high level Dignitaries and Federal Ministers including Mr. L. K. Advani, the head of BJP

Presentation of APPNA plaque to Mr. Advani, for his hospitality extended towards our members during the New Delhi reception was greatly criticized by a section of our membership because of his anti-Muslim views and his role in destruction of Babri Mosque. However, within three months of our India trip, Mr. Advani was invited to visit Pakistan by the Government of Pakistan. On the first day of Pakistan tour, he condemned the demolition of Babri Mosque. He distanced himself from "Akhand Bharat (Greater India)" and accepted the partition as an unalterable reality. He highly praised Mohammad Ali Jinnah, and while visiting his Mausoleum, he wrote in the register that "There are many people who leave an un-erasable stamp on history, but there are very few who actually create history; Mohammad Ali Jinnah was one such rare individual." For a hard line adversary to making such positive and genuine remarks about Pakistan and its founder was a great achievement for APPNA. One can speculate that he changed his mind about his past misdeeds, and that was partly due to our members' interaction with him during the reception in New Delhi.

From CME and sightseeing point of view, Dr. Shaukat Khan, past President of APPNA, did a remarkable job of organizing one of the best trips in the history of APPNA. During our visits to the historical cities of New Delhi, Agra, Jaipur and Mumbai, we were received with open hearts, not only by the Indian elites, but also by the ordinary people on the streets.

There was great turmoil during my Presidency year because some members perceived my stance on people to people link with India and Pakistan as anti-Pakistan. Their perception was wrong. I am a true Pakistani who believes in peace not war. I strongly believe that it was a political vendetta of some to undermine my Presidency. Though it was very painful for me to see many of my friends lined up against me, I hope that someday, APPNA will acknowledge my team's achievements.

Abdul Rashid Piracha
27th President, 2006

Dr. A. Rashid Piracha has been an active member of APPNA since the early nineteen eighties. He is a lifetime member of APPNA whose initial involvement in APPNA was through Nishter Alumni Association of North America (NANA). He was the President of NANA from 1985–1987 and also during 2002–2003. He started an endowment fund for Nishter Medical College and presently serves as the executive director of NANA.

Dr. Piracha was elected President elect of APPNA in a very closely contested election in 2004. His leadership capabilities surfaced when he tirelessly worked for the rehabilitation of the victims of the 2005 earthquake in Pakistan and Kashmir. He made four trips to Pakistan during APPNA's earthquake related efforts; a service that goes beyond the call of duty for an APPNA officer. APPNA was involved directly in earthquake relief efforts along with the help of numerous other Non-Governmental Organizations.

Ever since his Presidency, he has been a stalwart of APPNA, serving in various capacities. He has been a passionate worker for the issues of our young physicians; especially pertaining to their visa issuance and security clearance by the US authorities in the post September 11, 2001 era. For the same reason, he has been very active in the Young Physicians Committee (CYP) and Advocacy, Legislative, and Governmental Affairs Committee over the last decade. His resilience and leadership has brought results and many physicians, whose residencies were facilitated by the visa clearance efforts of Dr. Piracha, are now active members of APPNA and proud advocates for their communities. His contributions are also highlighted in the chapters of this book pertaining to advocacy, disaster relief, and young physicians. Dr. Piracha is serving as the Chair of board of trustees (2016).

Highlights of APPNA—2006

- APPNA embarked on a major relief and rehabilitation operation in the aftermath of the 2005 earthquake. The Rehabilitation Center and operation theatre for orthopedic surgeries at Rawalpindi General Hospital was built with APPNA donations.
- APPNA also funded the Mansehra Rehabilitation Unit and its operations from 2006–2008.
- A full time Executive Director was hired for APPNA Central Office in Westmont, Illinois.
- An updated APPNA Directory was launched, which was published in 2007.
- Ninety-two percent of Pakistani descent physicians who were accepted in residency programs were able to join on time in 2006 with the efforts of my advocacy team.
- APPNA active membership grew to 2,500.
- The fourth Day on the Hill was arranged by APPNA.
- APPNA website was upgraded to meet the needs of present day electronic communication.
- The CABL amendments were proposed for enhanced transparency including the impeachment of officer's clause.

Service to Pakistani & Muslim Community

Community: Past president of the Islamic Society of the Appalachian Region

Media: Spokesperson of the community; continues to appear on local TV, and writes opinion columns in local newspapers since 9/11 on Muslim issues.

ISNA: Member of ISNA Development Foundation and Founders Coordination Committee. A committee of volunteers that advises ISNA in its activities and missions, and promotes concepts of philanthropy

Service to Local American Community

Numerous interviews on TV & newspapers regarding medical issues and cardiology topics
Princeton Community Hospital Foundation member
Past Board Member of the Princeton Health and Fitness Center

Professional Activities Offices
Chief of Staff, Princeton Community Hospital, 1976–1979 & 1984–1988
Chief of Medicine, Princeton Community Hospital 1973–1983
Current Director, Cardiology Department, Princeton Community Hospital, 2015

Hospital Board
Board member, Princeton Community Hospital, 1998–2009
Vice President of the Board and Chairman Princeton Community Hospital 2008–2009

PHO: Chairman, PHO-Preferred Care of the Virginias, an organization of Physicians and Hospitals in southern West Virginia and southwestern Virginia, from inception (1995) to 2005

Scientific Societies
Fellow, American College of Cardiology
Fellow, American College of Chest Physicians
Fellow, American College of Physicians
Fellow Royal College of Physicians and Surgeons of Canada

Perspective

On October 8, 2005, Pakistan was hit by an earthquake that brought devastation, death and injury to thousands of Pakistani citizens. APPNA immediately began the relief work, gathering monetary donations as well as medical supplies and equipment. My supplication at that time was this: *"O Allaaho Julla Jalaalo Ho*! *"If this earthquake is retribution from **You**, we admit our errors and beg Your forgiveness. If it's a trial, fill our hearts with strength of Faith and our actions with purity of Your obedience. If it's a lesson intended to teach, teach those of us who did not suffer how to lift those who did suffer!"*

We welcomed and quickly joined M.A.S.H unit field hospital in Muzaffarabad in order to provide triage and care in the immediate area of the injuries. APPNA physicians were regularly deployed there. Through the generous donations of our members, APPNA was able to equip two operating rooms at PIMS and built a rehab center at Rawalpindi General Hospital; complete with an orthotics lab, as well as a Rehab Center. We also helped in Mansehra, Melody Center, PIMA Clinics, and several other projects. With the dedication and assistance of many devoted APPNA members, we were able to accomplish a great work in numerous relief settings. It was perhaps the most notable and best-documented achievement of APPNA's relief work to date in which record number of funds and medical equipment were delivered with the help of large number of APPNA members from 2005–2007. APPNA's achievement could have not been possible without collaboration with IMANA, PIMA, APPNA Sehat, Mercy USA, Hidaya Foundation, Development in Literacy, MASH, Rotary Club of Pakistan, the Citizen Foundation, CAIR, Medhelp, Children of Abraham, Dosti Foundation, ERFO, PMA, Islamic Relief and many other organizations as well as support from military and government of Pakistan.

I was first introduced to the concept of an "APPNA House" when I was running for the office of APPNA President. My vision was to initiate a process that provides temporary subsidized accommodations to young Pakistani physicians who would be spending a few months in the US in order to do electives, research, and appear in residency interviews. I continued to advocate for that project throughout my tenure as president and in subsequent years. Eventually, in 2009 the APPNA House project was approved by the APPNA Council. The first APPNA House was rented in July, 2009, and was managed by volunteers of the committee. It was a spacious residential facility in Bronx, NY, with capacity to accommodate 10 to 15 residents at a time. It was within walking distance of super markets and public transport. Residents paid $25.00 per week or $100 per month in rent and shared in the cost of groceries.

My passion to help our young physicians specially those who arrive every year to start their residency training kept me going in APPNA. I have consistently served on Advocacy and Young Physician's committees over the last decade for the same reason. In the spring of 2015, U. S. Representatives Grace Meng (D-NY) and Tom Emmer (R-MN) introduced a legislation that would direct the State Department to speed up the visa approval process for international physicians slated to work at hospitals in the United States. Expected to become law, this legislation will mandate that the J-1 Visa applications be processed in a timely manner so that our young physicians can join their programs on time.

It has been my privilege and honor to serve.

Nadeem Kazi
28ᵗʰ President, 2007

Dr. Nadeem Kazi graduated in 1986 from Sindh Medical College (SMC), Karachi, Pakistan. His first exposure to APPNA was in 1995 when he attended the annual APPNA meeting in St Louis, Missouri. Dr. Kazi is credited for organizing the successful effort to have SMC Alumni Association of North America (SMCAANA) recognized as a component society of APPNA in 1997. His efforts were instrumental in getting different factions of SMC Alumni organized under one organization. He became the President of SMCAANA in 2000. Dr. Kazi also helped in organizing the first Basic Cardiac Life Support (BCLS) program in Pakistan along with his Alumni members including Dr. Saeed Akhtar, Dr. Pervez Mussarrat, and Dr. Moin Fikree. Gradually, he became more involved in APPNA and helped with the creation of the Arizona chapter in 2002. He has served the Association as treasurer in 2004, secretary in 2005, and was elected APPNA President for 2007 with an overwhelming majority. Dr. Kazi is a board certified Gastroenterologist. He serves as the Chair of Medicine at Casa Grande Medical Center in Arizona and also manages to run a busy Gastroenterology practice at the center. He served as the Chair of APPNA Board of Trustees in 2015. He is also serving as a member of the Board of Directors of the Arizona Medical Association. He lives in the suburbs of Phoenix with his wife Shani, and two sons Faraaz and Farhan. Nadeem feels indebted to his family for their relentless support that enables him to contribute to the betterment of the organization.

APPNA Highlights—2007

Launching of MERIT:

I designated my year of Presidency to be a year dedicated to the promotion of medical education. We launched Medical Education and Research Investment Taskforce (MERIT) and APPNA *Sukoon* (Palliative Medicine

Initiative) to improve health care in Pakistan. The Nationwide Insurance Company donated seed money of $25,000 to help launch this program. It was a great honor to have Dr. Naheed Usmani to lead APPNA MERIT program because of her passion for education. Dr. Naheed Usmani and her husband Hasan Usmani worked day and night for this program leading to its successful launch in 2007 and its continued success for several years.

APPNA also started a primary school project, together with a dispensary in the remote Sindh area with the help of Rangers. Currently, there are 12 schools, established with the help of private donors, running in and around Thar region. The teachers and compounders for these schools/dispensaries were provided by the Rangers. Each school costs from $10,000 to $12,000. We also started a free tutoring pilot program in Los Angeles, CA with the help of Dr. Asif Mahmood (President of California chapter).

APPNA Center and Organization

In 2007 council approved policies and procedures for our committees to run the organization smoothly and with transparency. I appreciate the efforts of Dr. Tariq Cheema, the executive director of APPNA, who diligently worked for three months on these policies for council approval. The stock market was doing well in 2007 and there were surplus funds available in the lifetime dues. I made a decision to buy the building next to the APPNA central office which was approved by the council and the board. The new office building was inaugurated on December 16, 2007, which is now home to APPNA free clinic and other activities. We also registered the trademark "APPNA" with federal patent so no one can misuse the "APPNA" acronym.

Civil Rights Initiative

We formed a coalition with other organizations which were actively fighting for the civil rights issues faced by Muslims after 9/11 in USA. The council approved a contribution of $100,000 to Muslim Advocates (MA) to fight for APPNA members' rights in USA and to advise us on a case by case basis if our members face any such predicament. MA produced a DVD on racial profiling which explains our rights under the law as citizens and provides guidance to our community. We also worked with Muslim Public Action Committee (MPAC) and the Institute for Social Policy and Understanding (ISPU). APPNA and Salaam Maryati, Executive Director of MPAC, met with the US Department of Defense to discuss the psychological needs of the prisoners in Guantanamo Bay. We funded ISPU for the study of Muslim Impact on American Society, which was published in 2009. In July 2007 after the car bomb attack at Glasgow Airport we suffered a backlash in the media. We started a coalition among other Muslim groups and partnered with One Nation to tackle the situation and to educate the law makers. This issue was resolved within weeks due to the appropriate approach of this coalition. Senator Hillary Clinton (D-NY) attended APPNA annual meeting in 2007 as aspiring candidate for the US presidency.

Social Welfare and Relief Work

The earthquake relief work continued in 2007. We inaugurated the Police Hospital in Abbottabad on October 8, 2007 and Girls School in Kathai on December 23, 2007. The financial commitment for APPNA's orthopedic center at Rawalpindi General Hospital was fulfilled in 2007. The APPNA dispensary at Topa Soon was completed in May 2007. The Citizens Foundation—APPNA School in District Bagh was constructed. In November 2007, we started a new project in Mansehra jointly with Hope for Humanity called Shamdara dispensary. This center also serves as a mother and child care center. All donated equipment for earthquake relief was distributed to the Ministry of Health in Azad Kashmir and NWFP.

The Cytogenic Lab at National Institute of Children's Health in Karachi was inaugurated on December 27, 2007 by the children who had received services by this Lab. The SWDR committee started several new programs and APPNA donated $10,000 to Bangladesh Medical Association for flood relief, $15,000 to LRBT, $15,000 for Pakistan flood relief ($10,000 to Red Crescent and $5,000 to PMA). Another $7,500 was given as a loan to young physicians. The Red Crescent Pakistan trained our employee Mr. Zeeshan Paracha in Pakistan for rapid response and planning during disaster situation.

Membership issues

In 2007 our membership finally crossed the 3,000 mark. Dr. Shahid Usmani organized the annual meeting which was attended by a record number and 3,020 attended the annual banquet. Education was the theme of our Annual meeting, which included discussions on democracy and justice, a CME program in collaboration with the University of Florida, and sports competitions. Thanks to the efforts of Dr. Salim Afridi, youth debate was held during the annual meeting. The topic of the first debate was "Islamic institution have failed the Muslim youth." There were excellent arguments for and against the topic, which gave us an insight on the mindset of our youth and how they perceive Islamic institutions.

Election Reform

The re-election of President 2008 ended in a tie. This put APPNA in a very difficult situation. The only option, per our constitution, was to have third election between the same candidates, which most of our members opposed by expressing their feelings through emails and phone calls. I took the initiative to resolve this matter, requesting the candidates for their help. Dr. Zeelaf Munir and Dr. Mahmood Alam both acted as mature leaders and came to a resolution. I appreciate and admire Dr. Zeelaf Munir's decision to withdraw her candidacy for the President-2008 in favor of Dr. Mahmood Alam in the greater interest of the organization. We learned a great deal from the lawsuit of 2006 and several corrective measures were implemented. I appointed an election reform committee chaired by Dr. Amjad Hussain. The committee's recommendations on election reforms were approved next year during Dr. Mahmood Alam's presidency.

Perspective

I was first exposed to APPNA in 1995. I felt it was a group of elite physicians just having fun. In 2002, my best friend Dr. Alay Safdar Zaidi was killed in Karachi by religious extremists. Dr. Mohammed Suleman was President of APPNA at that time. He took this incidence seriously and arranged a meeting with the State Department and Pakistani Embassy, which led to the arrest and punishment of the four culprits. My perspective of APPNA changed after this action by the organization. To me, APPNA has emerged as a strong platform for our community to launch social and educational projects. I got involved with full faith and commitment in 2002 and, ever since, I have found APPNA to be a great democratic organization of expatriates that has a lot to her credit. I feel that we still need to work on the governance of the organization. The most crucial factor in failing of good governance in APPNA is the lack of implementation of its own rules and regulations. Institutional memory rarely makes its way to the planning meeting at the change of guard every year. The activation of Long Range

Planning Committee (LRPC) this year (2015) and the ad hoc committee for improved governance of APPNA is working on the solutions for this issue which will hopefully improve the overall functioning of the organization. I am sure that this organization will continue to flourish as a strong platform for Pakistani Americans.

It has been an honor and privilege to serve APPNA in various capacities.

Mahmood Alam
29th President, 2008

Dr. Mahmood Alam hails from Lahore, Pakistan, where he graduated from Allama Iqbal Medical College (AIMC) in 1983. Dr. Alam came to the US in 1987, and in the next nine years he completed his research in Molecular Cardiology, his Residency in Internal Medicine, and his Fellowship in Cardiovascular Medicine and Interventional Cardiology, at State University of New York (SUNY), Downstate Medical Center, Brooklyn, New York. Dr. Alam started his professional career as the Director of Coronary Care Unit at Kings County Hospital Center in Brooklyn in 1996. He also served as Director of Interventional Cardiology Program at SUNY Downstate Medical Center from 1999–2000.

Dr. Alam had the faculty appointment at SUNY from 1996 to 2001 as Assistant Professor of Medicine and Cell Biology. During these years Dr. Alam consistently mentored numerous young physicians and successfully assisted many of them with placement into residency programs. Presently, Dr. Alam is Director of Non-Invasive Cardiology at Raritan Bay Medical Center, New Jersey, where he also serves on the faculty of the Internal Medicine Residency Program. In addition, he is a Clinical Assistant Professor of Medicine at Rutgers School of Medicine in Newark, New Jersey. Dr. Alam has published several scientific papers in peer reviewed medical journals.

Dr. Alam got involved in the activities of the Association of Physicians of Pakistani descent of North America (APPNA) in New York City in 1995, and helped found the Allama Iqbal Medical College Alumni Association of North America (AIMCAANA) in 1996. He became the New York Chapter's secretary in 1997 and played a significant role in the revitalization of the chapter. On August 6, 2000, as president of the NYC chapter, Dr. Alam organized and directed the first APPNA Young Doctors' Seminar. Following this initiative, in 2003, he was among the founding members of the APPNA Task Force on Young Physicians. Dr. Alam also founded the New Jersey Chapter of APPNA in 2003. He has served on the APPNA Council several times; representing the NYC chapter in 2000,

Region 2 in 2001, and AIMCAANA in 2002. He then rose through the ranks in APPNA on a national level: serving as Treasurer 2005, Secretary 2006, President Elect 2007, and President of APPNA in 2008.

Dr. Alam continues to serve APPNA in various capacities as deemed necessary by the organization. He served as the chair of the Constitution and Bylaws Committee in 2011 and 2014. His efforts in this capacity paved the way for the approval of amendments that were made to reform election procedures and enhanced transparency. He also served as the editor of the APPNA Journal in 2011. He was appointed as first chair of the Long Range Planning Committee (LRPC) and Director of the APPNA history project in 2015.

Dr. Alam has been very active in the community for the Advocacy on the issues of profiling and civil liberties. Within the last decade, he has helped with organizing four of APPNA's Day on the Hill events. He has personally participated in the medical relief efforts needed as a result the 2004 Tsunami in Asia, Hurricane Katrina in the US, and in the Pakistan Earthquake of 2005–2007. Dr. Alam has also served on the Board of Trustees and Board of Directors of Human Development Foundation (HDFNA). He has similarly helped to organize and fund numerous other educational and charitable projects for women and children through various non-governmental organizations. Most recently, he co-founded American Muslims for Democracy (AMD) in 2014; a grass-roots organization that empowers Muslim citizens through civic engagement and political activism in New Jersey. He was elected as the founding president of AMD. AmericanMuslimsforDemocracy.org

Highlights of 2008

APPNA Health Center: The first APPNA Health Center was inaugurated in August 2008 at APPNA headquarters, Westmont, IL. The clinic was equipped with donations from APPNA members and is being run very successfully by volunteers of the Pakistan Physician's Society (PPS), an Illinois chapter of APPNA. This clinic for indigenous populations at APPNA Center has served as an icon that has led to the opening of several free clinics by APPNA Chapters throughout America in recent years.

MERIT: The Medical Education and Research Investment Taskforce (MERIT) was launched in 2007. It was given the status of a standing committee of APPNA at the fall council meeting, 2008.

The Code of Conduct for APPNA Elections: The Council approved the final version of an Election Code of conduct by an overwhelming majority. This document now serves as the policy and procedure for elections overseen by the election and nominating committee.

Relief work for Baluchistan Earthquake: The Social Welfare and Disaster Relief Committee (SWDRC) established a fund to provide emergency relief to the victims of Baluchistan. APPNA built 58 new homes in one of the remotest villages in Ziarat, Baluchistan through its staff and collaborators.

Advocacy for Civil Liberties: APPNA had organized a series of events in collaboration with its partners at the summer meeting to address the issues of visa issuance due to delays in their security clearance of young physicians. The post 9/11 ethnic profiling of our community and delays in the issuance of green cards and citizenships was highlighted. (See details in chapter on advocacy).

Support for Democracy and Justice in Pakistan: APPNA felt that the lawyers' movement (2007–2008) for the promotion of justice and democracy was a significant event in Pakistan. The Chief Justice of Pakistan Mr. Iftikhar Chaudry visited the US to receive a Medal of Freedom from the Harvard Law School for his courageous commitment to up-hold the supremacy of law in Pakistan. APPNA also presented an award to the Chief Justice on November 22, 2008 at a prestigious gathering in NYC organized by Doctors for Democracy.

APPNA E-Newsletter: The first ever e-newsletter was launched in October 2008 with the efforts of Dr. Khawar Ismail.

The Canadian Chapter of APPNA was established and formally incorporated as the component society of APPNA in the fall council meeting. Its credit goes to Dr. Arshad Saeed who spearheaded the efforts. Dr. Syed Abdus Samad, president 2009, also played a significant role in the creation of Canadian chapter.

The Committee for Young Physicians continued to provide assistance to our incoming young physicians in pursuit of their training in the US. The

Young Physicians' Research Seminar was held in Lahore and abstracts of research were published in a special issue of the Pakistan Medical Journal.

The Society for future Physicians (student section of APPNA) and **Ayub Omayya Memorial Lecture and Scholarship:** These two important initiatives were approved by the fall Council meeting in 2008. However, these long-range projects never materialized due to lack for support from subsequent leaders.

Perspective

Why has APPNA not been able to build a stable infrastructure and governance system that are vital for achieving our greatest potential? It's a mind boggling question. What is your experience with APPNA? I asked Michael Thompson, the first executive director of APPNA who served the association for few months during the 2004–2005 period. He replied, "APPNA's greatest asset is its selfless force of devoted volunteers and its worst aspect is the conflicting work relations among its officers."

Arguably, APPNA could have done much better had the leadership worked in harmony to achieve our objectives over the years. Several past presidents have also expressed their views on this issue in *APPNA Qissa* (2004) and in APPNA journals. Past president (late) Raana Akbar has explained it more eloquently,

"The fact that APPNA is constitutionally a President-dominated organization and that the term of office for the President is only one year does not help develop a long-term well-defined agenda. Since different power blocs tend to elect different candidates every year, the thought process changes and the ultimate goals of the organization realign frequently. Officers should be ready to accept certain checks on their authority, which will actually deepen their influence and legitimacy. Frequently, officers forget that political process is a continuum and not a single event. Therefore, there is a constant effort at reinventing the wheel, which basically creates a lot of backsliding. If the aim is to improve service to the ordinary member, then the effort should be to develop systems which would help the whole organization."[1]

Strategic Planning in APPNA: During the last 12 years, numerous Presidents have organized special brainstorming sessions at the beginning of their terms to develop a long term strategic vision for APPNA. These sessions received a great deal of attention and had meaningful participation by junior and senior, alike. I had the opportunity to participate in most of these retreats. A lot of work and effort went into these meetings. Unfortunately, nothing significant materialized out of these discussions. There had been a dire need to have a long-range strategic plan for APPNA. It is such an important aspect of our work that it was supposed to be overseen by the Board of Trustees as per our bylaws: "The Board of Trustees shall oversee long-range and strategic planning for the Association."[2]

In 2015, by launching the Long Range Planning Committee (LRPC), the issue of APPNA's governance was given a top priority. Dr. Mubasher Rana, president 2015, has set the stage for broader cooperation amongst the leadership of APPNA. He asked president elect, Dr. Nasar Qureshi to lead the (Ad hoc) Committee on Improved Governance of APPNA (CIGA) and appointed past president Dr. Mahmood Alam as the chair of LRPC (2015). We believe the APPNA Council approved structure and procedures of LRPC will generate trust and promote unity of purpose among officers.[3] A maximum of seven members sit on this committee. The President Elect, President, and Immediate Past-President are permanent members of this committee. The Board of Trustees (BOT) nominates one member amongst themselves who serves for three years. The other 3 members are nominated. This committee structure with all of the stake-holders being represented is paramount to the development of successful long-range planning. A much-needed culture of harmony among APPNA officers is anticipated.

The LRPC felt that the elected leaders will have the opportunity to conceive long term projects of their interest early enough to have them discussed by this committee with due diligence before the final approval by the APPNA Council. Once approved, these projects will have longitudinal oversight by LRPC. I am optimistic that the assigned role of LRPC in 2015 will be respected by all the future leaders of APPNA in order to develop well founded projects in the years to come. The highest potential of APPNA may then be achieved!

End Notes:

1   *APPNA Qissa*, Chapter 7, page 216, a perspective by Dr. Raana Akbar
2   APPNA constitution and Bylaws; page 14, article 16.7.2
3   The minutes of APPNA Spring Council meeting, 2015

Syed Abdus Samad
30th President, 2009

Dr. Syed Samad is an adjunct clinical professor of medicine at the University of Arkansas for Medical Sciences and Medical Director of Arkansas Surgery & Endoscopy Centers in Pine Bluff and Little Rock, Arkansas.

After graduating with honors and receiving the gold medal from Dow Medical College in 1983, he completed his internal medicine residency at the University of Texas Health Science Center in Houston and Gastroenterology fellowship from Wright State University in Dayton, Ohio. He is board certified in internal medicine, gastroenterology and obesity medicine. He is a fellow of the American Gastroenterology Association, American College of Physicians, American Society of Gastrointestinal Endoscopy and American College of Gastroenterology.

Dr. Samad has served APPNA and its component societies as President of APPNA, President Dow Graduates Association of North America, Chairman Board of Trustees of Dow Endowment, and founding President of Arkansas APPNA chapter.

He has served his local communities as Co-chairman of the Arkansas Physician Advisory Board, member of the National Congressional Committee for Leadership in the area of healthcare reform, and Past President of the Muslim Association of Arkansas and Islamic Center of Pine Bluff. He currently resides in Little Rock with his wife, Ayesha, and three children, Ahmed, Rabiya and Ahad.

Highlights of APPNA 2009

APPNA started 2009 with a strategic planning conference on February 14 in Little Rock, Arkansas. Extensive deliberation identified seven major areas that were central to APPNA's vision: The enhancement of membership, financial strength with fiscal conservatism, advocacy, building organizational infrastructure, streamlining policies, procedures and operations, improving governance, and regulatory compliance.

The most important achievement of 2009 was regaining full accreditation from ACCME after being put on probation in 2007. A comprehensive response was undertaken including the revision of all CME policies and procedures, appointment of a full-time trained CME coordinator, and complete digitalization of all CME documentation; full accreditation was restored.

In the summer of 2009, GEO TV reported avoidable deaths of children in Faisalabad as result of a critical shortage of ventilators at the Allied Hospital. APPNA collaborated with General Electric, Islamic Relief and Punjab Medical College Alumni Association of North America. Eighteen ventilators with a five-year maintenance contract worth $460,000 were immediately sent, saving many lives immediately and years to come.

In 2009, we reached an amicable agreement over two long-standing lawsuits filed by Digital Broadcast Network (DBN) in 2007. After extensive deliberation and no financial compensation, these lawsuits were dropped. Under the terms of the settlement, DBN provided cost effective and excellent entertainment services during the summer and fall APPNA meetings.

APPNA took concrete steps toward fiscal discipline and restored financial stability by reducing the entertainment budget by 50% for all our meetings by contracting the services of an event management company. As a result, with all our meetings, including two international trips to Australia and New Zealand, and an Alaska cruise, we ended up with a significant profit.

In May 2009, the newly established APPNA house in Bronx, New York opened its door to young physicians visiting from Pakistan. Countless young physicians benefitted from the subsidized accommodations during electives, interviews and CSA exam.

In order to streamline all chapters and component societies of APPNA, an ad hoc chapters committee was formed under the leadership of Dr. Shahid Sheikh. Uniform chapter bylaws, financial disclosure Excel sheets and yearly reporting systems to central APPNA were established, and approved by the council. This led to Wednesday being designated as "Chapters Night" during the annual summer meeting. Now our chapter bylaws are in synchrony with central APPNA bylaws, a prerequisite for an organization with a 501(c) (3) status. APPNA soared to historic proportions, with 2,760 registered members in 2009.

In collaboration with Aga Khan University and Dow University of Health Sciences, we had a very successful winter meeting in Karachi.

Other than the excellent CME programs, there were two exceptional events: "Young Physicians Research Seminar" and the "Career Counseling Seminar," where APPNA members provided guidance to those students pursuing medical training in the U.S. These events exposed APPNA's work to its potential future members. The "DAWN" Newspaper featured a six-page supplement on the meeting, which highlighted APPNA projects.

In 2009, unprecedented efforts were made by APPNA members and Khyber Medical College through SWDRC to help millions of internally displaced Pakistanis as a result of the Swat crisis. Over $300,000 were dispersed through the Red Crescent and Edhi Trust in Pakistan. We provided three state-of-the-art ACLS capable ambulances for the people of Peshawar and Swat. During these humanitarian crises, Khyber Alumni took initiative in coordinating relief efforts with APPNA and provided medical camps along the route of migration. I express my deepest appreciation to Dr. Syed Mohammad Taqi, Arshad Rehan and Naeem Khan for their contributions.

First National Health Day was organized by APPNA in 2009 in response to healthcare initiative by President Barack Obama. APPNA physicians and volunteers offered free health screening services at 19 clinics across the U.S, in an effort to rekindle APPNA's commitment to serve the nation through community-centered efforts.

APPNA's resource committee, in collaboration with FJMC Alumni and under the leadership of Dr. Nasar Qureshi and Dr. Shaheen Mian, established an electronic library with 26 workstations at FJMC Lahore. This project has provided the students and staff with access to web-based medical education.

On April 11, 2009, Women Physicians of APPNA (WAPPNA) was formerly founded. This non-political group planned to enhance and facilitate the social, educational and professional networking of its members. Dr. Humeraa Qamar, Dr. Shaheen Mian, Dr. Naheed Chaudary and Dr. Sarwat Iqbal facilitated this historic occasion.

From September 25 to September 27, 2009, APPNA members met in Niagara Falls, Ontario for the fall meeting, which was the first national APPNA meeting in Canada. The President of American Medical Association, Dr. Nancy H. Nielson was the keynote speaker.

APPNA MERIT Committee played a key role in the approval of the new specialty in "Critical Care and Emergency Medicine" by the College of Physician and Surgeons of Pakistan.

The Electronic Teaching Initiative was started in 2009. The Neurology e-Conference was beamed from APPNA's summer meeting in San Francisco to all medical schools in Pakistan. The Anesthesiology e-Conference was televised in October to the National Conference of the Pakistan Association of Cardiothoracic Anesthesia. These interactive programs proved to be highly effective teaching events.

APPNA members were also on the Capitol Hill, along with Pak-Pac, lobbying to get "Enhanced Partnership with Pakistan Act" passed in 2009. We requested more financial assistance and debt relief than $1.5 billion proposed in the Kerry/Lugar Bill. During personal meetings with legislators we discussed our concerns in regards to profiling, immigration and young physician Visa delays.

In 2009, we applauded the call by the President and the Prime Minister of Pakistan to overhaul the healthcare system in Pakistan. We proposed a set of regulations, a system of medical error prevention and robust checks and balances to be implemented nationwide. We proposed an urgent need for comprehensive healthcare reform to implement the existing medical laws, establish the patient's bill of rights and mandate the Pakistan Medical and Dental Council to come up with comprehensive reform in handling medical negligence cases. We also proposed the formation of an Advisory Council with representation from medical professionals, the pharmaceutical industry, and administration with recommendations to be made into law and implemented over the next five years.

The Communication Committee, under the leadership of Dr. Nadeem Zafar, revamped the APPNA website and kept the membership informed through electronic newsletters and "blast e-mails."

Perspective

Our membership faced an important challenge in 2009. The hotly contested election resulted in a narrow margin of outcome which divided the membership. In order to bring this cycle of suspicion and discord to an end, we brought comprehensive reform in the membership criteria, reviewed ambiguities in our constitution and bylaws, voting eligibility, and the overall election process. During the fall meeting, APPNA council approved landmark changes to everyone's satisfaction and our membership came together by building new bridges through mutual trust, cooperation and respect for each other. We rooted out the differences that threatened our organization. Our organization learned an important lesson that year (2009): true partnership and progress requires constant work, substantial sacrifice, and building on common ground. We all needed to work in harmony to emerge stronger than before and restore our membership's faith in APPNA's leadership.

My presidency was based on the principles of transparency, accountability and professionalism. Even though we faced some difficult and politically divisive issues, it was always my belief that civility and professionalism should never be compromised. These were my election promises that I fulfilled. All of the landmark achievements of my tenure would not have been possible without the guidance and outstanding hard work by Drs. Zia Moiz Ahmad, Nadeem Zafar, Zahid Asgher, Omar Atiq, Mufiz Chauhan, Adeel Butt, Shahid Shaikh, S. Tariq Shahab, Jamil Farooqui, Nasar Qureshi, and Dawood Nasir.

Zeelaf B. Munir
31st President, 2010

Dr. Zeelaf Munir graduated from Dow Medical College in 1989 and received her residency training at Washington University School of Medicine in St. Louis, MO. After obtaining her board certification in Psychiatry and Neurology, she earned both an MPH and a certificate in Finance and Management from Johns Hopkins University.

Dr. Munir served as the Medical Director of Fellowship Health Resources, which provided 40 psychiatric and psychosocial programs in 5 states, before forming her own company, Synergies Behavioral Health and Wellness. She was also the Chief of Psychiatry of Beebe Medical Center in Lewes, DE.

Throughout this time, Dr. Munir maintained active involvement in several professional medical associations. She was the President of the district branch of the American Psychiatric Association, namely the Psychiatric Society of Delaware. She joined the Dow Alumni Association in North America (DOGANA), ultimately serving as Councilor, Secretary/Treasurer and President. Prior to becoming President of APPNA in 2010, Dr. Munir participated in many aspects of the organization, notably: Secretary, Treasurer, Chair of the Finance Committee, Chair of the Membership Committee, and Chair of the Young Physicians Task Force.

In addition to medical associations, Dr. Munir has been involved with several humanitarian and cultural organizations, both in Pakistan and the US. She is a former board member of the Human Development Foundation of North America and the founding member of the American Pakistan Foundation. She currently sits on the Board of the iCare Foundation and the Community Development Program-Govt. of Sindh. She is partner in Acumen Fund for social entrepreneurship and member of the Asia Society for art and culture.

Her dedication to helping humanity is matched by her loyalty to family and her spirit of entrepreneurial innovation. In 2012 at the request of her father, she relocated to Pakistan, joining the family business. She is now a prominent corporate leader of one of Pakistan's largest food companies and currently resides in Karachi. She and her husband, Khawaja Munir Mashooqullah have raised three sons.

Highlights of 2010 and Perspective

When I reflect upon my journey in APPNA, role as President, and hopes for its future, my vision and abiding goal remains constant: building a stronger institution by making it relevant, resourceful, and in keeping with modern times.

Dr. Iltifat Alavi introduced me, then a second-year resident, to DOGANA and APPNA. Although their memberships had been relatively stagnant for a decade, I joined both and became actively involved. In 2000, I was the first woman and youngest president of DOGANA. Working with passionate and dedicated people in DOGANA's executive committee, by 2001 DOGANA had become the largest alumni association of APPNA with membership increasing from 150 to 450. The same year, I was appointed the Chair of APPNA's membership committee by then-president Dr. Riaz M. Chaudhry. With APPNA's membership committee, we had initiated outreach to the next wave of physicians.

The crux of our APPNA outreach was that new members should become active participants, building the organization's contemporary and forward-thinking identity. Our efforts were immediately reflected by growth. In two years, APPNA membership nearly doubled from 1200 to 2000+ members. Three constituencies played an important role: alumni, women and young physicians. Alumni were reinvigorated, the Women Physicians Caucus and Young Physicians Task Force formed in 2003. They later became the Women Physicians Chapter of APPNA and the Young Physicians Committee. Enthusiasm flourished.

Many believed that APPNA was poised for change, but change never happens spontaneously. After having served as Treasurer and Secretary, in 2004 I lost my bid for Presidency to opponents who as per their own campaign communication "wanted to durust the Qibla of APPNA." The challenges required courage, bold decisions and sacrifice, and I was one of those committed to the task. When I ran for President in 2006, the election outcomes revealed irregularities in institutional functioning. External adjudication was needed. The findings did support my position, but I voluntarily declined to run again at that time; it was not in APPNA'S best interests to mire itself in constitutional deliberations. Nevertheless, the objective of focusing attention upon the need for institutional reform was achieved.

In 2008, I ran for President on the same platform: a progressive APPNA, institutionally strengthened and increasingly relevant in our communities, both here and in our homeland. The election results affirmed an unequivocal widespread support.

Modernizing APPNA involved initially unpopular decisions that later proved to be the prudent course. Together with my Executive Committee, including Secretary Dr. Nasar Qureshi and Treasurer Dr. Mubasher Rana, and an effective Board, led by Dr. Ihsan-ul-Haq, we undertook several measures to improve governance, such as changing the central office infrastructure and improving APPNA's financial health. We initiated outstanding audits for several years, processes to meet long overdue regulatory requirements, and an election code of conduct, including membership verification. We also enacted comprehensive website, digital and print communications to reflect a contemporary organization. The quality of publications soared. All of these measures, which required significant time to enact, will continue to bear fruits for years to come.

In 2010, the Dallas annual convention, and the NYC spring, the Miami fall and the Lahore winter meetings were each more successful and profitable than the next, thanks to the grueling effort of the host committees. Impeccably organized, they incorporated innovative programs, contributing significantly to our mission-forward goals.

For instance, we initiated successful outreach to career-bound young adults with interests other than medicine through the Youth Leadership Conference. Our relationship with other professional organizations, which had previously been cultivated by people such as Dr. Busharat Ahmad, was rekindled with the attendance of the AMA President Dr. James Rohac and other representatives at our meetings.

APPNA's history of outreach to elected representatives to further physician and Diasporan causes reached new heights through presence of prominent legislators at our meetings in 2010. I had initiated similar outreach prior to 2010. My state's Congressional representative had been Sen. Joe Biden, Chair of the Senate Foreign Relations Committee. Years before I became President, I had introduced him to APPNA, seeking his help for physician visa issues. His 2008 Biden-Lugar bill supporting non-military aid to Pakistan made his subsequent interactions at Pak-Pac events even more meaningful.

By mid-2010, with stronger internal organization, enhanced communications and many new members, we reinvigorated our base and embarked on one of the most innovative and meaningful programs during my Presidency: *The APPNA National Healthcare Day*. Members provided free health care in 40+ different sites across America to thousands of people, a truly grassroots mobilization effort.

By holding National Healthcare Day as part of the larger APPNA Healthcare Initiative, we engaged the national debate in the wake of the Affordable Care Act (Obamacare) deliberations, highlighting the work routinely done in our communities and demonstrating publicly that we are committed to advancing healthcare for all people in the United States. An additional byproduct was that smaller APPNA chapters in every region, even rural North America, felt recognized, included and honored. Local press throughout the US covered the event.

I am particularly proud that APPNA National Healthcare Day remains an annual event.

By far, the most unexpected tragedy during my tenure was the 2010 flood in Pakistan, a humanitarian disaster of unprecedented scale.

Fortunately, APPNA was poised to respond. Through the SWDR Committee efforts, we raised over $1M in humanitarian aid, and APPNA members provided emergency healthcare services and supplies. I traveled to Pakistan on APPNA's behalf, visited 19 towns and villages and met with several agencies to help coordinate relief.

Reflecting upon my presidency, I am reminded of an early 2000s APPNA journal editorial: "The challenge of APPNA is to incorporate the past into the new future." This challenge remains to the present day. Vision, long term planning and policy continuity, regardless of ideological or political affiliations, are essential for APPNA to reach the next level of effective organization.

I am proud of all that APPNA has achieved through its founders' vision and the hard work of countless dedicated people, and I am grateful to all my supporters and the membership for the honor and privilege of serving APPNA.

Manzoor Tariq
32nd President, 2011

Dr. Manzoor Tariq graduated from Quid-e-Azam Medical College Bahawalpur, Pakistan, in 1980. He did his Internal Medicine training from St. Luke Hospital, St. Louis, and subsequently completed his fellowship in cardiology in 1995 from the University of Missouri, Columbia. He has been practicing Interventional Cardiology in St. Louis, Missouri for the last 20 years.

Dr. Tariq has been an active member of the community in the greater St. Louis area that is also home to large group of Pakistani-descent physicians. He joined APPNA very early in his career. In 2001, he led the efforts of handful of his Alma Mater graduates and founded Quid-e-Azam Medical College Alumni Association of North America (QMCAANA). QMCAANA became a component society of APPNA and Dr. Tariq served as its founding President until 2003. He started his leadership role in APPNA from the grassroots and served APPNA Chapter of St. Louis in the capacity of its Treasurer, Secretary, and President from 2005–2007. His leadership abilities surfaced in 2006–2007 when he singlehandedly managed to raise funds, acquired data, and published an updated APPNA membership directory.

Dr. Tariq's services to local St. Louis community, to his Alma Mater, and to APPNA were soon recognized by the membership. Despite belonging to perhaps the smallest Alumni Association, he rose through the ranks of Treasurer and Secretary to become the President of APPNA in 2011.

Highlights of 2011 and Perspective
Strategic Planning Meeting: This meeting was held on February 9 at St. Louis, MO. Over 90 members were in attendance; this was a record number for such meetings. It was professionally conducted by a visiting faculty expert, Professor Rafik Beekan from University of Nevada at Reno. Its recommendations were later summarized in APPNA's Spring Newsletter; 2011. The major focus of the meeting was to develop a contemporary

strategic vision, mission, and goals for the organization based on the very fundamental objectives for which this organization was created.[1]

Central Office Affairs: APPNA's charitable status was restored on February 17, 2011 from the Illinois Attorney General's office. It had lapsed due to a lack of compliance with state rules. A system was then established for APPNA to follow the regulatory requirements on a continuous basis, allowing APPNA to comply with all rules and regulations. Following these guidelines, APPNA's audits for the past three years were completed and filed as required by law.

Effective Communication with membership: The web site was revamped to make it a more effective tool of communication. I took the initiative to come out with the President's Monthly Message. It was an electronic way to inform membership about our activities. Their feedback helped me to take APPNA in the right direction, fulfill membership needs, and better serve the community.

Young Physicians' Guide to Residency Training: APPNA mentors volunteered and offered their support and advice in assisting our Young Physicians to gaining valuable US clinical experience. A booklet was published and was also made available on our website to guide our young Pakistani medical graduates seeking residency training in the US.

APPNA Free Clinics: APPNA conducted "APPNA CARES" Clinic Day to continue our tradition of annually giving back to the community. APPNA provided free health screening, testing and administered free flu vaccines throughout the United States. On this day, the Alabama Chapter also unveiled the newest APPNA Free Clinic. Besides Alabama, APPNA chapters of St. Louis, MO, Los Angeles, CA, Atlanta, GA, and North Carolina also initiated their free clinic services in 2011. We appreciate their penchant for giving back through charitable efforts, and their help in expanding the APPNA Free Clinic initiative.

Peace Walk at Summer Meeting: One of our most unique and innovative events at the summer meeting was the Peace Walk in protest of targeted physicians killing and journalists who have lost their lives in Pakistan.

Hepatitis C Initiative: The Hepatitis C Initiative was started in 2011 and it has been an extremely beneficial educational project in the past few years. Dr. Maqbool Arshad developed disease prevention literature and organized several activities across Pakistan to help educate the population about the risks of Hepatitis C and how it could be prevented. We also participated in World Hepatitis Day on July 28, 2011 by sponsoring Hepatitis C awareness activities throughout Pakistan. I am optimistic that its continuation will help to prevent millions of innocent victims from contracting Hepatitis C.

Bone Marrow Registry Drive: APPNA launched a Bone Marrow Registry Drive in response to a shortage of Pakistani and South Asian donors on February 25, 2011. We collaborated with other organizations to successfully create a Bone Marrow Registry in the National Marrow Donor Program for persons of South Asian descent. As a community we were also able to collect over $260,000.

Medical and Monitory Assistance to victims of Natural Disasters in America and around the world: The spring season in 2011 was accompanied by a series of storms and tornadoes that severely affected the city of Joplin, Missouri, as well as many Southern states, including Alabama. Our APPNA community stood together and members traveled to the affected areas to provide immediate relief assistance and medical goods and services. We raised significant sums of money and APPNA was able to purchase and donate a truck for the relief efforts in Alabama.

APPNA remained committed to global causes by fund raising and providing relief equipment to those in need around the world, including those affected by the earthquake and tsunami in Japan, the famine in Somalia, and the earthquake in Turkey. In response to the 2010 flooding in Pakistan, APPNA adopted a flood affected village in Munirabad. We were able to build a total of 128 homes in the village. The Munirabad APPNA village was officially inaugurated on December 24, 2011. Revisiting the village after a year, it was amazing to see the world of difference APPNA made for the villagers. In September 2011, the Sindh province was hit by floods. As always, we rose to our call of duty and raised money for relief efforts in those areas. We have also adopted a village in Sajawal in Sindh after seeing the successful outcomes in the village in Munirabad. The village was officially inaugurated on December 30, 2011.

National Affairs: The Secretary of State, Hillary Clinton, hosted a USAID Global Diaspora Forum in Washington, D.C. on May 16–18, 2011, which I attended. APPNA has partnered with USAID to provide global relief efforts and, in particular, aid to Pakistan. The mission and achievements of APPNA were shared with everyone at the forum. On July 20, 2011, several APPNA members and I traveled to Washington, D.C. to share a constructive conversation with key officials on how to best advance relationships between the U.S. and Pakistan. We met with several Senators, Congressmen, and Marc Grossman who was United States Ambassador to Afghanistan and Pakistan. It was the first time that APPNA was invited to the White House for the annual Ramadan Dinner on August 10, 2011. I had the opportunity to speak with the President at the event. President Obama knew all about APPNA and was very appreciative of what APPNA had done for the community. I updated him on our recent activities and charitable contributions throughout the world and, of course, Pakistan. I also told him about our ongoing fund raising efforts for Somalia, which was the subject of his Ramadan greetings speech in 2011.

American Medical Association (AMA) and APPNA: The AMA Meeting took place in New Orleans, Louisiana on November 11–13, 2011. It was my honor to introduce APPNA to the AMA and present our society and its mission to them. As a result, after years of struggle, APPNA joined the AMA's SSS (Specialty and Service Society Caucus). This was a great accomplishment and a source of pride for all of us.

Advocacy: APPNA returned to Washington, D.C. on December 6, 2011 for a "Day on the Hill." The item of particular concern that we focused on was lingering visa and security clearance issues for young Pakistani physicians. Several APPNA members spent the day meeting with key officials, such as Timothy Lenderking, Director of Pakistan Affairs at the State Department, Department of Homeland Security staff, Thomas Frye and Chris Walker. We were promised that serious attention on the matter will be given to make the process of security clearance on a fast track basis for those coming to join Residency Training programs next year.

Membership Benefits Program: Most importantly, I want to appreciate the APPNA members by thanking them for their hard work that has made APPNA a grassroots organization. It was my pleasure to enact the Membership Benefits Program. The package offers discounted malpractice insurance, reduced rates at most hotels, discounted airfare on major airlines, and many more benefits.

Long live America & Pakistan *Zindahbad.*

End Notes:

1   APPNA Newsletter, 21:1, Spring 2011, 6–7.

Saima Zafar
33rd President, 2012

Dr. Saima Zafar graduated from King Edward medical College in 1987. She was awarded All Round Best Graduate with eight Gold medals and seven Silver medals. She completed her Residency in Internal Medicine in 1994 and Fellowship in Cardiology in 1997. She received an MBA from the University of Iowa in 2013, with focus on Management and Entrepreneurship. Dr. Zafar is board certified in Cardiology, Coronary CT Angiography, and Nuclear Cardiology. She has been practicing Non Invasive Cardiology since 1997 in Des Moines, Iowa. She is a member of the Iowa State Board of Ethics and Campaign Disclosure—appointed by the Governor of Iowa since 2009.

She is the Co-Founder and CEO of Neutrino Medical, a Digital Health Platform company with Mobile patient monitoring. She served APPNA as its Treasurer in 2009 and as President in 2012. She is married to Mr. Abid Butt, has 3 Children, Maeshal Abid, Roshan Abid, and Kaamil Abid

Highlights of 2012 and Perspective

> "Unless commitment is made, there are only
> promises and hopes… but no plans."
> PETER DRUCKER

As the clock struck midnight and the year 2012 unfolded for the next President of APPNA, I set off to follow the tracks of the previous APPNA presidents, who had sacrificed their personal time, funds, family commitments and time away from work for APPNA.

I had studied management for two years and felt that we could possibly apply a somewhat different approach to the year with a clearly spelled out strategy for the key issues.

I set off by creating S.M.A.R.T goals (Specific, measurable, achievable, realistic and time-bound) on every project that I had set for 2012 for APPNA.

The goals had to be set in line with the Constitution and Bylaws of APPNA and the expectation of the membership. These included increasing its membership, arranging financially sustainable quarterly meetings, charitable projects, solving visa issues for young physicians, capital and operational planning, office infrastructure, and attracting the best and most qualified staff that understood the values of APPNA. As I worked through the year, it was a constant cycle of identifying opportunities, analyzing problems, establishing priorities and allocating available human and financial resources.

Major staffing changes allowed us to organize finances through a bookkeeper. Mr. Nick Suh brought us great experience from his IT background. Ms. Jennifer Wozniak worked diligently to supervise the office routine.

The venue of Summer Meeting was Gaylord Resort at Washington DC. The location was very attractive to the membership and with record attendance, APPNA made record income from the summer meeting events thanks to the host committee's hard work.

APPNA's main office in Westmont, Illinois was in dire need of structural improvement and updated furniture and technology. We were able to completely remodel the office with redesigning the interior. Apart from staff offices, we set up a state of the art audiovisual room that was capable of hosting international videoconferencing. The APPNA-PPS Free clinic was also remodeled in the same building, to better serve the community. The credit for this project goes to Dr. Arif Agha, Chair, Office management Committee.

Our membership increased by 18% compared to the previous year. All 36 young physicians who applied for J-1 visas were able to get their visas in a timely fashion, thanks to the effort of our Advocacy committee and Young Physicians' Committee.

The International meetings in Samarkand and China were exciting and eye opening.

Our final culminating events in Pakistan during the winter meeting included a one-day symposium on Burn Management with participation from International experts including Dr. M. A. Jawad and Dr. Ashok Gupta. This was mainly held in light of the menace of acid burns inflicted on women in Southeast Asia. Ms. Sharmeen Obaid-Chinoy, the first Oscar winner from Pakistan graced us with her presence.

Countless heroes in APPNA made the year a success.

Overall, the social, human, talent and intellectual capitals in APPNA are unlimited. Every member is an incredible asset to the organization. To predict the future is difficult, however, future leaders of APPNA may gain tremendous insight through effective leadership coaching and training. APPNA will advance in multiple ways with the approach of entrepreneurial ideas from appropriately directed coaching for the leadership role.

> "Effective leadership is not about making speeches or being liked; leadership is defined by results not attributes."
> PETER DRUCKER

Javed Suleman
34th President of APPNA, 2013

Dr. Javed Suleman graduated from Sindh Medical College, Karachi, Pakistan in 1986. He completed his Internal Medicine Residency from North Shore Medical Center, Salem, MA in 1996. He received his cardiology fellowship from St. Vincent Hospital, Worcester, MA in 1999. He completed his fellowship training in Interventional Cardiology at Mount Sinai Medical Center at New York City in 2000. Dr. Suleman is in an Interventional Cardiology practice for the last 15 years. He is the Director of Interventions at Queens Hospital Center for Mount Sinai Medical Center. He has a faculty appointment as clinical Associate Professor of Medicine at Mount Sinai School of Medicine, New York.

Dr. Suleman joined APPNA at the time when he started his residency training in 1993. He served as president of Sindh Medical College Alumni Association of North America (SMCAANA) in 2004. He has served in the Research, Education, and Scientific Affairs (RESA) Committee of APPNA over the past decade and was instrumental in organizing numerous continuing medical education activities. He has also served on the membership committee and was its Chair in 2006. He was elected as APPNA president and served his term in 2013.

Dr. Suleman is the founding president of the Association of Pakistani Cardiologists of North America (APCNA), which was established in 2004. APCNA has provided a platform for Pakistani-descent cardiologists over the last decade with its main focus on cardiac health and philanthropy. APCNA has been providing substantial help to the most deserving patients in Pakistan; where the poor cannot even afford lifelong cardiac medications, let alone receiving cardiac stents and pacemakers when needed for lifesaving indications. Dr. Suleman and his colleagues have established a Pacemaker Bank in Pakistan that provides free pacemakers for the needy. (A detailed account of APCNA work and services is included in the Appendices of this book). Dr. Suleman was honored with "Tamga-e-Imtiaz" in 2009, which is a civilian award given to a Pakistani citizen with distinguished record of public service.

Javed resides in Old Westbury, NY, with his very loving family. His wife, Rana Suleman, is also a graduate of SMC and a lifetime member of APPNA. She practices as an internist. They are blessed with 3 children, Sanam, Omar, and Hasan.

Highlights of 2013

- The membership fee was reduced by 40% that included the proportional reduction in lifetime membership dues. This was in line with the vision to increase participation of Pakistani descent physicians in APPNA. We had the highest gain in membership, with addition of more than 500 lifetime members.
- The Advocacy Committee worked hard to help with the looming issue of visa issuance after security clearance of incoming resident physicians from Pakistan. We had 100% success in assisting 47 such physicians.
- Social justice in Pakistan is very close to my heart. We held two seminars addressing these issues. The targeted killing of Physicians was at the top of the agenda of one such seminar. Whereas, "Death of Religious Freedom in Pakistan—An end to Jinnah's Legacy," was the title of a very successful seminar at our Summer Convention in Orlando.
- APPNA Scholarship Fund was initiated and about $600,000 were collected for this noble cause.
- Through the MERIT program, we continued to support our live presentation of medical education to Pakistan throughout the year.
- APPNA Institute of Public Health was initiated at JPMC, Karachi.

Perspective

It was a great honor for me to serve as 34th President of APPNA. We started with a clear vision for the future of APPNA. Transparency and accountability in all functioning of APPNA had been our guiding light and inclusion and diversification was the key approach throughout my tenure. My team's goal was to steer APPNA in the direction where mutual respect, positive attitude and productive outcomes are achieved consistently. With this spirit, we have worked hard to increase membership, provide unwavering support for our young physicians, extend continuing support for social and philanthropic causes, and provide support for research and education.

The theme for the year 2013 was "Heart Healthy Communities." With the cooperation from APCNA, we have been working on a program to educate our communities, both in North America and in Pakistan regarding heart healthy lifestyle to prevent future cardiac events. We also realized that in our efforts to support the medical infrastructure in Pakistan, the biggest bang for the buck is in "Prevention" rather than "Cure." With this thought, we initiated the "first APPNA Institute of Public Health" in collaboration with Jinnah Sindh Medical University in Karachi, Pakistan. This effort can lead to a long lasting impact and will help significantly in reducing the morbidity and mortality in preventable diseases in public sector.

Asif Rehman
35th President, 2014

Dr. Asif Rehman was born and raised in Mirpur, Azad Kashmir. He graduated from Nishtar Medical College, Multan, Pakistan. He completed his postgraduate training in the US at the prestigious National Institute of Health (NIH), Bethesda, Maryland and Tufts University, Boston, Massachusetts. He has a busy interventional cardiology practice in long Island, NY. He also serves as the Associate Director of the Cardiac Catheterization Lab at South Nassau Communities Hospital in Oceanside, New York.

Prior to serving his term as the President of APPNA, Dr. Rehman served the organization for more than a decade as President of the New York Chapter, President of APCNA (Association of Pakistani decent Cardiologists of North America) and President of his own alumni association. He also served on several committees in various roles, including Chair of the Membership and Constitution and Bylaws Committees.

Dr. Rehman conducts himself on the strong principles of fairness and transparency and has been an advocate for the same in the organization. He is unafraid to make difficult decisions and to speak out on important and often controversial issues. He set his goal to lead APPNA to the highest level of professionalism, moving away from regional politics and focusing instead on global issues, with the goals of strengthening the organization and securing its future. He reached out to establish important relationships, brought APPNA annual convention to the Capitol, and took important steps towards protecting the rights of the next generation of physicians.

Asif believes that one of the most important roles APPNA will play in years to come is in the evolution of the health care delivery in this country. Not only will Pakistani physicians be recognized for their contributions in providing healthcare across the nation but they will also lead the change in direction in improving patient access and quality of healthcare. Dr. Rehman took the steps to develop APPNA as a bridge between professional organizations and the government with the mission of working together for the future of an effective health care system.

Highlights of 2014 and Perspective

- The creation and registration of the APPNA Foundation as a 501(3) C organization which will raise endowment funds for education and healthcare in Pakistan and the United States.
- The concept of an APPNA medical school was brought to fruition after a significant commitment of donations. An Ad hoc Committee was created to collaborate with different states to facilitate APPNA's involvement in the U.S. healthcare system.
- A Scholarship Committee was created by accepting a generous donation of $1,000,000 from an anonymous donor that required a matching fund of same amount raised from APPNA affiliated Alumni Associations. This target was successfully achieved in 2015.
- Constitutional amendments for well-needed election reforms were introduced, approved, and ratified by the general body in a historical one year period.
- Dr. Rehman reached out to numerous lawmakers. He also had a meeting with the U.S. Vice President Joe Biden, representing APPNA and sharing its work and mission. APPNA was able to educate lawmakers, convincing them to initiate legislation GRAD Act-H.R.5735 to help young foreign graduates coming from anywhere in the world. Dr. Rehman is passionate about this lobbying activity which will help all young physicians coming to this country, specifically from Pakistan, as they are the future of this organization.
- Asif Rehman strongly believes that APPNA's future depends heavily on young physicians. This includes not only those coming from Pakistan, but also the physicians born and raised in the US who have attended local and regional medical schools. He has made special efforts to lead the organization in a direction, which will attract to the next generation of physicians.
- APPNA gave a loan of $250,000 to the Chicago Chapter in 2014 to buy "APPNA House" that will provide housing for young residents while continuing to support and upgrade existing APPNA houses.
- Multiple sub-specialty societies in APPNA were created including pulmonary, nephrology and psychiatry to name a few, which will give a platform for different specialties to work under APPNA as the umbrella organization.

- Dr. Rehman strongly believes in outreach and collaboration with different organizations. An MOU was signed with several medical societies as well as UNICEF to educate people about polio in Pakistan. This effort included APPSUK, "Association of Pakistani Physicians and Surgeons of UK" in order to work together for improvement of healthcare and education in Pakistan. The plan is to build bridges between several organizations across the Atlantic, leading to a significant positive impact on future generations.
- Dr. Rehman strongly believes in addressing the social injustices in Pakistan especially violence against the minorities and targeted killing of physicians. He feels that protecting the rights of women and children should be an integral part of APPNA's mission. Dr. Rehman created an Ad hoc Committee on Social Justice to voice these concerns. A video presentation highlighting some of these issues was shown during the Summer Convention, 2014.
- Dr. Rehman believes that APPNA should continue its active participation in social welfare projects and that it should be taken to next level. APPNA should continue to offer free health clinics in the US to serve the less fortunate population of this country.
- The spring meeting of APPNA was held in Los Angeles, California after several decades. The summer convention in Washington DC resulted in a record attendance. The convention was addressed by Senator Tim Kaine of Virginia who Chairs Foreign Affairs Subcommittee for Southeast Asia. For the first time in the history of APPNA, Pakistan Day was celebrated on August 14, 2014 as part of the APPNA summer convention. Flags of Pakistan and USA were raised together followed by a special address by Senator Richard Lugar of Indiana.

It has been an honor and privilege to serve APPNA.

Mubasher Ehsan Rana
36th President of APPNA, 2015

Dr. Mubasher Rana is a graduate of King Edward medical college (KEMC), Lahore, class of 1981. He serves as Medical Director of Walnut Creek Dialysis Center. He is Chief of Nephrology at Diablo Service Area, KFH Northern California where he is in the practice of Nephrology since 1990.

Dr. Rana's journey with APPNA started in 1998, when he participated in APPNA Summer Meeting in Los Angeles. It was a motivational event that inspired him to join. The first thing that came out of that activism was the formation of APPNA Northern California Chapter, which he accomplished with the help of few others. He served as the founding President of the chapter from 1998–2000. It was the beginning of his love and dedication to serving the community in North America, and giving back to his country of birth, Pakistan.

Over the past 17 years, Dr. Rana has had the honor to serve APPNA and KEMC Alumni Association of North America (KEMCAANA) at numerous positions. He represented Region 8 in APPNA executive council in 2002 and 2003. He served KEMCAANA in various capacities since 2004 to become its President in 2008. He has helped in organizing numerous meetings for APPNA and KEMCAANA from 2002 to 2012. He has served on several standing committees of APPNA and chaired the Social Welfare and Disaster Relief (SWDR) committee in 2012. After serving APPNA as Treasurer in 2010 and its Secretary in 2011, he rose to Presidency of APPNA in 2015.

Dr. Rana is a chartered member of USPAK foundation, an organization that works to strengthen the Pakistani American community by training the next generation of Pakistani American leaders. It educates the community and government officials on important issues such as immigration, civil liberties and U.S. Pakistan relations.

Dr. Rana sits on the Board of Directors of Zaytuna College, Berkley, CA. Zaytuna College is the first accredited Muslim liberal arts college in the United States. It was founded in 2009 under the leadership of Shaykh Hamza Yusuf, Imam Zaid Shakir and Dr. Hatem Bazian.

Mubasher is blessed with a most loving and supportive family. His wife, Farah is a graduate of Fatima Jinnah Medical College, a practicing Neurologist, and a Lifetime APPNA member. They have 2 grown children, Saad and Iman.

APPNA Highlights 2015:

1. **APPNA Telemedicine:** APPNA Telemedicine program was launched. Through this initiative, APPNA members will be able to securely interact with physicians in Pakistan and around the world, discuss cases and provide expert advice as needed.

2. **Centralized electives, observerships and research program:** A new program was developed that helps young physicians in finding clinical electives and research positions through a centralized online process.

3. **APPNA Medical Corps (AMC):** A group of volunteer physicians have been organized who are ready to serve as medical team of first responders in disaster relief. AMC would also serve in peacetime for medical and surgical care of patients, especially women and children.

4. **Support of New Free Clinics:** APPNA has established a new free specialty clinic in Richmond, Virginia, and another APPNA supported free clinic in Birmingham, Alabama in 2015; more clinics are in the planning phase.

5. **Increased number of Specialty Based Networks:** Six new Specialty Networks: Nephrology, Radiology, Pediatrics, Hematology/Oncology, and Anesthesia/Pain Medicine were formed in 2015. This will enable them to network and do specialty specific projects.

6. **Long Term Strategic Planning committee:** The Long Range Planning Committee was launched. One of its tasks is to evaluate present governance structure of APPNA and to make recommendations for more effective governance that is transparent.

7. ***APPNA Qissa* Volume II:** This book covers APPNA history from 2004–2016. It is in your hands and also available as an e-book. This project was completed under the leadership of Dr. Mahmood Alam.

8. **Comprehensive Membership Benefit package:** A new Membership benefits program has been launched. An agreement was signed with an internationally renowned credit card processing company, World-pay, obtaining 1.9% credit card service charges for APPNA and its members. An agreement with a marketing company was signed to manage the APPNA membership benefit program.

Besides the above programs, several other projects were implemented in 2015:

1. **Helping Young Physicians:** Young physicians' committee assisted around 90 young physicians during the post-match SOAP week from March 16–21, 2015. Over 180 young physicians who got matched in different residency programs contacted YPC for visa-related issues. All of them got their visas cleared.

   The financial burden of over $60,000 per year for the maintenance of New York and Detroit APPNA Houses on central APPNA was completely eliminated. The YPC website, cyponline.net was updated. Many features including residency match (lists of Pakistani-Descent Residents and Program Directors), US clinical experience (list of YPC mentors), and Educational material have been uploaded. A soft loan program (Qarz-e-Hasana) for the deserving young physicians was launched.

2. **APPNA Charities:** During the Heat Wave crisis in Karachi early in 2015, $121,000 was raised. APPNA physicians worked on the ground and medical supplies and equipment was donated to different hospitals in Karachi. APPNA also held 12 free eye camps in various cities in Pakistan and over 150,000 patients benefited. Water-borne diseases account for 60% of all hospital admissions in Pakistan. APPNA SWDRC and LMC Alumni raised $130,000 for the clean water project in Thar, Pakistan. Clean water supply through a pipeline

has been provided to 3 remote villages in Thar. It will benefit around 7,000 people in the area.

3. **Advocacy:** APPNA continued its lobbying efforts for the **Grant Residency for Additional Doctors (GRAD) Act of 2015.** APPNA has lobbied to have this bipartisan legislation introduced in the congress. It would direct the State Department to expedite the visa approval process for international physicians who are slated to start their residencies in the United States.

4. **Election Reform and Electronic balloting:** New APPNA election reform was introduced and Electronic balloting was successfully implemented for the first time in 2015.

5. **APPNA Institution of Higher Learning:** This will be one of the most important projects of APPNA. Work is actively under way for the establishment of a School of Allied Health based in Chicago with focus on Echocardiography and Ultrasound training. Our vision is to establish a School of Health Sciences with focus on Public Health and Hospital Administration, followed by establishing a Hospital with Residency training programs and eventually a Medical School.

6. **APPNA Qatra Fund:** This fund is based on the concept of: *"Qatra Qatra Darya Ban Jata Hai"* and is created to enable monthly donations by APPNA members for APPNA Projects. Even if 200 APPNA members donate $50 per month for a year, it accumulates $120,000 per year for our ever increasing charitable endeavors.

7. **New APPNA website** was launched.

Perspective

APPNA First: It was an incredible and extremely rewarding experience to serve APPNA as its 36th President. The theme for 2015 was "APPNA First" which is based on my firm belief that as long as we put APPNA before our personal interests, we can achieve whatever we strive for. APPNA's greatest strength lies in the commitment and volunteerism of its members and they do so in the spirit of giving back.

Unity and Teamwork: I feel my greatest accomplishment has been bringing people together and form cohesive teams. I remember that in 1997 when we were celebrating the 50ᵗʰ Anniversary of Pakistan's Independence, the community in San Francisco Bay Area was divided and could not agree on a joint celebration. My efforts brought everyone together and we were able to hold a very successful joint event attended by about 8,000 people. During my Presidency, I have tried to do the same. I worked very closely with president elect, Dr. Nasar Qureshi and took him in confidence on all APPNA projects with future implications. I have brought people together on a single platform to work on APPNA projects with unity of purpose and clear objectives.

Three Pillars of APPNA: After several years of serving APPNA, I have realized that APPNA's mission is based on 3 pillars:

1)   Education, Research and Transfer of Expertise

2)   Helping Young Physicians

3)   Health related charities.

I feel all APPNA's programs besides the institutional building initiatives, should be focused on these 3 objectives and that is what I have tried to do during my presidency. We are very fortunate that we have an organization, which provides a platform for its members to bring forth their ideas and pursue their passion for serving humanity.

So, let us Stand up for APPNA. Let us all be proud, strong and resolute and let us work together to make a difference in the lives of people we serve. *God Bless APPNA, Pakistan and United States of America*

M. Nasar Qureshi
37th President of APPNA, 2016

Dr. Nasar Qureshi graduated from DOW Medical College in 1983. During his medical college years, besides academic pursuits, he was actively involved in student union activities, and leadership development, especially as a member of the Junior Chamber International (JCI). JCI is an international youth leadership development organization and he served as its executive vice president for Pakistan, and as an international senator of the organization, before proceeding to the United States for post-graduate studies. He received his PhD from Tulane University in New Orleans in 1991, before proceeding to New York, where he did his residency training and fellowships. He briefly worked at a community hospital in New Jersey before joining the faculty at Columbia Presbyterian Medical Center, from where he proceeded to private practice in New Jersey. During his career, Dr. Qureshi has maintained his interest in academics and is well published in peer-reviewed journals and has extensively presented at various national and international meetings.

Dr. Qureshi was first exposed to APPNA at its council meeting in New Orleans in 1988. Since then Dr. Qureshi became actively involved in APPNA starting as a counselor in his alumnus, DOGANA, and serving on every post in the executive committee, as well as its president in 2008. Dr. Qureshi also was a founding member of the NJ chapter of APPNA and served on various posts on the executive committee of APPNA-NJ before having the honor of serving as the local chapter's president in 2007. Dr. Qureshi concomitantly served on various APPNA committees, before serving as secretary of APPNA in 2010 and as president in 2016.

APPNA Highlights 2016
APPNA-USAID Memorandum of Understanding: Under the term of this historical MOU, APPNA and its physicians will perform health care related activities, including, but not limited to, supporting medical camps

and consultations at USAID facilities in Pakistan. APPNA will also provide continuing medical education to the staff at USAID facilities through their MERIT Program, besides providing telemedicine support to the physicians at USAID facilities through the APPNA Telemedicine Program. USAID will in return provide logistical support and local coordination for APPNA programs. Once successful, this also opens doors for APPNA to work with USAID supporting their healthcare-related programs internationally.

Collaboration with Rotary International in promoting support for eradication of Polio in Pakistan: APPNA has collaborated with Rotary International to promote supporting efforts for the eradication of polio in Pakistan and highlighted the polio eradication drive in various forums. The President of Rotary International, Mr. John F. Germ, Guest of Honor on Alumni night at the 2016 Annual Convention, highlighted the ongoing relationship.

APPNA US College Scholarship: This need-based scholarship fund for Pakistani descent students in college, is a first in ensuring APPNA's involvement in the larger community, and providing support to our future generations.

Adopt a Medical Students in Pakistan: A scholarship has been established in association with the ICare foundation in Pakistan to support tuition for medical students in public medical schools on a need-basis. Nearly 50 scholarships have been given in the inaugural year of this program.

Limited Term Loan Program for Need Based Support of Pakistani Physicians for USMLE Exams and Interview Process: Although APPNA has supported this over the years under various programs, this program guarantees continuous support from donors year after year, with reasonable guarantee of return of funds and recirculation for future graduates.

APPNA Medical Corps: APPNA's first peace time mission was sent to Guatemala. This serves as a basis for expanded role of APPNA in international community for providing health care services, not only in emergent situation and natural disasters, but utilizing its potential fully as a peace time Medical corp.

APPNA Job board: A much needed job exchange was created for the first time on APPNA website.

APPNA Find a Doctor Program: A new program was initiated to allow larger community, especially Pakistani descent patients, to be able to search for Pakistani-descent physicians in their areas.

APPNA free Medical Clinic in Karachi: A permanent APPNA medical clinic was started in Karachi in 2016. If successful, this provides a framework to replicate such clinics throughout Pakistan.

A new webinar program for young graduates was established and has initially focused on residency applications and interview processes, through the committee on Young Physicians.

Perspective
Prevent, Heal, Empower

The theme of APPNA in 2016—"Prevent, Heal, Empower" reflects what I believe is the core of APPNA mission and values. Although the theme, at first glance, may appear to be related to health care and patients, it is beyond that and reflective of how, as an organization, we should be approaching our mission directed towards healthcare, education and empowering, not only our patients with their health, but our communities here in USA and Pakistan with being able to navigate their lives for a better tomorrow.

Community Involvement

There is no doubt in my mind that besides the work we do in Pakistan, as an organization we have to take ownership of our communities and future generations in North America and help them become a proud community of Americans and Canadians of Pakistani descent. The need-based college scholarship for Pakistani-Descent students going to college is just a first step. It is crucial for our growth and respect in the community to bring additional programs such as this to APPNA. Just one community based program, which was initiated in 2010, the APPNA National Health Care Day, has become a flagship program of APPNA, and brings APPNA well deserved coverage and prominence in our communities every year.

The Path Forward for APPNA

The most important thing today for APPNA is to consider how it can improve itself, and what organization building steps we can put in place to ensure the survival, growth and increased relevance of APPNA in future. To this end, Dr. Mubasher Rana (President 2015) initiated the Committee on Improved Governance of APPNA. The committee worked diligently in 2015, with wide ranged discussions in various groups of APPNA members, seeking to understand the issues for APPNA and listening to the members on how they believe we can improve the governance of APPNA as a first step. The consensus recommendations were presented to the Long Range Planning Committee and approved last year. This year the discussions continued unofficially including a retreat called to discuss just "how we can improve APPNA" in the start of the year. The council gave a green light to Constitution and Bylaws Committee (CABLC) to prepare and present a draft of changes to the CABL for its consideration. The CABLC is planning to present their recommendations to the Council at its fall meeting in 2016. This will likely be the first step in discussion and consensus towards appropriate changes. Interestingly, none of what is being proposed and what we have heard from the membership is new! If we peruse the pages of *APPNA Qissa* (2004), or minutes of previous Council meetings, we will find many previous Presidents and Councils have made all of these suggestions in one form or the other. Then what has kept us from implementing them? One issue which has been pointed out ad nauseum is the discontinuity of processes from year to year, with the annual change of President. The organization has become slave to its structure, and is president-centric, instead of the structure being organization-centric. Possibly, also the biggest obstacle to change always is "the fear of change itself!" Someone has to do it, let's make it happen, so we can take on the strengths of our thirty-nine years and ensure a vibrant and growing organization for the next hundred.

13

APPENDICES

THE HIGHLIGHTS OF APPNA HISTORY[1]

(1976–2016)

October 30, 1976: A plenary session was held at the Hyatt Regency Hotel in Dearborn, Michigan. Approximately 20 physicians participated. This landmark meeting was the result of the background work initiated by Zaheer G. Ahmad in West Bloomfield, MI. Most of the early meetings were held at Dr. Ahmad's house. Those who were dedicated enough to take part in the initial work were: (late) Dr. Malik Mirza, Dr. Ahsan-ul Haq, Dr. Khalid Latif, Dr. Sattar Choudhary, (late) Dr. Aurangzeb Sheikh, Dr. Rauf Sheikh, Drs. Tariq and Rehana Siddiqui, (late) Dr. Chaudhary Mohammad ldris, (late) Dr. Zafar Mahmud, and Dr. Basharat Ahmad.[1]

Before APPNA was created, a few physicians who graduated from King Edward Medical College in Lahore met as a group every year concurrent with the annual meeting of American Medical Association (AMA). This group effort was initiated by Dr. Amanullah Khan from Dallas, TX. The late Dr. Malik Mirza was one of the regular participants in this group. He initiated a dialogue with this group on behalf of APPNA (in the making) and arranged a meeting at the residence of Dr. Sadiq Mohyuddin in St. Louis, MO, in 1978.[2]

1　Besides APPNA Qissa published in 2004, various short accounts on APPNA history were also written and could be found in the newsletters and journals of the association. These synopses on APPNA history were authored by, Zaheer G. Ahmad, S. Amjad Hussain, Hassan I. Bukhari, Raana S. Akbar, and Mubasher E. Rana. Nevertheless, a comprehensive account of historical highlights of APPNA was needed from its inception to present. Author has made an effort to achieve that goal by gathering information from all the available resources.

August 29, 1977: The Association was formally incorporated as the **Association of Pakistani Physicians (APP).** The first constitution was drafted by a committee chaired by Dr. Basharat Ahmad (MI). It was based on the AMA framework. The constitution was then presented to the membership at the Hyatt Regency Hotel in Dearborn (MI) in 1977. In the same meeting Dr. Zaheer G. Ahmad was elected as the President and (late) Dr. Malik Mirza as the Secretary-Treasurer of the association. The APP was also registered as a Michigan based non-profit organization in 1977.[3]

June 20, 1978: The first formal meeting in USA was held in Dearborn, Michigan.

Later, a national dinner meeting was held at the Hyatt Regency Dearborn on September 22, 1978. Pakistani Ambassador Sahabzada Yaqub Khan was invited as chief guest. This meeting was well attended and some physicians from Canada also participated.

September 15, 1979: The first national symposium called "**Health Care in Pakistan**" was sponsored by APPNA on September 15, 1979 at the Detroit Plaza Hotel - Renaissance Center.

December 20, 1980: The first meeting in Pakistan was held at the Hotel Intercontinental, Karachi. President of Pakistan General Zia ul Haq inaugurated the meeting. After the Karachi meeting, a number of winter meetings were held by rotation on the campuses of various alumni affiliates. The first ever CME meeting was held in King Edward Medical College, Lahore, and also in Karachi in March/April, 1980. The topic was "Update in Medicine and Surgery." The summer meeting was held in Washington, DC. The Alumni of KE, Dow, and Khyber started negotiations to join APPNA.

1981: A committee was commissioned to draft a new set of rules for governance. The summer meeting was held in Detroit, MI, and winter meeting went to Lahore.

1982: APPNA launched Pakistan Research Society of Pakistan under the direction of Dr. Nausherwan Burki. The Society encouraged research in

Pakistan and held regular research forums in Pakistan. There have not been any reports on the activity of this society after its initial years. In the 1982 fall meeting, it was decided that in addition to medical education and welfare projects in Pakistan, APPNA should also direct its efforts towards similar causes within the US and Canada. Also in 1982, at the request of the Government of Pakistan, APPNA prepared a comprehensive plan for postgraduate medical education and training in Pakistan. As is the wont of Pakistani bureaucracy, it was never implemented as intended.[4]

In the initial years, the association was called Association of Pakistani Physicians (APP). In 1982 letters "NA" were added to reflect the geographic location of the association. The name was thus changed to **Association of Pakistani Physicians of North America (APPNA).**

During 1982, the central office of APPNA was shifted to Fort Worth Texas. Initially the office was located in Dr. Aslam Malik's office. The first ever Executive Secretary, Barbara Birgel, was hired who worked in the first free standing APPNA office in Dallas for three years. Ms. Birgel was instrumental along with Dr. Aslam Malik to apply and obtain APPNA's tax-exempt status as a 501-C-3 organization in 1982.[5] The summer meeting was held in New York and winter meeting was held in Peshawar in 1982.

Regular publication of the newsletter was started, and became a means of communication and an instrument of enunciating the manifesto of this organization. The final draft of APPNA constitution and bylaws prepared by the committee led by Dr. S. Sultan Ahmed was presented and approved.

APPNA membership was at 200 in 1982. Liaquat Medical College Alumni was formed in 1982.

Also in 1982, months before he was to assume presidency of APPNA, Dr. Iftikhar Salahuddin resigned as president elect and returned to Pakistan permanently. That created two vacancies that had to be filled simultaneously. Dr. Amjad Hussain was nominated and elected as president 1982–83 and Amanullah Khan was elected president-elect to succeed him a year later.

1983: The summer meeting was held in Washington, DC and winter meeting was held in Multan in 1983.

1984: Just about the time that APPNA was organized, another organization called, International Association of Pakistani Physicians (IAPP) was being formulated on the East Coast. The late Dr. Bunyad Haider, was among others from the US and Canada who started this organization independent of APPNA. Serious negotiations were held between the two groups and the other organization magnanimously agreed to merge into APPNA in 1984.[6'7]

APPNA established the first **audiology laboratory** in Pakistan. APPNA membership was at 600. Fatima Jinnah Medical College Alumni Association came into being and joined APPNA.[8]

In July 1984, APPNA appealed to the American Medical Association (AMA) on the issues faced by Foreign Medical Graduates (FMG). The Executive Council unanimously passed a resolution asking the AMA to establish a mechanism by which qualified foreign medical graduates are given equal chance to compete with American medical graduates for entry-level programs in postgraduate education.[9] The summer meeting was held in Detroit, MI, and winter meeting was held in Hyderabad in 1984.

1985: APPNA spearheaded the formation of the **National Alliance of All International Physicians** and was accorded the status of Co-Chairman. This Alliance consisted of the following physician organizations; APPNA, American Association of Physicians from India (AAPI), Association of Philippine Physicians of America (APPA), American College of International Physicians (ACIP), Islamic Medical Association (IMA), and Latin American Physician Association (LAPA). This alliance evolved into the International Association of American Physicians (IAAP) in 1988. The struggle of the IAAP for the rights of FMGs resulted in numerous remarkable accomplishments. The effective lobbying with congress eliminated the amendment to the Budget Reconciliation Bill in 1986 that had proposed elimination of all funding for FMG training in the US. The summer meeting was held in Anaheim, CA, and winter meeting was held in Karachi in 1985.

1986: Downer Grove (IL) was approved as the permanent headquarters for the Association and the office moved from Dallas, Texas in March 1986. APPNA held a joint session with IAAP in Washington, DC. APPNA/ KEMCAANA **Post Graduate Education (PGE)** Program was initiated and an endowment fund was collected with donations of $450,000. The idea of this successful PGE program was conceived by Dr. Arif Toor (CT), president APPNA (1989–90). The endowed residency program in internal medicine was launched at the New Britain General Hospital in Connecticut that helped about eighty Pakistani doctors to obtain and complete three-year residency training over the period of two decades. The summer meeting was held in Washington, DC, and winter meeting was held in Lahore.

1987: The Youth Program was initiated for the first time. **Lifetime membership** was also instituted and an endowment fund from the lifetime dues was initiated. The summer meeting was held in Oakbrook, IL, and winter meeting was held in Peshawar in 1987.

1988: The concept of **APPNA SEHAT**, a primary healthcare program was proposed by the President Nasim Ashraf and it was approved in July 1988. The summer meeting was held in Terrytown, New York, and winter meeting was held in Lahore.

1989: APPNA SEHAT, a primary healthcare project to serve rural areas in Pakistan, was launched. The premise was simple: inoculate children, use of homemade oral rehydration salt to prevent infectious diarrhea related morbidity and mortality, help installation of hand pumps for potable water, training of lady health visitors, and teach villagers the value of proper sewer drainage from their homes. It was mostly a self-help program and was initiated in 4 villages in different parts of Pakistan. Within a few years the results showed dramatic success. It was later expanded to include adult literacy and vocational training. It is interesting to note that this self-help program was run at the cost of $1 per person per year. In later years, some international charities and AID programs gave financial assistance to the program. The program was later expanded to include dozens of villages in Pakistan. Because of its success, APPNA Sehat model was adopted by some of the 3rd world countries in South America.[10] It also received the **Richard and Hinda Rosenthal Award** by the American College of Physicians.

APPNA/KEMCAANA PGE program, which was initially started to help KE graduates, was opened to all Pakistani medical graduates. APPNA also became the first organization to endorse Imran Khan's Cancer Hospital.

The AMA yielded to the advocacy efforts of the IAAP and created a section for International Medical Graduates (IMGs), to address the issues of foreign trained physicians in organized medicine. Also in 1989, major bills were passed in the Senate as well as in the Congress that brought

IMGs at par with US medical graduates; once a physician was licensed in the US, there would be no distinction as to where that physician received medical training.

In 1989, the summer meeting was held in Detroit, MI, and winter meeting was held in Multan.

1990: The political action committee or **PAK-PAC**, initially conceived as the political arm of APPNA, was registered as a separate entity.

Also in 1990, the **Children of Association of Pakistani Physicians of North America (CAPPNA)** was formed to organize the children of APPNA under one banner and the Youth Advisory Committee was formed to oversee and to advise on the activities of this group.[11] The summer meeting was held in Washington, DC, and winter meeting was held in Lahore.

1991: The **Publication Committee** was created for the first time and the newsletter was again resumed. APPNA Sehat completed and presented the Village Improvement Model (VIM) on which all subsequent APPNA Sehat projects would be based. The summer meeting was held in Chicago, and winter meeting was held in Islamabad.

1992: The newsletter was revamped; a standardized format was conceived and the post of an editor as a separate entity was formed. The practice of awarding the **APPNA Gold Medal** as the most prestigious recognition of APPNA was started on the initiative of Dr. Khalid J. Awan. Chapter presidents were given voting rights in the Executive Council. The Single Physicians Group was formed that was subsequently known as the **Social Forum**. The first complete **directory of Pakistani physicians** was created. In June 1992, APPNA purchased the property for its central office in Westmont, Illinois.

Also in 1992, with the help of IAAP which APPNA partnered with for lobbying, the Health Professional Reauthorization Act was passed resulting in the establishment of the National Council on Medical Licensure; allowing the Council to make recommendations to the US Department of Health and Human Services on how to insure non-discriminatory medical licensing practices. This greatest victory was called the Solarez/Kennedy/Simon bill for its major sponsors, which finally put to rest the issues of Medicare and Medicaid funding for the training of international medical graduates. The bill mandated that residency programs receiving federal funds could not discriminate based upon the country of origin and medical school graduation.[12]

In 1992, the summer meeting was held in New York City, and winter meeting was held in Lahore.

1993: An accountant was appointed for the first time and the fiscal policies were defined for the organization. **The Society of Young Adults (SAYA)** was created in October of 1993 to have youth between the ages of 18–28 in one group and CAPPNA's membership was then limited to the age group of 12–17. In 1993, The summer meeting was held in Washington, DC, and winter meeting was held in Peshawar.

1994: Sindh Medical College Alumni Association joined APPNA. Washington/Baltimore became the first chapter to gain recognition as a Component Society. This was the first expansion of the Executive Council since the early years of the Association.

Constitution and Bylaws were amended to incorporate Regional Chapters and Physicians-In-Training Section as Components Societies of APPNA, to define the role and functions of various committees, and to change the term of office to correspond to the fiscal year.

The summer meeting was held in Dallas, TX, and winter meeting was held in Hyderabad.

1995: A tradition was set that all meetings whether Annual or Regional should be profitable. The Local Host committees were empowered to run their meetings and solicit funds from pharmaceutical companies. CME was reintroduced after a hiatus of a few years. **APPNA Alliance,** and the Task Force on HDF was appointed. In 1995, the summer meeting was held in St. Louis, MO, and winter meeting was held in Islamabad.

1996: A Resource Center was organized at the central office to help the physicians in training with placement opportunities, and visa related issues. The summer meeting was held in Detroit, MI, and winter meeting was held in Multan.

1997: APPNA, (SIH) Society of International HELP, and Noor Foundation cosponsored the Human Development Foundation of North America (HDFNA). The mission of HDFNA was to launch a non-political movement for positive social change and community empowerment through mass literacy, enhanced quality of education, universal primary health, and grass root economic development. This was a gift to the people of Pakistan on the occasion of the 50th anniversary of Pakistan's independence.

Allama Iqbal Medical College Alumni Association (AIMCAANA) was formally recognized as a component society of APPNA. The summer meeting was held in New York City, and winter meeting was held in Lahore.

1998: The Committee for Research, Education and Scientific Affairs (RESA) was revamped and was charged with the provision of CME programs at all APPNA meetings and for acquisition of independent accreditation from the Accreditation from the Accreditation Council for continuing Education (ACCME). The second APPNA directory was printed. Dr. Durdana Gilani became the first female president of APPNA. **NAMA (North American Medical Alumni Association)** was recognized as a component society of APPNA. Rawalpindi Medical College Alumni Association (RMCAANA) also achieved the status of recognition by APPNA. The summer meeting was held in Los Angeles, CA, and winter meeting was held in Peshawar.

1999: The APPNA journal was printed for the first time. $50,000 was donated to LRBT (Layton Rehmatullah Benevolent Trust) for building an APPNA wing in their Quetta, Pakistan unit. Another sizable donation was given to the Smithsonian for what was subsequently an educational internet program on The Mughal Gardens. The concept of international trips was approved. The post of Executive Director was defined and also approved by the Executive Council. The summer meeting was held in New Orleans, LA, and winter meeting was held in Lahore.

2000: It was decided that APPNA elections were to be held by an outside agency. Aga Khan Alumni Association joined APPNA. The first international trip by APPNA to Egypt was arranged. APPNA Listserv was started. The summer meeting was held in Atlanta, GA, and winter meeting was held in Lahore.

2001: APPNA strongly condemned the atrocious and brutal acts of terrorism on September 11, 2001. Shocked by the enormity of the events, first response of APPNA and its members were to show support and solidarity with their adopted homeland, America. APPNA Disaster Management Committee and the New York (NY) Chapter launched APPNA NY Crisis Management Center on September 18, 2001 in Franklin Square NY. This effort received much positive attention in the media, and showed APPNA's concern for those affected by the terrorist acts. President Riaz M. Chaudhry changed the venue of fall meeting from Florida to NYC to extend APPNA's support to the families of the victims. It was held on November 10 at LaGuardia Marriott where 9/11 heroes were honored and $35,000 was raised and donated to Fire Fighters Association and American Red Cross.

In NYC, a coalition of various Pakistani organizations was put together under the APPNA NYC Chapter in 2002. The coalition was called FAPA, Federation of Pakistani American Associations. It worked in close collaboration with various nonprofit organizations in New York working on the detainees and undocumented Pakistanis. It arranged for financial and legal help for the detainees.

APPNA received its **accreditation by Accreditation Council for Continuing Medical Education (ACCME)** in April 2001 after three-year-long hard work of the Association spearheaded by Drs. Juzar Ali and Raza Dilawari.[13] Quaid-e-Azam Medical College Alumni Association (QMCAANA) was accepted as a component society in APPNA. Dr. Raana Akbar was elected as the second woman president of APPNA to serve in 2003. The summer meeting was held in Chicago and winter meeting was held in Multan.

2002: APPNA held its summer meeting in NYC to express membership's support to the city after the 9/11 atrocities. The process of revision of Constitution and Bylaws was started for the third time since 1982. The second international trip to Spain and Morocco took place. APPNA applied for an affiliate organization status to AMA. APPNA membership approached close to 2,000 mark. The summer meeting was held in New York City, and winter meeting was held in Karachi. A book detailing APPNA's history was requisitioned.[14]

2003: The Constitution and Bylaws had a major revision and the first reading of that revision was done. **APPNA's Task Force on Young Physicians** was constituted to review and lobby against problems faced by Pakistani physicians in getting US training post 9/11. Less than 30% of the Pakistani physicians accepted by the US residency training programs were able to join on time due to visa delays under the new US policy of security clearance in 2003. APPNA was represented for the first time in the AMA at the SSS (specialty and service section). The summer meeting was held at Gaylord Resort in Orlando, FL, and winter meeting was held in Karachi and Hyderabad.

The webpage was revitalized. Online registration for the APPNA Summer meeting was started. The official APPNA Listserv was closed and APPNA page was revitalized. *APPNA Qissa* (history book) was endorsed. An effort was made to resolve the differences between HDFNA and APPNA. The first **Day on the Hill** was held by APPNA independently of any organization.[15]

2004: APPNA budget was formally presented and approved by the Council for the first time. The hiring of Executive Director of APPNA was approved. Mr. Michael Thompson was hired to that effect. APPNA Committee on **Advocacy, Government and Legislative Affairs was established**. APPNA Day on the Hill during the Annual Meeting established advocacy as a key objective of the organization. A standing **Committee on Young Physicians** was established. A web based, Young Pakistani Physicians Resource Center, (ypprc.org) was created. Collaboration with national civil rights organizations, like ACLU, NAACP, CAIR, NIF, was initiated. Liaison with Bangladeshi American and Indian American physician associations (AAPI) was established. Strategic Planning Conference for establishing short and long-term goals for APPNA was held. MOUs with HDFNA and PAKPAC were provisionally approved. The concept of APPNA Charitable Foundation and the decision to assist Cytogenetic Laboratory at the National Institute of Child Health in Karachi were approved. APPNA SEHAT was revived.[16] APPNA had its third International CME trip to China. *APPNA Qissa*, book on the history of APPNA was published. The summer meeting was held in Washington, DC, and winter meeting was held in Peshawar.

Constitution and Bylaws amendments, which were started in 2002 were ratified and adopted in 2004. The name of the organization was changed to Association of Physicians of Pakistani-descent of North America (APPNA). Far-reaching amendments to the constitution and bylaws were adopted in the Preamble, Aims and Objectives, Structure and Function of the Association.

2005: APPNA helped Tsunami victims in Southeast Asia (with $155,250). APPNA helped Katrina victims in New Orleans, USA (with S91,278). APPNA raised $1,520,342) for earthquake victims in Pakistan.[17] Over and above this, APPNA donated in kind donations and medical supplies and equipment at least three times the cash donations. About 200 physicians and medical students from North America volunteered and went to work on sight in the aftermath of earthquake in Pakistan.

The **APPNA Charitable Foundation** was approved and launched. The fourth International trip to India was undertaken. Annual summer meeting generated over $200,000 for APPNAs running expenses. The third APPNA Day on the Hill was run in collaboration with PAK-PAC. The summer meeting was held in Houston, TX, and winter meeting was held in Islamabad.

2006: APPNA embarked on a major relief and rehab operation in the aftermath of 2005 Earthquake. The cash donations crossed the $ 2M mark. The funding of a rehabilitation center as well as building of an operation theatre for the Rawalpindi Medical College were accomplished. APPNA also funded the Manshera Rehabilitation Unit for the next three years. All the money raised for the Pakistan Earthquake was utilized to serve the earthquake victims. The first full time executive director was hired by President A.R. Piracha. The issue of delays in visa issuance for young physicians from Pakistan was nearly resolved. 92% of Pakistani physicians who had been accepted in an accredited US residency programs arrived in the US on time after expedited security clearance.[18] APPNA membership grew to 2500. The Cytogenetics lab in Karachi was completed. The fourth Day on the Hill was run by APPNA in collaboration with CAIR and other civil rights organizations. The website was revitalized. The CABL amendments were proposed for enhanced transparency including the impeachment of officer's clause. The updated APPNA Directory was launched. The fifth International trip to Greece and Turkey took place. The summer meeting was held in Chicago and winter meeting was held in Rawalpindi.

2007: APPNA launched **Medical Education and Research Investment Taskforce (MERIT)** and **APPNA** *Sukoon* (Palliative Medicine Initiative) to improve health care in Pakistan.[19] APPNA inaugurated and put to operation seven healthcare and educational facilities across NWFP and Kashmir. Summer meeting registration crossed the 1,000 mark for the first time. APPNA provided relief to the victims of floods in Sindh, Pakistan. The updated APPNA Directory was published. APPNA council approved policies and procedures for the committees to run the organization smoothly and with transparency. APPNA bought the building next to the APPNA central office, which has become home to APPNA free clinic and other activities. The "APPNA" acronym was registered with federal patent as a trademark of APPNA. The summer meeting was held in Orlando, FL, and winter meeting was held in Karachi.

2008: The **First APPNA Community Health Clinic** was inaugurated at APPNA headquarters in Westmont, IL. Ayub Omaya Scholarship was approved. The Society of Future Physicians (APPNA's student section) was also approved. The fifth APPNA Day on the Hill was organized along with a trip to the Capitol. A meeting with Homeland Security Officials on Pakistani physicians and students on delays in visa clearance was held. First Young Physician Research Assembly was held in Lahore. APPNA collaborated with a Tele-Health Pilot Project that was launched in District Mardan, NWFP Pakistan. The first formal **APPNA e-Newsletter** was launched by Dr. Khawar Ismail. The first Canadian Chapter was recognized as the component society. Dental APPNA was approved as an affiliate organization. Punjab Medical College Alumni Association of North America (PMCAACA) was approved as the component society of APPNA. The MERIT committee was given the status of a standing committee of APPNA. The Council approved the final version of an **Election Code of conduct**, which was initially written in 2007. The Social Welfare and Disaster Relief Committee (SWDRC) established a fund to provide emergency relief to the victims of Baluchistan earthquake. APPNA built 58 new homes in one of the remotest villages in Ziarat, Baluchistan through its collaborators in Pakistan.[20] Dr. Zeelaf Munir was elected as the third woman president of APPNA to serve in 2010. The sixth international CME trip went to Italy. The summer meeting was held in Washington, DC, and winter meeting was held in Lahore. A mini-trip to Dubai was also conducted in December.

2009: First Canadian Chapter was established and APPNA fall meeting was organized in Niagara Falls. CME Desk was established in the central office and ACCME accreditation was renewed. The 7th International CME) trip was taken to Australia/New Zealand besides a CME trip to Alaska. The annual summer meeting was held in San Francisco, CA, and winter meeting was held in Karachi. The sixth Day on the Hill was held in collaboration with PAK-PAC. On April 11, 2009, Women Physicians of APPNA **(WAPPNA)** was founded. In May 2009, the newly established **APPNA house** in Bronx, New York opened its door to young physicians visiting from Pakistan. The young physicians benefit from the subsidized accommodations at APPNA house during electives, interviews and CSA exam. The Electronic Teaching Initiative was started in 2009. The Neurology e-Conference was beamed from APPNA's summer meeting in San Francisco to all medical schools in Pakistan. The Anesthesiology e-Conference was also televised in October to the National Conference of the Pakistan Association of Cardiothoracic Anesthesia.

The unprecedented efforts were made by APPNA members and Khyber Medical College through SWDRC to help millions of internally displaced Pakistanis as a result of the Swat crisis. Over $300,000 were dispersed through the Red Crescent and Edhi Trust in Pakistan. APPNA provided three state-of-the-art ACLS capable ambulances for the people of Peshawar and Swat. During these humanitarian crises, Khyber Alumni took initiative in coordinating relief efforts with APPNA by raising funds and providing assistance in holding medical camps along the route of migration.[21]

2010: APPNA National Health Care Day was initiated. APPNA Facebook Page was introduced to have APPNA presence in social media. The website was upgraded and new traditions were set to improve the outlook of APPNA Journal. The National Math Bee, a community youth development program was started. Committee for Young Physicians continued its efforts through seminars, research competitions, counseling and mentorship throughout the year. A Youth Leadership Conference was also held to guide Pakistani-descent youth for better opportunities. The summer meeting was held in Dallas, TX, and winter meeting was held in Lahore.

APPNA had its eighth International CME trip to Malaysia, Thailand, and Singapore.

APPNA's efforts towards the **2010 floods** were supported generously by the membership and communities all across the continent and raised a total of $1,343,630.00. APPNA adopted Samar Bagh, a village in the flood affected area in collaboration with the Human Development foundation (HDF). The village was reconstructed by building houses, a school, and a community health unit. The cost of the project was $777,357.00. This cost was equally shared by HDF and APPNA. Dr. Saima Zafar was elected as the fourth woman president of APPNA to serve in 2012.[22]

2011: APPNA Hepatitis C Awareness Initiative was launched in Pakistan. The APPNA Vision and Mission Statements were developed at the strategic meeting in St. Louis.[23] APPNA helped to establish a **bone marrow registry** for Southeast Asians and held its first National Bone Marrow Registry Drive. APPNA CARES Clinic Day (ACCD) was celebrated all over USA by providing free medical examinations and Free Flu vaccines. **APPNA Free Clinics** were established in MO, AL, NC, GA and CA. APPNA rejoined the AMA Specialty and Service Society Caucus (SSS). A booklet was published and made available on the website to guide young doctors seeking residency training in the US.

APPNA adopted flood-affected **Munirabad village**.[24] A total of 128 homes were built at a cost of $1,000 per residence. In the same year, the St. Louis chapter provided the initial money for a dispensary that was also established in the Munirabad village that treated about 400 patients a month. APPNA built a primary school in Munirabad that opened its doors in 2011. Four dedicated teachers provide quality education to sixty-five girls and sixty boys every day up to fifth grade.

Also in 2011, Ms. Jennifer Wozniak was hired as APPNA Administrator. The summer meeting was held in St. Louis, MO, and winter meeting was held first time ever in Bahawalpur. The ninth International CME trip went to South America and the 10th trip was taken to African Safari and adjacent areas.

In September of 2011, areas of Sindh province were badly hit with floods. SWDRC helped build 100 homes in village Rahib Amaro in Sajawal Sindh in partnership with "Shine Humanity." The money for this project was donated by APPNA Southern California Chapter.

2012: Pakistan flood relief work continued. To help with earnings for the families in the flood affected areas of Sanghar, Badin, and Mirpurkhas, APPNA raised funds and distributed 34 Rickshaws. APPNA also provided clothing and 1,600 pair of shoes to the children of Munirabad village adopted in 2011. APPNA also contributed $50,000 to Hurricane Sandy for relief work in NY and NJ.

Major staffing changes allowed APPNA to organize finances through a bookkeeper. Mr. Nick Suh was hired and brought great experience from his IT background. APPNA's central office was completely remodeled. New audiovisual equipment was installed which was capable of hosting international videoconferencing. The APPNA-PPS Free clinic was also remodeled in the same building in order to make it a better facility to serve the community. The **APPNA House in Detroit, MI** was launched. Four apartments (3 males, and 1 female) were acquired by Dr. Majid Aized (MI). KEMCAANA, Woman Physicians of APPNA, Dr. Nasar Qureshi (NJ), and Dr. Muhammad Suleman (LA) were among the sponsors of this effort.

APPNA membership increased by 18% compared to the previous year. All the young physicians who applied for J-1 visas were able to get their visas in a timely fashion with the effort of Advocacy committee and Young Physicians' Committee. Constitution and Bylaws amendments of 2006 and 2007 were finally ratified by the general body.[25]

The 11th International CME trip went to Central Asian countries and the 12th CME tour went to China. The summer meeting was held in Washington, DC, and winter meeting went to Lahore.

During the winter meeting, a one-day symposium on Burn Management was held with participation from International experts including Dr. M. A. Jawad and Dr. Ashok Gupta. This was mainly held in light of the menace of acid burns inflicted on women in Southeast Asia. Ms. Sharmeen Obaid-Chinoy, the first Oscar winner from Pakistan also attended the meeting.

2013: The membership fee was reduced by 40% that included the proportional reduction in lifetime membership dues. APPNA had an addition of more than 500 lifetime members.

All physicians who applied for visa were able to get in timely manner. Two seminars were held addressing social justice issues in Pakistan. The targeted killing of Physicians was at the top of the agenda in one of the seminar. **APPNA Scholarship Fund** was initiated with a generous donation of $1,000.000 by an anonymous donor that required a matching fund of same amount raised from APPNA affiliated Alumni Associations. **APPNA Institute of Public Health** was initiated at JPMC, Karachi. Two International CME trips were conducted. The 13ᵗʰ International trip went to Eastern European countries and 14ᵗʰ trip was taken to Middle East including Palestine. The summer meeting was held in Orlando, FL, and winter meeting was conducted in Karachi.

2014: APPNA Foundation was revitalized and registered as a 501(3) C organization to raise endowment funds for education and healthcare in Pakistan and the United States. **Constitutional amendments** for election reforms were introduced and approved. APPNA was able to educate lawmakers, convincing them to initiate legislation **GRAD Act-H.R.5735** to help young foreign graduates coming from anywhere in the world. APPNA gave a loan of $250,000 to the Chicago Chapter to buy "**APPNA House**" that would provide housing for young residents. **Sub-specialty societies** in APPNA were created including pulmonary, GI and psychiatry.

An MOU was signed with several medical societies as well as UNICEF to educate people about polio in Pakistan. This effort included APPSUK, "Association of Pakistani Physicians and Surgeons of UK" in order to work together for improvement of healthcare and education in Pakistan. An active collaboration with Rotary International in Pakistan was established to launch joint Polio Eradication efforts. An ad hoc **Committee on Social Justice** was created to raise concerns against social injustices in Pakistan especially violence against minorities, women, and targeted killing of physicians. A video presentation highlighting some of these issues was shown during the Summer Convention, 2014.[26] The 15ᵗʰ International CME trip went to Jordan and Palestine and adjacent countries and the 16ᵗʰ CME tour went to Mediterranean cruise. The summer meeting was held in Washington, DC, and winter meeting was conducted in Multan.

2015: APPNA Telemedicine program was launched. A new **centralized online program** was developed to help young physicians find clinical electives and research positions.

Munirabad school (established in 2011) became a model school. It was declared the best among thirty local schools by National Commission of Human Development (PK). In 2015, there were 125 students enrolled, who otherwise would not have attended school. APPNA donated $26,000 for the maintenance of this school. APPNA managed the school with its local partner, *Tameer-e-Millat* Foundation (PK). **APPNA Medical Corps** was organized to conduct volunteer medical missions by APPNA physicians during peace time and disaster. APPNA physicians volunteered after the Nepal earthquake. APPNA established a new **free specialty clinic** in Richmond, Virginia, and another APPNA supported free clinic in Birmingham, Alabama. Six new **Specialty Networks**: Nephrology, Radiology, Pediatrics, Hematology/Oncology, and Anesthesia/Pain Medicine were formed to do specialty specific projects.

The **Long-Range Planning Committee** was revitalized. One of its tasks was to evaluate the governance structure of APPNA and to make recommendations for more effective and transparent governance. *APPNA Qissa Volume II*, the book which covers APPNA history from 2004–2015 was approved.

Committee on Young Physicians assisted doctors during the post-match SOAP week from March 16–21. Over 180 young physicians who got matched in different residency programs got their visas cleared on time, a well-deserved tribute to CYP and Advocacy Committee over the years. The financial burden of over $60,000 per year for the maintenance of New York and Detroit APPNA Houses on central APPNA was completely eliminated. The CYP website, cyponline.net was updated. Many features including residency match (lists of Pakistani-Descent Residents and Program Directors), US clinical experience (list of YPC mentors), and Educational material were made available on website. A soft loan program (Qarz-e-Hasana) for the deserving young physicians was launched. **APPNA Scholarship Fund** of $1,000.000 by an anonymous donor required a matching fund of same amount to be raised from APPNA affiliated Alumni Associations. This target was successfully achieved in 2015.

The $121,000 was raised during the Heat Wave crisis in Karachi in 2015. APPNA physicians worked on the ground and medical supplies and equipment were donated to different hospitals in Karachi. APPNA also held 12 free eye camps in various cities in Pakistan and over 150,000 patients benefited. APPNA SWDRC and LMC Alumni raised $130,000 for the clean water project. Clean water supply through a pipeline was provided to 3 remote villages in Tharparker-Sindh, Pakistan. It benefits around 7,000 people in the area.

A new APPNA **election reform** was introduced and **Electronic balloting** was successfully implemented for the first time. Work on **APPNA Institution of Higher Learning** was initiated. The proposed School of Allied Health based in Chicago with focus on Echocardiography and Ultrasound training be initially established. **APPNA Qatra Fund** was created based on the concept—Qatra *Darya Ban Jata Hai*—to procure monthly donations by APPNA members for APPNA Projects. **APPNA website** was redesigned. A new contract was signed with World Pay to reduce APPNA's credit card bank fees. The same benefit was provided to APPNA membership. In December 2015, after auditing APPNA's CME program from 2011 to 2014, ACCME declined to renew APPNA's accreditation. The 17th International CME tour meeting went to Australia and New Zealand and 18th Meeting was taken to Baltic cruise. The summer meeting was held in Orlando FL, and APPNA went to Lahore for winter meeting.[27]

2016: APPNA signed a Memorandum of Understanding with USAID. Under the terms of this MOU, APPNA and its physicians would perform health care related activities, including, but not limited to, supporting medical camps and consultations at USAID facilities in Pakistan. APPNA would also provide support through its MERIT and Telemedicine Programs to the physicians at USAID facilities through the APPNA Telemedicine Program. USAID will in return provide logistical support and local coordination for APPNA programs. The President of Rotary International, Mr. John F. Germ, was Guest of Honor on Alumni night at the 2016 Annual Convention, to highlight ongoing relationship in polio eradication in Pakistan.

APPNA US College Scholarship was started. This need-based scholarship would fund for Pakistani descent students in the US colleges. **Adopt a Medical Students in Pakistan** was established in association with the ICare foundation in Pakistan to support tuition for medical students in public medical schools on a need-basis. Nearly 50 scholarships were given. **Limited Term Loan Program for Need Based Support of Pakistani Physicians for USMLE Exams and Interview Process** was formalized. This program would guarantee continuous support from donors' year after year, with reasonable guarantee of return of funds and recirculation for future graduates. APPNA's first peace time mission was sent to Guatemala through its Medical Corps initiative. The 19ᵗʰ International CME trip went to Spain and Morocco and the 20ᵗʰ meeting was taken to Tanzania and Zanzibar. The summer meeting was held in Washington, DC.

A **job exchange board** was created for the first time on APPNA website. A new **Find a Doctor** program was initiated to allow larger community, especially Pakistani descent patients, to be able to search for Pakistani-descent physicians in their areas. A permanent **APPNA medical clinic** was started in Karachi. A new webinar program for young graduates was established that focused on residency applications and interview processes, through the Committee on Young Physicians. *APPNA Qissa II* was published, which would also be available as an e-book.[28]

Endnotes:

1   Zaheer G. Ahmad: A short historical perspective of the Association of Pakistani Physicians of North America, APPNA Journal, 4:1, Summer 2002, 11–12.
2   Ibid, 11
3   Ibid, 11
4   Dr. S. Amjad Hussain: A short history of APPNA (unpublished). It was written in 2014.
5   Dr. M. Aslam Malik (TX), personal communication
6   Ibid. Also by personal communication with late Dr. Bunyad Haider (NJ) and Abdul Rehman (NY).
7   Hassan I. Bukhari: Association of Pakistani Physicians of North America, Historical Perspective, First 25 Years, APPNA Journal, 4:1, Summer 2002, 13–16.
8   Raana Akbar: A Historical Synopsis of the Association of Physicians of Pakistani descent of North America, APPNA Journal, 8:3, Winter 2006, 22–24.
9   Minutes of APPNA Executive Council, July 14, 1984

10   Dr. S. Amjad Hussain: A short history of APPNA (unpublished). It was written in 2014.
11   *APPNA Qissa*, 2004, in chapter 4 page 74
12   *APPNA Qissa*, A history of Association of Pakistani Physicians of North America, 1978–2003; Political Activism and the FMG Issue, page 18–28, 2004.
13   The Maturing of an Organization, chapter 4, *APPNA Qissa*, 2004, 71.
14   APPNA Newsletter, 12:2, Fall 2002, message from the president, 1
15   APPNA Journal, 5:2, Winter 2003, message from the president, 5
16   Minutes of the special council meeting held in Chicago, November 2004 and Presidential Perspective of Omar Atiq in *APPNA Qissa II*.
17   APPNA Journal, 6:3, Summer and Fall, 2005, treasurer's report, 9
18   APPNA Journal, 8:3, Winter 2006, CYP report, 31
19   APPNA Newsletter, 17:1, Spring 2007, 1
20   APPNA Journal, 10:2, Winter, 2008, 5
21   APPNA Journal, 11:2, Winter, 2009, excerpts from various reports
22   APPNA Journal, 12:2, Winter, 2010, excerpts from various reports
23   APPNA Newsletter, 21:1, Spring 2011, 6–7.
24   APPNA Journal, 13:2, Winter, 2011, excerpts from various reports
25   APPNA Journal, 14:2, Winter, 2012, excerpts from various reports
26   APPNA Newsletter (magazine), 24:2, August, 2014, excerpts from various reports and also from Presidential Perspectives from Dr. Asif Rehman in *Qissa II*
27   APPNA Newsletter (journal), 25:2, Fall, 2015, excerpts from various reports and also from the minutes of Spring meeting 2016
28   APPNA 39th Annual Convention's special publication edition and general body meeting proceedings, 2016

APPNA Constitution and Bylaws
—A Brief History of its Evolution[1]

1978: After its inception in 1978, APPNA adopted a constitution and bylaws (CABL) modeled after the American Medical Association (AMA). The first constitution and bylaws was a good enough document for a nascent organization that outlined the purpose of its creation and provided a framework for its governance, due process, conflict resolution, and assurance of the preservation of assets and programs.

1981 and 1982: Subsequently in 1981, a committee was constituted to draft a new set of rules under the leadership of Dr. S. Sultan Ahmed. The draft constitution was adopted after numerous modifications in 1982—a process that demonstrated the maturity of the organization and its ability to reach consensus and make compromises.

The new constitution and bylaws provided for one governing body for the legislative and management functions of the organization. Custodianship of assets and financial controls were assigned to this body, called the "Executive Committee." Due to limited membership in the organization at that point, some of the structural concepts of AMA—like the creation of House of Delegates—were not feasible. The Board of Trustees (BOT), the original incorporators of the association, acted as ombudsmen. Several other amendments were also made in the bylaws in **1984, 1985, 1986, 1987, 1988 and 1989**.

In **1994,** the constitutional amendments incorporated Regional Chapters and Physicians-In-Training Section as Components Societies of APPNA. The role and functions of various committees were also defined and the term of office was changed to correspond to the fiscal year.

---

1 The information on this account is partly obtained from the piece that was contributed by Dr. S. Sultan Ahmed to *APPNA Qissa* 2004, in Appendix I, a brief history of APPNA Constitution, 258–59

2001 and 2002: The continued growth and stature of the organization by the end of second millennium generated discussions on improved governance and transparency in the organization. A committee was commissioned by president elect Dr. Muhammad Suleman in 2001 to draft new set of rules. Dr. M. Khalid Riaz chaired this committee and its recommendations were presented to the general membership at a special constitutional meeting in Chicago in May 2002. These changes proposed to enhance governance by reassigning vital roles of three bodies. The **BOT** was given the new responsibility as the custodians of the assets and control of finances; a policy-making **Council** represented by the five officers and representatives of all the component societies. This council was previously known as executive council, and an **Executive Committee (EC)** comprising of five officers was created to execute the approved policies and to conduct day to day affairs of the organization. The proposed changes had to go through contentious discussions in the subsequent meetings held in Orlando, Chicago, and New York before their eventual approval at the executive council meeting held in October 2002 in Scottsdale, Arizona.

2004: These amendments were finally enacted in 2004 after their ratification by the general body by an affirmative vote of more than 50%. After the 2004 amendments, bylaws were also amended in 2006, 2007, and 2014.

In **2006 and 2007** several back to back amendments in the bylaws were proposed to accommodate recommendations of council and general body and to streamline the functionality of the rapidly growing organization. President A. R. Piracha and President Nadeem Kazi appointed CABL committees that were chaired by Dr. Omar Atiq and Dr. M. Nasar Qureshi in 2006 and 2007, respectively. The salient features of these amendments were the following; a procedure for the recall of an officer, moving of the election schedule for the officers until after the summer meeting and to be concluded at the fall meeting, omitting the physicians-in-training section as a component society, committee appointments on a three-year staggered term basis, requirement of active membership for all members of APPNA Council and the Committees, clearly defining the function of the component societies, and clarity in the CABL language were proposed after due diligence. These changes could not be incorporated into the constitution and bylaws until after their ratification by the general body in December of 2012.

In **2014**, APPNA President Asif Rehman, (NY) appointed Mahmood Alam (NJ) chair of the CABL committee to amend the bylaws in order to accommodate some of the changes, which Dr. Rehman had worked on as the chair of the CABL committee and had subsequently gone through intense discussion in the fall council meeting in 2009. The following changes in the bylaws pertaining to election procedures were approved in 2014. Besides life-time members, all current annual dues paying members could only be eligible to vote provided they had at least 1 paid membership in the Association during the last 2 years preceding the elections. *(This was a fiercely debated decision taken to curb the "seasonal" annual paid membership in APPNA that was primarily sought by the aspiring candidates for increasing their voters' bank.)*

The provision of electronic balloting was added. New requirements for officers contesting the elections were introduced. All nominees for president elect, secretary, and treasurer should have served for at least one year on the Council as the President of a recognized component society. Past Treasurer or Secretary of central APPNA could also be eligible to run for any office in future. Any member whose dues were not received by the central office by July 7 will be considered in arrears and will not be eligible to vote in the elections that year, was also added. It was the first time in APPNA history that after council approval ratification by the general body was achieved during the same year (2014).

In **2015**, President Mubasher Rana appointed Dr. Mohammed Haseeb to lead the CABL committee to do an editing of the constitution and bylaws in order to improve the language and remove redundancies. The CABL committee also proposed to rewriting the clause that authorizes the North American medical graduates (NAMA) to register as one Alumni Association in APPNA. The new proposal includes the option of organizing Alumni Association(s) of Pakistani-descent doctors from any medical school around the globe. These organizations like Dental APPNA or Caribbean medical school Alumni Association(s) could become component societies of APPNA as long as they fulfill the criteria. These amendments also propose a pathway for provisional (ad hoc) committees that remain active for at least three years to become standing committees' after the council approval without going through the process of bylaws amendment(s). Moreover, Asset Management Committee is proposed to be a separate committee appointed and overseen by the

BOT. Similarly, APPNA Medical Corps would be a Standing Committee working independent of the social welfare and disaster relief committee. These amendments were presented and approved by the Council at its spring meeting on May 2, 2015. Their ratification by the general body is pending.

Also in 2015, Dr. Mubasher Rana commissioned a task force to start ground work on improved governance in APPNA (CIGA). President elect M. Nasar Qureshi was appointed its chair. CIGA reported its recommendations to newly revitalized Long Range Planning Committee (LRPC) at its summer meeting in Orlando, FL. The LRPC approved the concept that encompasses the modifications in all the major areas of APPNA's governance namely, board of trustees, council, executive committee, and standing committees. This concept was then taken up by an advisory group on governance in October 2015. The group completed its recommendation in July 2016. It has been proposed that the present body of board of trustees (BOT) should be replaced with a larger body of eleven members as the board of governors (BOG). The BOG will have all the provisions of BOT at present with responsibility of oversight in the implementation of APPNA policy and procedures. The BOG will be nominated by the general membership on staggered term basis from eight different geographical areas representing the entire North American territory. APPNA Council has been proposed to be renamed as House of Delegates, which would eventually elect the nominees to BOG once they are vetted by the governance committee appointed by BOG. President, president elect, and immediate past president are also ex-officio members of the BOG. The executive committee (EC) comprising of five officers will also include executive director and financial officer as ex-officio non-voting members. The major standing committees will be represented in the proposed "commissions" to streamline and organize the work of similar nature done by various committees. In 2016, by the time this book was going to print, CABL committee had completed its first draft of the proposed changes on governance in the constitution and bylaws. This work will be presented to the next council meeting(s) for discussion and approval.

The following excerpt from the constitution and bylaws that was originally ratified in 1982 gives the timeline of its amendments and the names of the signatories involved.

Enacted on the 12th day of June in the year one millennium, nine hundred, and eighty-two.

Ayub K. Ommaya
President
1981–82

S. Amjad Hussain
President
1982–83

Amanullah Khan
President-Elect
1982–83

Sajid Maqbool
Secretary
1981–82

S. Sultan Ahmed
Committee Chairman

M. Aslam Mailk
Secretary
1982–83

Amended on the 19th day of November in the year two millennium and four.

Omar T. Atiq
President

Hussain G. Malik
President-Elect

Mohammad Suleman
Chair CABL Committee

Amended on the 31st day of December in the year two millennium and twelve.

Saima Zafar
President

Mohammad Suleman
Chair CABL Committee

Amended on 8th day of December in the year two millennium and fourteen

Asif Rehman
President

Mahmood Alam
Chair, CABL Committee

ONE APPNA
—ONE COMMUNITY—ONE MISSION

Jennifer E. Wozniak-Watson, J.D.
APPNA Director of Operations

As I write this article for *Qissa* volume II, I think about my six years with APPNA and many themes come to mind: family; commitment; passion; community; assistance and evolution. These themes have been present in the past, are currently present and will be present in the future of APPNA. I cannot write about APPNA without thinking of these themes and I cannot write about the future of APPNA without also discussing its past.

APPNA; at its heart, is a family. I knew that from the first days on the job. That concept is something that is important to me and that is how I knew that it would be a good decision to give the blood, sweat and tears to the organization as I and many others do on a daily basis. APPNA will always have the family mentality and that is one of the great things about the organization. We are there for each other and we work together to strive to make things better for those around us.

APPNA equals commitment. Commitment from the staff that make the daily operations occur, commitment from the Executive Committee, the Board of Trustees, the component societies, the membership, host committees, committee chairs, etc. At times, these groups do not always work well together, there has been strife amongst them in the years I have been at APPNA, but in the end, all of these groups have the same commitment to the same goals of following the mission of APPNA. We all want to be the best we can be and there have been times when certain perspectives have clashed amongst us, but when you look at how many goals that we have achieved, goals that APPNA has met, everyone's perspectives become the same. It is a 'ONE-APPNA' mentality. This is something that needs to continue for the future.

APPNA has an extremely passionate membership. The passion can be good and bad at times. There have been times when that passion has driven staff to become very upset or even quit their positions. It has also driven members to argue at meetings and carry anger with them in their daily lives. On the other hand, that passion has also created high membership numbers, years of profits from meetings, numerous sessions of continuing medical education, 100% clearance of visas for those who need assistance, hundreds of social welfare projects, numerous scholarships, numerous events for day on the hill, vigils, national healthcare days, etc. The passion is exceptional, but as we all can learn from the past, I believe in the future of APPNA, we can all take a breath at times and try to work as a group, not be against each other, this will make for a smoother year and ultimately a smoother existence for the organization.

Community is a main feature of APPNA. We as a staff at central office are a community with all of our component societies and all of the membership in general due to our website, the eblasts, and the meetings. APPNA has definitely become more vocal in the last few years in terms of getting up-to-date information to our membership on a daily basis. We have streamlined a great deal of our delivery mechanisms to make sure that membership is able to have the current information. The best examples of community within APPNA are the national healthcare day and the free clinics that we provide and work with every year. This is something that will continue and needs to be a major priority for the future of APPNA.

Assistance is a mission in APPNA. Assistance coming in the form of philanthropy, of raising funds for all of the social welfare projects, the Qatra project, providing guidance to our young physicians, helping physicians attain their visas to come work in the United States and also the opportunity of the giving of scholarships and loans to our younger generation. APPNA can only survive with membership and will only survive and continue to thrive if we continue to provide assistance to those in need. We need to instill these values into our young physicians so they will continue on the traditions as they become APPNA members.

Evolution is something that is always occurring and has been for the best for APPNA in my opinion. In my six years, I have seen an evolution of the staff, an evolution of finance- reporting, an evolution of office processes and procedures and an evolution in the overall thinking of the organization. Now change can definitely be difficult and there is always a period of adjustment in any change situation, but change is something that APPNA goes through every year just based upon our make-up; APPNA can handle it.

The themes discussed in this article have been the cornerstone of APPNA and will continue for the future. They are not the only themes, but just a wonderful snapshot of an organization that is made up of hard-working individuals that in most cases would do anything for each other. I am proud to call myself the Director of Operations of the organization and I know that if we all continue to work together that we can make APPNA even better! APPNA is an organization that at its heart is about helping others. I know that we can always improve processes in the future, we can improve some attitudes, change some behaviors and assure that our great organization will thrive for years to come.

APPNA QISSA: APPNA MERIT[1]

Naheed Usmani, MD

Dr. Naheed Usmani with MERIT coordinator

In Fall of 2006, President Elect Dr Nadeem Kazi invited me to chair a committee whose aim would be to improve the medical education in Pakistan. With my firsthand work experience in Pakistan, this project connected with me deeply and I decided to embark on this journey. Our goal was to enable APPNA to contribute in a systematic way to the improvement of medical education in Pakistan. Our first task was to identify the issues and then to elicit ideas on how APPNA could contribute

---

1   Dr. Naheed Usmani wrote this article for *APPNA Qissa* on the author's request. This report on APPNA MERIT showcases on how a concept is transformed into a reality and how success is achieved by facing the challenges with relentless efforts and commitment of our volunteers. This scenario is also true for the success of numerous other committees of APPNA as well.

in a substantial and meaningful way to the improvement of medical education and research in Pakistan. APPNA MERIT, Medical Education & Research International Training & Transfer-of-Technology Committee of Association of Physicians of Pakistani-descent of North America, was established in 2007 to collaborate with Pakistan's medical teaching institutions to help them develop 21st century medical education, research, and practice. MERIT wanted to mobilize 15,000 physicians of Pakistani descent in North America to contribute their expertise to improve physician training in Pakistan. APPNA is an organization has consistently sought to maintain professional relationships with physicians, medical researchers, and medical institutions in Pakistan. It has organized research conferences, arranged faculty interaction, and provided advice on health policy as well as emerging issues in health management. It has also mobilized resources for investment in key sectors and programs, including earthquake relief, basic health, and quality of medical education and research. After the intense engagement of APPNA physicians in 2005 earthquake relief work, concerns surfaced that the health management system in Pakistan had not responded adequately to emerging challenges, both in terms of health delivery system, but also at the medical education and research level. This is the result in part of the absence of a strong national research tradition and in part of the deterioration rather than steady improvement in the quality of medical education. Given the potential of APPNA for accessing global technical expertise, mobilizing financial resources, and interacting with national policy circles, there was an expectation both by key stake holders in Pakistan as well as expatriate Pakistani physicians that the association would accept the challenge to channel broad based investments in medical education and research in Pakistan. The initial activities planned by APPNA MERIT fell into two major phases:

1. Diagnostic Phase, in which the key issues in medical education were identified and analyzed.
2. Prescriptive Phase, in which the findings and recommendations were compiled and presented to APPNA membership and Pakistani stakeholders, and finalized after further refinement, prioritization, and adaptation for implementation.

APPNA Council voted at its Fall 2008 meeting in New Jersey to make APPNA MERIT a permanent standing committee of APPNA from the ad-hoc education initiative that MERIT had been since 2007.

DIAGNOSTIC PHASE: Dr Nadeem Kazi APPNA President Elect and MERIT members who attended the December 2006 APPNA meeting in Pakistan, met with key stakeholders to discuss initial concepts and seek their advice and support. Subsequently, APPNA MERIT representatives held extensive follow-up discussions during January, February, and March 2007, in Pakistan. Multiple meetings were held to refine initial concepts with a large number of key Pakistani stakeholders including:

- **Medical university vice chancellors** at University of Health Sciences (Lahore), Dow University of Health Sciences (Karachi), King Edward Medical University (Lahore)
- **Post-graduate medical institution heads** and medical college principals at Pakistan Institute of Medical Sciences (Islamabad), Shaukat Khanum Memorial Cancer Center (Lahore), Rawalpindi Medical College, Allama Iqbal Medical College (Lahore), Lahore Medical College, Fatima Jinnah Medical College and Wah Medical College
- **Leaders at regulatory and funding bodies**, including Pakistan Higher Education Commission, College of Physicians and Surgeons of Pakistan, Pakistan Medical and Dental Council, Pakistan Medical Association, Federal Ministry of Labour's National Talent Pool VEPCON program, and Federal Ministry of Health. A large number of issues surfaced during initial meetings:

  - Medical education curriculum reform and need for continuous updates
  - Uneven quality and lack of standardization of health education: many startup medical institutions with shortage of trained medical faculty leading to institutional variability
  - Medical colleges given university charter status without development of research capabilities and other aspects integral to a medical university
  - Lack of planned programs and system for continuous medical education (CME) throughout Pakistan
  - Lack of systems to measure quality and outcomes in teaching

hospitals
- Lack of linkages between major medical training centers and community and district outreach hospitals, with subsequent inequity of healthcare availability
- Multiple layers of bureaucracy throughout health education, leading to confusion and obfuscations of roles
- Need for observerships for Pakistani medical students in US hospitals
- Lack of international linkages in research and shortage of basic science researchers and faculty for new research labs. and post-graduate programs

The diagnostic phase resulted in the compilation of first draft paper in Spring 2007 and APPNA MERIT Presentation in a CME session at the Summer Meeting 2007. This *CME MERIT Symposium* was very well received and the Visiting faculty program was presented. The symposium had the best attendance for the CME program. There was overwhelming Affirmative response by the APPNA attendees to the question: "I believe medical education improvement in Pakistan should be a key goal for APPNA." Good feedback was generated from the presentations and discussion.

Based on the assessments of issues of medical academic institutions and the available resources at APPNA, our committee decision was to focus on improving health education in the public sector, with emphasis on specialty-to-specialty support and development of new areas of medicine that were not available at all in the country or were in dire shortage. The development of research collaboration and transfer of technological advances then would be a direct benefit of such interactions.

Convergence Towards An Actionable Proposal: APPNA MERIT went back to stakeholders with two key concepts to address some of their needs and desires: a CME initiative for physicians in practice and a Centers of Excellence program in which APPNA will help with creation of medical education and research centers of excellence. Based on additional feedback from Pakistani stakeholders APPNA MERIT gave shape to a Visiting Faculty Program for Centers of Excellence in Medical Education and CME. This concrete proposal has received unanimous support from Pakistani stakeholders.

PRESCRIPTIVE PHASE:

- **APPNA Visiting Faculty Initiative:** The Visiting Faculty Initiative was envisioned as a year round program that placed APPNA specialists in assignment throughout the year. APPNA Specialty coordinators were designated to work out details of the 2-week assignment program with their Specialty counterparts at the host institutions. Visiting Faculty would receive reimbursement of their travel and local lodging/transport through HEC or VEPCON visiting faculty programs. APPNA MERIT was to manage the overall initiative and negotiate overall terms of reference with the host and funding institutions. The Government of Pakistan National Talent Pool's **Visiting Expatriate Pakistani Consultant (VEPCON)** program processed 6 APPNA consultants initially in 2008 for sponsorship who went to Pakistan. **Higher Education Commission** of Pakistan (HEC) incorporated sponsorship of APPNA MERIT as a specific line item in their budget for the fiscal year that started in July 2007. HEC and APPNA approved the Terms of Reference (TOR) for selection and approval of HEC sponsored APPNA Visiting Scholars in 2008. This APPNA Merit engagement with VEPCON and HEC laid a solid institutional foundation for long term sponsorship of APPNA MERIT by two key government of Pakistan (GOP) entities, while also made APPNA's contribution to medical education improvements in Pakistan very visible to GOP. DUHS set up a specific committee for organizing the visiting faculty program. We also developed a 360 degree system of reporting and evaluation for ongoing monitoring of the effectiveness of this program. Unfortunately, VEPCON process was laborious and difficult for our physicians and we could only send a dozen physicians on this program. About 30 US faculty members applied to go on short-duration Visiting Faculty visits to Pakistan under HEC program in 2010; and 10 were approved for teaching visits to DUHS, a reflection of the great organizational infrastructure by that institution. Applications sent to KEMU, UHS, LUHS, NUST were never fully processed according to HEC guidelines by the universities before HEC could give its final approval to them. The extensive logistical follow-up required with applicants and Pakistani universities and HEC made it difficult to continue the program without APPNA Central Office support. While there continued to be great interest in APPNA consultants to go on Visiting Faculty programs, no further applications could be processed from 2011 onwards in absence of office support for MERIT program. The program continues at the alumni level, with well-established visiting faculty programs at DUHS and KEMU.

- **APPNA SUKOON** (APPNA Palliative & Hospice Care Educational Program): In Pakistan, Palliative care is in its infancy. There is no established formal hospice care. There is non-availability of morphine orally except at some large/well known hospitals. There are few elderly or chronic care facilities; main focus of inpatient care is on acute care. In Fall, 2007 APPNA SUKOON, palliative medicine initiative was launched with Dr Mahjabeen Islam as the program director.

- **AIM OF APPNA SUKOON:** To educate the medical system and increase the awareness in the lay public about palliative medicine and hospice care. To do so, MERIT scholars would visit different medical teaching institutions in Pakistan and teach individually or in symposia the core curriculum of palliative care. APPNA SUKOON wanted to introduce Palliative and hospice care into medical curriculum and develop the subspecialty for college of physicians and surgeons of Pakistan (CPSP). We wanted to educate the Pakistan governmental health department/s about the vital importance of morphine and derivatives and ensuring their easy availability for relief of pain in suffering in the ailing.

SUKOON ACHIEVEMENTS:

1. **HOSPICE AND PALLIATIVE EDUCATION IN PAKISTAN IN DECEMBER 2007:** Palliative Care conferences were held in Karachi, Islamabad and Lahore.
2. We held meetings with Pakistan Health Ministry officials.
3. We considered a proposal for setting up an APPNA Sukoon at Shifa International in Islamabad in December 2007 and Institute of Child Health Karachi.
4. In 2008, APPNA MERIT endorsed the INCTR Clinical Guidelines for Palliative Care in low resource countries.

5. IN 2008, I visited Shaukat Khanum Hospital, INMOL hospital, Children's' Hospital, Mayo Hospital and Jinnah Hospital to evaluate the availability of hospice and palliative care facilities in Lahore. There were no designated beds available any where in Lahore. Dr Haroon Hafeez at SKMCH and Dr Riaz ur Rehman at Jinnah hospital are both palliative care physicians. There are palliative care nurses at SKMCH, who have also been conducting free training programs for nurses at other institutions in Lahore. I participated in a meeting with "Friends of INMOL" who agreed to fundraise for an independent hospice for INMOL. Dr. Mahmud Shaukat declared that Mayo Hospital musafir-khana could easily be adapted to develop palliative care/hospice beds. At Jinnah Hospital, Prof Zeba Aziz promised 6 beds in her new oncology ward to be dedicated to palliative care and at Children's Hospital 6 beds were also dedicated to pediatric palliative care. All centers requested help with design and program details. Over the last 6 years, we now have dedicated palliative care beds in all of the above institutions, morphine is more easily available and there are annual palliative care conference organized at Shaukat Khanum Hospital.

6. With INCTR help, Childrens' Hospital Lahore won an international palliative care grant from "My Child Matters" program.

7. APPNA faculty joined with INCTR and participated in a Palliative Care Seminar held at SKMCH in November 2011. This SKMCH palliative care symposium is an annual event that I attend regularly.

SPECIALTY-SPECIFIC MERITNETS: To organize the visiting faculty program and our teaching initiatives, we found it imperative to organize the APPNA membership based on their professional specialties **as Vehicles for Collaboration & Joint Action**. In 2008 we launched the Specialty-Specific MERITnets, to mobilize the 15,000 APPNA specialists to help create Centers of Excellence in post-graduate training in specific specialty areas in Pakistani medical institutions. These APPNA specialists could volunteer for 2-week visiting faculty assignments, create curriculum enrichment in "Top Ten" topic areas for their specialty, deliver seminars and training programs when they visited Pakistan, and volunteer for

Telemedicine Panels to facilitate training and consultation from the US/
Canada. The Critical care, Anesthesia, Neurology and Dermatology were
the initial MERIT specialty networks created. We developed an e-list and
a webpage for each network to facilitate their interaction. Anesthesiology
MERITnet participants on Oct 19, 2008 organized a lunch get-together
at the American Society of Anesthesiology Annual meeting, Orlando, to
get acquainted and plan out activities. They decided that their MERITnet
could be a great professional networking initiative not only to collaborate
on initiatives for Pakistani medical institutions but also as a Pakistani-
American Anesthesiologists' professional network in the US/Canada for
jobs, research, and other activities. They discussed arranging teaching and
clinical workshops with major anesthesia conferences in Pakistan, clinical
training in target Pakistani teaching institutions with collaboration of their
faculty, international conference in Dubai for the SAARC and Mid-East
countries, a Journal of Anesthesia for Pakistan with peer-reviewed articles,
and collaboration with Pakistan Society of Anesthesia and its branches.
They wanted to build the Anesthesiology MERITnet web site to include
more teaching material, presentations and videos, create a more comprehensive database of Pakistani Anesthesiologists and establish links with
Anesthesiology departments in Pakistani medical institutions.

Anesthesiology MERITnet Website:http://sites.google.com/site/
anesthesiologymeritnet/

Anesthesiology MERITnet E-List: http://groups.google.com/group/
anesthesiology-meritnet

APPNA Anesthesiologists Total: 357

Critical Care MERITnet Website: http://sites.google.com/site/
intensivistsmeritnet/

Critical Care MERITnet E-List: http://groups.google.com/group/
intensivists-meritnet/

APPNA Critical Care Physicians Total: 252

Dermatology MERITnet Website: http://sites.google.com/site/
dermatologymeritnet/

Dermatology MERITnet E-List: http://groups.google.com/group/
dermatology-meritnet

APPNA Dermatology Physicians Total: 32

Neurology MERITnet Website: http://sites.google.com/site/
neurologymeritnet/
Neurology MERITnet E-List: http://groups.google.com/group/
neurology-meritnet/
APPNA Neurology Physicians Total: 374

These networks undertook arranging MERIT seminars during APPNA annual meetings, workshops in Pakistan as well as coordinating visiting faculty.

MEDICAL CURRICULUM REFORM: In 2008, APPNA MERIT was invited by KEMCAANA president Dr Mubasher Rana to help them with the undergraduate medical curriculum reform at KEMU. A curriculum reform committee was put together that opened the dialogue at KEMU with other academic medical universities engaged in updating the undergraduate medical curriculum. APPNA physicians involved in medical curriculum efforts in US/Canada medical schools volunteered their time and ideas to help Pakistani medical institutions update their medical curriculum for 21st century medical teaching and practice. I visited KEMU in November to discuss issues and reforms needed with the Vice Chancellor and academic council at KEMU as well as other medical institutions in Pakistan. Armed with the copy of the MBBS curriculum, we held meetings with medical education experts within APPNA, locally in US as well as other institutions in Pakistan who were also trying to update their curriculum, we planned a day long Medical Curriculum Reform Colloquium on December 24, 2008 at King Edward Medical University as part of APPNA's Winter Meeting in Pakistan. The King Edward Medical University Auditorium was the venue for a standing-room-only gathering of KE faculty for an all-day international colloquium on Undergraduate Medical Curriculum Reform. The colloquium brought together Vice Chancellors, Deans, Professors, and medical students from the US and Pakistan. Presentations focused on the current state-of-the-art in evidence-based, competencies-oriented undergraduate medical education internationally, the status and challenges of MBBS teaching in Pakistan, and the lessons from recent pioneering educational reform initiatives in Pakistan.

KEMU Vice Chancellor, Prof. Dr. Zafar Ullah Khan, required the full KE faculty to attend the colloquium, as an indication of KEMU's seriousness about medical education reform. The perspectives included those of medical students, international faculty, medical education reformers in Pakistan, and medical regulatory bodies, including:

- **Introduction of Symposium: KEMU vision of needed Curriculum Reform**, by Prof Mahmood Shaukat, Registrar, KEMU.
- **Medical Education Experience at KEMU**, by Final year medical students, Mehreen Zarin and Sanad Saad, and recent MBBS graduate and Fulbright scholarship winner, Dr. Madiha Shams.
- **US Medical Student Perspective,** by Asima Ahmad, a University of Chicago medical student and a Master's student in Harvard University's School of Public Health
- **Competency-Based Medical Curriculum: The New International Goal Post,** by Naheed Usmani, MD Assoc. Prof. at University of Massachusetts Medical School, and Chairperson, APPNA MERIT
- **Clinical Clerkship: Medical Student Transition from Classroom to Clinical Practice,** by Adeel Butt, MD, University of Pittsburgh Medical School
- **Medical Curricular Reform at Dow University of Health Sciences: Successes and Challenges,** by Prof. Masood Hameed Khan, Vice Chancellor DUHS, Karachi
- **Implementation of Problem based Learning in Medical Education at Aga Khan University,** Prof. Rukhsana Zuberi, Dean of Medical Education, AKU, Karachi
- **An Integrated Curriculum based on Social and Biological Context of Disease at Shifa College of Medicine,** by Prof. Mujtaba Quadri, Assoc. Dean, Shifa College of Medicine, Islamabad
- **The Medical Curriculum—Some Observations,** Prof. Ijaz Ahsan, Dean, University of Lahore
- **Pakistan Medical & Dental Council Perspective on Medical Education Reform,** by Prof. Sibtul Hasnain, President PMDC
- **Modernization of Existing MBBS Program with the Help of Best International Practice,** by Prof. Syed Muhammad Awais, Pro-Vice Chancellor, KEMU, Lahore
- **Wrap Up of Curriculum Reform Colloquium,** by Prof. Muhammad Zafar Ullah Khan, Vice Chancellor, KEMU.

Following the colloquium he met with KEMCAANA and APPNA leadership to announce a set of concrete reform steps, including:

1. Establishment of a Medical Education dept. at KE immediately under Prof Mahmud Shaukat's leadership
2. Resolve to update the curriculum and teaching methodology
3. Request for KEMCAANA and APPNA MERIT help to revise the first 2 year curriculum based on semester system, modular integrated teaching and early introduction of clinical medicine
4. A steering committee of KEMU faculty and administration to be established to shape the curriculum reform initiative, with international members contributed by KEMCANA and APPNA MERIT. MERIT curriculum reform committee, which included the Late Dr Reza Dilawari visited the vice chancellor and the Academic council in 2009 as well for follow up discussions and advice.
5. Subsequently, senior faculty from KEMU participated in medical education reform conferences and courses at Aga Khan University.

This colloquium was the catalyst for much needed medical education reform at KEMU and contributed to the reform discussion and initiatives in medical education in Pakistan in general, and now there is a modern curriculum being introduced across the country, at DUHS, KEMU and many UHS affiliated institutions.

Establishment of New Fellowships in Emergency Medicine, Critical Care Medicine and Pediatric Hematology Oncology:

Prof. Masood Hameed Khan, Vice Chancellor Dow University of Health Sciences, met with APPNA MERIT chairperson, Naheed Usmani, MD at the APPNA Winter Meeting in Lahore 2008 and outlined a number of new DUHS initiatives in which he would like help from APPNA MERIT. These include:

- **Emergency Medicine Fellowship**. DUHS would like APPNA Emergency Medicine Specialists to help design curriculum for a new Emergency Medicine Fellowship at Dow and to volunteer to be Visiting Faculty for 2-week short-duration teaching visits. Till then there were no Emergency Medicine specialization training in Pakistan.

- **Critical Care Medicine Fellowship**: DUHS asked APPNA Critical Care Medicine Specialists to help design curriculum for a new Critical Care Medicine Fellowship at Dow and to volunteer to be Visiting Faculty for 2-week short-duration teaching visits as there was no Critical Care Medicine specialization training in Pakistan

APPNA MERIT made a commitment to help DOW with these initiatives. **Critical Care MERITnet,** which was launched in 2008, took the lead on the Critical Care Fellowship. A new **Emergency Medicine MERITnet** was started to address the need for an Emergency Medicine fellowship.

College of Physicians & Surgeons of Pakistan (CPSP), held two working meetings with APPNA and KEMCAANA leadership during the Winter Meeting 2008 to discuss the many initiatives CPSP had launched to maintain the high standard of post-graduate certification and training in Pakistan and requested collaboration from APPNA to help in launching new training programs and improving existing ones.

CPSP plays the role in Pakistan that American Board of Medical Specialties do in the US. CPSP offers Fellowship training in 53 disciplines and Membership in 10. FCPS training varies from 3–5 years depending upon specialty. Prof. Zafar Ullah Chaudhry, President CPSP, and Prof. Khalid Masood Gondal, Regional Director CPSP, hosted the APPNA team. CPSP invited APPNA to collaborate on the following initiatives:

- Help develop fellowship programs in new specialty areas currently lacking in Pakistan: Critical Care Medicine, Emergency Medicine, Pediatric Hematology Oncology. This collaboration included establishment of training standards, curriculum, visiting training faculty and finally examiners for certification of trainees.
- APPNA faculty to participate as CPSP examiners for fellowship certification and serve on specialty curriculum panels. The college would be willing to pay the travel cost as well as hosting of the examiners. An examiner for CPSP has to meet CPSP requirements for foreign examiners, board certification and faculty position in a teaching institution for 10 years.
- APPNA faculty to participate in training-videoconferences that CPSP arranges for its members at various CPSP sites. CPSP has state of the art video conferencing hardware installed in all it's offices, and this facility is available for their post graduate trainees.

We quickly got Critical care and Emergency Medicine networks together and asked them to take on the charge of coming up with fellowship proposals in their respective fields that would work in the local environment. By summer of 2009, we had delivered on our promise to our partners in Pakistan. All three fellowships were approved by the CPSP.

Critical Care Fellowship:
Author: **Muhammad Jaffar, MD**, Co-Chair CC MERITnet, Assoc. Prof. of Anes. & Critical Care, U of Arkansas Medical School
Contributors: **Iqbal Ratnani, MD. Noormahal Kabani, MD**, Co-chairs MERITnet
- 2-Year Fellowship, after FCPS Part 1&2
- Multi-institution partnership proposed: DUHS & AKU
- Visiting Faculty Drawn from 250+ APPNA Critical Care Specialists
CPSP has approved the new fellowship: July 1, 2009

Emergency Medicine Fellowship
- Request from CPSP, DUHS
    - Drs. Mahmood Alam and Bakhtiar Ishtiaq from APPNA collaborated with Dr Junaid Razzak (AKU) to draft a fellowship proposal that has been approved.

Pediatric Oncology Fellowship: This had been my ardent wish since my work at Shaukat Khanum Hospital in 1994–1999. While I was there, I had submitted a draft proposal for the fellowship but I had been told by CPSP officials at that time that CPSP had too many fellowships to manage, and they were not considering new fellowship proposals. After discussing with Pakistani Society of Pediatric Oncology group, Dr Alia Zaidi, Shaukat Khanum Hospital and Dr Zehra Faddoo Aga Khan Hospital, in collaboration with APPNA MERIT resubmitted the fellowship proposal to CPSP. The fellowship was approved in 2009 as well.

APPNA MERIT E-TEACHING INITIATIVE
Because of our inability to send large number of physicians to Pakistan, numbers sufficient to make a difference, in 2009 we decided to evaluate options of distance learning. In APPNA Spring meeting 2009, in Dallas,

I was approached by Dr. Jamal Mubarak, an intensivist and APPNA member, that he had an IT company working on long distance learning and he would like to volunteer his talents and services to set it up for APPNA MERIT. After discussing with the APPNA Executive committee, we decided to take him up on his offer and started the APPNA MERIT e-teaching initiative. We tested a pilot program in APPNA Summer 2009 meeting of live Grand Rounds in Neurology for Pakistan, beamed to medical universities and colleges via internet-based videoconferencing. Faculty and post-graduate trainees attended in hundreds in major Pakistan cities.

"Electronic Conference" Delivered Live Over the Internet w. Q&A Pilot: Neurology MERITnet Conference (half-day)
Organizer: **Shahid Rafiq, MD,** *Co-Chair, Neurology MERITNET*
MERIT Technology Co-Chair: **Jamal Mubarak, MD**
Pakistan sites: AKU, DUHS, UHS, KEMU, RMC, LMC
- **Childhood Epilepsies**. *Nadeem Shabbir, MD, Asst. Prof., SUNY Friday 9am-noon, July 3 Pakistan/Thurs. July 2 even. San Fran*
- **Multiple Sclerosis: Current and Future Treatment Options**. *Syed Asgher Rizvi, MD, Assoc. Prof., Brown University Medical School*
- **Sleep in Children—Linking Multiple Neurological Problems Together**. *Amer Khan, MD, Sutter Neuroscience Medical Group*

Dr. Jamal Mubarak built a technology infrastructure for APPNA MERIT to support videoconferences, online courses, and online collaboration between US and Pakistan. It used public domain software and dedicated servers. In May 2010 APPNA funded APPNA MERIT E-Teaching System and MERIT launched Grand Rounds immediately. Live broadcasted Grand Rounds became regular, weekly feature in 2010 and twice-weekly (Saturday and Monday at 8:30 am Pakistan time) in 2011, attended by faculty and post-graduate trainees in videoconference rooms across Pakistan including KEMU, DUHS, UHS Lahore, Liaquat U. Jamshoro, AKU, Quaid-e-Azam MC Bahawalpur, FJMC, Services Hospital MC Lahore, Liaquat National MC Karachi, AIMC, Fatima Memorial MC, Lahore, Shifa Intl MC, Islamabad, NICH Karachi, and others. A US faculty member covered the topic in a PowerPoint presentation of 30–40 minutes followed by live questions from Pakistan for another hour or so.

The live Q&A was considered the most valuable and unique aspect of these Grand Rounds, allowing faculty and trainees in Pakistan to explore issues important to them in a Pakistani context related to the presentation topic with the US faculty expert. The grand rounds were recorded and a video library was developed that was available for physicians to review at www.appnamerit.com. These videos were regularly viewed not just in Pakistan but internationally in countries such as India and Bangladesh. The IT team organized these talks into specialty specific course folders, that could eventually be developed into individual courses for which attendees could receive certification of attendance from Pakistani medical universities, with pre and post quizzes. This library would meet the requirements for the Pakistan general practitioners online CME training courseware as requested by Prof Masood Hameed Khan, vice-chancellor DUHS.

These MERIT programs were designed through close collaboration with Pakistan's medical teaching institutions, including Aga Khan University, Dow University of Health Sciences, King Edward Medical University, Khyber Medical University, Liaquat University of Medical & Health Sciences, University of Health Sciences Lahore, College of Physicians & Surgeons Pakistan, Allama Iqbal Medical College, Army Medical College, Rawalpindi, Armed Forces Institutes Rawalpindi, CMH Lahore Medical College, Fatima Jinnah Medical College, Pakistan Institute of Medical Sciences, Punjab Medical College Faisalabad, Quaide Azam Medical College Bahawalpur, Nishtar Medical College, Services Institute Lahore, Rawalpindi Medical College, Fatima Memorial Hospital & Medical College, Liaquat National Hospital & Medical College, Shifa International Islamabad, National University of Science & Technology. APPSUK (Association of Pakistani Physicians and Surgeons, United Kingdom) also asked to participate in our e-Teaching initiative and were willing to fund a 3rd Grand round for an afternoon session in Pakistan, organized by UK physicians.

Financial Issues: In 2011, the annual operating budget for APPNA MERIT totaled $60,000 ($50,000 for eCME and $10,000 for Office support). This budget was presented in APPNA 2011 spring executive council meeting. During EC meeting, $22,000 were pledged in a fundraiser managed by Dr Saima Zafar and Dr Waheed Akbar. The remaining funds were approved by EC to be used from RESA funds. $20,000 were paid to MDLS (Dr Mubarak's company) for the eCME initiative. The RESA chair and executive committee decided that RESA funds could not be used to finance the APPNA MERIT and it's eCME initiative. Without sustainable funding, this successful program could not grow and successfully develop as one of the main anchors of APPNA initiatives for improving healthcare in Pakistan.

APPNA MERIT TELEMEDICINE Initiatives

Through out the MERIT development phase, the committee was approached by both APPNA physicians in US as well as our partners in Pakistan about the possibility of starting a telemedicine initiative. I have been a volunteer consultant in a humanitarian international telemedicine project with Swinfen Trust for the last 13 years. Initially in the APPNA MERIT infancy, Dr Rizwan Naeem, who was the Co-Chair of the committee in 2007, rolled his Telemedicine project into MERIT which was a telemedicine/tele-training project funded by HEC and USAID that aimed to train lady health visitors using ICT based Tele-Health-care. He presented his experience "Capacity Building of Lady Health care Workers in Rural Mardan, NWFP through the use of ICT-Based Telemedicine," at Pakistan-U.S. Science and Technology Conference Islamabad. The Mardan facility was a key partner in delivering healthcare to the internally displaced people as well as flood victims in 2007–2011. Another Telemedicine initiative was being run by Dr Khalil Khatri, as a Dermatology Telemedicine initiative for Pakistan-based doctors at the same time. In December 2014, I was approached by Dr Mubasher Rana, President Elect APPNA to chair a committee in charge of developing a telemedicine initiative for APPNA. Our mission was to improve health care quality and access to specialist medical care in Pakistan, for underserved populations, by setting up Internet based consultations between specialists in USA and referring doctors from Pakistan in order to improve patient care through recommendations for latest treatments and timely access to specialist knowledge. This will result in updating Pakistani physicians on the principles of evidence-based medicine as practiced in USA. We have worked hard over the past 8 months, recruited almost 200 APPNA physicians as consultants, developed our own web-based platform that is secure and dedicated to these consultations, and developed partnerships with two Pakistani institutions and an NGO that serves indigent population. We are hoping to have a robust pilot up and running in September, and in December' 2015 we will broaden our engagement with Pakistani institutions across the country.

All this work is the result and dedications of an army of volunteers. First of all, I would like to thank my APPNA MERIT committee chairs, MERITnet chairs and members of my committee who worked selflessly to make this project a success:

Dr. Nadeem Kazi; Dr Iqbal Ahmed, MA; Dr Iqbal Ratnani, TX; Dr Noormahal Kabani, AR; Dr Mustafa Saad Siddique, NC; Dr Zulfiqar Ahmed, MI; Dr Khalil Khatri, MA; Dr. M Jaffar, AR; Dr Rizwan Naeem, NY; Dr. Shahid Raffique, MD; Dr. Jamal Mubarak, TX; Dr. Khalid Aziz, NC; Dr. Nusrum Iqbal, AZ; Dr. Tariq Mahmood. MD; Dr. Dawood Nasir, TX; Dr. Babar Rao, NY; Dr. Iftikhar Syed, MA; Dr. Zahid Imran, LA; Dr Mahjabeen Islam, OH; Dr. Asif Mohyddin, MO; Dr. Mubasher Rana, CA; Dr. Ayyaz Shah, FL; Dr Fauzia Rana, FL; Dr Saad Usmani, AR; Dr Naeem Tahirkheli, OK; Dr. Jalil Khan, TX.

As I was developing this initiative, I was very lucky to be mentored and guided by two of my closest friends:

1. Dr Adil Najam, Dean, The Frederick S. Pardee School of Global Studies Professor, International Relations, Boston University
2. Dr Tariq Banuri, Professor, Economics Department, University of Utah

Last but not least, my husband, Hasan Usmani has been my guide, mentor, sounding board and I heavily relied on his public policy background and business training to run this committee and make it successful.

APPNA LEADERSHIP 2004–2016

APPNA LEADERSHIP 2004			
Executive Committee			
President	Dr. Omar Atiq	President-Elect	Dr. Hussain Malik
Secretary	Dr. Zeelaf Munir	Treasurer	Dr. Nadeem Kazi
Immediate Past President	Dr. Raana Akbar	Interim Executive Director	Michael Thompson, PhD
Alumni Association Presidents			
Aga Khan	Dr. Tahseen Mozaffar	Allama Iqbal	Dr. Iqbal A. Nasir
Dow	Dr. Zia Moizuddin Ahmad	Fatima Jinnah	Dr. Syedah S. Gilani
Khyber	Dr. Mohammad Khalid	King Edward	Dr. Mohammad Jahanzeb
Liaquat	Dr. Izhar Ul Haque	Nishtar	Dr. Najeeb Ur Rehman
Quaid-I-Azam	Dr. Manzoor Ahmad Tariq	Rawalpindi	Dr. Amer Akmal
Sindh	Dr. Javed Suleman	NAMA	Dr. Nadia S. Afridi
Chapter Presidents			
Arizona	Dr. M Yousuf Khan	Florida	Dr. Shahid Farooq Usmani
Georgia	Dr. Shahid Rafique	Illinois	Dr. M. Omar Nasib
Michigan	Dr. Busharat Ahmad	Mid-South	Dr. Sadeem Mahmood
Missouri	Dr. Zia M. Ahmad	Nevada	Dr. Muhammad Nasir Tufail
New England	Dr. Naheed Usmani	New Jersey	Dr. Shaukat A. Chaudhery
New York	Dr. Mohammad Aslam	North Texas	Dr. Jalil A. Khan
Northern California	Dr. Zubeda A. Seyal	Ohio	Dr. Shahid I. Sheikh
Pennsylvania	Dr. Zahid Rashid	Southern	Dr. Zahid Imran
Southern California	Dr. Ahsan U. Rashid	South Texas	Dr. Asaf R. Qadeer
Three River	Dr. Adeel A. Butt	Upstate New York	Dr. Ashraf Sabahat
D.C. & Baltimore	Dr. Mubashar A. Choudry	Physicians-In-Training	Dr. Sajid Rashid Chaudhary
North Carolina	Dr. Waheed Khalid Bajwa		
Board of Trustees			
Chairman		Dr. S. Sultan Ahmed	
Dr. M Jafar Shah		Dr. Shabbir H. Safdar	
Dr. Arif Muslim		Dr. M. Afzal Arain	

APPNA LEADERSHIP 2005			
Executive Committee			
President	Dr. Hussain Malik	President-Elect	Dr. Abdul R. Piracha
Secretary	Dr. Nadeem Kazi	Treasurer	Dr. Mahmood Alam
Immediate Past President	Dr. Omar Atiq	Executive Director	
Alumni Association Presidents			
Aga Khan	Dr. Asad Ansari	Allama Iqbal	Dr. Mohammad Tariq
Dow	Dr. Syed A. Samad	Fatima Jinnah	Dr. Saadia I. Khan
Khyber	Dr. Roh Afza Afridi	King Edward	Dr. Furhan Yunus
Liaquat	Dr. Kimat G. Khatak	Nishtar	Dr. Shahid Latif
Quaid-I-Azam	Dr. Shabbar Hussain	Rawalpindi	Dr. Raza Bokhari
Sindh	Dr. Qazi K. Haider		
Chapter Presidents			
Arizona	Dr. Akhtar S. Hamidi	Florida	Dr. Mohammad H. A. Qazi
Georgia		Illinois	Dr. Shabbir A. Chowdhry
Kentucky & Indiana	Dr. Aftab Ahmed	Michigan	Dr. Busharat Ahmad
Mid-South	Dr. Nadeem Zafar	Missouri	Dr. Zafar Quader
Nevada		New England	Dr. Naheed Usmani
New Jersey	Dr. Avais Masud	New York	Dr. Muhammad Haque
North Carolina	Dr. Waheed K. Bajwa	North Texas	Dr. Adnan Nadir
Northern California & Oregon	Dr. Fayaz Asghar	Ohio	Dr. Shahid I. Sheikh
Pennsylvania	Dr. Abdul Rashid	Southern	Dr. Zahid Imran
Southern California	Dr. Ahsan U. Rashid	South Texas	Dr. Muhammad Yaqoob Shaikh
Three River	Dr. Adeel A. Butt	Upstate New York	Dr. Ashraf Sabahat
D.C. & Baltimore	Dr. Mohammad Akbar	Physicians-In-Training	Dr. Mohammad Zaim Nawaz
Board of Trustees			
Chairman		Dr. M. Jafar Shah	
Dr. Shabbir H. Safdar		Dr. Arif Muslim	
Dr. M. Afzal Arain		Dr. Iltifat A. Alavi	

APPNA LEADERSHIP 2007			
Executive Committee			
President	Dr. Nadeem Kazi	**President-Elect**	Dr. Mahmood Alam
Secretary	Dr. Shahid Usmani	**Treasurer**	Dr. Rizwan Naeem
Immediate Past President	Dr. Abdul R. Piracha	**Executive Director**	Dr. Tariq H. Cheema
Alumni Association Presidents			
Rawalpindi	Dr. Shahid Rafiq	**Aga Khan**	Dr. Rizwan Khalid
Dow	Dr. Farid Ullah Qazi	**Khyber**	Dr. Afzal Bangash
Liaquat	Dr. Azra S. Haque	**Nishtar**	Dr. Muhammad Javed Iqbal
Qaid-I-Azam	Dr. M. Khawar Ismail	**Sind**	Dr. Joseph Emmanuel
Allama Iqbal	Dr. Ashraf Sabahat	**Fatima Jinnah**	Dr. Naheed Chaudhry
King Edward	Dr. Ijaz Mahmood	**NAMA**	Dr. Nadia S. Afridi
Punjab	Dr. Shahid Rafiq		
Chapter Presidents			
New Jersey	Dr. M. Nasar Qureshi	**Southern California**	Dr. Aamir Jamal
Arizona	Dr. M. Asim Khwaja	**Connecticut**	Dr. Atique Azam Mirza
South Florida	Dr. Iqbal Zafar Hamid	**Heartland**	Dr. Syed Faisal Jafri
Kentucky & Indiana	Dr. Zaka U. Rahman	**Mid-South**	Dr. Muhammad Ilyas Shakir
Nevada	Dr. Salman Akhtar	**Upstate New York**	Dr. Abdul Qadir
Ohio	Dr. Mohammad Almas Ahmed	**Pennsylvania**	Dr. Abdul Rashid
Southern	Dr. Ghayas Ahmed	**South Texas**	Dr. Kamran Sherwani
D.C. & Baltimore	Dr. Tariq Mahmood	**Northern California & Oregon**	Dr. Munir Javed
Greater Cincinnati	Dr. Farooq Mirza	**Florida**	Dr. Muhammad Ashraf Ch.
Georgia	Dr. Khalique U. Rehman	**Illinois**	Dr. Arif Agha
Michigan	Dr. Dr. Zakir H. Qureshi	**Missouri**	Dr. Sajid M. Zafar
New England	Dr. Syed Iftikhar Hussain	**New York**	Dr. Abdul Majeed
North Carolina	Dr. Waheed K. Bajwa	**Oklahoma**	Dr. Asim Jafar Chohan
Physicians-In-Training	Dr. Syna Hamidi	**North Texas**	Dr. Imran Shahab
Three River	Dr. Adeel A. Butt		
Board of Trustees			
Chairman		Dr. Arif Muslim	
Dr. M. Afzal Arain		Dr. Iltifat A. Alavi	
Dr. Ihsan Ul Haq		Dr. Pervez Rasul	

APPNA LEADERSHIP 2009			
Executive Committee			
President	Dr. Syed Abdus Samad	President-Elect	Dr. Zeelaf B. Munir
Secretary	Dr. Manzoor Tariq	Treasurer	Dr. Saima Zafar
Immediate Past President	Dr. Mahmood Alam	Executive Director	Dr. Tariq H. Cheema
Alumni Association Presidents			
Aga Khan	Dr. Faiz Y. Bhora	Allama Iqbal	Dr. Rizwan Akhtar
Dow	Dr. M. Muslim Jami	Fatima Jinnah	
Khyber	Dr. Mohammad Taqi	King Edward	Dr. Mohammad Haseeb
Liaquat	Dr. Abdul Sattar Shaikh	Nishtar	Dr. Abdul Jabbar
Punjab	Dr. Muhammad Ashraf	Quaid-e-Azam	Dr. Dawood Nasir
Rawalpindi	Dr. Tanveer Ahmad	Sindh	Dr. Suhail H. Siddiqui
Chapter Presidents			
Alabama	Dr. Samia S. Moizuddin	Arizona	Dr. Syed Taqi Azam
Northern California & Oregon	Dr. Munir Javed	Southern California	Dr. Kamran A. Qureshi
Greater Cincinnati	Dr. Rashid Masood Khan	Connecticut	Dr. Atique A. Mirza
Florida	Dr. Riffat N. Qureshi	South Florida	Dr. Rahat Abbas
Georgia	Dr. Mohammad Y. Abubaker	Heartland	Dr. Muhammed Salman Haroon
Illinois	Dr. Fatima Ahmad	Kentucky & Indian	Dr. Sohail Ikram
Michigan	Dr. Naeem Ahmed	Mid-South	Dr. Muhammad Jaffar
Missouri	Dr. Nadeem Ahmed	Nevada	
New England	Dr. Fauzia Wali-Khan	New Jersey	Dr. Zafar Jamil
New York	Dr. Asif M. Rehman	Upstate New York	Dr. Ashraf Sabahat
North Carolina	Dr. Waheed K. Bajwa	Ohio	Dr. Raheela A. Khawaja
Oklahoma	Dr. Asim Jafar Chohan	Pennsylvania	Dr. Mohammad Khawar Ismail
Physicians-In-Training		Southern	Dr. Zahid Imran
North Texas	Dr. Khalid Mahmood	South Texas	Dr. Afaf Zahra Shah
Three River	Dr. Mehboob K. Chaudhry	Virginia	Dr. Salman Siddiqui
D.C. & Maryland	Dr. Tariq Mahmood	Northern Indiana	Dr. Sophia Janjua Khan
Board of Trustees			
Chairman		Dr. Iltifat Alavi	
Dr. Ihsan Haq		Dr. Pervaiz Rasul	
Dr. Javed Akhtar		Dr. Kimat Khatak	

APPNA LEADERSHIP 2010			
Executive Committee			
President	Dr. Zeelaf B. Munir	President-Elect	Dr. Manzoor Tariq
Secretary	Dr. M. Nasar Qureshi	Treasurer	Dr. Mubasher E. Rana
Immediate Past President	Dr. Syed Abdus Samad	Executive Director	
Alumni Association Presidents			
Aga Khan	Dr. Faiz Y. Bhora	Allama Iqbal	Dr. Tahir Latif
Baqai	Dr. Amir M. Qureshi	Caribbean	Dr. Shahid Usmani
Dow	Dr. Shazia Malik	Fatima Jinnah	Dr. Manzar J. Shafi
Khyber	Dr. Mohammad Taqi	King Edward	Dr. M. Masood Akbar
Liaquat	Dr. Abdul Sattar Shaikh	Nishtar	Dr. Haroon H. Durrani
NAMA		Punjab	Dr. Muhammad Siddique
Quaid-I-Azam	Dr. M. Farooq Khokhar	Rawalpindi	Dr. Sophia Janjua Khan
Sindh	Dr. I. Zafar Hamid		
Chapter Presidents			
Alabama	Dr. Samia S. Moizuddin	Arizona	Dr. Syed Taqi Azam
Northern California & Oregon	Dr. Munawar Alvi	Southern California	Dr. Asif Mahmood
Canada	Dr. Naheed Masood Chaudhry	Greater Cincinnati	Dr. Rashid Masood Khan
Connecticut	Dr. Atique A. Mirza	Florida	Dr. Riffat N. Qureshi
South Florida	Dr. Rahat Abbas	Georgia	Dr. Adnan Abbasi
Heartland	Dr. Muhammed Salman Haroon	Illinois	Dr. Javed Suleman
Kentucky & Indiana	Dr. Asim Rashid Piracha	Northern Indiana	Dr. Bilal Ansari
Michigan	Dr. Muhammad Sohail Jilani	Mid-South	Dr. Mohammad Saif Siddiqui
Missouri	Dr. Mujtaba A. Qazi	Nevada	
New England	Dr. Fauzia Wali-Khan	New Jersey	Dr. Nadeem Ul Haque
New York	Dr. Salman Zafar	Upstate New York	Dr. Taseer Cheema
North Carolina		Ohio	Dr. Nasim Sheikh
Oklahoma		South Central Pennsylvania	Dr. Rahat Taswir
Physicians-In-Training		Southern	Dr. Zahid Imran
North Texas	Dr. Khalid Mahmood	South Texas	Dr. Khawaja Azimuddin
Three River		Virginia	Dr. Attique Samdani
D.C. & Maryland	Dr. Sohail M. Qarni		
Board of Trustees			
Chairman		Dr. Ihsan ul Haq	
Dr. Pervez Rasul		Dr. M. Javed Akhtar	
Dr. Kimat Gul Khatak		Dr. Aftab Ahmad Naz	

APPNA LEADERSHIP 2011			
Executive Committee			
President	Dr. Manzoor Tariq	President-Elect	Dr. Saima Zafar
Secretary	Dr. Mubasher E. Rana	Treasurer	Dr. Asif Rehman
Immediate Past President	Dr. Zeelaf B. Munir	Director of Operations	Jennifer Wozniak-Watson, JD
Alumni Association Presidents			
Aga Khan	Dr. Syed J. Sher	Allama Iqbal	Dr. khurram Nazeer
Army		Baqai	Dr. Amir M. Qureshi
Caribbean	Dr. Shahid Farooq Usmani	Dow	Dr. M. Sohail Khan
Fatima Jinnah	Dr. Nosheen Mazhar	King Edward	Dr. Tariq Jamil
Khyber	Dr. Arshad Rehan	Liaquat	Dr. Shahnaz Maria Saber
NAMA	Dr. Shahnaz Maria Saber	Nishtar	Dr. Haroon H. Durrani
Punjab	Dr. Mehboob K. Chaudhry	Quaid-I-Azam	Dr. Shabbar Hussain
Rawalpindi	Dr. Shahida S. Rehmani	Sindh	Dr. Aftab Ahmed
Chapter Presidents			
Alabama	Dr. Khalid Matin	Arizona	Dr. Azhar Rafiq Jan
Arkansas	Dr. Muhammad Arshad	Northern California & Oregon	Dr. Shahid Abbasi
Southern California	Dr. Kamran A. Qureshi	Canada	Dr. Aamer Mahmud
Cincinnati	Dr. Amir Izhar	Connecticut	Dr. Atique A. Mirza
Florida	Dr. Masood Hashmi	South Florida	Dr. Rahat Abbas
Georgia	Dr. Roohi Abubaker	Heartland	Dr. Muhammad Salman Haroon
Illinois	Dr. Zubair M. Syed	Kentucky & Indiana	Dr. Asim Rashid Piracha
Northern Indiana	Dr. Bilal Ansari	Michigan	Dr. Muhammad Sohail Jilani
Mid-South	Dr. Mohammad Saif Siddiqui	Minnesota	Dr. Nadeem Iqbal
Missouri	Dr. Mohammed Haseeb	New England	Dr. Khalil A. Khatri
New Jersey	Dr. Shahnaz Akhtar	Nevada	Dr. Muhammad Sabir
New York	Dr. Pervaiz Qureshi	Upstate New York	Dr. Ashraf Sabahat
North Carolina	Dr. Khalid Aziz	Ohio	Dr. Naghma Malik
South Central Pennsylvania	Dr. Mohammad Khawar Ismail	Southern	Dr. Zahid Imran
Tennessee		North Texas	Dr. Hasan F. Hashmi
South Texas	Dr. Ghyasuddin Syed	Virginia	Dr. Agha Suhail Haider
D.C. & Maryland	Dr. Sohail M. Qarni	Wisconsin	Dr. Imran Nadeem
Board of Trustees			
Chairman		Dr. Pervez Rasul	
Dr. M. Javed Akhtar		Dr. Kimat Gul Khatak	
Dr. Aftab Ahmad Naz		Dr. Nadeem A. Kazi	

APPNA LEADERSHIP 2012			
Executive Committee			
President	Dr. Saima Zafar	President-Elect	Dr. Javed Suleman
Secretary	Dr. Asif M. Rehman	Treasurer	Dr. Farid Ullah Qazi
Immediate Past President	Dr. Manzoor Ahmad Tariq	Director of Operations	Jennifer Wozniak-Watson, JD
Alumni Association Presidents			
Aga Khan	Dr. Sadaf Khan	Allama Iqbal	Dr. Abid Hussain
Army	Dr. Rashid Masood Khan	Baqai	Dr. Amir M. Qureshi
Caribbean	Dr. Riaz. A. Chaudhry	Dow	Dr. Talha Siddiqui
Fatima Jinnah	Dr. Farhat Osman	Khyber	Dr. Arshad Rehan
King Edward	Dr. Muhammad Hamid	Liaquat	Dr. Imtiaz A. Arain
NAMA	Dr. Shamail S. Tariq	Nishtar	Dr. Khalid A. Rao
Punjab	Dr. Amjad Ghani Sheikh	Quaid-I-Azam	Dr. Massoud Elahi Mian
Rawalpindi	Dr. Mirza Qasim Hasan	Sindh	Dr. Rukhshinda R. Hameedi
Chapter Presidents			
Alabama	Dr. Saeed Shah	Arizona	Dr. Faran Bashir
Arkansas	Dr. Muhammad Arshad	Canada	Dr. Shabnam Hussain
Connecticut	Dr. Inam U. Kureshi	Florida	Dr. Masood Hashmi
Georgia	Dr. Sarah Hayat	Greater Cincinnati	Dr. Amir Izhar
Heartland	Dr. Amam U. Khan	Illinois	Dr. M. Waseem Kagzi
Kentucky & Indiana	Dr. Jamil Farooqui	Michigan	Dr. Adil Akhtar
Mid-South	Dr. Mohammad Saif Siddiqui	Minnesota	Dr. Nadeem Iqbal
Missouri & Greater St. Louis	Dr. Naseem A. Shekhani	Nevada	Dr. Nayab M. Zafar
New England	Dr. Jamila Khalil	New Jersey	Dr. Shahida M. Abbas
New York	Dr. Ahsan Nazir	North Carolina	Dr. Javed Masoud
North Texas	Dr. Hasan F. Hashmi	Northern California & Oregon	Dr. Sabir Ali Khan
Northern Indiana	Dr. Zeba Ali	Northern Tennessee	Dr. Shahram Malik
Ohio	Dr. Naghma Malik	South Central Pennsylvania	Dr. Rashid K. Anjum
South Florida	Dr. Syed Javed hashmi	South Texas	Dr. Mubashir Tufail Chaudhry
Southern California	Dr. Hyder Jamal	Southern	Dr. Naveed Malik
Upstate New York	Dr. Ashraf Sabahat	Virginia	Dr. Agha Suhail Haider
D.C. & Maryland	Dr. Mubarik Khan	Wisconsin	Dr. Iram Nadeem
Board of Trustees			
Chairman		Dr. M. Javed Akhtar	
Dr. Kimat Gul Khatak		Dr. Aftab Ahmad Naz	
Dr. Nadeem A. Kazi		Dr. Abdul Rashid Piracha	

APPNA LEADERSHIP 2013			
Executive Committee			
President	Dr. Javed Suleman	President-Elect	Dr. Asif M. Rehman
Secretary	Dr. Farid Qazi	Treasurer	Dr. S. Tariq Shahab
Immediate Past President	Dr. Saima Zafar	Director of Operations	Jennifer Wozniak-Watson, JD
Alumni Association Presidents			
Aga Khan	Dr. Sadaf Khan	Allama Iqbal	Dr. Abid Hussain
Army Medical	Dr. Rashid M. Khan	Baqai	Dr. Amir M. Qureshi
Caribbean	Dr. Riaz A. Chaudhry	Dental APPNA	Dr. Mohammad Arshad
Dow	Dr. Sajid Zafar	Fatima Jinnah	Dr. Tabassum Saeed
Khyber	Dr. Sajjad Savul	King Edward	Dr. Maqbool Arshad
Liaquat	Dr. Imtiaz A. Arain	Nishtar	Dr. Mohammad Imran Ata
NAMA	Dr. Shamail S. Tariq	Punjab	Dr. Shahid Sheikh
Quaid-I-Azam	Dr. Massoud Elahi Mian	Rawalpindi	Dr. Hina Naushad
Sindh	Dr. Syed Taqi Azam		
Chapter Presidents			
Alabama	Dr. Saeed Shah	Arizona	Dr. Nusrum Iqbal
Arkansas	Dr. Asif Masood	Canada	Dr. Mahjabeen Ammad
Connecticut	Dr. Inam Kureshi	Florida	Dr. Humeraa Qamar
Georgia	Dr. Haroon Rashid	Greater Cincinnati	Dr. Tanvir Sajjad
Heartland	Dr. Abdul Ahad Haleem	Illinois	Dr. Saima Sabah
Kentucky & Indiana	Dr. Vasdev Lohano	Michigan	Dr. Adil Akhtar
Minnesota	Dr. Nadeem Iqbal	Missouri & Greater St. Louis	Dr. Shahid Badar
Nevada	Dr. Rizwan Qazi	New England	Dr. Jamila Khalil
New Jersey	Dr. Rabia Awan	New York	Dr. Muhammad Hamid
North Carolina	Dr. Javed Masoud	North Texas	Dr. Dawood Nasir
Northern California & Oregon	Dr. Tanvir Sattar	Northern Tennessee	Dr. Zia Ur Rahman
Ohio	Dr. Bushra Siddiqui	South Central Pennsylvania	Dr. Zahid Khan
South Florida	Dr. Danyal Khan	South Texas	Dr. Sardar Daud Khan
Southern California	Dr. Hyder Jamal	Southern	Dr. Naveed Malik
Upstate New York	Dr. Zahid S. Asgher	Virginia	Dr. Abdul Qadir Mohiuddin
D.C. & Maryland	Dr. Rashid Nayyar	Wisconsin	Dr. Iram Nadeem
Board of Trustees			
Chairman		Dr. Kimat Gul Khatak	
Dr. Nadeem A. Kazi		Dr. Aftab Ahmad Naz	
Dr. Abdul Rashid Piracha		Dr. Mufiz Chauhan	

APPNA LEADERSHIP 2015			
Executive Committee			
President	Dr. Mubasher Rana	President-Elect	Dr. M. Nasar Qureshi
Secretary	Dr. Shahid Rashid	Treasurer	Dr. Iqbal Zafar Hamid
Immediate Past President	Dr. Asif M. Rehman	Director of Operations	Jennifer Wozniak-Watson, JD
Alumni Association Presidents			
Aga Khan	Dr. Faisal Qureshi	Allama Iqbal	Dr. Raza Khan
Baqai	Dr. Amir M. Qureshi	Caribbean	Dr. Naveed Chowhan
Dental APPNA	Dr. Dean Nadeem Ahmad	Dow	Dr. M. Asif Mohiuddin
Fatima Jinnah	Dr. Samina Hijab	Jinnah Sindh	Dr. Sabir Ali Khan
Khyber	Dr. Sajjad Savul	King Edward	Dr. Ahmed Mehdi
Liaquat	Dr. Abdul Majeed	Nishtar	Dr. Safdar Ali
Punjab	Dr. Mohammad Khalid Waseem	Quaid-I-Azam	Dr. Mohammad Khalid Iqbal
Rawalpindi	Dr. Sohail Minhas		
Chapter Presidents			
Alabama	Dr. Ehtsham Haq	Arizona	Dr. Habib Ur-Rehman Khan
Arkansas	Dr. Sunbal Zafar	Canada	Dr. Humaira H. Ali
Connecticut	Dr. Momina Salman	Delaware Valley & Pennsylvania	Dr. Sarwat Iqbal
Florida	Dr. Ayyaz Shah	Georgia	Dr. Mirza W. Ahmed
Greater Cincinnati	Dr. Muhammad Aslam	Heartland	Dr. Hussain Haideri
Illinois	Dr. Hasina Javed	Kentucky & Indiana	Dr. Asad Ismail
Michigan	Dr. Kashif Qureshi	Minnesota	Dr. Bushra Dar
Missouri & Greater St. Louis	Dr. Hasan A. H. Ahmed	New England	Dr. Muhammad Ramzan
New Jersey	Dr. Razia Awan	New York	Dr. Syed Tariq Ibrahim
North Carolina	Dr. Mohammad Anjum Bhatti	North Texas	Dr. Mohammad Zaim Nawaz
Northern California & Oregon	Dr. Muniza Muzaffar	North East Tennessee	Dr. Adil Warsy
Ohio	Dr. Fouzia Tariq	Oklahoma	Dr. Iftikhar Hussain
South Central Pennsylvania	Dr. Mohammad K. Ismail	South Floriad	Dr. Mian Ahmed Hasan
South Central Texas	Dr. Mehmood Khan	South Texas	Dr. Muhammad Yaqoob Shaikh
Southern California	Dr. Hyder Jamal	Southern	Dr. Muhammad Shuja
Virginia	Dr. M. Rehan Khan	D.C. & Maryland	Dr. Samia Waseem
Wisconsin	Dr. Danish Siddiqui		
Board of Trustees			
Chairman		Dr. Nadeem Kazi	
Dr. Abdul Rashid Piracha		Dr. Mufiz Chauhan	
Dr. Imtiaz Arain		Dr. Farrukh Hashmi	

APPNA COMMITTEES LEADERSHIP

2004–2016

Advocacy, Legislative & Governmental Affairs Committee*		
Name	**Position**	**Year**
Dr. M. Saud Anwar	Chair	2004
Dr. Hussain G. Malik	Chair	2005
Dr. Abdul R. Piracha	Chair	2006
Dr. Nasir Gondal	Co-Chair	2007
Dr. Asim Malik	Co-Chair	2007
Dr. Abdul R. Piracha	Chair	2008
Dr. Zia Moiz Ahmad	Chair	2009
Dr. Asif Mahmood	Chair	2010
Dr. Zaffar Iqbal	Chair	2011
Dr. Manzoor Tariq	Chair	2012
Dr. Talha Siddiqui	Chair	2013
Dr. Abdul R. Piracha	Chair	2014
Dr. Hameed Peracha	Chair	2015–2016

*President Raana Akbar appointed a Taskforce on the Visa and Security Clearance issues of young physicians from Pakistan in 2003. Asim Malik and Dr. Nasir Gondal were appointed Chair and Co-chair, respectively. The members of the Taskforce were Mahmood Alam, Sajid Chaudhry, Zaffar Iqbal, Waheed Akbar, Faisal Cheema, M. Saud Anwar, Busharat Ahmad, Saeed Akhtar, Omar Atiq, Javed Suleman, Adnan Khan, and Nadeem Zafar. This task force led to the formation of a standing committee on Advocacy, Legislative and governmental affairs in 2004.

Alumni Scholarship Committee		
Name	**Position**	**Year**
N/A	Chair	2004–2012
Dr. M. Masood Akbar	Chair	2013–2016

Constitution & Bylaws Committee		
Name	**Position**	**Year**
Dr. Mohammad Suleman	Chair	2004
Dr. Mushtaq Sheikh	Chair	2005
Dr. Omar Atiq	Chair	2006
Dr. M. Nasar Qureshi	Chair	2007
Dr. Riaz M. Chaudhry	Chair	2008
Dr. Asif Rehman	Chair	2009
Dr. Suhail H. Siddiqi	Chair	2010
Dr. Mahmood Alam	Chair	2011
Dr. Mohammad Suleman	Chair	2012
Dr. Ahsan Rashid	Chair	2013
Dr. Mahmood Alam	Chair	2014
Dr. Mohammed Haseeb	Chair	2015
Dr. Mahmood Alam	Chair	2016

Communications Committee		
Name	**Position**	**Year**
Dr. Adeel A. Butt	Chair	2004
Dr. Sajid Chaudhary	Chair	2005–2006
Dr. Muhammad Ali	Chair	2007
Dr. M. Khawar Ismail	Chair	2008
Dr. Nadeem Zafar	Chair	2009
Dr. Mohammed Taqi	Chair	2010
Dr. M. Shahid Yousuf	Chair	2011 –2016

Ethics & Grievance Committee		
Name	**Position**	**Year**
Dr. Farooq Ahmad Mirza	Chair	2004
Dr. Busharat Ahmad	Chair	2005
Dr. S. Latafat Hamzavi	Chair	2006
Dr. M. Javed Akhtar	Chair	2007
Dr. S. Sultan Ahmed	Chair	2008
Dr. Adeel A. Butt	Chair	2009
Dr. S. Sultan Ahmed	Chair	2010
Dr. M. Ishaq Chishti	Chair	2011
Dr. Roh A. Afridi	Chair	2012
Dr. Mahmood Qalbani	Chair	2013

Ethics & Grievance Committee		
Name	**Position**	**Year**
Dr. Riaz A. Chaudhry	Chair	2014
Dr. Asim Malik	Chair	2015
Dr. Naeem Qazi	Chair	2016

Finance Committee		
Name	**Position**	**Year**
Dr. Nadeem A. Kazi	Chair	2004
Dr. Mahmood Alam	Chair	2005
Dr. Shahid Usmani	Chair	2006
Dr. Rizwan Naeem	Chair	2007
Dr. Manzoor Tariq	Chair	2008
Dr. Saima Zafar	Chair	2009
Dr. Mubasher E. Rana	Chair	2010
Dr. Asif Rehman	Chair	2011
Dr. Farid Ullah Qazi	Chair	2012
Dr. S. Tariq Shahab	Chair	2013
Dr. Shahid Rashid	Chair	2014
Dr. Iqbal Zafar Hamid	Chair	2015
Dr. Dawood Nasir	Chair	2016

Hotel Selection & Negotiations Committee		
Name	**Position**	**Year**
Dr. Riaz A. Chaudhry	Chair	2004–2008
Dr. Shahid Usmani	Chair	2009–2010
Dr. Riaz A. Chaudhry	Chair	2011–2012
Dr. Aftab Ahmed	Chair	2013
Dr. Munir A. Shikari	Chair	2014
Dr. Syed Taqi Azam	Chair	2015
N/A	Chair	2016

International Meetings Committee		
Name	**Position**	**Year**
Dr. Riaz A. Chaudhry	Chair	2004–2009
Dr. Zia Moiz Ahmed	Chair	2010
Dr. Riaz A. Chaudhry	Chair	2011–2012
Dr. Aftab Ahmed	Chair	2013
Dr. Riaz A. Chaudhry	Chair	2014

International Meetings Committee		
Name	Position	Year
Dr. Adnan Zaidi	Chair	2015
Dr. Aftab Ahmed	Chair	2016

Committee for Liaison with Professional Organizations		
Name	Position	Year
Dr. Ayaz Samadani	Chair	2004
Dr. Mohammad H. A. Qazi	Chair	2005
Dr. Busharat Ahmad	Chair	2006
Dr. Ayaz Samadani	Chair	2007–2008
Dr. Javed Suleman	Chair	2009
Dr. Zahid Imran	Chair	2010
Dr. Busharat Ahmad	Chair	2011
Dr. I. Zafar Hamid	Chair	2012
Dr. Zahid Imran	Chair	2013
Dr. Tariq Jamil	Chair	2014
Dr. Ayesha Najib	Chair	2015
N/A	Chair	2016

Medical Education & Research International Training Committee (MERIT)		
Name	Position	Year
Dr. G. Naheed Usmani	Chair	2007–2011
Dr. Babar Rao	Chair	2012–2016

Membership Committee		
Name	Position	Year
Dr. Sadeem Mahmood	Chair	2004
Dr. Syed A. Samad	Chair	2005
Dr. Javed Suleman	Chair	2006
Dr. Asif Rehman	Chair	2007
Dr. Asif Rehman	Chair	2008
Dr. Sajid R. Chaudhary	Chair	2009
Dr. Sophia Janjua Khan	Chair	2010
Dr. Haroon Durrani	Chair	2011
Dr. Sajjad Savul	Chair	2012
Dr. Joseph Emmanuel	Chair	2013
Dr. M. Khawar Ismail	Chair	2014

Membership Committee		
Name	**Position**	**Year**
Dr. Jamil Mohsin	Chair	2015
Dr. Joseph Emmanuel	Chair	2016

Nomination & Election Committee		
Name	**Position**	**Year**
Dr. Nisar Chaudhry	Chair	2004
Dr. Mohammad Suleman	Chair	2005–2006
Dr. Ahsan Rashid	Chair	2007
Dr. Mufiz Chauhan	Chair	2008
Dr. Ahsan Rashid	Chair	2009
Dr. Ahsan Rashid	Chair	2010
Dr. Farooq A. Mirza	Chair	2011-2012
Dr. Jamil Farooqui	Chair	2013
Dr. Sajjad Savul	Chair	2014–15
Dr. Jamil Farooqui	Chair	2016

Office Management & Oversight Committee		
Name	**Position**	**Year**
Dr. Iltifat A. Alavi	Chair	2004
Dr. Riaz Akhtar	Chair	2005
Dr. M. Mushtaq Sharif	Chair	2006
Dr. M. Omar Nasib	Chair	2007
Dr. Imtiaz Arain	Chair	2008–2009
Dr. M. Mushtaq Sharif	Chair	2010
Dr. Imtiaz Arain	Chair	2011
Dr. Arif Agha	Chair	2012
Dr. Mansoor Alam	Chair	2013
Dr. Aftab Khan	Chair	2014
Dr. Mansoor Alam	Chair	2015–2016

Publications Committee—APPNA Journal and Newsletter		
Name	**Position**	**Year**
Dr. Furrukh Sayyer Malik	Chair	2004
Dr. Zia Moiz Ahmad	Co-Chair	
Dr. Rizwan Naeem	Managing Editor (English)	
Dr. Naeem Kohli	Urdu Editor	
Dr. Abdul Rahman	Managing Editor (Urdu)	
Dr. Mufiz A. Chauhan	Chair	2005
Dr. Zia Moiz Ahmad	Co-Chair	
Dr. Rizwan Naeem	Managing Editor	
Dr. Naeem kohli	Urdu Editor	
Dr. Abdul Rahman	Urdu Co-Editor	
Dr. Rizwan A. Karatela	Chair	2006
Dr. Raana Akbar	Co-Chair	
Dr. Zia Moiz Ahmad	Editor	
Dr. Naeem kohli	Editor (Urdu)	
Dr. M. Shahid Yousaf	Chair	2007
Dr. Shahab Arfeen	Co-Chair	
Dr. Furrukh S. Malik	Editor	
Dr. Salman Zafar	Editor (Urdu)	
Dr. Shahid Athar	Chair	2008
Dr. Salman Zafar	Co-Chair	
Dr. Farrukh S. Malik	Editor	
Dr. Asaf Ali Dar	Editor (Urdu)	
Dr. Syed Tariq Shahab	Chair	2009
Dr. Jamil Farooqui	Co-Chair	
Dr. Zia Moiz Ahmad	Editor	
Dr. Salman Zafar	Editor (Urdu)	
Dr. Syed Nadeem Ahsan	Chair	2010
Dr. Lubna Pal	Co-Chair	
Dr. Salim Chowdhrey	Editor	
Mohammad Taqi	Editor (Urdu)	

Publications Committee—APPNA Journal and Newsletter		
Name	**Position**	**Year**
Dr. Asaf Ali Dar	Chair	2011
Dr. Mahmood Alam	Editor	
Dr. Wasique Mirza	Co-Editor	
Dr. Asaf Ali Dar	Editor (Urdu)	
Dr. Javaid Akbar	Co-Editor (Urdu)	
Dr. Tanveer M. Imam	Chair	2012
Dr. Zimran Chaudhary	Editor	
Dr. Ghazala Kazi	Editor (Urdu)	
Dr. Syed Mansoor Hussain	Chair	2013
Dr. Abid Rasool	Co-Chair and Editor	
Dr. Tanveer M. Imam	Chair	2014
Dr. Javaid Akbar	Co-Chair	
Dr. Muniza Shah	Co-Chair	
Dr. Abdul Rahman	Editor (Urdu)	
Dr. Tahir Latif	Chair and Editor	2015
Dr. Javaid Akbar	Co-Chair and Editor (Urdu)	
Dr. Intikhab Ahmad	Chair	2016
Dr. Fariya Afridi	Co-Chair	
Dr. Tariq Alam	Co-Chair	
Dr. Mohammad Taqi	Co-Chair	
Dr. Shamim Zafar	Co-Chair	
Dr. Salman Zafar	Advisor	

Qatra Fund Committee		
Name	**Position**	**Year**
Dr. Mahjabeen Islam	Chair	2015–16

Research, Education & Scientific Affairs Committee		
Name	Position	Year
Dr. Raza Dilawari	Chair	2004–2007
Dr. Shabbir Safdar	Chair	2008
Dr. Adeel A. Butt	Chair	2009
Dr. Raza Dilawari	Chair	2010
Dr. Tariq Jamil	Chair	2011
Dr. Ayaz Samdani	Chair	2012
Dr. Rizwan C. Naeem	Chair	2013
Dr. Mohammad Jahanzeb	Chair	2014
Dr. Jawad Hasnain	Chair	2015
Dr. Raheel R. Khan	Chair	2016

APPNA SEHAT Committee		
Name	Position	Year
Dr. Hassan I. Bukhari	Chair	2004–2006
Dr. Abdul R. Piracha	Chair	2007
Dr. Hassan I Bukhari	Chair	2008

Social Welfare & Disaster Relief Committee (SWDRC)		
Name	Position	Year
Dr. M. Javed Akhtar	Chair	2004
Dr. Nadeem Zafar	Co-Chair	
Dr. M. Javed Akhtar	Chair	2005
Dr. M. Javed Akhtar	Chair	2006
Dr. Saima Zafar	Co-Chair	
Dr. Saima Zafar	Chair	2007
Dr. Shahabul Arfeen	Chair	2008
Dr. Nadeem Zafar	Chair	2009
Dr. Jamil Farooqui	Chair	2010
Dr. Humeraa Qamar	Co-Chair	
Dr. Aisha Zafar	Chair	2011
Dr. Mubasher Rana	Chair	2012
Dr. Shahid Sheikh	Chair	2013
Dr. Naeem Khan	Co-Chair	
Dr. Babar Cheema	Chair	2014
Dr. Aisha Zafar	Chair	2015– 2016

Spring Meeting Committees		
Name	**Position**	**Year**
Dr. Mahmood Alam	Chair	2004
Dr. Habib Bhuta	Chair	2005
Dr. Hameed Peracha	Chair	2006
Dr. Asim Khwaja	Chair	2007
Dr. Zaka Ur Rahman	Chair	2008
Dr. Khalid Mahmood	Chair	2009
Dr. Noor Khan	Chair	2010
Dr. Naveed M. Chowhan	Chair	2011
Dr. Nayab Zafar	Chair	2012
Dr. Pervaiz Iqbal	Chair	2013
Dr. Asif Chaudhry	Chair	2014
Dr. Talha Siddiqui	Chair	2015
Dr. Mian Ahmed Hasan	Chair	2016

Summer Meeting Committee		
Name	**Position**	**Year**
Dr. Zahid W. Butt	Chair	2004
Dr. Asaf Qadeer	Chair	2005
Dr. Parvez Rasul	Co-Chair	2006
Dr. M. Mushtaq Sharif	Co-Chair	
Dr. Shahid Usmani	Chair	2007
Dr. Hameed Peracha	Chair	2008
Dr. Mubasher Rana	Chair	2009
Dr. Jalil Khan	Chair	2010
Dr. Shabbir H. Safdar	Chair	2011
Dr. Zahid W. Butt	Chair	2012
Dr. Iqbal Zafar Hamid	Chair	2013
Dr. Hameed Peracha	Chair	2014
Dr. Shahid Usmani	Chair	2015
Dr. Talha Siddiqui	Chair	2016

Fall Meeting Committee		
Name	**Position**	**Year**
Dr. Arif Agha	Chair	2004
Dr. Shazia Kirmani	Chair	2005
Dr. Riaz A. Chaudhry	Chair	2006

Fall Meeting Committee		
Name	**Position**	**Year**
Dr. Asim Khwaja	Chair	2007
Dr. Mohammad A. Zubair	Chair	2008
Dr. Arshad Saeed	Chair	2009
Dr. I. Zafar Hamid	Chair	2010
Dr. Riaz A. Chaudhry	Chair	2011
Dr. Arif Agha	Chair	2012
Dr. Shagufta Naqvi	Chair	2013
Dr. Nasir Gondal	Co-Chair	2014
Dr. Asim Malik	Co-Chair	
Dr. Munir Javed	Chair	2015
Dr. Aamir Ehsan	Chair	2016

Winter Meeting Committee		
Name	**Position**	**Year**
Dr. Javed I. Bangash	Chair	2004
Dr. Raza Bokhari	Chair	2005
Dr. Nasir Gondal	Chair	2006
Dr. Farid Ullah Qazi	Chair	2007
Dr. Mubasher Rana	Co-Chair	2008
Dr. M. Babar Cheema	Co-Chair	
Dr. Adeel Butt	Chair	2009
Dr. Arif Toor	Chair	2010
Dr. Dawood Nasir	Chair	2011
Dr. Mubasher Rana	Chair	2012
Dr. Rizwan Naeem	Chair	2013
Dr. Haroon Durrani	Chair	2014
Dr. Mohammed Haseeb	Chair	2015
Dr. M. Azim Qureshi	Chair	2016

Committee on Young Physicians		
Name	**Position**	**Year**
Dr. Zeelaf Munir	Chair	2004
Dr. Tahseen Mozaffar	Co-Chair	
Dr. Rashid Piracha	Chair	2005
Dr. Rubina Inayat	Chair	2006
Dr. Rizwan Khalid	Chair	2007

Committee on Young Physicians		
Name	**Position**	**Year**
Dr. Faisal Cheema	Chair	2008
Dr. Rashid Piracha	Chair	2009
Dr. Rizwan Naeem	Chair	2010
Dr. Rubina Inayat	Chair	2011
Dr. Jalil Khan	Chair	2012
Dr. Zahid Imran	Chair	2013
Dr. Sajid Chaudhary	Chair	2014
Dr. Shahzad Iqbal	Chair	2015
Dr. Faisal Khosa	Chair	2016

APPNA AWARDS

In 1989, Dr. Khalid J. Awan (VA) proposed the idea of a Gold Medal Award to honor members who had provided meritorious services to APPNA over and above the call of duty. Dr. Awan also donated the seed money for the award. A committee was appointed in 1991 to develop selection criteria. A Lifetime Achievement Award was started later and first award was given in 2006. This award honors APPNA members who have excelled in their medical career and also contributed to achieving organizational goals in education and philanthropy. A Humanitarian Award was recently added and first award was given in 2014. The recipient of Humanitarian Award could be anyone—a person or an organization—whose services to humanity made a difference in the lives of people across the globe. Another award was also added in 2014—the Chapter or Alumni Association of The Year Award—to recognize any extraordinary achievement that stands out among the component societies. APPNA Awards Committee appointees should include at least two past presidents, two board of trustees' members, and at least one past gold medal awardee. The Chair of the committee is appointed by the sitting president of APPNA.

Besides these formal awards, a tradition of giving out "Presidential Awards" has been seen intermittently in the last several years. In general, these awards are given at the behest of the sitting president to various individuals and/or fraternal organizations in recognition for their contributions to APPNA or community.

RECIPIENTS OF APPNA GOLD MEDAL AWARD	
1991	Dr. Zaheer Gukhar Ahmad (MI)
1992	Award not given
1993	Dr. Nasim Ashraf (MD)
1994	Dr. Arif Muslim (NY)
1995	Dr. S. Amjad Hussain (OH)
1996	Dr. Hassan Bukhari (TX)
1997	Dr. Arif A. A. Toor (CT)
1998	Dr. M. Khalid Riaz (IL)
1999	Dr. M. Mushtaq Sharif (IL)
2000	Dr. Durdana Gilani (CA)
2001	Award not given
2002	Dr. Iltifat Alavi (IL)
2003	Dr. Mushtaq Khan (IL)
2004	Award not given
2005	Award not given
2006	Dr. M. Aslam Malik (TX)
2007	Dr. S. Sultan Ahmed (NJ)
2008	Dr. Shabbir H. Safdar (MO)
2009	Award not given
2010	Award not given
2011	Dr. Raana S. Akbar (MI)
2012	Dr. M. Ishaq Chisti (MO)
2013	Award Not Given
2014	Dr. Omar T. Atiq (AR)
2015	Dr. M. Shahid Yousuf (MI)
2016	Dr. Amanullah Khan (TX)

RECIPIENTS OF LIFETIME ACHIEVEMENT AWARD	
2006	Unknown
2007	Dr. Busharat Ahmad (MI)
2008	Dr. Ghaus Malik (MI)
2009	Award Not given
2010	Award Not given
2011	Dr. Raza A. Dilawari (TN)
2012	Dr. S. Amjad Hussain (OH)
2013	Award Not given

RECIPIENTS OF LIFETIME ACHIEVEMENT AWARD	
2014	Dr. Mohammad Suleman (LA)
2015	Award not given
2016	Dr. Zeenat Anwar (MI)

RECIPIENTS OF HUMANITARIAN AWARD	
2014	Dr. Nadeem Zafar (TN)
2015	Dr. Atiya Khan (MD)
2016	Award not given

RECIPIENTS OF COMPONENT SOCIETY OF THE YEAR AWARD	
2014	Pakistan Physicians Society (IL)
2015	Award not given
2016	Award not given

APPNA ALLIANCE PRESIDENTS

2004	Shahia Sheikh
2005	Bushra Sheikh
2006	Sajida Arain
2007	Hameeda Tariq
2008	Mehreen Atiq
2009	Rukhsana Mehmood
2010	Samrina Haseeb
2011	Rania Asif
2012	Fatima Elahi
2013	Hajra Kazi
2014	Samrina Haseeb
2015	Jabeen Bukhari
2016	Farah Haider

(L-R) Dr. Faiqa Qureshi (VA), Dr. Riffaat Bangash, Dr. Ishtiaque Bangash (r)(CA), Mrs. Farzana Naz (CA), Dr. Aftab Naz (r), Dr. Talat Bukhari (TX), Mrs Shani Kazi, Dr. Nadeem Kazi (r) (AZ), Dr. Atiya Khan (NY), Dr. Khalid Mahmood(r), Dr. Ejaz Mahmood(r) (KY), Mrs. Hameeda Tariq, Mrs. Rukhsana Mahmood, Mrs. Shazia Mahmood (KY), Farhaan Kazi, Dr. Manzoor Tariq(MO), Dr.Tariq Khan (NY).

Alliance Banquet 2009

BARACK H. OBAMA ON APPNA

Barack Obama

June 28, 2008

APPNA
c/o Mahmood Alam, MD, President
6414 S. Cass Avenue
Westmont, IL 60559

Dear Friends,

I am happy to welcome all of you to the 31st annual banquet of the Association of Physicians of Pakistani-descent of North America. I enjoyed the last time we met, and I am sorry that I could not be with you tonight.

Since its founding in 1976 by a handful of physicians, your organization has taken great strides. Today APPNA represents over 15,000 physicians across the United States. You have been more successful in bringing together Pakistani Americans than any other organization. And you have harnessed that success to provide vulnerable communities with medical assistance when and where it is most needed.

I value the humanitarian work your organization does, both here in the U.S., and around the world. From Hurricane Katrina to your work in Pakistan during 2005 and 2006, to this year's devastating earthquake in Indonesia, APPNA has funded relief efforts and put hundreds of doctors and medical students on the ground. Time and again, your organization has used its network and resources to relieve human suffering, and I commend you for that.

Thank you for the long-standing support that so many APPNA members have given me over the years, and for your service. I wish you continued success in all of your future endeavors.

Sincerely,

Barack Obama

OBAMA'08

Obama for America • PO Box 8210 • Chicago, IL 60680 • BarackObama.com

Paid for by Obama for America

APPNA AFFILIATED MEDICAL SPECIALITY NEWORKS

Association of Pakistani Cardiologists of North America (APCNA) was the first APPNA affiliated medical specially that was organized independent of APPNA. It was inaugurated on March 4, 2004 at the auspices of American College of Cardiology Meeting in New Orleans, Louisiana. During 2013–2014, the idea of developing medical **Specialty Societies** in APPNA sparked and small groups in the sub-specialties of Pulmonary, Gastroenterology, and Psychiatry began to organize. Six new groups in the specialties of Nephrology, Radiology, Pediatrics, Hematology/Oncology, and Anesthesia/ Pain Medicine were formed in 2015 to do specialty specific projects. Most of the work is being focused on increasing awareness of preventive healthcare issues by providing health education and strategies. Some of the specialties have also embarked on providing hard core treatment by donating medical equipment as well as staff training in the likes of ventilators and hemodialysis units. The beneficiaries are indeed poor people of Pakistan. The introductory accounts on the themes of some of these groups are included below to showcase their evolving commitment to improving healthcare in countries like Pakistan.

Chest Physicians of Pakistani Descent of North America, Inc. (APPNA CHEST)

APPNA Chest specialty network which includes Pulmonary and Critical Care physicians was formed in 2014. Its first President was Dr. Riaz A. Chaudhary (NY). The other members of the executive committee were Dr. Nadeem Ahmad (MO)—President Elect, Dr. Maqbool Arshad (WI)—Secretary and Dr. Abdul Majeed (NY)—Treasurer.

Dr. Mehboob Chaudhry (PA), Dr. Nisar Akbar, Dr. Imtiaz Arain (IL), and Dr. Bashir Chaudhry (GA) were appointed as the Board of Trustee members.

APPNA Chest launched a successful Anti-Tobacco campaign event throughout Pakistan in 2014. Awareness about the menace of tobacco smoking was highlighted in some of the major hospitals and medical colleges. APPNA CHEST developed and printed posters focusing on the health issues of tobacco smoking and the ill-effects of smoke pollution in the society.

A national non-governmental organization known as Akhuwat Foundation participated in this anti-tobacco campaign by putting APPNA posters throughout Pakistan in their offices. Akhuwat Foundation also asked their loan recipients to refrain from smoking. Vocational and special needs schools in Punjab participated in the anti-tobacco campaign as well.

Dr. Maqbool Arshad (WI) contributed to this report.

APPNA PEDS

APPNA Pediatrics Specialty Network was formally founded in 2015. Bylaws and constitution were approved. Office bearers were elected, and committees were formed. World renowned Professor of Global Health, Dr. Zulfiqar Bhutta agreed to be the Chairman of the Board of Trustees. The first inaugural meeting was held in August 2015 in Orlando, FL. Dr. Mubasher Rana and Dr. Ghulam Mujtaba's help and guidance was instrumental in its creation.

APPNA Pediatric network's objective is to have close ties with the Pakistan Pediatric Association to communicate, understand needs and disperse resources to assist in improving pediatric care in Pakistan. APPNA PEDS would also like to help young pediatricians in Pakistan to identify experienced pediatric specialists outside the country who could guide them in their field of interest and possibly get them some training opportunities abroad.

APPNA PEDS launched the following three projects in 2015:

1) Neonatology—headed by Dr. Mohammad Riaz, neonatologist, Pennsylvania

2) Academic PEDS—led by Khalid Kamal, pediatrician, Michigan—$1000 were distributed to ten Pakistani pediatricians for submission of comprehensive case reports.

3) PEDS Cardiology—led by Dr. Danyal Khan, pediatric cardiologist, Florida for transfer and distribution of cardiac instruments,

pacemakers and catheters for Pakistani children with congenital cardiac conditions.

The Neonatology Project: Pakistan has unfortunately one of the highest infant and neonatal mortality rates in the world. While infant mortality rate in general has gone down in Pakistan, there has been no change in infant mortality rate under one-month age during the past ten years. There are two main levels of care that need to be addressed. One is the introduction of the helping babies breathe (HBB) program at community level and the other is improvement of the neonatal Intensive Care Units (NICUs) in the country.

The major causes of infant mortality are asphyxia, infections, prematurity, hypothermia and feeding problems. APPNA PEDS will be training Lady Health Workers in "Helping Babies Breathe" (HBB) and "Helping Babies Survive" with essential care for every baby (ECEB) during the first 24 hours of infant's life. It would be demonstrated to the hospitals and government officials that this program (HBB) works. In 2015, three visits to Pakistan were made to assess the situation by Dr. Mohammad Riaz, Dr. Kaukab Naseer and Dr. Khalid Kamal.

NICUs in Pakistan lag far behind in the practice of evidence based medicine. There is an imperative need for more education. There is an acute shortage of nursing staff. Patient to nurse ratio is close to 1:15. There is overcrowding beyond the capacity of hospital beds and many babies with different needs have to be placed under one warmer. There is lack of central oxygen supply at District Headquarter level. There is minimal nasal CPAP use. Most places use only ventilator CPAP. APPNA PEDS plans to work with "One NICU at a time" and would help with education of nurses and physicians, alike. The NICU of Sir Ganga Ram Hospital is affiliated with Fatima Jinnah Medical University (FJMU). APPNA PEDS member, Dr. Saima Aftab visited FJMU in April 2016 to provide hands on training to the resident doctors on HBB, NRP and ECEB, bubble CPAP and on improving ventilator management. She provided pulse oximeters, laryngoscopes, self-inflating and flow inflating bags for the unit. Medical officers from the unit will visit the prestigious Women and Brigham's Hospital in Boston for a short-term training in Neonatology in near future.

APPNA PEDS is active on social media. A dedicated website AppnaPeds.org was launched. A Facebook group for APPNA pediatrics has over 200 members.

Dr. Khalid Kamal contributed to this report.

APPNA-HemOnc

APPNA-HemOnc was formally inaugurated and announced in August 2015. This new specialty society will encompass and represent hematologists, medical oncologists, surgical oncologists, radiation oncologists, cancer researchers, and other physicians involved in cancer care. Initial bylaws were developed. The inaugural meeting was held at the annual APPNA summer meeting in Orlando (FL) in August 2015. It was attended by large number of hematologist/oncologists who came to attend the meeting from all over the country. Most of them expressed their willingness to devote their time and expertize to support this project.

The mission of APPNA-HemOnc is to facilitate treatment and prevention of cancer and blood disorders through research, education, professional development, training and advocacy in the field of hematology and oncology with a goal to deliver high quality care for patients.

Following Officers were unanimously elected to serve the first term expiring at 12/31/2016. President: Dr. Aamer Farooq, Secretary: Dr. Sairah Ahmed, Treasurer: Dr. Farrukh Awan, and President-Elect: Dr. Mehdi Hamadani. Initial appointments on the Board of Trustees include Dr. Raza Khan, Dr. Omar Atiq, Dr. Muzaffar H. Qazilbash, Dr. Farid Qazi, and Dr. Mohammad Jahanzeb.

Several standing committees have been formed and work is underway to ensure smooth and transparent functioning of this new affiliate society of APPNA. The projects to improving the delivery of oncological care in Pakistan are the focus of intense debate at present in the APPNA-HemOnc. How to facilitate Pakistani-descent young physicians' interest in the HemOnc field in the US is another question in the minds of the founders. A new website will be developed. Continued support from all APPNA members is needed to make this venture a great success.

Dr. Sairah Ahmed contributed to this report.

THE STORY OF APCNA

Rizwan A. Karatela, MD, FACC
Executive Director

On March 7, 2004 something very profound happened. There was no fan-fare yet everyone heard it. There were no dazzling lights yet everyone's face was illuminated. There was a palpable energy in the air. People were excited, deep inside they felt something great was happening. In the Embassy Suites Hotel in New Orleans the banner went up, speeches were delivered and peo-ple heard the most melodious Jazz they had ever heard in New Orleans. The organization was born.

Professor Shahbuddin Rahimtoola (Dow class of 1954) addressing at the Inaugural Meeting of APCNA, March 7, 2004. Dr. S. Sultan Ahmed and Dr. Javed Suleman who were among the founders are sitting on the table. Photo courtesy, Mahmood Alam

APCNA's story is the story of love, respect for life, participation and commitment. Since its inception, it has become a great melting pot of self-less, enthusiastic, dedicated and committed workers. All of these people can claim to be progenitors of the lifeline of APCNA. No one member can claim to be the reason for APCNA. The collective will of these people have held this organization high above the self-projection, petty politics or corruption that may cast shadows on new beginnings. Each year brings new life, new zeal and new ideas. All new ideas unique in their own right.

Traversing our histories of industrious youthful age to when we first began to practice our professions, it has been a long and hard journey for many of us. Achieving that fulfillment, it was worth it. Then, there was a desire to give back to the community. What could be more satisfying than to fulfill this desire by harnessing the power of one's own profession. APCNA provided that platform for many of us. The past ten years are a testimony to what good work an organization of like-minded workers can achieve. Only the first chapter of the story of APCNA has been written, the real work will continue to inspire many more, and without a doubt, it will be a model of excellence for many to emulate. For us, it will strengthen our commitment towards our core mission.

We would like to present here some of the highlights of APCNA over the years. For more details information and getting involved in many of the APCNA work please visit our website at www.apcna.net.

APCNA cardiologists from the US during their visit to Indus
Hospital Karachi. Photo courtesy, Rizwan Karatela

APCNA
Journey Through Time; 2004–2014

With the active participation of many of our members we have been able to work towards our core mission. Here we will highlight a few of the major projects and activities through the years.

Cardiology Lectures:

More than 300 didactic lectures at Pakistan's institutions. Since 2004, APCNA had been committed to arrange annual winter meetings in various medical colleges of Pakistan on a rotation basis. Such meetings have been a great source of interest to the local faculty, and the house-staff.

Interventional Cardiology Workshops:

More than 75 workshops, > 500 PTCA cases with local faculty.

In addition to the lectures, hands-on workshops, especially in interventional cardiology, have been very useful in transfer of technology and expertise, which has been one of APCNA mission. This exercise is clearly mutually beneficial to both the APCNA members and the local faculty. **Echo and**

TEE workshops:

Annual workshops > 200 cases and lectures.

Non Invasive cardiology workshop are also as important and received by the local faculty and the house-staff enthusiastically. Here interesting cases are discussed and hands-on approach in Echo and TEE have been extremely useful.

Cardiology Supplies:

More than 5 million dollars worth of donations for patients.

The cardiac supplies collected and brought by APCNA members are certainly greatly appreciated by the local faculty who diligently care for these patients with meager means. These supplies over the years have helped many deserving and non-affording patients.

First Pacemaker Bank in Pakistan: in 2004 in Karachi

Hundreds of Pacemaker for the deserving non-affording patients in Pakistan.

It took a lot of effort on the Part of Dr. Wajid Baig to work in collaboration with Heartbeat International, Tampa, FL. To set up the First Pacemaker

Bank in Karachi. Over 150 devices implanted in the deserving patients who could not afford these devices.

Expansion of Pacemaker Banks throughout Pakistan by 2015
Hundreds of Pacemaker for the deserving non-affording patients in Pakistan.
With ongoing collaborative work in Pakistan
By 2015, APCNA was able to establish Pacemaker Banks in Karachi, Lahore and Peshawar with over 250 Pacemaker implanted.

CCU teaching rounds.
Annual sessions at various medical colleges in Pakistan
CCU rounds with the local faculty and case presentation is now a regular feature of APCNA winter meetings.

BLS training for healthcare workers.
Support of BLS training in Pakistan under APCNA members.
APCNA established BLS Training Center for health care providers at the Pakistan Medical Association (PMA) House in Karachi in 2008. >$6000 worth of supplies donated for this purpose. Hundreds of healthcare workers have been trained since.

First Peripheral Vascular Disease Workshop:
First hands on workshop in PVD in NWFP.
Dr. Arshad Rehan conducted the First Peripheral Vascular Disease workshop at his alma mater at Khyber Medical College in Peshawar. He presented the latest developments in this field

Collaboration with Societies:
Ten annual winter cardiology conferences in academic hospitals across Pakistan.
APCNA has established a good working relationship with the leadership of Pakistan Cardiac Society. A delegation of APCNA and PCS had an extensive meeting at Regency Plaza Hotel in Karachi in December 2008. It was decided to work on joint projects in promoting cardiac care. It was also discussed the possibility of holding joint conferences in Pakistan.

Interventions for the Deserving Patients
More than 600 cases performed by the visiting APCNA members in Pakistan.
APCNA members have been providing their services several times a year over the last 10 years in different hospitals in Pakistan. Interventional Cardiologists have performed hundreds of difficult PCI's in various institutions in Pakistan. They have participated in training post graduate Cardiology Fellows in performing high risk cases.

APCNA in AHA Heart Walk
AHA Heart Walk 2007, raised $1000 for AHA by APCNA youth.
APCNA members and their families have been actively participating in the AHA Heart Walk program in Florida. Dr. Karatela and his Children are at the forefront of this fund raising event. APCNA Members pledged money to the participants of walk.

First IVUS use in NWFP:
Transfer of expertise, first IVUS use at the Lady Reading Hospital, Peshawar.
APCNA members were the first to perform procedures with an IVUS at Khyber Medical College/Lady Reading Hospital in Peshawar in winter 2008.

Nuclear Cardiology Workshop:
Nuclear cardiology workshop Lady Reading Hospital, Peshawar
Nuclear cardiology workshops are very much liked by the local faculty and the house staff. Interesting cases discussed and many imaging examples reviewed by the APCNA for the house staff.

HUMAN DEVELOPMENT FOUNDATION

A Success Story

Dr. Atiya Khan

In *APPNA Qissa* Volume 1, the launching of HDF is mentioned as a dream of visionaries. These visionaries were aware of the situation in Pakistan, which was pretty drastic at the time; with the population reaching almost 160 million and increasing every day with hardly any family planning. The poverty, the illiteracy, the suboptimal public health, the scarcity of clean drinking water and the nonexistence of infrastructure in the rural areas (which is almost 75% of the total country) were all at unacceptable levels.

Realization of this huge dilemma gave rise to the idea of HDF. Two individuals who brought this idea to life were Dr. Nasim Ashraf and Dr. Khalid Riaz; with the objective of giving back to the country where they originally came from. They dreamt of helping people get access to better educational opportunities, gain access to quality health care, live in dignity and come out of the vicious cycle of poverty. They wanted to help people take control of their destiny and truly change it; as these two doctors did since they came to the US.

With this in mind, HDF was launched from the APPNA platform in 1997 as a gift to Pakistan on the 50th anniversary of its independence, with the deep commitment of a few individuals, and a goal to ensure long term sustainability and scalability of the projects in a way that the programs and services would impact generations to come.

The organization's core strength is its holistic model of development that constitutes an integrated set of development interventions. These provide a strong basis for comprehensive engagement and partnership with the local communities.

The organizational maturity and institutional strengthening of HDF has followed four phases. (1) Institution building (2) Implementation (3) Expansion (4) Excellence.

(1) Institution Building: This included registering as a 501(c)3 nonprofit organization, and the development of a broad based donor group in North America to provide a predictable source of funding to meet the program needs in Pakistan. The final step of institution building was to set up operations in Pakistan, and hire committed and passionate staff who would implement the projects with the same dedication and commitment that was in the people who came on board in America. This was successfully achieved by a few Board members who travelled to Pakistan for this very reason.

(2) Implementation: This phase included the execution of the holistic model. The back bone of the model is the social mobilization program. The idea is to build partnerships with communities in Pakistan and organize them into village development organizations. These organizations through a democratic process choose their own village leaders, and then help organize the development initiatives in health, education, sustainable environment, and economic development; thus striving to become independent, sustainable communities over time.

(3) Expansion: This was a phase with rapid vertical and horizontal growth in the program areas of HDF. Additional human resources, with experience in mature organizational systems, were brought on board to study the impact and results of HDF programs. These individuals conducted robust financial channeling, increased accountability through regular monitoring and evaluation, staff appraisals and data analysis before the projects started and after 5 and 10 years of service to document the successes of the holistic model executed by HDF.

(4) Excellence: This was a transformational stage for HDF. With successes in programs and increasing experiences in the field, HDF started aiming towards attaining excellence. This was sought through better financial systems, more efficient service delivery and growing our networks and partnerships with other organizations in the field (attached is a list of our partners). In order to take the governance and oversight of the organization to the next level we brought onboard committed volunteers; people with significant social and professional standing. These volunteers had better understanding and knowledge about development, and additionally possessed deep insight and sheer commitment to the cause and mission of HDF in the USA, Pakistan and Canada.

17 years later, with the passionate and sustained hard work and dedication of many people: including board members, volunteers, donors, supporters, friends, and the staff not only in North America but also in Pakistan the change in the lives of hundreds of thousands of people is really impressive. This impact on over a million people's lives has made HDF a globally recognized organization in the non-profit sector.

We can all take pride in HDF.

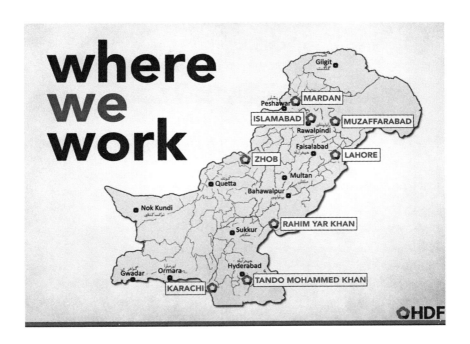

what we do

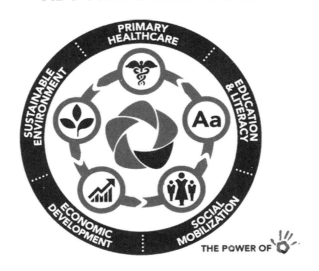

THE POWER OF

Provided in all 9 Regions of Pakistan

The HDF Holistic Model includes programs in 5 key areas:

Social Mobilization

By empowering local communities at a grass roots level, HDF encourages individuals to identify their own problems and provides them with the tools to solve them.

Education & Literacy

From building new schools and instilling a love of learning in children to providing local residents with specialized training, HDF strives to create a system and framework to educate all citizens.

Economic Development

By providing individuals with microloans and vocational skills training, HDF provides both the financial resources and skills needed for people to earn a sufficient living

Sustainable Environment

HDF works to reverse the loss of environmental resources and partners with local communities to develop new and sustainable infrastructure; including water filtration, paved roads, waste management and agricultural projects.

Primary Healthcare

HDF's healthcare efforts include reducing mortality rates for at-risk individuals and improving health behaviors through community education campaigns.

HDF impact

Around **10,000** children enrolled in school each year

287 Village Development Organizations

Over **1,000,000** people benefitted from HDF's Holistic Model and Partnerships

Infant mortality decreased from
85/1000 births to 23/1000 births

11,243 Participants Trained in Technical/Vocational Skills

862 Drinking Water Projects

HDF success stories
Education

Aqsa Bano

15 year old Aqsa Bano from HDF's Formal School in Basti Khandoo in Rahim Yar Khan secured 1st position in matriculation in the overall Humanities Group of Board of Intermediate and Secondary Education (BISE), Bahawalpur. We are extremely proud of her!

Rukhsama Parveen Khokar

"I have no words to express my gratitude for HDF. I belong from a very conservative area where there was no concept of education. But with the support of my parents, brother and HDF, I completed my education. HDF is my first institute for learning."

I have now finished my Master's degree and working for USAID. I just bought a car. This is how HDF changed my life.

Primary Healthcare

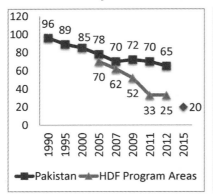

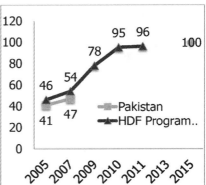

Economic Development

Shaista Jabeen

"I attended a training workshop conducted by HDF where I learned embroidery skills. This changed my life. I now sell my own embroidered products and also teach the craft to other women. I can support my family and hope to provide a better future for them."

Sustainable Environment

HDF partners

Adult Basic Education Society
(ABES)
APPNA
Bearing Point, Pakistan
COMSATS
Department for International
Development (DfID)
Development Alternatives, Inc.
(DAI Europe)
EMMA
Empowerment through Creative
Innovation (ECI)
Environmental Resource
Management, North America
Faysal Bank
FFBL
Foundation for Advancement
of Science and Technology
University (FAST)
Imran Khan Foundation
Khushali Bank
King Edward Medical College
Merlin Pakistan
Met Life Alico
MFF
NRSP
Pakistan American Grade
Association, Seattle (PAGS)
Pakistan Poverty Alleviation Fund
Pepsico Foundation
Planning and Development
Department, Sindh
Rawalpindi Medical College
(RMC), Pakistan
Right to Play
Rotary Club
Shifa Medical College,
PakistanSMEDA
Pakistan
Strengthening Participatory
Organization (SPO)
Sustainable Development Policy
Institute (SDPI)

Swat Relief Initiative (SRI)
Takeda Pharmeceuticals
The Asia Foundation (TAF)
Trust for Democratic Education
and Accountability (TDEA)
Ukaid
UNDP
United Nations FAO
University of Chicago
University of Illiois
UNOCHA
USAIDUNICEF
Wah Medical College
Whole Foods
World Health Organization
Zulekhani Gani Foundation

US recognition and awards

Charity Navigator
Guidestar
*Safeer-e-Pakistan
*Chinar
*APPNA
*KEMCAANA
*APPNA Richmond Network
*APPNA North Carolina Network
*Awarded to Dr. Atiya Khan for her
contributions and work with
HDF

Pakistan recognition and awards

IMCP Certification in 2007
PCP Certification in 2009 & 2012
Best Performing Alliance Partner
in 2011
Best Environment Award
2011–2012
9th Annual Environmental
Excellence Award 2012
Global Human Resource
Excellence Award
CSR Business Excellence Award in
2013 & 2014

HDF expense ratios

Expense Ratios

Program Services	84.08
Management & General	9.42
Fundraising	6.5

Expense Ratios Year 2014

■ Program Services   ■ Management & General   ■ Fundraising

Before we end this chapter, there are a number of people we must mention who have shown commitment and continuously worked hard for last 17 years: Dr. Khalid Riaz, Dr. Naheed Qayyum, Dr. Zeenat Anwar, Dr. Tariq Khan and Dr. Shahnaz Khan. We also want to thank all the donors, volunteers, supporter, and staff in North America and Pakistan who have made our work possible.

Please visit our Website at www.hdf.com for the rest of the Board of Directors, Board of Trustees, and Network chairs that have contributed a lot through the years.

We invite all APPNA members to visit our programs whenever they are in Pakistan. We can arrange it for you, whenever it is convenient, and where ever you want to go. You would have an experience never to be forgotten inshallah.

PAK-PAC

New leadership sets out on mission to engage Pakistani-Americans in Advocacy and political activism

Muhammad Suleman and Riffat Chughtai

Today, our adopted home, the United States, stands at difficult crossroads in regards to civil rights of immigrants and minorities. It has become one of the main focus of the Presidential campaign (2015–16). These issues directly impact us as Pakistani-Americans. Decisions made in Washington will affect our future generations here in the US and across the globe. PAK-PAC remains committed to educating our community and lobbying with policymakers on the pertinent contemporary issues.

PAK-PAC supports carefully vetted candidates who are committed to federal policies that promote good governance, enhance awareness and promote security and civil liberties in the United States as well as in Pakistan. It is observed that too often community members have been just an ATM used by the political candidates. PAK-PAC reminds Pakistani community that voting record of a candidate on issues relevant to our community be checked and issues of concern be raised when political donations are made in support of any candidate.

PAK-PAC is the only Pakistani-American organization registered with the Federal Election Commission. We are not affiliated with any political party in Washington or Islamabad. All PAK-PAC funding and expenditures are public record as required by federal regulations. PAK-PAC intends to elect a Pakistani American to federal office by the 2026 election. Meanwhile, we will continue to organize and educate our community.

Mission Statement: The mission of PAKPAC is to amplify the political voice of Pakistani—Americans by building long term relations with key elected officials through strategic and constructive dialogue and education.

PAK-PAC Governance: PAK-PAC activities are governed by its National Board. The board members are elected based on their leadership qualities and commitment to the mission of PAK-PAC. The board elects a President for a three-year term. Each member of the Board contributes at least $2,000 annually and is required to actively engage in local, state and national politics. The board is represented from all across the United States. The Advisory Council comprises passionate young professionals who volunteer over ten hours a month. The National Board and Advisory Council care deeply about the mission—and goals of PAK-PAC and always welcome input from like-minded politically active Pakistani-Americans.

PAKPAC Activities:

The new PAK-PAC leadership took over in May 2014. Since then, the organization has engaged the community and American elected officials in unprecedented ways. The following programs were held.

- Panel Discussions on Human Rights and Civil Liberties
- Political Organizing Seminar with Senator Tim Kaine, the former governor of Virginia and Chairman of the Democratic National Convention
- Advocacy Workshop drawing parallels from the Cuban-American Community with Congressman Albio Sires
- High Tea in Washington with Foreign Policy Leaders of the New Congress
- Muslim American Strategy Session with Congressman Andre Carson
- Youth Organizing with Congressman Eric Swalwell
- Muslim American Strategy Session with Congressman Keith Ellison
- Get out the Vote Rally with Senator Jeanne Shaheen

- Town Hall Meeting with Congressman Ted Deutch and Senator Bob Casey
- Discussion on "Republican Approaches to Foreign Policy" with Congressmen Mike Turner and Joe Wilson
- Quarterly update meetings with Ambassador Jalil Abbas Jilani
- Invitations to Presidential Debates

Founding of PAK-PAC: On the eve of the 1990 election in an increasingly complex world, our founders saw a need for greater political coordination, activism, and advocacy. PAK-PAC was established in 1989 on the initiative of Dr. Arif Toor and others. Dr. Nasim Ashraf was elected first president of the organization serving it from 1989–1991. Other presidents have included Dr. Hassan Bukhari (1991–1993), Dr. Naseem Ashraf (1993–1994), Dr. Ikram Ullah Khan (1994–1996), Mr. Akram Chaudhry (1996–1998), Dr. Arif Toor (1998–1999), Dr. Arif Muslim (1999–2002), Dr. Pervez I. Shah (2002–2004), Dr. M. Saud Anwar (2004–2006), Dr. Raza Bokhari (2006–2007), Dr. Muhammad Suleman (2008–2010), Dr. Salman Malik (2011–2012), Dr. Ijaz Mahmood (2013–2014) and Mrs. Riffat Chughtai (2014–2015).

Mr. Irfan Malik, past executive director of PAK-PAC also contributed to this report.

Board of Directors—2015

Riffat Chughtai (President)
Pennsylvania
(412) 612-6381

Muhammad Suleman
Louisiana
(504) 388-4525

Pervez Shah (Treasurer)
Maryland
(240) 441-6106

Salman Malik
New Hampshire
(603) 785-8789

Jalil Khan (Secretary)
Texas
(972) 672-5156

Babar Rao
New York
(212) 949-2516

Tariq Butt
Illinois
(312) 545-8471

Hanadi Nadeem
Nevada
(702) 569-7739

Masood Akbar
Pennsylvania
(570) 449-4067

Shazia Malik
Missouri
(314) 616-3596

Advisor: Ari **Mittleman**

DOCTORS WHO LOST THEIR LIVES TO VIOLENCE IN PAKISTAN[1]

ہم جو تاریک راہوں میں مارے گئے

1.	Syed Qasim Abbas	19.	Syed Hasan Alam
2.	Qasim Abbas	20.	Nasim Baber
3.	Nasim Abbas	21.	Noreen Bajwa
4.	Haider Abbas	22.	Shiraz Bajwa
5.	Naseem Abbas	23.	Ali Bangash
6.	Hadi Afzal	24.	Hasan Hyder Bokhari
7.	Shahid Ahmed	25.	Syed Asad Ali Bukhari
8.	Tahir Ahmed	26.	Nizam Chaudary
9.	Muzaffar Ahmed	27.	M Hussain Divjani
10.	Munawer Ahmed	28.	Sibtain Ali Dossa
11.	Shahnawaz Akhunzada	29.	Yousuf Ghori
12.	Babar Ali	30.	Shahid Nazir Gondal
13.	Kausar Ali	31.	Ali Haider
14.	Baber Ali	32.	Syed Raza Haider
15.	Sher Ali	33.	Syed Zulfiqar Haider
16.	Mohammad Ali	34.	Ali Haider
17.	Sher Ali	35.	Syed Abbas Hairder
18.	Hyder Ali	36.	Ghulam Shabbir Haji

---

1 This is an incomplete list that was compiled by some physicians and put together in alphabetical order. The information is deemed reliable. APPNA bears no responsibility of its authenticity.

37. Anees Ul Hasan
38. H S Baqar Hasnain
39. Mehdi Hassan
40. Hadi Hassan
41. Nayyar Hussain
42. Zahid Hussain
43. Karamat Hussain
44. Ghulam Hussain
45. Mansoor Hussain
46. Riaz Hussein
47. Ishart Hussein
48. Azhar Hussein
49. Javed Hyder
50. Syed Abbas Hyder
51. Hyder Raza Iarchevi
52. Syed Ibn-e-Hasan
53. Syed Ejaz Imam
54. Raza Mehdi Jaffery
55. Syed Raza Jaffery
56. Syed Ali Jah Jaffri
57. Syed Manzar H Jaffri
58. Naseer Hussain Jaffri
59. Ikhlaq Hussain Jaffri
60. Ch Ali Hassan Jafri
61. Syed Mohd Jamal
62. Abul Qasim Jiwa
63. Fayyaz Karim
64. Syed Shabih Kazmi
65. Syed Abbas H Kazmi
66. Mehtab H Kazmi
67. Saifullah Khalid
68. Mohammad Ali Khan
69. Sardar Riaz Khan
70. Mohammed Ali Khan
71. Agha Syed Abid Iqbal
72. Abdul Mannan
73. Baber Mannan
74. Faisal Manzoor
75. Faisal Manzoor
76. Syed Rashid Mehdi
77. Aslam Mina
78. Aslam Mirza
79. Jaffer Mohsin
80. Ali Nadir
81. Naimatullah
82. Syed Ali Raza Naqvi
83. Syed Baqar Naqvi
84. Syed Pervaiz A. Naqvi
85. Syed M Ali Naqvi
86. Syed Mohsin Naqvi
87. Mumtaz H Naqvi
88. S Asad Abbas Naqvi
89. Syed Iqtedar H Naqvi
90. Syed Nadeem Naqvi
91. Shahid Nawaz
92. Mohamad Raza Pirani

93. Adel Bin Abdul Qadir
94. Mehdi Ali Qamar
95. Hasan Ali Qureshi
96. Muteeur Rahman
97. Tabassum Raza
98. Abid Raza
99. Abid Raza
100. Mujeed Ur Rehman
101. S M Saqlain Rizvi
102. Syed Asif H Rizvi
103. S G Akbar Rizvi
104. Iafler Mohsin Rizvi
105. Asad Abbas Rizvi
106. Saqlain Rizvi
107. S Mohsin Ran Rizvi
108. Syed Mojavir Ali Rizvi
109. Syed Asad Raza Rizvi
110. S M Saqlain Rizvi
111. Muzzafar All Samoo
112. Zahid Ullah Sapal
113. Sarfaraz Ali Shah
114. Ibrahim Shah
115. Baqar Shah
116. S Saeed Hassan Shah
117. Junaid Shakir
118. Shamsul Haq Tayyab
119. Naushad A. Vallani
120. Naseen Zaidi
121. Syed Hassan A. Zaidi
122. Syed Qamar H Zaidi
123. S Raza Mehdi Zaidi
124. S Jaffer Abbas Zaidi
125. Syed Shakir H Zaidi
126. Syed M Haider Zaidi
127. Alay Zaidi, MD
128. Qamar Zaidi
129. Haider Zaidi
130. S Alay Safder Zaidi

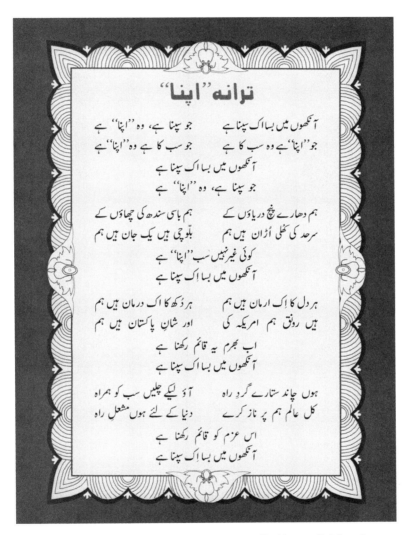

ترانہ "اپنا"

آنکھوں میں بسا اک سپنا ہے   جو سپنا ہے، وہ "اپنا" ہے
جو "اپنا" ہے وہ سب کا ہے   جو سب کا ہے وہ "اپنا" ہے
آنکھوں میں بسا اک سپنا ہے
جو سپنا ہے، وہ "اپنا" ہے

ہم دھارے پنج دریاؤں کے   ہم باسی سندھ کی چھاؤں کے
سرحد کی کھلی اُڑان ہیں ہم   بلوچی ہیں یک جان ہیں ہم
کوئی غیر نہیں سب "اپنا" ہے
آنکھوں میں بسا اک سپنا ہے

ہر دل کا اِک ارمان ہیں ہم   ہر دُکھ کا اِک درمان ہیں ہم
ہیں رونق ہم امریکہ کی   اور شانِ پاکستان ہیں ہم
اب بھرم یہ قائم رکھنا ہے
آنکھوں میں بسا اک سپنا ہے

ہوں چاند ستارے گردِ راہ   آؤ لیکے چلیں سب کو ہمراہ
کل عالم ہم پر ناز کرے   دنیا کے لئے ہوں مشعلِ راہ
اس عزم کو قائم رکھنا ہے
آنکھوں میں بسا اک سپنا ہے

APPNA Tarana (Anthem) was authored by Dr. Naeem Kohli and was first published in 2005 summer journal. This piece is taken from the back page of the booklet, which was printed to celebrate the "Mushaira" of 2011 summer meeting at St. Louis, MO

413

EDITORS

Zainab B. Alam

Zainab Alam is a Ph.D. candidate in political science at Rutgers University and has her masters in Global Affairs from NYU. She is the coordinator for a non-profit program that places female undergraduate students in leadership positions. Additionally, she has worked for a number of years in the field of immigration law and with various international NGOs.

Nasir M. Gondal

Dr. Nasir Gondal is a graduate of Rawalpindi Medical College, class of 1985. He is a Clinical Assistant Professor, Department of Medicine at New York University (NYU). He practices clinical Hematology and Oncology at NYU Langone at Columbus Medical in Queens, NYC.

Nasir Gondal is a life-time member of APPNA who has served the organization in various capacities for the causes of Young Physicians as well as Advocacy. He is also known for his frequent contributions to APPNA related listserves and on social media. Dr. Gondal belongs to a literary circle in NYC called Halqa Arbab-e-Zauq. He also writes a blog under Ghareebkhana, ghareebkhana.blogspot.com

M. Aslam Malik

Dr. Aslam Malik is a graduate of Nishter Medical College, class of 1963. He retired as Assistant Professor in surgery at the University of North Texas. He received general surgery training in Great Britain and was awarded fellowship in the Royal College of Surgeons in Edinburgh (FRCS). He practiced as a general surgeon in Fort Worth, Texas, since 1972. He was the president of Fort Worth Surgical Society, member of the Tarrant County Medical Board, and delegate to Texas Medical Association House of Delegates.

Dr. Aslam Malik has served APPNA as secretary, president, editor of the APPNA newsletter, and Chair Board of Trustees. Dr. Malik was the 6th president of APPNA, 1984–85. He is a recipient of APPNA Gold Medal Award (2006) for his meritorious services to APPNA and medical community. He is one of the signatories of the APPNA Constitution published in 1984.

Wasique Mirza

Dr. Wasique Mirza is a graduate of the Allama Iqbal Medical College, class of 1991. He practices Internal medicine in Scranton, PA and is a Specialist in Clinical Hypertension. He serves as the Medical Director of Scranton Primary Healthcare Center, a Federally Qualified Health Center (FQHC) and a faculty member as well as Acting Program Director for the Internal Medicine residency program at The Wright Center in Scranton, PA. Dr. Mirza is an Associate Professor of Medicine at The Commonwealth Medical college in Scranton. He has been actively involved in APPNA through his contributions to the Publication Committees over the years. He is an Op-Ed Columnist for The Times-Tribune of Scranton, PA and also contributes to the Huffington Post. In fiction writing, he is the author of a political thriller, Zero Point.

Mubasher E. Rana

Dr. Mubasher Rana is a graduate of King Edward Medical College, class of 1984. He is a Nephrologist practicing in the San Francisco, Bay Area. He is Chief of Nephrology at Diablo Permanente medical group and Medical Director of Walnut Creek Dialysis unit. Dr. Rana served on the Medical Advisory Board of National Kidney Foundation of Northern California. He is a Fellow of American College of Physicians and American Society of Nephrology.

He served as President of KEMCAANA in 2008. He is the founding President of APPNA Northern California chapter. He has chaired several APPNA committees including Chair of APPNA Summer meeting in 2009. Dr. Rana served as Treasurer and Secretary of APPNA and then as its 38th President in 2015. Dr. Rana is also a Board of Trustees member of the Zaytuna College in Berkeley, CA.

ABOUT THE AUTHOR

A 1983 graduate of Allama Iqbal Medical College, **Mahmood Alam** is a Clinical Assistant Professor, Department of Medicine, at the Rutgers School of Medicine in Newark, New Jersey. Currently, he is on the faculty of the Internal Medicine Residency Program at Raritan Bay Medical Center (RBMC), in Perth Amboy, New Jersey. He also serves as the Director of Non-Invasive Cardiology at RBMC. Dr. Alam is a fellow of American College of Cardiology (FACC) and American College of Physicians (FACP). Dr. Alam has been involved in teaching and academic medicine for the last twenty years. He has published several research manuscripts on cardiovascular medicine in peer reviewed journals.

Dr. Alam's interest in writing goes back to his medical school days, when he served as the managing editor of a quarterly magazine, *Sehar*[1]. In 1985, he was appointed as a member of the editorial board of "The Medical Tribune"—a fortnightly newspaper of Pakistan Medical Association (PMA) Punjab. Dr. Alam has served APPNA in various capacities. He was the 29th President of APPNA in 2008. He has been frequent contributor to APPNA newsletter and journal since 2003. Dr. Alam has also served as the editor of APPNA Newsletter/Journal in 2011. *APPNA Qissa II* is the first book he has authored.

---

1   *The "good old days" of non-profit publishing—when there were no computers. The editors used to collect handwritten material from the contributors, type-writing it themselves or taking it by the curbside typists before taking it to a professional type-setter or giving the Urdu material to a "Katib." They would then collect everything to do proofreading before it went to copy-pasting. Then it would get published after the editor would negotiate the right price. This venture wouldn't end there. The editor(s) would have to collect the published copies, carry them on their motorcycles and personally distribute them to the potential readers. This account could only be appreciated by those who have done this job. Author felt that his job of producing* APPNA Qissa II *was not much different!*

INDEX

Note: page numbers in italic refer to photos or accompanying captions.